THE SPIRIT OF VATICAN II

Vatican II profoundly changed the outlook and the message of the Catholic Church. After decades, if not centuries, in which Catholic public opinion appeared to be primarily oriented towards the distant past and bygone societal models, suddenly the Catholic Church embraced the world as it was, and it joined in the struggle to create a radiant future.

The Sixties were a time of great socio-cultural and political ferment in Europe as a whole. Especially the second half of the 1960s and the first half of the 1970s witnessed an astounding range of 'new' and 'old' social movements reaching for the sky. Catholic activists provided fuel to the fire in more ways than one. Catholics had embarked on the quest for new horizons for some years prior to the sudden growth of secular activism in and around the magic year of 1968. When secular radicals joined up with Catholic activists, a seemingly unstoppable dynamic was unleashed.

This book covers five crucial contributions by Catholic communities to the burgeoning atmosphere of those turbulent years: a) the theological innovations of Vatican II, which made such an unprecedented engagement of Catholics possible in the first place, but also post-conciliar theological developments; b) the resurgence of the worker priest experiment, and the first-ever creation of autonomous organisations of radical parish priests; c) the simultaneous creation of grassroots organisations—base communities—by (mostly) lay activists across the continent; d) the crucial roles of Catholic students in the multiform student movements shaping Europe in these years; e) the indispensable contributions of Catholic workers who helped shape—and often initiated—the wave of militant contestations shaking up labour relations after 1968.

Gerd-Rainer Horn is Professor of Twentieth-Century History at the Institut d'Études Politiques de Paris, Sciences Po.

D1559693

The Spirit of Vatican II

*Western European Progressive
Catholicism in the Long Sixties*

GERD-RAINER HORN

OXFORD
UNIVERSITY PRESS

OXFORD
UNIVERSITY PRESS

Great Clarendon Street, Oxford, OX2 6DP,
United Kingdom

Oxford University Press is a department of the University of Oxford.
It furthers the University's objective of excellence in research, scholarship,
and education by publishing worldwide. Oxford is a registered trade mark of
Oxford University Press in the UK and in certain other countries

Published in the United States of America by Oxford University Press
198 Madison Avenue, New York, NY 10016, United States of America

British Library Cataloguing in Publication Data
Data available

Library of Congress Cataloging in Publication Data
Data available

ISBN 978–0–19–959325–5 (Hbk.)
ISBN 978–0–19–884444–0 (Pbk.)

Acknowledgements

The material basis for the research leading to this book was furnished by a British Academy Research Development Award (BARDA), which allowed time away from teaching and administrative duties from the summer of 2011 to New Year's Eve 2012. It is my wish for future generations of historians that the uniquely generous British funding bodies, such as the British Academy, will continue to support major individual research projects of this sort.

Archival work for this book has been carried out in close to two dozen different institutions in Belgium, France, Italy, Netherlands, and Spain. Without this network of primary source deposits, all-too-frequently maintained and kept accessible by selfless volunteers, historians, especially historians of non-elite movements and intellectual currents, would literally have to close shop. In a day and age of mantra-like austerity politics across the European continent, it must be hoped that this lifeline for historians will continue to survive.

The list of individuals who have helped this monograph to become reality is far too long to recite in toto. I can only list a representative few. An indispensable conversation partner for the crucial Dutch dimension of Second Wave Left Catholicism was the erstwhile spiritus rector of Septuagint, Jan Ruijter. The various telephone calls to him I made over the past years have assisted me greatly in measuring Septuagint's national *and international* influence at a crucial moment in the development of Western European progressive Catholicism. My father-in-law, André Tanghe, lived the spirit of Vatican II as a dynamic and committed grassroots activist in the city of Ghent, Belgium. His patient advice and explanations helped me tremendously in understanding the meaning and the message of Vatican II.

The person who has consistently—by now for more than fifteen years—given me sound advice and a grounding in the vagaries of French progressive Catholicism is Yvon Tranvouez. I will never forget our first all-evening-long conversation in a neighbourhood bar in Milan, long after we first met during a workshop in Leuven. In Spain, Feliciano Montero performed a role in my discovery of the Spanish dimension similar to Yvon for the case of France. Our first meeting in the *Parque del Retiro* in Madrid made it clear—I think for both of us—that we operate on similar wavelengths, and yet another friendship organically emerged out of an intellectual affinity.

In Italy, two calm and generally rather reserved individuals played essential roles in allowing me access to what turned out to be indispensable resources. When we first met, Giovanni Avonto, a retired trade union and political activist of first-rate calibre, now the head archivist of the Fondazione Vera Nocentini, drew up a list of names and phone numbers of individuals and organizations that he felt I should contact in or near Turin; I was then at the very beginning of my series of archival journeys throughout Italy. Urbano Cipriani, in his unassuming way, played a similarly crucial role in my attempt to reconstruct the lifeworld and microcosm sui generis of Florentine progressive Catholicism. It is entirely due to him that a selection of photos emanating from the remarkable Historical Archive of the Comunità dell'Isolotto grace the pages—and the front cover—of this book. I should add that Urbano was also the photographer who in fact took most of the photos forty-five years ago as a young teacher and activist.

Two individuals deserve special mention in this sketchy and all-too-brief line-up of persons without whom this book would never have come to be. Carlo Carlevaris, who has an important cameo role in Chapter 2, hosted me twice for week-long stretches of time in his rooftop apartment in the San Salvario neighbourhood behind the Porta Nuova station in Turin, visits that usually lasted into the evening hours each day. His permission to give me free access to his copious personal archive opened up entirely unforeseen dimensions to the arguments in my book. His engaging accounts of his life story and the milieus which he helped to generate and flourish, spiced up with colourful anecdotes, did even more than his paper archive to make history come alive.

Vittorio Rieser, a key player behind the scenes in Turin and Italian New and Far Left politics ever since his engagement with the early *operaisti* in the late 1950s, knew Italian postwar history and politics like no one else. A secular non-conformist Marxist all of his life, he was consistently open to a kaleidoscope of viewpoints from a great variety of perspectives. An irregular participant in various events at the Waldensian study and retreat centre of Agape to the west of Turin high up in the Alps, Vittorio likewise frequented one of the early prototypes of subsequent base communities, the *Circolo Emmanuel Mounier*, in the early sixties. It was Vittorio who set me on the elusive track of the *Comunità del Vandalino*, and it was Vittorio who introduced me to Giovanni Avonto and Carlo Carlevaris. We usually met over some glasses of Nebbiolo at apero time in one of the outdoor cafés on the magnificent Piazza Vittorio Veneto. Vittorio Rieser died on 21 May 2014. It is hard to believe that there will be no more congenial hours spent chatting with and learning from Vittorio.

I wish to dedicate this book to the two individuals who, to me, incorporate the spirit of Torinese and Italian social movements in the age of Vatican II and the *sessantotto* more than anyone else: Carlo and Vittorio.

Contents

Introduction

Second wave Left Catholicism in Western Europe emerged in the course of the 1960s, especially in the wake of Vatican II, and it rode the crest of its popularity in the years, approximately, 1968–1975. Paradoxically, its period of maximum impact on European society coincided with a strengthening of counter-movements within the Catholic church. The honeymoon phase of second wave progressive Catholicism was thus limited to three short years: 1965–8.

This monograph forms the sequel to my 2008 *Western European Liberation Theology. The First Wave, 1924–1959*, but it also serves as a companion volume to my 2007 *The Spirit of '68. Rebellion in Western Europe and North America, 1956–1976*. For, when researching and writing *The Spirit of '68*, I already felt that, at some future time, I would want to devote special attention to the Catholic contribution to 'global 1968'. I thus decided to save the Catholic motivations and energies behind '1968' for a volume dedicated to this subject all on its own. Interestingly, of the wealth of, mostly rather favourable, reactions to *The Spirit of '68*, not one critic complained about the absence of the religious dimension in that volume.

This curious failure to observe what I would regard as a major lacuna in *The Spirit of '68*—even if wilfully designed to leave religion aside—highlights the general state of myopia within the historical profession with regard to the dynamic behind social movements in late modern Western European society. Characteristically, Eric Hobsbawm, in his quartet of stimulating introductory texts to Modern European History, no longer devoted specific chapters to Religion after 1848 on the grounds that Religion was no longer sufficiently important to deserve specific treatment. With few notable exceptions—the most recent laudable attempt to integrate religion into the story of social movements in and around 1968 is the edited volume on *Europe's 1968. Voices of Revolt*—the 1960s and 1970s are treated as virtually exclusively secular affairs. It is, in part, to correct this misconception that I have written this book.

The range of countries covered in some depth includes, above all, the Netherlands, Belgium, France, Italy, and Spain. *The Spirit of Vatican II* should thus also be seen as part of my continuous attempt to include Mediterranean

Europe in an overall assessment of Western European history and politics—
and the recognition of the centrality of the 'lands between'—in this case
Belgium and the Netherlands—as promising terrain for historical investigations. The range of countries could have easily been extended to include
Austria, Germany, Portugal, and Switzerland, but Lenin's dictum, 'Better
Fewer But Better', appeared to me of sufficient relevance to limit my gaze to
five countries alone.

In fact, not all chapters cover the five topics chosen in a comprehensive
manner with supporting evidence from all national cases studied. As in my
earlier monographs, I wish to highlight that I have never intended to present
an encyclopedic approach. It is often far more instructive to showcase particularly distinctive samples of the issues at hand, rather than to attempt the
impossible: a discussion of *all* relevant manifestations of a given trend.

Thus, Chapter 1 covers only what I regard as the most important and the
most promising theological conclusions of Vatican II. Also within this chapter,
I include a selective survey of the most stimulating and influential contributions by post-conciliar theologians. It may raise eyebrows that I open up this
monograph with a discussion of the intellectual heritage of progressive (Western European) theology in the 1960s and 1970s, rather than a hands-on
portrayal of grassroots radical action. I remain convinced, however, that,
certainly in this particular instance, Hegel won out over Marx. Without the
breakthrough achieved at Vatican II, without the imprimatur of the World
Council of the Catholic Church to positively engage with the hopes and the
challenges of the modern world, the second wave would have never come
about—or, at any rate, it may well have arisen in the wake of 1968, but it would
never have gone very far.

Chapters 2 and 3 take a closer look at the two most influential institutional
innovations of this second wave of Left Catholicism. Chapter 2 reveals the
hitherto virtually unknown history of radical priest associations, which shook
up the Catholic world in the late 1960s and early 1970s. Here my attention is
twofold. I first present a select survey of key moments in the development of
the second wave of the worker priest experience which, despite its far greater
social implantation when compared to the first, is to date far less well known
than the earlier wave of the late 1940s and early 1950s. And I then cast light on
an entirely unprecedented additional phenomenon of the sacerdotal experience in the long sixties: the rise and fall of the Christian Solidarity International Congress, an irreverent and fearless association of radical (mostly
parish) priests operating in all Catholic states.

Chapter 3 focuses on yet another innovation of second wave Left Catholicism: the truly impressive sudden emergence of Christian base communities
across Western Europe. Today often seen as a feature of radical Catholicism
peculiar to Latin America and, subsequently, other Third World states, I draw
attention to the equally vibrant European dimension of the attempt to

construct 'authentic Christian communities' outside the traditional structures (parishes, etc.) of the Catholic church, ceaselessly engaged in fraternal reflections as much as in concrete actions. It was in the course of penning this chapter that I decided to limit my analysis and description to one country only, Italy, and then only to the formative years of this experience up to 1970. This choice appeared to be the best way to get across the singularity, vitality but also the multiplicity of initiatives that can be justifiably included under the label of 'base community'.

Chapters 4 and 5 seek to portray the particular contributions of Left Catholic energies to the two overarching social movements which are readily associated with the long sixties: student movements and radical workers' movements. Chapter 4 traces the outlook of what I regard as the Catholic roots of '1968' in a variety of unexpected locations. This chapter perhaps comes closest to furnishing a survey of flagship personalities and capstone moments in a number of states. Chapter 5 attempts to do the same for the powerful wave of workers' struggles in the wake of 1968.

In both Chapters 4 and 5 significant attention is placed on events in Spain which, to some extent, formed an anomalous case in Western Europe. Here the radicalization of Catholic communities had already begun in the 1950s, a result of the peculiar political conditions of Francoist Spain. The Spanish contribution to second wave Left Catholicism in fact preceded the stimulus emanating from Vatican II. In one sense, then, Spanish Left Catholicism experienced a cycle of activism somewhat separate from most other Western European phenomena of this kind. Spanish Left Catholicism, virtually unknown to the north of the Pyrenees to this day, was not only a pioneering venture, but it may stand as a powerful reminder that, in the last analysis, it is material conditions which give rise to social movements, new theologies, and apostolic experiments, rather than new theologies spawning grassroots action as if by spontaneous generation—and thus, ultimately, that Marx may win out over Hegel after all.

The full list of what is missing in this book would be longer than its table of contents. I only wish to point to a few select topics which, given the constraints of time and space, I ultimately felt constrained to leave unaddressed in these pages. In the process of carrying out my archival research, I collected materials on a variety of organizations which I originally intended to include in my text. They include the rich holdings of the Italian wing of the Christian Solidarity International Congress, Sette Novembre, deposited in the Archive of the Italian Senate in Rome; the most important holding of materials on French base communities, the Fonds Bernard Besret at the Centre de Recherche Bretonne et Celtique in Brest; the wealth of papers on the history of the Gioventù Italiana di Azione Cattolica in the Istituto Paolo VI in Rome; and the Archive of the Juventud Obrera Cristiana in Madrid.

The same goes for those materials I collected in the archives of leading international associations of specialized Catholic Action. I barely scratched the surface in my closing subsections of Chapters 4 and 5 where I draw on the profusion of materials collected in the archives of the Jeunesse Étudiante Catholique Internationale in Nanterre and the Mouvement Mondial des Travailleurs Chrétiens in Leuven. Readers will also search in vain for references to the materials I collected in the archival holdings of the Jeunesse Ouvrière Chrétienne Internationale in Brussels and the Mouvement International de la Jeunesse Agricole et Rurale Catholique in Leuven—or the documents on the fascinating conjuncture of largely Catholic-inspired radical farmers' movements in the Loire Atlantique, which I collected in the Centre d'Histoire du Travail in Nantes.

Given that second wave Left Catholicism has not yet been succeeded by a third wave in more recent decades, there will be no sequel to this monograph. But I hope to find the time to process my documents from these aforementioned holdings on future occasions and in forthcoming publications—*si Dieu le permet.*

1

Vatican II and Post-conciliar European Theology

On Pentecost Sunday (3 June) 1963, Pope John XXIII died in the papal palace in Vatican City. Few other popes in history had ever caused so much upheaval within the Catholic church in so few years as Angelo Giuseppe Roncalli. Indeed, it is of more than symbolic relevance that one of the most iconoclastic gadfly intellectuals of the twentieth century, Hannah Arendt, entitled her review of the 1965 English translation of John XXIII's compendium of spiritual exercises and reflections 'The Christian Pope', an irreverent title whose multiple meanings were further enhanced by the *New York Review of Books*' editorial decision to drop the question mark from the published version of Arendt's views.[1]

Pope John XXIII died less than eight months after the commencement of the World Council of the Catholic Church, dubbed Vatican II. The council itself continued for another two-and-a-half years; yet already at the time of Roncalli's death, it was clear beyond a shadow of a doubt that his pontificate would leave a mark on world history in more ways than one. Nothing like this had been expected from Angelo Roncalli when he was chosen to succeed Pius XII on 28 October 1958.

GETTING VATICAN II OFF THE GROUND

As Étienne Fouilloux has recently reminded us, today's largely non-controversial assessment of the pontificate of John XXIII as a key moment of crisis and opportunity in church history clashes with virtually every single prediction made at the onset of his pontificate. Mostly seen as a relatively colourless bureaucrat in the diplomatic corps of the Vatican state, Roncalli had been chosen precisely because he was expected to fulfil his designated role as a

---

[1] Hannah Arendt, 'The Christian Pope', *New York Review of Books*, 17 June 1965.

pope of 'transition' in a dignified and, above all, calm and uncontroversial manner. After Pius XII, who had made his mark as a hardline opponent of progressive currents within the church, what was needed was an efficient mediator to calm the troubled waters. And, initially at least, it appeared to the papal curia that John XXIII would indeed become a worthy successor to Pius XII's conservative tradition.

In September 1959, the Secretary of the Holy Office, Cardinal Pizzardo, closed the last major remaining loophole for the continued operation of the worker priest experience, which had been at the centre of controversies within the European Catholic church in the late 1940s and early 1950s. And Pizzardo could count on the full support of Roncalli in this move.[2] Such conservative instincts were by no means rare survivals of 'the spirit of Pius XII' after the latter took leave of his earthly pursuits. Even as late as June 1962, four months before the official opening of the actual deliberations of Vatican II, the Holy Office warned all believers against the nefarious consequences of the thought of Teilhard de Chardin, who had attempted to bring the Catholic church in alignment with the insights of modern science. It comes as little surprise, then, that, commenting on the occasion of John XXIII's death, the Jesuit Robert Rouquette recalled that 'the least which one could say is that we expected nothing from his pontificate' when the papal conclave chose the former Vatican ambassador to Paris to succeed Pius XII.[3]

Even for the curia in Rome, the call to establish a new council, aired to a small group of cardinals, came as a surprise. The announcement of what eventually was called 'Vatican II' was largely a personal decision by John XXIII. At that time, of course, even Roncalli himself had as yet no clear idea of the precise dimensions of the forces that he would thereby unleash.[4] Slowly, efforts got under way to organize the institutional infrastructure which would permit the necessary preparation of such a world council. And such a gestation period was all the more necessary as literally no one had expected such a decision at this particular time. Even such a leading proponent of fundamental change as Yves Congar noted in his diary in July 1960: 'Personally, I have applied myself to activate the public so that it expects and demands quite a bit.

[2] Gerd-Rainer Horn, *Western European Liberation Theology 1924–1959. The First Wave* (Oxford: Oxford University Press, 2008), pp. 289–90.

[3] This information including the citation by Rouquette is taken from Étienne Fouilloux's recent reflections, 'Essai sur le devenir du catholicisme en France et en Europe occidentale de Pie XII à Benoît XVI', *Revue théologique de Louvain* 42 (2011), p. 534.

[4] For a more detailed reconstruction of the atmosphere and an assessment of the issues behind the official launching event for Vatican II in the early summer of 1959, see Giuseppe Alberigo, 'The Announcement of the Council. From the Security of the Fortress to the Lure of the Quest', in Giuseppe Alberigo and Joseph A. Komonchak (eds), *History of Vatican II*, Vol. I: *Announcing and Preparing Vatican Council II. Towards a New Era in Catholicism* (Maryknoll, NY: Orbis, 1995), pp. 1–54.

I have never ceased to say on all occasions: maybe only five per cent of that which we will have asked for will come to pass. One more reason to increase our demands.'[5]

If the erstwhile 'Left Opposition' within the Catholic church went on the offensive, their counterparts in the well-established seats of ecclesial power did the same, the latter appearing to have all the trump cards in their hand. In June 1960, ten preparatory commissions were established, each one dealing with a specific theme of the coming council. The curia naturally expected to call all the shots in the nomination of these all-important commissions which, in more ways than one, were to fix the agenda of the council itself. Yet there soon emerged countervailing forces at work, not the least of them Pope John XXIII himself, whose most important decision in this regard may well have been to keep the Supreme Congregation of the Holy Office, the ideological watchdog of the Catholic church, formerly known as 'The Inquisition', at arm's length in the preparatory period. In the end, despite the preponderance of the Roman curia in most commissions, many non-Italian bishops, unorthodox theologians, and even theologians hit by sanctions in the dark years of Pius XII's pontificate managed to find their way onto those preparatory commissions.[6]

Now began a tug of war. Yves Congar reports, for instance, that, when the preparatory commission for theology received some guidelines at the onset of their work, they were thoroughly imbued with the spirit of Pius XII. In fact, Congar wrote, the points of view expressed within this document were 'more or less similar to the way they would have been stated at the First Vatican Council in 1868'.[7] Despite notable improvements (from the point of view of progressive forces) in the process of elaborating the various schemes to guide the forthcoming council, when the schemes were sent to the bishops-at-large in the summer preceding the opening of Vatican II, their reactions 'expressed dissatisfaction, emphasizing the disparity between the perspectives indicated by the pope and the orientation of these schemata'.[8] Another historian adds: 'Disappointment and dissatisfaction were particularly widespread in Central European circles and among many missionary bishops who had some contact with them.'[9]

---

[5] Yves Congar, *Mon journal du Concile*, Vol. I (Paris: Cerf, 2002), p. 4.

[6] On the work of the preparatory commissions, note above all Giuseppe Alberigo and Alberto Melloni (eds), *Verso il Concilio Vaticano II (1960–1962). Passagi e problemi della preparazione conciliare* (Genoa: Marietti, 1993).

[7] Cited in Giovanni Turbanti, 'Vatican II et son monde', in Alberto Melloni and Christoph Theobald (eds), *Vatican II, un avenir oublié* (Paris: Bayard, 2005), p. 59.

[8] Giuseppe Alberigo, *A Brief History of Vatican II* (Maryknoll, NY: Orbis, 2006), p. 15.

[9] Gerald P. Fogarty, 'The Council Gets Underway', in Giuseppe Alberigo and Joseph A. Komonchak (eds), *Vatican II*, Vol. II: *The Formation of the Council's Identity. First Period and Intersession. October 1962–September 1963* (Maryknoll, NY: Orbis, 1997), p. 70. Fogarty is here referring to the Germanic-language areas from the Low Countries to the Austrian Alps as 'Central Europe'.

Already prior to the setting up of the preparatory commissions, John XXIII had taken the unusual step of inviting all bishops to freely formulate the issues and concerns which they felt should be considered at the forthcoming event, following no particular format in the drafting of their notes. About 2,000 bishops heeded this call. At this early stage of the proceedings, the episcopacy was still, for the most part, in sleep mode, cowed into submission by Pius XII's iron grip during his *ventennio*. 'The majority of these writings demonstrated surprise and disorientation. Rome was not issuing orders, but was asking for suggestions!'[10] With encouragement from the pope himself, before long the bishops' timidity and hesitations turned into proactive enthusiasm. The participant-observer and crucial player behind the scenes, Giuseppe Alberigo, continues: 'It was a gradual but rapid process, without any planning or management; the Council fathers were simply becoming aware of their role and of the vast and unforeseen horizons of the Council itself.'[11] The newly found self-confidence of the bishops meant that, at the end of the first (of four) council sessions, none of the schemata presented to them had been approved. The participants were in it for the long haul.

CONTRADICTORY PLURALISM

In assessing the milestones created by Vatican II, it is important to keep in mind that, not only did Vatican II experience the election of a new pope in mid-stream, which brought about a new configuration and a somewhat different dynamic to the procedures, but there is also the difficulty to determine what precisely are conciliar documents. Technically, of course, only documents approved by the entire body of council members are official contributions to the body of church doctrine by Vatican II. Yet, in the course of the three years of the various sessions, a host of other documents saw the light of day, notably papal encyclicals, such as John XXIII's testament of sorts, *Pacem in Terris*. Nominally not part of Vatican II procedures, the most important of such additional documents made public during the years of the council—and during the more than two years of the preparatory period— crucially influenced council procedures and attitudes. One should, moreover, note that such papal encyclicals were often more uncompromising and 'radical' documents than straightforward council decrees, declarations, and constitutions, as a pope did not have to heed expert advice by others in the course of the encyclicals' formulation to the same extent as the makers of products of council debates constantly reformulated by various committees.

---

[10] Alberigo, *Brief History*, p. 12.   [11] Alberigo, *Brief History*, p. 26.

In fact, council documents were invariably products of long-winded discussions, drafts, redrafts, and all sorts of negotiations, so that the final product was often a compromise solution, including hidden and not-so-hidden inbuilt contradictions that make interpretations of certain text passages difficult at best. Paul VI's tendency to go to greater lengths than John XXIII in order to soften the impact of the progressive majority's numerical preponderance at the council on the traditionalist and conservative minority further emphasizes the 'contradictory pluralism' which, in effect, in the end, often shaped the ultimate documents.[12] And literally the entire corpus of Vatican II documents was voted on and approved with Paul VI in the Holy See, rather than the less hesitant John XXIII! Small wonder that, in Giuseppe Alberigo's words: 'The Council as a whole, the Council majority, and the directive bodies coordinated by the majority gradually lost cohesion and efficiency. The sense that the body of bishops was the real main character of the Council, a sense that had been widespread during the first two periods, began to lose its intoxicating effect. What came to replace it, in addition to a greater sense of uneasiness, was a certain sense of fatigue.'[13] Still, Vatican II became the keynote event in twentieth-century Catholic history not because of the sometimes acrimonious dissensions amongst church fathers or its compromise formulations, but more importantly because of its conclusions voted on and approved.

A NEW ECCLESIOLOGY

By all means some of the central contributions of Vatican II were its pronouncements on the new ecclesiology which was to guide the Catholic church. Fundamental differences over the nature and the constitution of the church had already formed the basis for heated debates in the course of the rise and decline of what I have termed the first wave of Left Catholicism from the 1930s

---

[12] Note the cogent discussion of the multiple factors playing a role in the formulation of council documents in Peter Hünermann, 'Redécouvrir le "texte" passé inaperçu. A propos de l'herméneutique du concile', in Melloni and Theobald (eds), *Vatican II*, pp. 251–4. A brilliant guide towards an interpretation of key texts of official church doctrine, above all the documents emanating from Vatican II, can be consulted with much profit in the section entitled, 'Exkurs. Regeln zur Interpretation kirchenamtlicher Texte—und insbesondere des Zweiten Vatikanischen Konzils', in Otto Hermann Pesch, *Das Zweite Vatikanische Konzil (1962–1965). Vorgeschichte—Verlauf—Ergebnisse—Nachgeschichte* (Würzburg: Echter, 1993), pp. 148–60.

[13] Alberigo, *Brief History*, p. 90. The changing context and atmosphere of the later sessions are well described in Luis Antonio Gokim Tagle, 'The "Black Week" of Vatican II (November 14–21, 1964)', in Giuseppe Alberigo and Joseph A. Komonchak (eds), *History of Vatican II*, Vol. IV: *Church as Communion. Third Period and Intersession (September 1964–September 1965)* (Maryknoll, NY: Orbis, 2003), pp. 386–452, a week during which various tensions came to a head.

to the 1950s.[14] What happened at Vatican II is that, to a significant extent, the demands and expectations aired by this earlier generation of Catholic reformers now became official doctrine of the church. Discussions and negotiations surrounding various drafts and redrafts of what eventually became the *Dogmatic Constitution on the Church (Lumen Gentium* (LG)) took up a significant percentage of the council sessions. For it was, in fact, clear from the very beginning that the relevant texts presented by the preparatory commission were too timid to express majority opinion on this topic at the council. And a variety of alternative projects soon superseded the quickly abandoned original scheme.

Given several crucial interventions by John XXIII and Paul VI allowing bishops greater freedom to move within council deliberations, and given the fact that bishops—along with their theologian consultants—were the prime immediate beneficiaries of the new winds blowing at the Vatican, it comes as little surprise that some of the most innovative passages of *Lumen Gentium* concern the role of bishops within the newly defined church. LG 27 stipulated, for instance, in its opening passage that bishops are to be regarded as 'vicars and ambassadors of Christ', and that they should not be regarded as 'the vicars of the Roman pontiff, for they exercise an authority that is proper to them, and are quite correctly called "prelates", heads of the people whom they govern'. LG 22 had already prepared the terrain by stressing the importance of the principle of collegiality and the desirability of the creation of episcopal conferences to formulate policy, thereby suggesting that the episcopacy should have important powers returned to them which, over the past centuries, Rome had removed. And LG 22 also stipulated that bishops have 'supreme and full power over the universal Church, provided we understand this body together with its head the Roman Pontiff and never without this head.' Finally, in this select highlighting of the free space Vatican II was attempting to carve out for the episcopacy, LG 23 underscores that dioceses are 'particular churches' which already carry within themselves the essence of the universal church rather than constituting ever so many constituent parts of the church, with each diocese by itself lacking what it takes to be considered the church.

Yet it is also true that *Lumen Gentium* already carried within itself important qualifiers and latent contradictions. On the one hand *Lumen Gentium* includes formulations which clearly widened the space for autonomous manoeuvres by the episcopacy. And on 15 September 1965, Paul VI went yet one step further and indeed established a world council of bishops by his *motu proprio Apostolica Sollicitudo*. Yet this act fell short of a true emancipation of the episcopacy, as the pope retained the exclusive right to convoke the synod,

---

[14] See Horn, *Western European Liberation Theology, passim.*

to set its agenda, and to determine the remit of such synods.[15] And thus the discussion surrounding episcopal rights and liberties within the hierarchical constitution of the church showcased both the promises and the limitations evoked and set by Vatican II.[16]

If even the episcopacy could not legislate its own unequivocal emancipation within the upper rungs of the hierarchy, somewhat less was to be expected for the various members of the church on lower levels. True to form, on the one hand Chapter IV of *Lumen Gentium*, addressing the role of the laity, and the conciliar Decree on the Lay Apostolate, *Apostolicam Actuositatem*, certainly included important improvements in the role and status of laypersons in the church, which led Karl Rahner and Herbert Vorgrimmler, in their commentary on the corpus of documents approved by Vatican II, to suggest that to continue 'to keep down and to disenfranchise the laity within the church' must henceforth be regarded as an impossible path to pursue.[17] But, certainly in hindsight, the following prescient observation by Giuseppe Dossetti less than one year after the closure of Vatican II turns out to have been more appropriate. The Italian *éminence grise* of progressive Catholicism noted in his reflections that the entire range of council documents dealing with the role and status of laypersons turns out to have been 'particularly deficient and that, for all practical purposes, it has not marked much progress with respect to the very first preparatory schemes'.[18]

On the whole, however, *Lumen Gentium* is a milestone in the direction of greater autonomy for subordinate elements in the church's hierarchy, despite the fact that often the second half of a sentence partially rescinds the gains announced in the sentence's opening passage. In fact, the diplomatic manoeuvres surrounding the making of *Lumen Gentium*, including the wording of the final product, are an excellent example of the frequent observation by participant-observers that, quite often, the official documents emanating from the council, when placed under close textual scrutiny, fall short of the

---

[15] See the discussion of the *motu proprio* in Gilles Routhier, 'Finishing the Work Begun. The Trying Experience of the Fourth Period', in Giuseppe Alberigo and Joseph A. Komonchak (eds), *History of Vatican II*, Vol. V: *The Council and the Transition. The Fourth Period and the End of the Council. September 1965–December 1965* (Maryknoll, NY: Orbis, 2006), pp. 55–61.

[16] A number of contributions to the five-volume history of the Second Vatican Council edited by Alberigo and Komonchak include vital information on aspects of the fashioning of *Lumen Gentium*. Of particular detail is Alberto Melloni, 'The Beginning of the Second Period: The Great Debate on the Church', in Giuseppe Alberigo and Joseph A. Komonchak (eds), *History of Vatican II*, Vol. III: *The Mature Council. Second Period and Intersession. September 1963–September 1964* (Maryknoll, NY: Orbis, 2000), pp. 1–115.

[17] Karl Rahner and Herbert Vorgrimmler, 'Einleitung', in Karl Rahner and Herbert Vorgrimmler (eds), *Kleines Konzilskompendium. Alle Konstitutionen, Dekrete und Erklärungen des Zweiten Vaticanums in der bischöflich genehmigten Übersetzung* (Freiburg: Herder, 1966), p. 117.

[18] Giuseppe Dossetti, *Il Vaticano II. Frammenti di una riflessione* (Bologna: Mulino, 1996), p. 48.

proverbial 'spirit of Vatican II'. The Galician theologian Andrès Torres Queiroga put it like this: 'The extraordinary meaning of the Council far surpasses the actual letters of its texts which do not convey the true significance which animates them except when one places them in the context of the Council's grand design.'[19] And the ubiquitous Giuseppe Alberigo pointed out yet another rather important aspect of Vatican II, which has often been overlooked in the relevant literature, and which should be mentioned in this particular context. Whereas in the official council deliberations most of the bishops present played a rather passive role, the atmosphere in 'Off-Vatican' Rome presented a rather more lively picture. A constant flow of 'presentations, workshops, episcopal assemblies, informal conversations in cafés or inside buses during travel' to and from various venues contributed their own fair share to the fashioning of a positive view of the overall meaning of council deliberations by sympathizers of the progressive council majority.[20] It was at least in part due to this atmosphere surrounding the four sessions that the council deliberations were regarded by many as an open-ended and hopeful experience. Thus, despite the contradictory pluralism of quite a number of key text passages, what entered collective memory as the event of Vatican II was a perception of council procedures which did not always mesh with the reality of sometimes tense discussions in the corridors of power.

There was one aspect of the drafting of *Lumen Gentium* which symbolically captures the much invoked joyful and progressive 'spirit of Vatican II'. In October 1963, one year before the final approval of *Lumen Gentium*, the draft document on the constitution of the church, then still referred to as *De Ecclesia*, underwent an important change in the sequence of its chapters. Chapter 1 remained a reflection on the nature of the church, itself quite significant in part because, in its final passages, it is stressed that 'the Church encompasses with love all who are afflicted with human suffering, and in the poor and afflicted sees the image of its poor and suffering Founder' (LG 8). Yet the real novelty consisted in the reshuffling of Chapters 2 and 3. The original second chapter, which focused on the ecclesiastical hierarchy, was moved to Chapter 3. And the former third chapter, a discussion of the church as the People of God, now moved up to second place. The articles of what became Chapter 2 highlighted that all members of the church, via the act of baptism, were equal and united and thus form together the People of God. To place this enlightened discussion of the People of God prior to the disquisition on the hierarchy was a symbol-laden act and was understood as such on all sides of

[19] Andrès Torres Queiroga, 'Vatican II et sa théologie', in Melloni and Theobald (eds), *Vatican II*, p. 35.
[20] Giuseppe Alberigo, 'Vatican II et son histoire', in Melloni and Theobald (eds), *Vatican II*, p. 49.

the debate. 'The very succession of topics would demonstrate their decreasing theological importance.'[21]

THE ROAD TO *GAUDIUM ET SPES*

Compared to *Lumen Gentium*, the second major council document, the *Pastoral Constitution on the Church in the Modern World (Gaudium et Spes)* reads more straightforwardly, and its message thus comes across in less equivocal terms. Unlike most other council documents, it is almost entirely a product of the council deliberations themselves. For the preparatory commissions had never even attempted to address the relationship of the church to the world in one coherent schema. Comments on this—hitherto in church history—uneasy relationship had been interspersed within various schemata in an unorganized fashion.

Both *Lumen Gentium* and *Gaudium et Spes* can be traced back to the 20 October 1962 'Message to the World', officially proclaimed by the council on the tenth day of its first session. It had been drafted out of a growing sense of episcopal 'dissatisfaction with the schema drafted by the preconciliar commissions and from a determination to correct its direction'. In other words, it was a reflection of the bishops' rapidly growing self-awareness and their wish to have the progressive council majority determine the agenda of Vatican II, rather than the traditionalist minority entrenched in the bulwark of the Roman curia. Andrea Riccardi succinctly describes the message's content: 'This rather short text moves on two levels: one focused on the self-presentation of the Church and its mission, the second on showing the world the solidarity of Catholicism in regard to the great problems of the age.'[22] The first theme eventually mutated into *Lumen Gentium*, the second became *Gaudium et Spes.*

To place *Gaudium et Spes* in a larger context, brief mention must be made of what was perhaps the most important papal encyclical in the years of Vatican II. For the 11 April 1963 encyclical of John XXIII, *Pacem in Terris*, was a remarkable and astounding document in more ways than one. It was the first encyclical to be addressed to all of humanity—and not just to the members of the Catholic church. It broke with an age-old theological tradition by denying that there could be any such thing as a just war, certainly now in the atomic age. And *Pacem in Terris* for the first time proclaimed that human beings are invested with inalienable rights that are absolute values unassailable

---

[21] Alberigo, *Brief History*, p. 49.
[22] Both citations in this paragraph are from Andrea Riccardi, 'The Tumultuous Opening Day of the Council', in Alberigo and Komonchak (eds), *Vatican II*, Vol. II, p. 53 and p. 50.

by any authority.[23] But what is *Pacem in Terris*'s most important contribution in the context of the genesis of *Gaudium et Spes* is its repeated recourse to 'the signs of the times' as measures and tools with which to comprehend the reality of a constantly changing world. The innovation of this approach lies in its implied recommendation to study in all seriousness contemporary reality and society in order to determine in which way the values of the Gospel have materialized in today's world. Rather than relying on pre-established and traditional doctrine to judge present-day reality, Catholic believers are enjoined to place trust in investigatory methods that could be described as sociological, historical, and anthropological, before making value judgements on the phenomena of today's world.[24] And it is certainly in large part due to such methodological insights that *Pacem in Terris* was able to astound the world with its innovative insights and recommendations.

Perhaps Giovanni Turbanti puts it best when he points to the crucial impulses given by *Pacem in Terris* to subsequent deliberations in the making of *Gaudium et Spes*. For it openly encouraged efforts 'to observe in history and in the world the positive moments', rather than to view the world and humanity as primarily the source of most evils. 'This theological position implied a fundamental choice for an optimistic perspective, in sharp contrast to the negative vision which had characterized a large portion of theology and Catholic culture in prior decades.' Unsurprisingly, but importantly, such a novel vision also led to innovative conclusions. Rather than stressing the centrality of the gap dividing the contemporary world as being the opposition between communism and capitalism, the less blinkered assessment of *Pacem in Terris* would thus conclude that the world was divided into rich and poor.[25] *Pacem in Terris* was certainly the most explicit document in which John XXIII made use of such a historical and sociological method which had fallen into disuse within official circles of the Catholic church for quite some time.

In some respects, of course, this methodological approach is not all that far removed from what Alberto Melloni regards as the red thread behind John XXIII's personal and theological itinerary: Giuseppe Roncalli's distinct penchant to rely far more on close readings of the Bible than on various doctrinal 'traditions' established in subsequent centuries by the church.[26] In that sense, John XXIII echoed some central preoccupations of earlier reform theologians, who had engaged in a generational quest 'to return to the sources'.

---

[23] This last point is particularly stressed by Alberto Melloni, *Pacem in Terris. Storia dell'ultima enciclica di Papa Giovanni* (Bari: Laterza, 2010), pp. 69–70.

[24] A classic restatement of this social scientific method is presented by Marie-Dominique Chenu, *La Doctrine sociale de l'Église comme idéologie* (Paris: Cerf, 1979), pp. 64–5.

[25] Turbanti, 'Vatican II et son monde', citations on pp. 64 and 65.

[26] Alberto Melloni, *Papa Giovanni. Un cristiano e il suo concilio* (Turin: Einaudi, 2009), pp. 118–26.

GAUDIUM ET SPES

Gaudium et Spes (GS), Peter Hünermann suggests, was a document *sui generis*: 'Unlike previous treatises on ecclesiology, this document was to deal not with hierarchical structures and the prerogatives characteristic of the Church, but rather with the relationship of the Church to the people of the present age.'[27] Heeding the signs of the times, *Gaudium et Spes* became a sign of the times in its own right. For it is a commonplace in the literature on *Gaudium et Spes* to stress the fact that, in virtually all subsequent, post-conciliar debates within the Catholic church, the roots of the issues at hand were topics broached already in *Gaudium et Spes*. Or, to cite a Dutch theologian: '*Gaudium et Spes*, the pastoral constitution on the Church in the World of today, is *the* document of the Second Vatican Council.'[28]

'The joys and the hopes, the griefs and the anxieties of the men of this age, especially those who are poor or in any way afflicted, these are the joys and hopes, the griefs and anxieties of the followers of Christ' (GS 1). The opening sentence of *Gaudium et Spes*'s preamble already clearly points in the direction in which the church fathers were headed with this pastoral constitution. The document then quickly got to the point by stating in unequivocal terms that 'the Church has always had the duty of scrutinizing the signs of the times and of interpreting them in the light of the Gospel'. Whether the church had always actually conformed to such an attitude was tactfully left unaddressed. The church fathers at Vatican II were more concerned with present-day realities and the future of the church—as well as the world. Article 4 continued: 'We must therefore recognize and understand the world in which we live, its explanations, its longings and its often dramatic characteristics. Some of the main features of the modern world can be sketched as follows' (GS 4).

This is not the time and place to reconstruct the concrete sequence of arguments chosen by the drafters of *Gaudium et Spes*.[29] What is crucial, however, is to highlight the anthropocentrism of this document, as well as its consistent orientation towards an analysis and assessment of the most burning questions facing the modern world today. One echo of this—for conservative Catholic theologians—rather non-traditional approach can be easily detected in the structure of the document itself. In the first part of the constitution, entitled 'The Church and Man's Calling', in fact, despite its title, the relevant chapter on the church, 'The Role of the Church in the

---

[27] Peter Hünermann, 'The Final Weeks of the Council', in Alberigo and Komonchak (eds), *History of Vatican II*, Vol. V, pp. 422–3.

[28] Erik Borgman, 'Gaudium et Spes, les perspectives oubliées d'un document révolutionnaire', in Melloni and Theobald (eds), *Vatican II*, p. 105; emphasis in the original.

[29] The definitive work on the drafting process of the pastoral constitution will remain for quite some time Giovanni Turbanti, *Un concilio per il mondo moderno. La redazione della costituzione pastorale 'Gaudium et Spes' del Vaticano II* (Bologna: Il Mulino, 2000).

Modern World', stands in fourth (and last!) place in this section. Chapter 1, 'The Dignity of the Human Person', Chapter 2, 'The Community of Mankind', and Chapter 3, 'Man's Activity Throughout the World', take preference in this document. And even within each individual chapter, each theme is first addressed in general terms as well as judged in terms of its consequences in ways that could speak to all human beings, before finally being given an interpretation in light of church teachings.[30]

Two specific elements of *Gaudium et Spes* should be highlighted in order to grasp the full importance and novelty of this pastoral constitution. One pertains to the questions of war and peace, which were then, in the early-to-mid-1960s, in the wake of the Cuba Crisis and the rapidly quickening nuclear arms race, uppermost on people's minds. Though somewhat less clear-cut in its pacifist orientation than John XXIII's *Pacem in Terris*, *Gaudium et Spes* nonetheless contains strident condemnations of warfare in the modern age, and it refused to countenance the invocation of standard military procedures demanding unconditional obedience by subordinates and, another novelty for a conciliar document, it instead included a rousing praise and defence of soldiers who refuse to follow immoral orders:

> Even though recent wars have wrought physical and moral havoc on the world, the devastation of battles still goes on day by day in some part of the world. [...] Contemplating this melancholy state of humanity, the council wishes, above all things else, to recall the permanent binding force of universal natural law and its all-embracing principles. Man's conscience itself gives ever more emphatic voice to these principles. Therefore, actions which deliberately conflict with these same principles, as well as orders commanding such actions, are criminal, and blind obedience cannot excuse those who yield to them. [...] The courage of those who fearlessly and openly resist those who issue such commands merits supreme commendation. (GS 79)

Another trail-blazing argument central to *Gaudium et Spes* pertains to a matter which traditionally has been regarded as the social teaching of the church, in other words the questions of social inequality in the modern age, largely brought to the forefront during the industrial revolution in the course of the nineteenth century. *Rerum Novarum* (1891) and *Quadragesimo Anno* (1931) had set first benchmarks in slowly coming to terms with the conflictual relationship between capital and labour. As in so many other things, it was 'the Christian Pope', John XXIII, who finally expanded the boundaries of official church doctrine in this respect beyond what Leo XIII and Pius XI had dared to say. His encyclical *Mater et Magistra* (1961), but also to some extent certain passages in *Pacem in Terris*, proclaimed the need to strengthen workers' rights

---

[30] On this, I follow the argument put forth by Karl Rahner and Herbert Vorgrimmler in their 'Einleitung' to *Gaudium et Spes* in their *Kleines Konzilskompendium*, p. 427.

as well as the need for increasing the remit of organizations set up to collectively defend the rights of labour. Nonetheless, *Gaudium et Spes* broke further new ground in this respect.

Article 67, the first specific mention of labour and of workers in the constitution, already established the atmosphere within which the ensuing articles of the subsection, 'Certain Principles Governing Socio-Economic Life as a Whole', must be seen. It opened with an unequivocal statement highlighting that, in the conflictual relationship between capital and labour, the council's sympathies lie on the side of the weak: 'Human labour which is expended in the production and exchange of goods or in the performance of economic services is superior to the other elements of economic life, for the latter have only the nature of tools' (GS 67). As Pius XI had already mentioned in *Quadragesimo Anno*, Article 68 of *Gaudium et Spes* noted: 'Amongst the basic rights of the human person is to be numbered the right of freely founding unions for working people', adding that strikes may 'remain in present-day circumstances a necessary, though ultimate, aid for the defence of the workers' own rights and the fulfilment of their just desires.'[31]

Yet *Gaudium et Spes* goes beyond *Quadragesimo Anno* in explicitly enlarging the terrain of fruitful activity for unions and other workers' associations in general, recommending 'the active sharing of all[32] in the administration and profits of their enterprises in ways to be determined', a conciliar stamp of approval for various schemes of co-determination and workers' participation in the running of their enterprises. Amazingly enough, *Gaudium et Spes* went even one step further: 'Since more often, however, decisions concerning economic and social conditions, on which the future lot of the workers and of their children depends, are made not within the business itself but by institutions on a higher level, the workers themselves should have a share also in determining these conditions—in person or through freely elected delegates' (GS 68).

If the articles on labour's rights were already refreshingly clear calls for an attenuation of the prevailing social order, *Gaudium et Spes* reserved its most explicit condemnation of the status quo for class relations in the Third World:

In many underdeveloped regions there are large or even extensive rural estates which are only slightly cultivated or lie completely idle for the sake of profit, while the majority of the people either are without land or have only very small fields, and, on the other hand, it is evidently urgent to increase the productivity of the fields. Not infrequently, those who are hired to work for the landowners or who till a portion of this land as tenants receive a wage or income unworthy of a human being, lack decent housing and are exploited by middlemen.

---

[31] Rahner and Vorgrimmler add in their astute commentary: 'A right of lock-out for employers is not mentioned'; see Rahner and Vorgrimmler, *Kleines Konzilskompendium*, p. 440.
[32] That is, in the words of the constitution, 'owners or employers, management or labour'.

And the council fathers then, in full logic, mandated that 'reforms are necessary', notably including the socialization of landed estates: 'Indeed, insuffi-
ciently cultivated estates should be distributed to those who can make these
lands fruitful' (GS 71), a truly revolutionary measure of enormous relevance to
the majority of countries in the world of the 1960s and one of the driving
forces behind the genesis of Liberation Theology in subsequent years. It is easy
to see how such passages in *Gaudium et Spes*—and there were plenty of other
topics raised in this constitution which cannot be addressed in this context—
provided wind in the sails of social justice campaigners around the world,
certainly the small army of such activists drawing on inspiration for their work
from Catholic teachings.

   For the moment, however, it is necessary to return to the philosophic–
theological underpinnings of *Gaudium et Spes*, its single-minded focus on the
world as it was, and its option for the identification and support for those
elements which were hopeful and forward-oriented in today's world. And
such an orientation towards actually existing realities, rather than the time-
worn doctrinal certainties transmitted in repetitive and tiring manuals from
one generation of (neo)scholastic scholars to the next, had as consequence and
corollary what I earlier called the anthropocentrism of *Gaudium et Spes*. The
Catalan Benedictine monk from Montserrat, Evangelista Vilanova, formulated
this insight in these straightforward terms: 'Another central principle was both
anthropological and Christological: the central place of both the human
person and Christ emphasized the unity of the human vocation and the
importance of earthly values and activities.'[33] Article 2 of *Gaudium et Spes*
put it like this: 'Therefore, the council focuses its attention on the world of
men, the whole human family, along with the sum of those realities in the
midst of which it lives; that world which is the theatre of man's history, and
the heir of his energies, his tragedies and his triumphs; that world which the
Christian sees as created and sustained by its Maker's love, fallen into
the bondage of sin, yet emancipated now by Christ, Who was crucified and
rose again to break the stranglehold of personified evil, so that the world might
be fashioned anew according to God's design and reach its fulfilment.'

YVES CONGAR

If, apart from the Roman curia and the two popes, the bishops played the
central role at Vatican II, then it also stood to reason that theologians gained
more room to move at the very same time. Often intervening in their newly

---

[33] Evangelista Vilanova, 'The Intersession (1963–1964)', in Alberigo and Komonchak (eds),
History of Vatican II, Vol. III, p. 408.

found roles as experts and advisers for bishops congregating in Rome, theologians rose to new heights of prominence as well, if usually somewhat hidden behind the screens. One of the most tireless of them all, Yves Congar, almost two decades later reflected on the division of labour between bishops and theological advisers: 'One group utilized the work prepared by others; there was mutual interaction and exchange.' 'At Vatican II, council fathers and "experts" most frequently worked *together*.' 'We were aiding the bishops. It is true that one of the ways in which we supported them was by keeping them informed on the state of the art of Christian thought, by urging them to intervene, to prepare the materials that would shape their interventions. But,' Congar did not fail to note, 'they remained the judges, the masters.'[34]

Yet even the bishops were ultimately mostly pawns in a larger game. In fact, as noted above, Paul VI's September 1965 *motu proprio*, which (re-)established a synod of bishops as an institution within the hierarchical structure of the church, had already indicated in no uncertain terms that such episcopal assemblies would remain utterly dependent on the decisions and moods of papal authority. Post-Vatican II history proved pessimistic commentators right. The emancipation of the episcopacy, sketched in bold terms in *Lumen Gentium*, never truly came to be and, as the years went by, the independent powers of the bishops became a pale shadow of what many had hoped for when Vatican II deliberations were still in full force.[35] The growing silence and passivity of most, though not all, bishops after 1965, however, did not entail a similar attitude of quiet despair on the part of most theologians. Having smelled freedom, the newly enfranchised body of theologians were far more reluctant to accept the moderating course which could already be detected in the latter half of Vatican II, and which became more noticeable within a few years after the closing of council deliberations on 8 December 1965. It was, once again, Yves Congar who summarized the new rules of the game in his diary entry one month prior to the closing ceremony of Vatican II: 'The council was largely the result of the contributions by theologians. The period following the council will not retain the spirit of the council unless it carries on the work of the theologians.'[36]

Yves Congar has been repeatedly cited in part because he incorporated the presence and influence of theologians at Vatican II better than anyone else. For Congar's lifework came to fruition precisely in the thirty-eight months of

---

[34] Yves Congar, *Le Concile de Vatican II. Son église, peuple de Dieu et corps du Christ* (Paris: Beauchesne, 1984), p. 80; emphasis in the original.

[35] A telling assessment of the evolution of the inner workings of the Catholic church, by means of a shrewd and honest comparison of the synods of 1969 and 1985, can be consulted in Jan Grootaers, 'Collégialité et primauté dans l'application de Vatican II', in Leo Kenis, Jaak Billiet, and Patrick Pasture (eds), *The Transformation of the Christian Church in Western Europe 1945/2000* (Leuven: Leuven University Press, 2010), pp. 267–80.

[36] Congar, *Journal*, Vol. II, p. 465.

the council's duration. The Dominican hailing from the French Ardennes expressed this sentiment very well in the following succinct terms: 'I was content. The great causes which I had attempted to serve came into their own during the council: renewal of ecclesiology, tradition, reform efforts, ecumenism, laity, mission, ministries [...]'[37] Five months before the death of Congar, Étienne Fouilloux formulated it as follows: 'Thanks to the multiform activities which he undertook in order to have its message understood and received, Father Congar becomes *the* theologian par excellence of Vatican II,'[38] a well-deserved eulogy.

Yves Congar had established his international reputation as a forward-looking theologian since the second half of the 1930s, when he first made waves with his plea for the ecumenical approach in his 1937 *Chrétiens désunis. Principes d'un oecuménisme catholique*. Two contributions to the heated discussions concerning ecclesiology, a transnational debate which saw French theologians in vanguard positions, the 1950 *Vraie et fausse réforme dans l'Église* and the 1953 *Jalons pour une théologie du laïcat*, firmly established Congar's position as one of the leading theological defenders of church reform. But there was a price to be paid. Having already spent the years of World War II in German prison camps, it was now up to his church superiors to send him, from early 1954 to late 1956, into forced exile, first in Jerusalem and then Cambridge where Congar suffered from particularly severe restrictions imposed by the hierarchy, curtailing most meaningful contact with co-thinkers. The bishop of Strasbourg then offered Congar some respite from persecution by offering him a home in the Dominican convent in Strasbourg. Congar could now resume his intellectual work, though the shadow of church condemnation still clouded his various pursuits.[39] When, on 20 July 1960, Yves Congar learned from the pages of *La Croix* that he had been nominated as an expert at the forthcoming council, this news took him by complete surprise. Initially, he remained on the margins of the deliberations, but from spring 1963 onwards Congar was able to take on a leading role in council work. Ultimately, as hinted at above, 'Yves Congar had a hand in half of the Vatican II texts, at some stage.'[40] Yet the actual leading role of

---

[37] Yves Congar, *Une passion: l'unité. Réflexions et souvenirs 1929–1973* (Paris: Cerf, 1974), p. 90.

[38] Étienne Fouilloux, 'Frère Yves, Cardinal Congar, Dominicain. Itinéraire d'un théologien', *Revue des sciences philosophiques et théologiques* 79 (1995), p. 400; emphasis in the original. This is a text based on a presentation held in Paris in January 1995, five months before Congar's death on 22 June 1995.

[39] Apart from Fouilloux's 'Frère Yves', pp. 379–404, amongst the many biographical sketches one should note the intellectual biography by Joseph Famerée and Gilles Routhier, *Yves Congar* (Paris: Cerf, 2008).

[40] Fergus Kerr, *Twentieth-Century Catholic Theologians* (Oxford: Blackwell, 2007), p. 45.

Yves Congar in council procedures will not be dealt with in this study.[41] Instead, as with other theologians covered in this survey, emphasis will be placed on his activities and intellectual evolution once the council had closed shop.

THE PEOPLE OF GOD

'A new ecclesial climate was created by John XXIII in the space of a few weeks, then by the council. The most important opening came from above. Suddenly, the forces favouring renewal which, earlier on, had difficulties breathing fresh air, could unfold their activities.' Yves Congar then added: 'The timid examples of reform, which were mentioned in our text published in 1950, have largely been overtaken!'[42] Even a far-sighted reform theologian like Yves Congar could not but be affected by this new and promising conjuncture. With innovation no longer punished but encouraged, an unmistakable radicalization of ecclesiological thought soon set in. In Congar's case, it focused on the creative dynamic brought about by the fortuitous combination of two key concepts rediscovered and popularized in the 1930s and 1940s by theologians of the generation to which Congar himself belonged: the mystical body of Christ and the people of God.

Paralleling the growing social presence and organizational power of Catholic Action, the corresponding greater self-awareness of the laity had led to an important innovation in ecclesial thinking: the rise of the concept of 'the mystical body of Christ' as a novel view of what constituted the church. In my work on the first wave of Western European progressive Catholicism I merely stated the obvious when noting that, in the course of the 1930s, 'there is no doubt that the doctrine of the mystical body of Christ became what could be regarded as the theology of Catholic Action'.[43] The view of the church as 'the mystical body of Christ' allowed the inclusion of laypersons as a constituent part of the church, at the expense of the—earlier on—widely accepted vision of the church as being composed almost exclusively of members of the clerical strata from priests on up. Congar noted in 1971: 'Prior to the ecclesiological renewal of the past forty years, which has been to all intents and

---

[41] The definitive work on this subject is now Michael Quisinsky, *Geschichtlicher Glaube in einer geschichtlichen Welt. Der Beitrag von M.-D. Chenu, Y. Congar und H.-M. Féret zum II. Vatikanum* (Berlin: LIT, 2007).

[42] Yves Congar, 'Préface de la Seconde Edition', *Vraie et fausse réforme dans l'Église* (Paris: Cerf, 1968), p. 8, a text written at Christmas 1967.

[43] On the relationship between the rise of Catholic Action and the corresponding popularity of 'the mystical body of Christ', see Horn, *Western European Liberation Theology*, pp. 69–79, citation on p. 73.

purposes consecrated by the council, the vision of the church vulgarized by manuals was dominated by the notion of *societas inaequalis hierarchica*, not by notions of community or the people of God. The doctrine of the mystical body sometimes created a breach in the ramparts of clericalism but,' Congar then added, 'this doctrine itself was sometimes interpreted to strengthen the actually existing unequal and hierarchical society (*Mystici Corporis*).'[44]

Whatever the merits of the doctrine of the mystical body of Christ, from the late 1930s onwards, a number of theologians developed the notion of the church as 'the people of God' as an alternative vision. It was another way of defining and describing the new view of the church as being an organic whole, including everyone who has received the sacrament of baptism, notably both laypersons and the various rungs of the clerical ladder. The council documents emanating from Vatican II gave clear priority to the concept of 'people of God' over 'the mystical body of Christ'. Congar, a key proponent of this termino-logical innovation,[45] explained the choice of that concept by the conciliar preference for 'a certain sociological approach in the discussion of the church, at the expense of a more mystical vision',[46] and Congar likewise noted: 'The council wanted to distance itself from an exaggerated view of the homogeneity between Christ and the church. At the very moment when, for the first time in history, the church defined itself or, rather, declared and described itself, it wished to avoid an ecclesiocentrism' potentially implied by the reference to the mystical body of Christ.[47]

Yet the definition of the church as the people of God had other conse-quences as well. The more sociological approach permitted an easier under-standing of the church as being composed of clergy and laity, two distinct analytical categories 'differing from each other as a result of the different manner in which they participate' in the church's functions.[48] 'In effect, within the church, not everyone exercises the identical responsibilities, nor does everyone have the same means of communication and action. The entire church must stand for peace, but the means by which the pope can act is not the same as that of the Berrigan brothers: one does not see a pope burning the archives of military recruitment offices!'[49] Furthermore, the concept of the

---

[44] Yves Congar, *Ministères et communion ecclésiale* (Paris: Cerf, 1971), pp. 34–5. *Mystici Corporis* was an important encyclical by Pius XII in which he laid claim to the doctrine of the mystical body of Christ to reinforce existing ecclesiastical hierarchies.

[45] Note the clear-cut assertion: 'The central category of Congar's ecclesiology is that of the people of God'; in Rosino Gibellini, *Panorama de la théologie au XXème siècle* (Paris: Cerf, 2004), p. 234.

[46] Yves Congar, *Un peuple messianique. Salut et libération* (Paris: Cerf, 1975), p. 84.

[47] Congar, *Un peuple messianique*, p. 83.

[48] Yves Congar, 'L'Église comme peuple de Dieu', *Concilium* 1 (1965), p. 20.

[49] Congar, *Un peuple messianique*, p. 173. In one of the most prominent anti-war actions in the United States during the Vietnam War period, Daniel and Philip Berrigan, along with seven other United States Catholic peace activists, on 17 May 1968, removed 378 files from the military

people of God likewise underscored far more powerfully than the mystical body of Christ the rapidly growing emphasis on the central role of humanity in the life and definition of the church.[50]

Yet, as Congar came to realize in the course of the 1960s, the substitution of 'the mystical body of Christ' by 'the people of God' entailed some negative consequences as well. In particular, Congar affirmed, the eschatological and messianic potential of the church cannot be adequately expressed by the anthropocentric notion of the people of God. When considering the 'promises realized by the Incarnation of the Son and the gift of the Holy Ghost, the ones to whom the promises were made, i.e. the people of God, obtain a position which one can only adequately express by emphasizing the categories and the theology of the mystical body of Christ'.[51] Viewing the church as the mystical body of Christ could prove to be advantageous and 'necessary in order to take into account what the people of God had become after Incarnation, Easter and Pentecost'. 'The fault of Father Koster', the first theologian to have propagated the notion of the people of God as an alternative concept preferable to the mystical body of Christ, 'was not his praise of the use of the category "people of God", but to have built it up in opposition to the category of the body of Christ, the latter then still overshadowed by its medieval use' as a concept which largely excluded the laity.[52] Thus, Congar proposed a promising synthesis of both insightful concepts rather than viewing them as competing categories for a better understanding of what the church should be like as a constituent element of the modern world.[53]

Along with such a refinement of key ecclesiological concepts, Congar further concretized his ecclesiology as such. In the course of the 1960s, Congar began to criticize some of his own views he had put forth in his 1950 and 1953 studies on ecclesiology. What had been regarded as forward-looking and rebellious, netting Congar persecution and exile in the mid-1950s, Congar himself now regarded as no longer in tune with the *Zeitgeist*. In particular, Congar criticized his own retention of a linear view of the constitution of the church as divided into the categories of Christ, the priesthood, and the laity, all constituent elements of the church but not necessarily equal. He now, in hindsight, noted the 'danger of making the hierarchical priesthood into a mediator, implying the view of the faithful as disenfranchised, powerless and passive'. In his 1971 reassessment of his original ecclesiology, Congar now proposed a more egalitarian, dynamic, and thus circular view of the position

---

draft office in Catonsville, Maryland, took them to a parking lot outside the draft bureau, poured home-made napalm over the paper files, and burned them to a crisp.

[50] Or, in Congar's own terms, the notion of the people of God highlights that 'ecclesiology included an anthropology'; see Congar, 'L'Église', p. 22.

[51] Congar, 'L'Église', p. 32.   [52] Both citations are in Congar, 'L'Église', p. 32.

[53] Gibellini, *Panorama*, pp. 234–5.

and role of various elements constituting the church. 'One must thus substitute the linear view with a view in which the notion of community appears as the overarching reality within which the ministries, even the institutionalized and sacramental ministries, are regarded as services of what the community is called upon to be and to do.'[54]

THE MESSIANIC DIMENSION

The growing presence and self-confidence of the laity within the Catholic church, more securely positioned in the 1960s compared to earlier decades, ultimately explains the changing ecclesiology of a key theologian, such as Yves Congar. The socio-political context of the long sixties likewise helps to explain the growing attention to the messianic and liberatory mission of the church which increasingly became a reference point for Yves Congar, particularly in the 1970s. On the occasion of the tenth anniversary of the council, Yves Congar emphasized that 'Vatican II was accompanied and, even more so, followed by socio-cultural changes whose depth, radical nature, rapidity and cosmic character are without equivalent in any other historical epoch.'[55] In another publication at roughly the same time, he likewise noted how the doctrines put forth by Vatican II, 'which are neither outdated nor dead', coexist in a creative tension with even newer ideas, 'which aim to concretize themselves within the uncertainties of—and in dialogue with—current affairs. Solely to heed one while ignoring or repudiating the other appears to us as no solution. Attempting to unite the two risks to leave behind those who are committed to one approach at the exclusion of the other. Too bad! I envy those who, like Gustavo Gutiérrez or Joseph Comblin and quite a few others, attempt the same synthesis by means of an onerous, effective and concrete engagement in liberation movements. To each their own destiny and their vocation.'[56]

'Since 1968 (Medellín), we have seen a proliferation of "theologies of liberation", which stand in a line of continuity with "theologies of development" and "theologies of revolution".'[57] Congar writes elsewhere in *Un peuple messianique*: 'At the council, the church has realized that, to be Catholic, one must be Christian; in the post-conciliar period one has learned that, to be Christian, one must be a human being, i.e. one must take an active part from the inside in the building of the world, the great liberation movement, coextensive with the history of humanity.'[58] For Congar, however,

[54] Congar, *Ministères et communion*, pp. 18 and 19.
[55] Yves Congar, 'Les lendemains de conciles', in Yves Congar, *Concile de Vatican II*, p. 106.
[56] Congar, *Un peuple messianique*, p. 8.   [57] Congar, *Un peuple messianique*, p. 166.
[58] Congar, *Un peuple messianique*, p. 151.

engagement in the liberation movements operating in the here and now would clearly benefit from a simultaneous and ongoing, constant focus on the ultimate destiny of humanity in salvation. Human liberation and ultimate salvation are two sides of the same coin and organically interlinked.

Latin American liberation theologies, Congar asserts, 'show that revolutionary praxis, i.e. solidarity with the oppressed expressed in word and in deed and an efficient engagement in actions for liberation, constitutes the very point of departure for the elaboration of a valid theology of liberation'.[59] Yet ' "salvation" is more than "liberation". Salvation signifies something total and definitive: "one is done with all that" '.[60] For Congar, 'this utopia of a Kingdom to Come is a crucial touchstone, a point of comparison of our terrestrial accomplishments, always partial and provisory, in the area of justice and liberation'.[61] The biblical and utopian vision thus by no means hinders or precludes engagement and participation in the struggles of humanity today. Quite the contrary! 'The salvation of God and Jesus Christ as a matter of principle radicalizes the goals and demands of liberation.' Within the church, 'the awareness of the gap between the goals achieved and the ideal goal' has 'always' been a driving force behind reform efforts rather than constituting an obstacle.[62]

The following and final citation perhaps summarizes this fruitful and promising dialectic between liberation and salvation in optimal terms:

> Movements of authentic human liberation enter into the design of God; they form a constituent part of the latter. But the designs of God, of which Jesus and the Holy Ghost are the agents and which lead towards the Kingdom to Come, surpass all instances of human liberation, evaluate their accomplishments and radicalize their purpose. It is precisely because God's design transcends the options for humanity and human struggles that Christian salvation leaves such options and the corresponding battles as the tasks for history and in the full responsibility of human beings. Still, in the end, it is the project of divine salvation via Jesus Christ which overtakes, evaluates, and radicalizes the efforts of human beings to bring about temporal liberation.[63]

MARIE-DOMINIQUE CHENU

On 13 November 1964, after a gathering at one of the laboratories behind the scenes of Vatican II, Rome's Belgian College, where the think tank and study

---

[59] Congar, *Un peuple messianique*, p. 152.   [60] Congar, *Un peuple messianique*, p. 154.
[61] Congar, *Un peuple messianique*, p. 168.   [62] Congar, *Un peuple messianique*, p. 170.
[63] Congar, *Un peuple messianique*, p. 168.

group, called 'Church of the Poor', had its headquarters,[64] Yves Congar noted in his diary: 'Presentation by Father Chenu, a Chenu in two hundred per cent top form: intelligence, vitality, prophetic vision, presence. An analysis simultaneously of sensational prophetic vision and intellectual rigour.'[65] There were many ties which bound the two Dominicans together in their efforts to bring the church into the twentieth century and beyond. Chenu, nine years older than Congar, had taught Congar during the latter's theological studies at the (in)famous Le Saulchoir near Tournai in Wallonia from 1926 to 1931. Vatican II brought them into fruitful regular personal contact again.

Congar was 61 years old when the council ended in December 1965, Chenu already 70. Both theologians had, in effect, completed most of their lives' work in earlier decades. Chenu had shocked Vatican circles already in 1937 when he presented his ringing defence of scientific historical research within theological studies, later published as *L'École du Saulchoir*, in front of a small audience at Le Saulchoir in Kain, located between the first capital of the Frankish empire, Tournai, and the pilgrimage destination of Mont Saint Aubert. Quickly finding its way into the circuit of Catholic theologians, this pathbreaking volume was placed on the index in February 1942. And Chenu became one of the first reform theologians to bear the brunt of an early onslaught of Pius XII's manoeuvres in defence of 'orthodox' tradition, losing his position as director of research at Le Saulchoir.

Chenu soon made a name as the theologian who stood closest to the radical apostolic social movements created in the course of the first wave of Left Catholicism in Western Europe, likewise formulating innovative theologies of incarnation and theologies of labour. From 1954 to 1959, in the darkest years of Pius XII's pontificate, Chenu was removed from Paris and exiled to Rouen. It was as adviser to a former student of Chenu's at Le Saulchoir, the bishop of Madagascar, Claude Rolland, who participated in the Vatican deliberations, that Chenu returned to the limelight of ecclesial action. And Chenu immediately left a mark on council history as the author of the original draft of the opening salvo at Vatican II, 'The Message to the World', approved by the body of council fathers on 20 October 1962. As mentioned above, this programmatic manifesto prefigured the doctrinal innovations of both *Lumen Gentium* and *Gaudium et Spes*.[66]

---

[64] On this informal but influential grouping, see Denis Pelletier, 'Une marginalité engagée. Le Groupe "Jésus, l'Église et les Pauvres"', in Matthijs Lamberigts, Claude Soetens, and Jan Grootaers (eds), *Les Commissions conciliaires à Vatican II* (Leuven: Bibliotheek van de Faculteit Godgeleerdheid, 1996), pp. 63–89.

[65] Congar, *Journal*, Vol. II, p. 264.

[66] On the genesis of this document, note above all André Duval, 'Le Message au monde', in Étienne Fouilloux (ed.), *Vatican II commence...: Approches francophones* (Leuven: Bibliotheek van de Faculteit der Godgeleerdheid, 1993), pp. 105–18.

As in my discussion of certain aspects of Congar's oeuvre—and, in the subsequent subsection, the contributions by Karl Rahner—I leave largely unaddressed the particular role played by Chenu in the course of council deliberations.[67] Emphasis will be placed on post-conciliar publications by Chenu. An astute biographer, Antonio Franco, recently noted on this final period in Chenu's long and productive life: 'We can affirm that Chenu, from 1965 to the end of the 1970s, did no more than to comment on and to deepen several doctrinal elements of Vatican II, in the first place *Gaudium et Spes*.'[68] A close look at some of Chenu's writings in those crucial post-conciliar years will, however, discover that Chenu considerably developed 'several doctrinal elements of Vatican II'. Attention will be placed on two such elements: the 'signs of the times' and 'messianism', two dimensions of, as I will aim to show, the identical coin.

If there is one red thread that should be singled out in the personal and theological itinerary of Marie-Dominique Chenu, it is his consistent defence of the necessity for concrete engagements with historical reality, both in the past and in the present. Attention to historical texts, in Chenu's view, aids the modern-day theologian to discover long-forgotten and neglected church traditions that could become of great relevance for the revitalization of the church today. Attention to events and processes in the world today could not only open up one's vision to the realities of contemporary societies but at the same time open windows onto the ultimate destiny of humanity in the utopian Kingdom to Come. Past, present, and eschatological future are thus neatly linked in the historical theology of Marie-Dominique Chenu. It is instructive to point to some samples of Chenu's own relevant texts—but first a brief digression.

In October 1964, a Swiss Protestant pastor, Lukas Vischer, in the course of the deliberations of a conciliar subcommission, observed 'that, to recognize the signs of the times in the important historical phenomena of our epoch, we are not handed any criteria which permit us to distinguish the voice of God from any other misleading voice'.[69] Chenu, confronted with this observation, never delivered a social scientific, verifiable blueprint or user guide to facilitate a correct identification of such signs of the times which, at any rate, would have been difficult to deliver. Nor did anyone else. And, in fact, the question of how to sift the vast mass of concrete historical and social scientific data in order to distil the essence and the driving forces of concrete historical and social phenomena is, of course, fundamental to any historical or social

---

[67] Again, Quisinsky, *Geschichtlicher Glaube*, is now the definitive work on this subject.

[68] Antonio Franco, *Marie-Dominique Chenu* (Brescia: Morcelliana, 2003), p. 76. This slim volume is, in general, an apt and concise summary of Chenu's biography and theology.

[69] As reported by Marie-Dominique Chenu, 'Les Signes des temps. Réflexion théologique', in Yves Congar and Michel Peuchmaurd (eds), *L'Église dans le monde de ce temps. Constitution pastorale 'Gaudium et Spes'*, Vol. II: *Commentaires* (Paris: Cerf, 1967), p. 216.

scientific quest. Still, despite the absence of a systematic corpus of studies on this topic, in the course of Chenu's many ruminations on this theme, he developed important insights which transcend the field of theological studies and which have crucial bearing on any serious historical analysis of events and processes in the past and in contemporary society.

UTOPIANISM AND MESSIANISM

Perhaps Chenu's most powerful text in this regard was published in January 1965, when the council was still in full swing. Addressing the conundrum of how to recognize the signs of the times in concrete historical events, Chenu wrote:

> The storming of the Bastille in 1789 was, as the deed of a few Parisian insurgents, a fact of preciously little importance; such actions have occurred at countless times throughout history. Yet it was and became so significant that it could serve as a symbol for revolutionary disturbances, with many reverberations around the world, for the better part of a century. [...] What matters, then, is not so much to determine with much erudition how a specific event in the past occurred in all its details. We must instead strive to discover the hidden force within such an event, that element which constituted its soul [...] The directly tangible content of such an event—however important it may have been—is no longer the most crucial aspect, but the way in which it allowed the awakening of minds, capturing the energies and the hopes of human beings. [...] History consists indeed not so much out of a sequence of intricately related events, but instead out of collective, yes indeed, massive leaps forward by human beings, leading to qualitatively new levels of consciousness, a reorientation by means of which humanity suddenly steps into mental spaces of whose existence it had, for the longest time, not the faintest idea.[70]

Chenu here describes the process of human history as marked by a number of sudden leaps forward rather than a never-ending stream of countless individual tiny actions, all equally valid and of similar importance. It is a dynamic view of history, which has parallels in the writing of social scientists and even scientists *tout court*, not the least of which is a certain intellectual proximity to the Marxist view of history which pinpoints revolutions as 'locomotives of history'.[71]

---

[70] Marie-Dominique Chenu, 'Les Signes des temps', in Marie-Dominique Chenu, *Peuple de Dieu dans le monde* (Paris: Cerf, 1966), pp. 40–1. This contribution was a reprint of an article first published in the pages of *Nouvelle revue théologique* in January 1965.

[71] Note Thomas Kuhn, *The Structure of Scientific Revolutions* (Chicago: University of Chicago Press, 1962), together with Niles Eldrege and Stephen Jay Gould's theory of punctuated equilibria in evolutionary biology, for influential statements emerging from the world of natural sciences.

In an earlier work I have drawn attention to Chenu's recognition of such a moment of rapid change in the socio-political conjuncture at the very end of World War II when he suddenly realized 'that liberation would not only bring about the military expulsion of the enemy but, on a much more profound level, the joyful and triumphant explosion of a social and political aspiration in existence for some time'; that 'large numbers of hitherto amorphous human beings' suddenly were becoming conscious 'of their own power', just as 'we have witnessed in the demonstrations of 1936: this arrival of the masses at a consciousness of themselves'. 'In this manner, the human being chained to the assembly line, dehumanized and proletarianized; in this hour [i.e. during the final assault on the last redoubts of Nazi occupation strongholds], when he practises hatred to the maximum extent, he will simultaneously discover what one may call his myth, his ideal goal, his secret enthusiasm, his massive energies: the sense of a brotherly community of human beings.'[72]

In mid-twentieth century, Marie-Dominique Chenu had placed his hopes in the liberatory potential of the most visible radical social agent at that time. The blue-collar working class then appeared to incorporate the signs of the times. Twenty years later, Chenu's focus broadened, though the underlying concepts and categories remained identical: 'The 1955 Bandung Conference was something entirely different from a mere encounter of representatives from underdeveloped countries. The emancipation of women in the contemporary world is more than an improvement in economic, psychological and cultural life conditions. The gathering at the Second Vatican Council was more than an assembly of 2,500 bishops for deliberations and common decisions.'[73] Hope was now invested in such unforeseen movements and unpredicted developments. What had changed, however, were not only the precise agents of the desirable changes symbolized and indicated by the signs of the times. The eschatological dimension of such moments of crisis and opportunity was now stated far more explicitly than in Chenu's earlier texts.

The true significance of the study of the signs of the times for Chenu was precisely the way in which such facts or actions prefigured the ultimate salvation of humanity and the world in the Kingdom to Come, the ultimate state of grace. 'One must commence with the facts, "events" which determine the actual human condition and its profound mutations in order to

---

I have attempted to theorize the relevance of such crucial 'moments of crisis and opportunity' in modern history in my *European Socialists Respond to Fascism. Ideology, Activism and Contingency in the 1930s* (New York: Oxford University Press, 1966), pp. 11–12 and 157–66, with some empirical studies of recent moments of transition showcased in Gerd-Rainer Horn and Padraic Kenney (eds), *Transnational Moments of Change. Europe 1945, 1968, 1989* (Lanham, Md.: Rowman and Littlefield, 2004).

[72] All citations taken from my *Western European Liberation Theology*, pp. 108–9, punctuation and translation slightly amended.

[73] Chenu, 'Réflexion théologique', p. 210.

recognize the implicit resource of the capacity of grace';[74] 'the process of considering and identifying the signs of the times is part and parcel of the intelligence of belief, which grasps the mystery in its making and its historical realities in the past, present and future';[75] or, as Chenu put it elsewhere in the same article: 'It is therefore the "movements of history" which are the field of dialogue between the church and the world.'[76] 'The encounter with the world is an evangelical operation, which renders the church unto itself, according to the rules of incarnation of the word of God. God is immersing himself within history.'[77] The phenomena of the present obtain their true significance as signs of the times precisely 'because of the leap they introduce, not without ruptures, in the continuity of human history'.[78]

Similar to Congar, Chenu now became firmly convinced that the anticipation of the ultimate state of grace can only be grasped by means of concrete engagements in temporal reality, in the here and now. Salvation and human liberation are thus two sides of the identical coin for Chenu as much as for Congar. Earthly pursuits and millennial goals are intimately and indissolubly interlinked. 'The same distinction and the same unity', argues Chenu, 'can be seen in the hopes of human beings. There exist, to be sure, analytically speaking, two kinds of hope: temporal hope, so often praised and so fascinating, and Christian hope, all too often discussed and then forgotten.' Chenu then comes to the point by stressing that 'these two hopes do not only stand in no opposition to each other but they are linked to each other. Terrestrial hope appeals to the other, Christian hope nourishes the former: giving a sense of purpose to human beings, fighting against hunger in the world, installing justice, fraternity and peace, promoting the orderly and peaceful unification of nations, etc. [. . .] Human history is henceforth saintly history in the course of fulfilling its messianic promises. For that juncture between creation and redemption, within a unique history, has a name, a specific name, within Scripture and the Judeo-Christian tradition: it is *messianism*.'[79]

Christian Bauer, in his important two-volume study of the theology of Marie-Dominique Chenu, summarizes his findings in the following precise fashion: 'The messianic dimension is the decisive element of Chenu's theology. [. . .] The messianic dimension heads the entire theology of Chenu just like a mathematical "sign".'[80] My sole dispute with Bauer on this point regards the chronology of Chenu's messianism. Though always implied and sometimes

---

[74] Chenu, 'Réflexion théologique', pp. 212–13.
[75] Chenu, 'Réflexion théologique', p. 213.   [76] Chenu, 'Réflexion théologique', p. 215.
[77] Chenu, 'Réflexion théologique', p. 219.   [78] Chenu, 'Les Signes des temps', p. 42.
[79] Marie-Dominique Chenu, 'Une constitution pastorale de l'Église', in Chenu, *Peuple de Dieu*, pp. 31–2; emphasis in the original.
[80] Christian Bauer, *Ortswechsel der Theologie. M.-Dominique Chenu im Kontext seiner Programmschrift 'Une école de théologie: Le Saulchoir'*, Vol. II (Berlin: LIT, 2010), p. 774. Bauer's magnum opus, over and above its detailed intellectual biography of Chenu up to 1942, the

explicitly stated even in pre-Vatican II publications, the suddenly unfolding signs of the times in the course of the long sixties pushed Chenu further along a road he had already entered when he first ascribed redemptive powers to the working class within the social conflicts of the twentieth century. The awakening of the Third World, the unpredicted millennial flashpoint in the course of 'global 1968', and the inspiration and hopes unleashed by Vatican II made Chenu, not unlike Congar, a leading interpreter of the messianic message in the final decades of his life.

KARL RAHNER

If Yves Congar was the most influential theologian at Vatican II, Karl Rahner was by all accounts the most prominent theologian from Germany present at the deliberations in Rome. Yves Congar described Rahner's intellectual engagement in the work of the all-important theological commission in the following evocative terms. The group of advisers sat at a table separate from the actual commission members. 'If my memory serves me right', Congar recalled twenty years on, 'there were three microphones available on both tables.' The veteran reform theologian, Gérard Philips, the nominal leader of the periti advising the Doctrinal Commission, needed one of the microphones for himself. The two remaining microphones were there to serve the other ten experts. 'Rahner, however, seemed to have taken over one of these microphones, and that for a good reason. He contributed to the debate more frequently than anyone else, and certainly never in order to say anything that was of no importance.'[81] Henri de Lubac once confided to Bernard Sesboüé at the time of the council: 'Rahner is the most outstanding theologian of the twentieth century', an authoritative and enthusiastic claim, which is not diminished by de Lubac's subsequent revaluation of Rahner's heritage when he informed Sesboüé in 1983: 'I would no longer say the same today.'[82]

Whatever the precise position of Karl Rahner at Vatican II, it is clear beyond a shadow of a doubt that Rahner operated at the centre of a distinct

---

declared topic of this study, in its second volume also includes more than 200 fascinating pages on the overall theological contribution by Chenu.

[81] Yves Congar, 'Erinnerungen an Karl Rahner auf dem Zweiten Vatikanum', in Paul Imhof and Hubert Biallowons (eds), *Karl Rahner. Bilder eines Lebens* (Zurich: Benziger, 1985), p. 65.

[82] Bernard Sesboüé, *Karl Rahner* (Paris: Cerf, 2001), p. 26. By the late 1960s, Henri de Lubac, along with other reform theologians, including such figures as Urs von Balthasar and Joseph Ratzinger, who, earlier on, had formed part of the team of enthusiastic supporters of the council deliberations, distanced themselves from the grouping of theologians most committed to the spirit of Vatican II, leading to the formation of rival publications and a notable deterioration in personal relationships between the two blocs.

shift in the geography of theological innovation, a shift which occurred in the course of the 1960s, a move away from the near-total dominance of French or, at any rate, francophone thinkers as the shapers of the reform agenda in Catholic theology, towards Germans and, most certainly, germanophone theologians as the leading movers and shakers of forward-looking intellectual debates within such circles. It is beyond the remit of this particular study to investigate the causes of this secular shift, but the reality of such a sea change is clear. Congar, Chenu, de Lubac, and other francophone theologians were still in the limelight of council discussions as such, so that the deliberations of Vatican II themselves are, in fact, a poor indicator of this subterranean shift. Yet, in hindsight, it is clear that Vatican II constituted a watershed of sorts or, better, a moment of transition from the uncontested hegemony of French theology towards a new paradigm of German predominance.[83]

Karl Rahner was born less than six weeks earlier than Yves Congar and, like Congar, he reached adulthood and carried out his post-secondary studies in the late 1920s and the turbulent decade of the 1930s. A Heidegger student in his native Freiburg, in 1936 the Jesuit Rahner moved to Innsbruck, Austria. This quaint Tyrolean alpine town was then at the centre of a theological renewal effort organized around a group of theologians including Josef Andreas Jungmann and Rahner's elder brother, Hugo. Though never wholly convinced of the key theses of kerygmatic theology then formulated in Innsbruck,[84] certain features of it were clearly closely related to Rahner's own theological innovations, which he developed in the subsequent forty-five years before his death in 1984.

Jungmann's theology of predication (*Verkündigungstheologie*) emphasized the need for a theology touching the emotional and mystical needs of human-kind. Finding traditional theology, as then taught and practised for some time, far too focused on questions of methodology and painstaking theological detail, theologians at Innsbruck felt that the optimistic, utopian, eschatological dimension of Christian belief was in dire need of being restored to a central place in theological practice. Keeping an eye on the prize of the ultimate goal and fulfilment in salvation, so the kerygmatic theologians contended, would rekindle interest in Christian belief which had become too bogged down in excruciatingly formalistic and thus counterproductive efforts to contend with liberal modernist ideologies. Amongst other things placing greater weight on the figure of Jesus Christ than orthodox theologians, kerygmatic theologians

---

[83] For a stimulating *aperçu* of this intellectual paradigm shift in Catholic theology, note Christian Sorrel, 'La Théologie francophone au lendemain du concile Vatican II. Dominante ou dominée?', in Dominique Avon and Michel Fourcade (eds), *Un nouvel âge de la théologie? 1965–1980* (Paris: Karthala, 2009), pp. 181–91.

[84] 'For good reasons, this theory elicited no interest', claims Rahner retrospectively in his entry for 'Kerygmatische Theologie', in Karl Rahner and Herbert Vorgrimmler, *Kleines theologisches Wörterbuch* (Freiburg: Herder, 1963), p. 196.

likewise strove to give greater recognition and expression to the views and needs of human beings as such.[85]

In a rather tangible sense, then, during a brief but important period in the late 1930s and early 1940s, kerygmatic theology played a distinct role as a current of renewal within the German-speaking world, not entirely dissimilar to *Le Saulchoir* in francophone Europe. Yet, as Rosino Gibellini correctly notes, unlike the school of *Le Saulchoir*, which frontally attacked the dominant paradigm of theological tradition, the Innsbruck school left mainstream theology largely untouched, preferring to offer kerygmatic theology as a parallel or supplemental theology rather than as a superior alternative to the theology taught in seminaries and manuals far and wide. This may well have been a factor behind the less turbulent relationship between Rahner and the church hierarchy. For, regardless of Karl Rahner's precise involvement with kerygmatic theologians in the late 1930s, Rahner—unlike Congar and, most certainly, Chenu—did not run afoul of church authorities for quite some time.

What, then, were some of the key features of the theology developed by Karl Rahner? As in all other sections of this chapter, the investigative focus will be placed on just *some* of the main arguments of the theologian under review, with the selective focus on those elements which are of greatest relevance to the increasingly active Left Catholic communities on Western European soil.

One central theme of Rahner's thought is his constant concern to give prominence to the transcendental dimension of Christian belief. From early on, Rahner kept stressing the eschatological utopia of the ultimate state of grace as an important feature of human practice and human concern. Forever in constant dialogue with secular philosophers, scientists, and philosophers of science, Rahner by the 1950s developed a distinct theology of science which underscored the transcendental destination of humanity. Researchers, whether operating in the field of human or natural sciences, carry out their work motivated by the desire to stretch and enlarge the boundaries of knowledge. Yet, Rahner contended, the more scientists discover, the more they realize that the realm of potential knowledge grows ever more vast. Rather than slowly narrowing the limits of science, scientific pursuits enlarge the contours of the yet-to-be-discovered in a never-ending quest for knowledge. Knowledge engenders concrete insights, at the same time as it enables new open questions to be formulated. Most certainly, Rahner avers, science will never be able to discover everything and definitely never the ultimate mysteries of the world and of life. This ultimate destiny will remain the prerogative of religion and belief.

'As long as one is young, the danger is present to overestimate science. As one grows older, one realizes that science is not at all about deciphering the ultimate puzzles of existence. Instead, one grows more understanding vis-à-vis

---

[85] Rosino Gibellini furnishes a pithy summary of the Innsbruck school of kerygmatic theology in his *Panorama*, pp. 241–7.

those persons who expound the word of God', wrote Rahner in a 1957 contribution.[86] 'All learning about the world, all views of the world, all classifying comprehension of the multitude of phenomena in this world thus occur in anticipation of the unimaginable, the incomprehensible, that which is not part of this world and the image of the world, but which is an infinity, which cannot be comprehended as a manifestation of this world and its laws, that which stands behind the multitude of earthly realities', explained Rahner in a 1954 article attempting to grapple with the relationship between science and belief.[87]

Yet, what could easily have become a conception of the limits of science leading to passivity and an attitude of quiet, step-by-step and detailed empirical earthly pursuits in expectation of the eventual certainty of the ultimate salvation and the Kingdom of God, takes on a wholly activist and dynamic dimension in Rahner. For the focus on the transcendental redemption of life on earth goes coupled with a deep-going and equally fundamental concern with what is often called 'the anthropological approach of his theology'. Unlike much traditional theology, which then continuously strove to teach human beings the supposedly eternal values of theological doctrines, Rahner was most interested in the lived experience of humanity which, when placed in juxtaposition with the message of much religious belief, often clashed with the latter. Rahner concluded with a maxim which made many traditionalists frown: 'At the very beginning stands the human being, not the Church's statement of faith.'[88]

Transcendental destiny and everyday life became two sides of the same coin for Rahner, whose theology 'represents the most vigorous contribution emanating from the world of theology to what has been called the "anthropological turn" in theology', writes Rosino Gibellini in his informative survey of twentieth-century theological trends.[89] 'Transcendental experience', in the eyes of Rahner, is 'cause, condition of possibility and horizon of the experience of everyday life',[90] or, as Rahner formulated it towards the end of his life: 'If this experience of transcendence, lived by human beings in everyday life, where they are constantly going beyond all limits, can be called "mystique", then one could say that mystique happens already right in the middle of

[86] Karl Rahner, 'Der Akademiker. Notizen zur Frömmigkeit des Akademikers', in Karl Rahner, *Sendung und Gnade. Beiträge zur Pastoraltheologie* (Innsbruck: Tyrolia, 1959), p. 312.
[87] Karl Rahner, 'Wissenschaft als "Konfession"?', in Karl Rahner, *Schriften zur Theologie*, Vol. III: *Zur Theologie des geistlichen Lebens* (Einsiedeln: Benziger, 1956), p. 459.
[88] Karl-Heinz Weger, *Karl Rahner. Eine Einführung in sein theologisches Denken* (Freiburg: Herder, 1978), citations on pp. 22 and 23. I have only partially relied on the English translation of this text, Karl-Heinz Weger, *Karl Rahner. An Introduction to his Theology* (New York: Seabury, 1980), pp. 14–15.
[89] Gibellini, *Panorama*, p. 269.
[90] Karl Rahner, 'Ideologien und Christentum', in Karl Rahner, *Schriften zur Theologie*, Vol. VI: *Neuere Schriften* (Einsiedeln: Benziger, 1965), p. 68.

everyday life, hidden and unnamed, the condition of possibility for the most simple and elementary experience in everyday life.'[91]

RAHNER'S THEOLOGY OF HOPE

An orientation towards humanity and the seemingly mundane problems encountered in the process of living rendered Karl Rahner sensitive towards the hopes and desires of everyday individuals. From the early-to-mid-1960s onwards, doubtless under the influence of actually developing social movements and the mystique of Vatican II, Rahner increasingly coupled his reflections on the production of ever-greater knowledge with considerations on the necessity to bring about ever-growing freedom and autonomy for human beings.[92] 'Christendom is the religion of the future. It conceives of itself—and it can solely be understood—from the vantage point of the future, which it knows as an absolute future coming towards individual human beings and towards humanity as a whole. [...] Christian belief is thus the religion of becoming, the religion of history, of self-transcendence, of the future.'[93] Yet this absolute future, the ultimate salvation and the final experience of the state of grace, should not be viewed as a utopian goal which will arrive by itself regardless of human actions in the present. Belief in the coming of the absolute future must be coupled with the striving for a better future in the here and now.

> The hope for the absolute future of God, the hope for eschatological salvation, which is nothing other than the absolute God itself, does not legitimate a conservatism which—petrified and petrifying—prefers the safe present over an unknown future; it is not the 'opium of the people' which assures a passive attitude vis-à-vis present-day realities, even when reality is full of pain and suffering. It enables and commands the exodus out of the present into the future, notably including a better worldly future, something which can be trusted in and which must be constantly embarked upon.[94]

Improvements within the world we live in and belief in the reality of the ultimate state of grace are intimately related elements that must guide Christian action. 'Thus, where Christianity means genuine commitment to

---

[91] Karl Rahner, *Erfahrung des Geistes. Meditation auf Pfingsten* (Freiburg: Herder, 1977), p. 29.

[92] The caesura of the mid-sixties as the moment when Rahner's eschatology of hope takes on ever-more concrete contours is stressed by Walter Schmolly, *Eschatologische Hoffnung in Geschichte* (Innsbruck: Tyrolia, 2001), especially on pp. 261–88.

[93] Karl Rahner, 'Marxistische Utopie und christliche Zukunft', in Karl Rahner, *Schriften zur Theologie*, Vol. VI (Einsiedeln: Benziger, 1967), p. 78. 'Absolute future', for Rahner, denoted the ultimate destiny of humanity, the state of grace, utopia or the Kingdom to Come.

[94] Karl Rahner, 'Zur Theologie der Hoffnung', in Karl Rahner, *Schriften zur Theologie*, Vol. VIII (Einsiedeln: Benziger, 1967), p. 576.

this world and, at the same time, an affirmation of the absolute future, both necessitating each other, it creatively generates utopia, which criticizes present-day conditions and spurs us on towards a new historical future.'[95] 'The Kingdom of God will only come to those who are constructing the future worldly kingdom, always utilizing the means given to us within a given historical epoch, and thus changing the overall design continuously.'[96] 'It is strange that we Christians, who are engaged in the radical attempt to link concrete hope with the intangible absolute future, cast suspicion on ourselves—and are suspected by others—that, for us, the desire to conserve constitutes the fundamental virtue of life.'[97] Instead, it is precisely 'the hope for the absolute future, which we cannot fashion ourselves, which requires of us an engagement with concrete historical utopia, whose critical spirit makes history restless and moves it forward, thus generating the concrete societal manifestations' of utopian longing.[98]

It needs no further comment to realize the inspirational value of Rahner's seemingly esoteric and *weltfremd* transcendental theology for an activist generation of Christian students and others, who, by the mid-to-late-1960s, were coming into their own and, in a virtuous circle, in turn influenced the further development and radicalization of Catholic theology in the aftermath of Vatican II. The colleague and biographer of Karl Rahner, Herbert Vorgrimmler, repeatedly stressed Rahner's 'daring [and] courage to engage in dialogue'[99] or 'courage to engage with utopia'.[100] Rahner, perhaps more than any other German-speaking theologian active at Vatican II, thus performed a crucial role as intellectual pathfinder to create a situation in which the spirit of Vatican II soon became image, myth, and reality all at the very same time. Given the *Zeitgeist* of the 1960s and 1970s in particular, it comes as little surprise that some of Rahner's students soon began to embark on even more unorthodox and non-traditional pathways.

JOHANN BAPTIST METZ

Born in 1928 in Franconia, Johann Baptist Metz obtained his first university degree in 1951 with a work on Rahner's teacher, Martin Heidegger,

---

[95] Karl Rahner, 'Die Frage nach der Zukunft', in Karl Rahner, *Schriften zur Theologie*, Vol. IX (Einsiedeln: Benziger, 1970), p. 537.

[96] Karl Rahner, 'Christlicher Humanismus', in Rahner, *Schriften*, Vol. VIII, p. 256.

[97] Rahner, 'Zur Theologie der Hoffnung', p. 578.

[98] Rahner, 'Die Frage nach der Zukunft', p. 538.

[99] Herbert Vorgrimmler, *Karl Rahner. Gotteserfahrung in Leben und Denken* (Darmstadt: Primus, 2004), p. 263.

[100] Vorgrimmler, *Rahner*, p. 235.

and ten years later his doctorate in theology with Karl Rahner as supervisor.[101] Entirely educated at germanophone institutions, Metz's writings are significantly devoid of any major references to the first (almost exclusively) francophone generation of progressive Catholics, who had opened a breach for a radical reappropriation of Christian theology from the 1920s to the 1960s. The theology of Johann Baptist Metz, perhaps the internationally most influential radical reformer in the Western European Catholic church for some decades after 1968, is thus a powerful indicator that progressive Catholic theology had come of age. It was sufficiently developed, with multiple intellectual branches leading beyond its original francophone core, no longer to necessitate an obligatory filiation to Maritain, Mounier, Chenu, or Congar.[102]

Another *novum* with regard to Johann Baptist Metz in this genealogy of second wave Left Catholicism was the centrality of various germanophone secular unorthodox Marxist philosophers as key influences on Metz's thinking. Jacques Maritain in the 1930s and 1940s, as well as Marie-Dominique Chenu at all stages of his life, had certainly been engaged in sophisticated dialogue with the thought of Karl Marx, but Marx was a thinker safely removed in time and more a classic author than a contemporary threat. Herbert Marcuse, Theodor Adorno, and Ernst Bloch were contemporary neo-Marxists with a considerable following in the emerging, largely secular New Left. A close colleague and intellectual companion of Metz, his biographer Tiemo Rainer Peters, contends that Metz was 'influenced by no one else to the same extent as by Ernst Bloch'.[103]

Ernst Bloch, born in 1885, by the 1960s was a well-known German non-conformist Marxist philosopher, for whom the old anarchist adage, *ni dieu, ni maître*, fitted perfectly, having experienced exile in the 1930s in Czechoslovakia and, after 1938, living in the United States, then teaching in East Germany where he was forced into retirement because of his unorthodox opinions, leaving for Tübingen after the construction of the Wall in 1961. His magnum opus remains doubtless his 1959 three-volume *Das Prinzip Hoffnung*, in which he employed his encyclopedic knowledge of the natural sciences, philosophy, social theory, and theology to develop his vision of history and utopia as harbingers of a future unalienated life. His profound

---

[101] An informed introduction to the apprenticeship period of Johann Baptist Metz is Giacomo Coccolini, *Johann Baptist Metz* (Brescia: Morcelliana, 2007), pp. 13–50.

[102] Karl Rahner, of course, also developed his theology largely independently of the elaboration of French *nouvelle théologie*, but French philosophers like Maurice Blondel did exercise significant influence on Rahner's philosophico-theological itinerary, for which there are no equivalents in Metz's biography.

[103] Tiemo Rainer Peters, *Johann Baptist Metz. Theologie des vermißten Gottes* (Mainz: Matthias Grünewald, 1998), p. 24.

knowledge of biblical texts and theological doctrines found its crystallized expression in Bloch's 1968 *Atheismus im Christentum*. After his transfer to West Germany, his Tübingen home became a magnet for an imaginative mix of New Left and Left Christian students and co-thinkers, amongst them Jürgen Moltmann and Johann Baptist Metz.[104]

The first trail-blazing work of progressive Christian theology to emerge out of the creative confluence of Bloch's Marxist utopian messianism, the bright light cast by civil rights activism in the United States, the ebullient atmosphere of Vatican II, and emerging student activism across Europe and the wider world, belonged to the Protestant tradition. It was a fitting theological expression of the atmosphere of hope and expectation of a better future in the here and now, characteristic of the early-to-mid-1960s. The 1964 *Theologie der Hoffnung* by the Bloch-pupil Jürgen Moltmann lit up the sky of Christian theology like a bolt of lightning and immediately became a modern classic.[105] Within the rapidly growing circles of progressive theologians at that time, Moltmann's *Theologie der Hoffnung*, for theologians, performed a role similar to E. P. Thompson's *The Making of the English Working Class*, published one year earlier, which quickly became a standard reference work for forward-looking historians. It opened up radically new perspectives for theologians, facilitating a reconceptualization of their relationship to the modern world, the utopian project, and the interrelationship between theology and activist engagement in the present.

Johann Baptist Metz developed his political theology precisely in these years of radical optimism, when large numbers of activists believed in the seemingly unlimited possibilities for improvements in the human condition, the period up to and including the calendar year of 1968, when radical and utopian visions caught on like wildfire, similar to the heady atmosphere of the years leading up to and including 1848 in an earlier historical period. In the subsequent years of heightened radical activism, the red decade after 1968, no other theologian influenced progressive theologians and church activists in Europe and the world more than Johann Baptist Metz. Many of his key theses can, in fact, be clearly discerned already in the first publications pointing the way, appearing in the early-to-mid-1960s. In fact, his trail-blazing *Zur Theologie der Welt*, a compendium of articles on this theme published in the 1960s, was sent to the printer in February 1968, literally on the eve of 'May '68'.

---

[104] The most accessible and insightful biography of Bloch remains Arno Münster, *Ernst Bloch. Messianisme et utopie* (Paris: PUF, 1989).

[105] Hubert Goudineau and Jean-Louis Souletie, *Jürgen Moltmann* (Paris: Cerf, 2002).

ANTHROPOLOGY AND APOCALYPTIC
ESCHATOLOGY

Standing on the shoulders of earlier giants, Johann Baptist Metz first elaborated what became known as political theology within the conceptual framework of a 'theology of the world'. Taking note of the ever-growing de-sacralization of the modern world, which was habitually interpreted as an indicator of the waning of religion, Metz, to the contrary, took delight in this move on the part of humanity to determine itself. For Metz, it is precisely the logical consequence of the transcendental nature of God for humanity to have obtained such significant autonomy. God wants to have the world develop under its own worldly precepts and laws, reserving his own role for more important functions. It would have been completely wrong-headed to imagine Christendom as progressing in the world via a growing presence of God in this world. The 'increasing importance of profane elements in this world' and the 'de-deification' of the world, in fact, is a solid indicator of the presence and design of God behind the scenes.[106] 'Christendom, one could argue, is still in the opening stages of its worldly history.'[107] It is part of God's design for the world to develop largely autonomously in the historical present. It is part of the trajectory of humanity to eventually arrive at the promised state of utopian grace. The fact that 'human beings in the contemporary age no longer experience the world passively as fate, but influence its parameters in a positive direction'[108] is part and parcel of God's will. 'God wants this world',[109] wrote Metz, and the secularization of the world should not be cast aside as an impasse on the road to the Kingdom of God, but should instead be viewed as a preliminary and necessary stage.

This fundamentally positive acceptance of the modern world was, from the very beginning, coupled with a firm belief in the eschatological dimension of Christian belief; small wonder, given that Karl Rahner was Metz's most crucial early theological influence. But Rahner soon became creatively conjoined with Ernst Bloch, and Metz's writings rapidly became suffused with references to the 'principled and constant openness of humankind towards the singular, the unobtainable, the unexpected and the surprising in this world which, as such, becomes in its manifold details increasingly more obtainable and calculable',[110] although, and here Bloch's influence came even more strongly to the fore, Metz soon began to add immediately to his argument after such transcendental reflections: 'That which is emerging, the not-yet-being, the up-to-now-never-having-existed, the "new" cannot, by definition, become

---

[106] Johann Baptist Metz, *Zur Theologie der Welt* (Mainz: Matthias Grünewald, 1998), p. 30.
[107] Metz, *Theologie der Welt*, p. 64.   [108] Metz, *Theologie der Welt*, p. 139.
[109] Metz, *Theologie der Welt*, note 51 on p. 45.   [110] Metz, *Theologie der Welt*, p. 68.

40

the object of a merely contemplative consciousness (Bloch).'[111] 'Each eschatological theology must therefore become a political theology, a socially critical theology.'[112] 'The relationship vis-à-vis the future is operatively defined, the theory of this relationship is notably linked to action.'[113] Political theology, Metz noted in his first public presentation of his *political* theology, 'renders the world primarily as a social and historical world, history primarily as eschatological history, belief primarily as hope, theology primarily as eschatological and socially critical theology.'[114]

On one level, of course, as we have seen, for Rahner, too, anthropology was coupled with eschatology in his transcendental theology. But, as Metz never tired of underscoring from the mid-1960s onwards, 'in its transcendental, existential and personalist orientation', even the forward-looking theologians of his day—amongst them, crucially, Rahner—gave insufficient attention to the socially critical, practical dimension of theology that could respond to the needs and hopes of today. Though having identified some key issues preoccupying contemporary society, such theologians 'treat the relevant societal dimension of the Christian message, secretly or openly, as not crucial, as secondary,' essentially privatizing this social message and thus reducing 'the practice of belief into a supra-worldly decision for each individual',[115] with attendant nefarious consequences. 'By doing so, the utopian predications are stripped of their conflictual and contradictory characteristics vis-à-vis contemporary reality, and thus they are robbed of any socially critical powers.'[116]

For Metz, then, as for Rahner, the human being stood central in his role as mediator between world and God. But for Metz not only the 'subject' but also the intimately interlinked notion of human 'praxis' was an utterly crucial concept guiding his theology.[117] Rahner had theorized the need for an active engagement of Christians within their present-day societies to help usher in the absolute, i.e. eschatological, future, but such comments, as prescient and inspiring as they were to many of his readers and students, did not occupy a central place in his—after all—transcendental theology. Furthermore, in the course of the 1970s, Metz increasingly underscored the apocalyptic dimension of his eschatology, underscoring the necessity of a radical, if not revolutionary, break.[118] Given the parameters of Metz's emerging political theology, it comes as little surprise that critics within the church quickly began to accuse Metz of providing, over and above all else, and despite his continued emphasis on the centrality of belief and Christian faith, a thinly disguised Marxist theology.

---

[111] Metz, *Theologie der Welt*, p. 90. [112] Metz, *Theologie der Welt*, p. 106.
[113] Metz, *Theologie der Welt*, p. 78. [114] Metz, *Theologie der Welt*, p. 76.
[115] Metz, *Theologie der Welt*, p. 100. [116] Metz, *Theologie der Welt*, p. 102.
[117] Johann Baptist Metz, *Glaube in Geschichte und Gesellschaft* (Mainz: Matthias Grünewald, 1978), pp. 45–6.
[118] For instance, note pp. 71 and 156 in Metz, *Glaube in Geschichte*.

To the great surprise and consternation of friend and foe alike, Metz, in the face of such claims, went on the counteroffensive. Refusing to accept the view of some critics that he was merely providing a thin theological veneer for a materialist belief in progress and earthly utopia, Metz began to emphasize an element of his theology which had hitherto been rather underdeveloped within his argumentation, or at any rate not very central to it. Not only are the present and the future intimately linked, argued Metz, but he now increasingly projected his vision equally into the past as he did into the future. If Metz had done so in earlier years, it had usually been to contrast human suffering on earth with the eschatological absolute future. He now began to note with much greater stress that solidarity with the suffering, compassion with the op-pressed, must include the recognition of the crimes against freedom experi-enced by human beings in the past. 'What is true is that which is relevant for all subjects, also for the dead and the defeated.'[119] And Metz coupled this concretization and revaluation of the human past with a new emphasis on '"memory" and "narrative" as categories of salvation'.[120] 'By this is meant that dangerous memory, which narrows the margin of manoeuvre of the present and questions it, because it reminds one of the not-yet-present future. Such memories pierce right through the aura of ruling consciousness. They pin-point repressed and not-yet-happened conflicts and unrequited hopes. In the face of the dominant paradigm, they flag up experiences from earlier periods and thus render the present less self-evidently assured.'[121] And for the voice-less, weak and subordinate, the recapture of historical memory constitutes a primary weapon in their quest for redemption. Memory, whether kept alive through oral tradition or in semi-clandestine written format, constitutes a 'category crucial for the recapture of historical identity, a category of liberation'.[122]

Marxism, Metz of course knew, was also crucially interested in memory and narrative as tools for liberation. But Metz immediately diagnosed the blind spot in much Marxist ideology and the practice of states purporting to incorporate the Marxist tradition. Marxists tend to succumb to a naive optimism in the future, investing the proletariat with magic powers and liberation movements with unquestioned virtues. Yet a quick glance at recent history shows 'that the history of revolution can result in new histories of violence and oppression, that within emancipatory societies new histories of suffering develop'; or, in the words of Ernst Bloch here cited by Johann Baptist Metz: 'Within the citoyen of the French Revolution lurked the bourgeois; may God help us when we realize what is hidden within the comrade.'[123]

---

[119] Metz, *Glaube in Geschichte*, p. 57. [120] Metz, *Glaube in Geschichte*, p. 63.
[121] Metz, *Glaube in Geschichte*, p. 176. [122] Metz, *Glaube in Geschichte*, p. 64.
[123] Metz, *Glaube in Geschichte*, p. 106.

Like Moltmann's theology of hope, which, in the apt words of Claude Geffré, 'one must read as a theology of history elaborated on the basis of the concept of the future',[124] Johann Baptist Metz developed his political theology as a theology organically linking past, present, and future, informed by human praxis as the connective tissue. Like his teacher, Karl Rahner, Metz placed great emphasis on the combination of anthropology and eschatology in his theological constructions. But, whereas Rahner, when contemplating about God, 'closed his eyes', Metz advocated a 'mystique of open eyes'.[125] Rahner, though never shying away from linking his theological insights with public statements and interventions on political questions of the day, on the whole preferred the study chamber and meditation to the microphone and pulpit, though he made ample use of the latter, and not only at Vatican II. Johann Baptist Metz was far more proactive, and he went much further in the adaptation of Marxist precepts.

Still, Metz's recognition that there are potentially deep flaws in human beings, even the apparently most selflessly acting activist for liberation in the here and now, made him sceptical about casting his lot with any one particular programmatic vision for human liberation. Only the ultimate utopian vision, the belief in the redemptive powers of God, found Metz's unmitigated and total support. In fact, Metz contended, the missing sense of the potential and actual dangers of all (merely) human liberation movements rendered Marxism susceptible to a false sense of blind and naive optimism in the inevitable coming of a better future. Over and above the historic blind spot with regard to the failed promises of movements for human emancipation, such linear optimism in the future, Metz added, rendered Marxism likewise an easy victim to the trappings of evolutionary thinking and corresponding (political) behaviours.[126]

The true apocalyptic revolutionary, then, for Metz, remained the Christian. The message of utopia was thus best preserved and authenticated in religious language. Given the state of the world in the wake of global 1968, it is small wonder that Metz quickly became enormously popular with students searching for the utopian vision amongst the thinkers active in their day. Not only was Metz a much-invited guest and speaker at workshops and conferences in Europe and the world, but students from far and wide, including notably the Hispanic world, 'were now very noticeably represented in the circle of tutees taught by Metz, and they were the source, at the end of the Sixties, of exciting and stimulating discussions in seminars and colloquia'.[127]

---

[124] Claude Geffré, *Un nouvel âge de la théologie* (Paris: Cerf, 1972), p. 104.

[125] Peters, *Johann Baptist Metz*, p. 146.

[126] This is best argued in Metz, *Glaube in Geschichte*, p. 72, where, *inter alia*, Metz assesses in particular structuralist Marxism of the Althusserian kind, then much in vogue in intellectual circles, as 'in effect the neutralization of dialectics by means of evolution'.

[127] Peters, *Johann Baptist Metz*, p. 115.

ERNESTO BALDUCCI

The utopian and messianic dimension of the Christian message, a hallmark of second wave Western European Left Catholicism, characterized Balducci's theology in the post-Vatican II era just as much as it played a role amongst progressive thinkers north of the Alps. Born in 1922, Balducci, however, unlike Metz, lived a significant period of his years as a young adult in the circumstances of fascist rule, first under Mussolini's iron fist, then under the subsequent German occupation. Then followed the volatile conjuncture of liberation and the immediate post-liberation period. Having opted in his teenage years for a life dedicated to the church, his education took place under the aegis of the Piarist Order, a member of which he remained until his tragic death in a car accident in 1992. As was to be expected from a future noncon-formist, already as a seminarian Balducci was noted for his 'highly pro-nounced autonomy'[128] vis-à-vis the mainstream teachings of his Roman seminary, which he attended from 1938 to 1944.

As was the case with Karl Rahner and other protagonists of Left Catholicism who came of age before the end of World War II, Balducci was drawn towards French thinkers, notably Maurice Blondel, whose emphasis on the importance of subjective volition and existential queries appealed to him.[129] Though Balducci did not develop a distinct interest in political affairs until the aftermath of World War II, an October 1943 flyer by a radical Communist Catholic current, with a strong presence particularly in Rome, stuck in Balducci's diary for 1944, showcases an openness for a variety of traditions on offer in the crucible of Italian politics at the moment of liberation.[130]

Balducci's further education benefited tremendously from his presence in Florence from the autumn of 1944 onwards, after graduating from the Monte Mario Calasanctianum. Newly liberated Florence was then a laboratory of political and cultural experimentation second to none in all of Italy. Non-traditional Catholic thinkers coexisted in the Tuscan capital city in fruitful interaction with radical democratic spokespersons and intellectuals emerging from the Partito d'Azione, side-by-side with open-minded representatives of the Communist tradition. This exceptionally vibrant and stimulating atmosphere, which persisted for several important postwar decades, provided an ideal envir-onment for Balducci, who was then in search of defining his life's calling.[131]

---

[128] Bruna Bocchini Camaiani, *Ernesto Balducci. La Chiesa e la modernità* (Bari: Laterza, 2002), p. 16.

[129] Bocchini Camaiani, *Ernesto Balducci*, p. 4.

[130] On the presence of the flyer in Balducci's diary, see once again Bocchini Camaiani, *Ernesto Balducci*, p. 63. On the Italian 'Catholic Communist' current in the late 1930s/early-to-mid-1940s, see Horn, *Western European Liberation Theology*, pp. 124–36.

[131] A highly informative, detailed survey of the Florentine laboratory of cultural and political innovation is Ettore Rotelli (ed.), *La ricostruzione in Toscana dal CLN ai partiti*, Vols I and II (Bologna: Il Mulino, 1980–1).

What characterized Florence in his formative decades, in Balducci's own words, was 'a culture which was organically related to the process of liberation, an activist culture, even if diversified in accordance with the variety of [local] traditions. One of the characteristics of Florentine culture of which I am speaking is its ability to anticipate later developments.'[132] Focusing solely on Catholic manifestations of nonconformity in post-1944 Florence, Balducci felt inspired to proclaim thirty years after the events: 'I dare to say that in Florence one experienced the [Vatican II] Council [long] before the Council.'[133] The undisputed principal figure of Florentine Catholic politics in the postwar decades was Giorgio La Pira, one of the three most prominent figures in the left-wing opposition *within* Italian Christian Democracy of the immediate post-liberation period.[134]

Repeatedly elected mayor of Florence, La Pira was noted for his keen attention to social questions, frequently clashing with the local elites and conservative members of the ecclesiastical hierarchy. In addition, La Pira became internationally famous for making Florence the organizational hub of a series of international peace conferences, assembling leading representatives of the Eastern and the Western bloc—in the middle of the Cold War!—to search for a non-military solution to bloc confrontation. What aided the development of this peculiar Florentine Catholic microcosm was the presence of Cardinal Elia Dalla Costa as archbishop of Florence from 1931 to 1961. Virtually nowhere else in Italy—and probably nowhere else in Europe and the world at that time—could lay and Catholic observers witness the spectacle of a cardinal extending his welcoming hand to the acting mayor of Moscow in a location of such venerable tradition as Santa Croce in downtown Florence on the occasion of one of the spectacular international peace initiatives animated by La Pira.[135]

Despite Balducci's growing interest in social questions and the vagaries of war and peace—the central preoccupations of Giorgio La Pira from early on—it took a few years before direct contact was established between the enterprising mayor and the young Piarist. In the course of the 1950s, however, Balducci became a frequent contributor to the never-ending cycle of workshops and conferences organized by activists and intellectuals under the spell

[132] Ernesto Balducci, *Fede e scelta politica* (Milan: Mondadori, 1977), p. 217.

[133] Balducci, *Fede e scelta politica*, p. 9.

[134] A solid and informative short introduction to this remarkable figure in Cold War Italy and Cold War Europe is Massimo de Giuseppe, *Giorgio La Pira. Un sindaco e le vie della pace* (Milan: Centro Ambrosiano, 2001). The superior early biography, written in the middle of La Pira's activist phase, remains Marcel Jacob, *Giorgio La Pira. Der seltsame Bürgermeister von Florenz* (Colmar: Alsatia, 1955).

[135] In Balducci's own words: 'At the time, what caused a huge uproar was the most scandalous fact that Cardinal Elia Dalla Costa reached out his hand to greet the mayor of Moscow in [. . .] Santa Croce.' See Balducci, *Fede e scelta politica*, pp. 222–3.

of La Pira. In 1952–3, Balducci founded Il Cenacolo, a group of young Catholic activists, whose goals were to provide social assistance to underprivileged sectors of the Florentine population 'side-by-side with religious and spiritual education and expressions of socio-political preoccupations'.[136] Occurring in a city then already on the worry-list of the Vatican hierarchy, Balducci thus began to earn a certain reputation at that time. By 1958, he upped the ante by creating a new journal, *Testimonianze*, which, in the course of the 1960s, evolved into a leading mouthpiece of Italian progressive Catholicism. In 1959 the worried curia struck back. Under pressure from the Holy See, the superior of his order in effect exiled Balducci from Florence to take up a position in Rome. As the irony of history would have it, however, his first exile from Florence soon brought him into close personal contact with leading international reform theologians, who were teeming in the Eternal City when Vatican II eventually convened.

THE TURN TO THE TEMPORAL

If, prior to Vatican II, Giorgio La Pira had been Balducci's lodestar in socio-political affairs, in matters of theology a similar role was fulfilled by Jacques Maritain. The most influential philosopher in the ambit of Left Catholicism from the 1930s to the 1950s, Maritain had successfully defended freedom of choice for Catholics in secular matters, while emphasizing the overall primacy of the spiritual.[137] Following Vatican II and its call for an embrace of the modern world, such an approach, emphasizing the duality of temporal and spiritual spheres, no longer appeared to conform to the new *Zeitgeist*. Vatican II's enthusiastic embrace of 'the signs of the times' now caught the imagination of progressive Catholics such as Balducci. The primacy of the spiritual no longer appeared to provide answers to the questions of the day.[138] As was to be expected, Balducci became an energetic supporter of the innovations propounded by Vatican II. And *Testimonianze*, initially operating within a perfectly Maritainian 'contemplative atmosphere',[139] began to turn its attention

---

[136] Bocchini Camaiani, *Ernesto Balducci*, p. 156.

[137] A brief survey of the central figure of First Wave Left Catholicism can be consulted in Horn, *Western European Liberation Theology*, pp. 89–97.

[138] Balducci's move from convinced Maritainian to post-Maritainian advocate of new departures in the relationship between church and state is well argued in Daniele Menozzi, 'Chiesa e società nell'itinerario di Ernesto Balducci', in Bruna Bocchini Camaiani (ed.), *Ernesto Balducci. La chiesa, la società, la pace* (Brescia: Morcelliana, 2005), pp. 61–7; see also Mary Malucchi, *Ernesto Balducci. Cattolicesimo, Marxismo, etica planetaria* (Florence: Chiari, 2002), pp. 26–7.

[139] A phrase used by Luciano Martini in the conversation transcripts composing Balducci's *Fede e scelta politica*, p. 221.

increasingly to the here-and-now. By 1966, *Testimonianze* began to organize national conferences on various themes related to the message of Vatican II, causing conservative representatives of the curia to worry about the journal constituting, in effect, 'a political movement of the Catholic Left'.[140]

Ernesto Balducci first obtained a distinct degree of national notoriety when, in 1962–3, he publicly came out in full support of the first Italian Catholic conscientious objector to the military draft, Giuseppe Gozzini. Balducci's interventions resulted in judicial prosecutions by both civilian and ecclesiastic authorities, receiving much media coverage.[141] From then on, Balducci received constant invitations to engage in public debates, to give talks and furnish interventions in radio and television programmes. Likewise, he now received an endless stream of personal letters from (frequently) young Catholics in search of advice on how to reconcile their faith with concrete social and political engagements.[142] Balducci now emerged as the leading activist–reformer within the Italian Catholic church.

By the late 1960s, Balducci's personal–political–theological itinerary began to execute another turn. In the face of growing opposition by the hierarchy vis-à-vis the concrete implementation of the progressive message of Vatican II, Balducci began to air his growing doubts about the possibility for a thorough reform of the church. He began to fear that 'the sole effect of the Council would consist in a superficial reordering of the Church and a marginal renovation which would fail to affect profoundly public awareness'.[143] Monica Galfré dates this growing scepticism more precisely to 1968.[144] And, in fact, one symbolic measure of this increasing pessimism as to the self-reforming mechanism of the Catholic church can be seen in Balducci's relationship with Pope Paul VI. In 1966, Balducci was allowed to return to Florence due to the intervention of Paul VI, who was able to overcome the powerful opposition by Alfredo Ottaviani and the archbishop of Florence, Ermenegildo Florit. But in the wake of 1968, 'the elements of critique and dissent with regard to papal decisions become much more accentuated'.[145] In April 1969, Balducci could thus confide to his diary: 'The line of Paul VI, which is constantly more propelled by fear, finds echoes in the strengthening of the reactionary institutions of the episcopacy.'[146]

[140] Bocchini Camaiani, *Ernesto Balducci*, p. 209.

[141] Bocchini Camaiani, *Ernesto Balducci*, pp. 71–9.

[142] Note here the insightful comments by Nicoletta Silvestri, 'Archivio Privato Sezione I', in Bruna Bocchini Camaiani, Monica Galfré, and Nicoletta Silvestri (eds), *Percorsi di archivio. L'archivio di Ernesto Balducci* (Florence: Edizioni Regione Toscana, 2000), pp. 57–61.

[143] Malucchi, *Ernesto Balducci*, p. 42.

[144] Monica Galfré, 'Alle frontiere dell'inquietudine. Balducci e la Chiesa', in Bocchini Camaiani, Galfré, and Silvestri (eds), *Percorsi di archivio*, p. 177.

[145] Bocchini Camaiani, *Ernesto Balducci*, p. 224.

[146] Entry for 24 April 1969 in Ernesto Balducci, *Diari (1945–1978)* (Brescia: Morcelliana, 2009), p. 818.

By about 1968, Balducci began to cast aside his recently acquired 'progressive optimism' and began to search for new yardsticks. 'If the "yes" to the Council was due to its reconciliation with reason and modernity, his [now emerging partial] "no" to the Council was a result of the Council's non-critical manner of that reconciliation.'[147] In tandem with the evolution of Balducci's personal convictions, *Testimonianze*, in the second half of the 1960s, began to engage in an interpretation of *Gaudium et Spes* and Vatican II from the standpoint of constructive criticism, 'pointing in a more radical and theologically well-versed direction'.[148]

THE TURN TO MARX

During Italy's 'red decade', i.e. roughly the years 1968 to 1978, Ernesto Balducci embraced Marxism as a sociological tool towards an understanding of society. As was usually the case with Left Catholics, it was the prophetic and utopian dimension of Marxism which had most attracted Balducci to Karl Marx's thought, though up to the late 1960s this dimension of Balducci's spiritual quest had been on a backburner. In the wake of the student uprisings of 1968, followed by the worker-dominated Hot Autumn of 1969, class analysis rapidly became a stock-in-trade of Balducci's ideological arsenal. And along with this adoption of Marx's epistemology came the open recognition and embrace of the working class as vehicle for liberation.[149] 'One characteristic of workers is that, when they talk of justice and injustice and social equality, the worker does not express himself in difficult concepts but reflects everyday life and sees clearly what is at fault, who are the exploiters and who are the exploited.'[150]

Ernesto Balducci now embarked on a marriage of Marx and Christ without parallel in the contemporary Italian context. Up to now, Balducci wrote in his 1971 manifesto, *La Chiesa come eucaristia*, the perfect Christian was always seen to be a contemplative, passive Christian. 'At the apex stood the ideal of the saving of the soul, which, to achieve, one needed to live ascetically. Against this type of religion, Marxist criticism had an easy go for more than one century', with Marxism providing much-needed hope for liberation in the real world. Today, Balducci affirmed, we are witnessing the dawn of a new age.

---

[147] Note the relevant important passage in Raniero La Valle, 'Balducci e il Concilio', in Bocchini Camaiani (ed.), *Ernesto Balducci*, p. 334.

[148] Giovanni Turbanti, 'La lettura e i commenti di Ernesto Balducci al Concilio', in Bocchini Camaiani (ed.), *Ernesto Balducci*, p. 264.

[149] The crucial bibliographic reference for Balducci's Marxist turn is now Mary Malucchi's central second chapter of her *Ernesto Balducci*, pp. 61–84.

[150] Balducci, *Fede e scelta politica*, p. 54.

'The heritage of the past was that, in fact, frequently the men of faith [i.e. Christians] had no hope, and the men of hope [Marxists] were without faith.'[151] Now, perhaps, these two enemy brothers might successfully merge their efforts. In his 1975 programmatic article, 'Le speranze vissute all'interno della storia', Balducci had already sounded a more cautionary note, warning against secularization as a possible consequence should this meeting of erstwhile hostile traditions not occur. But, here too, Balducci fully supported the creative admixture of Marxist and Christian energies. For Balducci, 'taking up the cause of the working class [la scelta di classe] is the way in which I can translate my desire for a society conforming to human values. This is the way to express one's love for all of humanity.' The opposition to class rule under capitalism does not have to take the route of the physical elimination of one's opponents, 'but the elimination of those structures which create the conditions for human beings to become an adversary of humanity and humankind. And, therefore, class struggle is the historically necessary way to establish universal love.'[152]

From the late 1960s to the late 1970s, Ernesto Balducci was firmly convinced of the concrete possibility of human emancipation.[153] This view was closely related to a process which Balducci at one point described in the following manner: 'Are we indeed faced with, as Rahner writes, an anthropological turn? The characteristics of this turn lie in the fact that humanity takes back into its own hands the destiny of the world',[154] an expression which has a more than circumstantial affinity to certain Marxist tenets. Another central platform point of the Marxist philosophy of history, the postulated forward march of humanity from necessity to freedom, is of course closely related to the classic Marxist view of man making himself—or humanity making itself, in the language of today. Balducci likewise incorporated this prophetic insight into his theology. 'The Kingdom of God exists to the extent that one moves from a condition of inferiority towards liberty.' And Balducci affirmed that 'human history is a constant movement, never fully accomplished, from a regime of necessity to a regime of freedom. That is what the Kingdom of God is all about.'[155] In a further passage of one of his sermons transcribed and published in *La politica della fede*, Balducci dots all the remaining i's: 'In the

[151] Ernesto Balducci, *La Chiesa come eucaristia* (Brescia: Queriniana, 1971), citations on pp. 121 and 122.
[152] Ernesto Balducci, 'Le speranze vissute all'interno della storia', in Ernesto Balducci and Roger Garaudy, *Cristianesimo come liberazione* (Rome: Coines, 1975), p. 41.
[153] Note the clear statement to this effect by one of the closest co-workers and co-thinkers of Balducci for several crucial decades, Luciano Martini, 'La cultura di Ernesto Balducci', in Bocchini Camaiani (ed.), *Ernesto Balducci*, p. 119.
[154] Balducci, *Chiesa come eucaristia*, p. 121.
[155] Ernesto Balducci, *La politica della fede. Dall'ideologia cattolica alla teologia della rivoluzione* (Rimini: Guaraldi, 1976), p. 64.

past we measured the progress of Christianity by the quantity of devotional acts and by the degree of docility in accepting orders. Today we must move forward to a Christian world in which our maturation is measured by the capacity for autonomy. Not just any sort of autonomy. An autonomy which is, to the contrary, defined by its sense of responsibility. But nonetheless autonomy. Wherever there exists inertia and passivity, we are witnessing the opposite of the Kingdom of God.'[156]

Even in his openly Marxist phase, Balducci, it should be stressed, never conflated faith and human liberation in simplistic fashion. Balducci firmly held on to his conviction that Christian faith alone provides the key and the deeper meaning to the ultimate destiny of humanity. Yet, from the late 1960s onwards, the root cause of 'the contemporary degenerative phenomena' was no longer identified with 'ecclesiastical institutions, immobile and reactionary as they may be', but with the continued survival of class society.[157] The earlier ecclesiocentrism of Balducci's activism and teachings had become a thing of the past, though not yet entirely abandoned. Faced with the growing realization that the church would probably never change at the apex of the hierarchy, sometime in the second half of the 1960s Balducci began to seek ecclesial salvation in the revalorization of the church at the local, grassroots level.[158]

Given the extraordinarily precocious and vibrant emergence of a rapidly growing number of base communities in Italy, about which more in Chapter 3, it is thus wholly unsurprising that Balducci sought salvation in grassroots experiments of ecclesial action. Still, though very close to the colourful movement of base communities, Balducci never wholly identified with their various causes, similar to the way in which Balducci fundamentally supported all sorts of 'dissident' currents within the Catholic church without abandoning his critical distance to their various concretizations. A case in point is Balducci's bold and public defence of the most famous conflict pitting base communities against the Catholic church, the case of the Florence base community in the Isolotto neighbourhood (again, see Chapter 3 for further details), at the same time as this experience reinforced Balducci's reluctance wholeheartedly to cast his lot with radical grassroots Catholic dissent.[159] Taking a critical view of protest cultures in general, Balducci confided to his diary in January 1970:

---

[156] Balducci, *La politica della fede*, p. 65.

[157] Note here the stimulating passage in Malucchi, *Ernesto Balducci*, pp. 83–4, citation on p. 84.

[158] On this development note, amongst others, Martini, 'La cultura', pp. 115–16. Menozzi, 'Chiesa e società', pp. 71–2, dates this switch to sometime in the late 1960s and early 1970s. Maria Paiano, 'Cultura cattolica e chiesa italiana dal secondo dopoguerra al post-concilio', a stimulating introductory text to Ernesto Balducci's *Diari*, on pp. 117–18 dates this turn to the years 1966 and 1967.

[159] Note, in this context, the astute assessment of Balducci's somewhat guarded relationship with Catholic grassroots radicalism, including the classic case of the Isolotto, in Turbanti, 'La lettura', p. 270. Likewise, Paiano, 'Cultura cattolica', pp. 121–4, highlights the identical

The role models age rapidly. Two years ago, Marcuse was a luminary. Who still mentions him today? [. . .] Today's atmosphere is characterized by an acceleration of perceptions and appropriations. Each encounter is consummated instantly, and one moves on to the next. It is not necessarily the case that the values they encounter are outdated. Perhaps they are barely worked through, so that— especially amongst the young—the processes of intellectual growth take on the overtones of something unripe and hurried.[160]

From the late 1970s onwards, the fertile mind of Ernesto Balducci executed a further—and his final—intellectual turn. He began to formulate critiques of Marxism which roughly paralleled his earlier friendly critiques of Vatican II. Perhaps under the influence of several crucial defeats of Italian social movements in general and the Italian working class in particular, after 1976 Balducci increasingly took a critical distance from Marxism which, just like *Gaudium et Spes*, he now regarded as representing an overly simplistic embrace of modernity.[161] His belief in the possibility of human emancipation gave way to a growing pessimism and catastrophism over the future of this world.[162] Similar to other creative thinkers of his generation and intellectual calibre—Rudolf Bahro or André Gorz come to mind—Ernesto Balducci, after years of serious attention to the Marxist world view, now devoted his attention to the ecological and planetary dimensions of the socio-political questions of his day. His 1990 *L'uomo planetario* can thus be seen as his ultimate legacy,[163] yet this final evolution reaches far beyond the chronological purview of this monograph.

JOSÉ MARÍA GONZÁLEZ RUIZ

If Italy constituted the open laboratory par excellence of Left Catholics in the long sixties, Spain must be regarded as the country where progressive Catholics in all likelihood played, when placed in a comparative context, the most crucial roles in the overall social movement culture in the course of the 1960s. A number of reasons may account for this Iberian anomaly, but one of the most important rationales was the unusual status of Catholic institutions in the Spanish state. With political parties and trade unions outlawed since the Spanish Civil War, the Catholic church, an ideological prop for

mixture of instinctive sympathies and intellectual distance of Balducci towards the more radical variants of *il dissenso cattolico*.

[160] Diary entry for 15 January 1970 in Balducci, *Diari*, p. 824.

[161] La Valle, 'Balducci e il Concilio', p. 334.   [162] Martini, 'La cultura', p. 119.

[163] Ernesto Balducci, *L'uomo planetario* (San Domenico di Fiesole: Edizioni Cultura della Pace, 1990).

Franco's dictatorship in the forty years of its existence, was one of the very few 'organizations' outside the regime proper, which retained a certain degree of autonomy and independence. It was thus in part for these somewhat circumstantial reasons that opposition movements challenging the Francoist order— other than the organizations which had supported the Spanish Republic and which had then opposed Franco on the battlefields of the Civil War—first began to arise under the umbrella of the Catholic church.[164] Until the very end of the brutal dictatorship in 1975, church organizations and institutions, notably their facilities and buildings, often provided all-too-rare protection from the repressive strongarms of the state, even for groups of underground activists not hailing from the church milieu.

Benefiting from its special status, some initially rather marginal elements within the Catholic church in Spain constituted the first Catholic-inspired oppositional groups, above all certain sections of specialized Catholic Action operating within the working-class milieu (see Chapter 5), dating back all the way to the late 1940s and early 1950s. By 1956, Catholic students made headline news as university students suddenly became the unexpected mainstay of political unrest (see Chapter 4), and the subsequently emerging underground Spanish New Left, perhaps more powerful and influential for the course of national opposition politics than in any other European state,[165] was initially almost exclusively inspired and dominated by Left Catholic traditions and currents. The peculiarity of the Iberian political and ideological traditions helps to explain why the most radical theologian in the line-up of illustrious thinkers covered in this opening chapter hailed from Spain.

Six years older than Balducci and twelve years older than Johann Baptist Metz, José María González Ruiz, born on 5 May 1916, thus belongs to a generation located halfway between Chenu, Rahner, and Congar and the notably younger scholars discussed in the preceding subchapters. Born into a relatively well-off middle class family in Seville, the Andalusian sociopolitical context helped shape González Ruiz in ways that would be unthinkable and most unlikely in most other regions of Europe at that time. Andalusia was then a stronghold of anarchism, and the anarcho-syndicalist Confederación Nacional del Trabajo (CNT) exercised hegemony within the labour movement in Seville. In 1921, a series of strikes led by the CNT, then in its

---

[164] A similar situation enabled Portuguese progressive Catholicism to play a prominent role in the opposition movement facing the most long-lived right-wing dictatorship on European soil, the Salazarist regime. Here pioneering works include João Miguel Almeida, *A oposição católica ao Estado Novo. 1958–1974* (Lisbon: Nelson de Matos, 2008), and Joana Lopes, *Entre as brumas da memória. Os católicos portugueses e a ditadura* (Porto: Ambar, 2007).

[165] The standard work on the—outside Spain—little-known but vital and imaginative Spanish New Left remains Julio Antonio García Alcalá, *Historia del Felipe (FLP, FOC y ESBA). De Julio Cerón a la Liga Comunista Revolucionaria* (Madrid: Centro de Estudios Políticos y Constitucionales, 2001).

phase of temporary and ill-fated flirtation with the Bolshevik tradition—from 1919 to 1922 opting for membership in the fledgling Communist 'Third' International—paralysed Seville. González Ruiz's father was then the managing director of a leading vegetable oil manufacturing plant, and the factory was one of the very few large plants in Seville where the workforce, on its own volition, had decided not to heed the strike call. José María González Ruiz many decades later recalled a number of visits by one of the national leaders of the CNT, Salvador Seguí, to his father, hoping to convince him to use his moral influence over his workforce for the latter to join the general strike. 'My father, who, in very many ways, sympathized with the revolutionary ideas of that movement [the CNT], responded in a friendly manner, smiling: "I would agree with you, if it were not for Him . . .". "Him" referred to the crucifix prominently affixed on his office walls.'[166]

The syncretism of Andalusian culture and politics left a lasting memory in González Ruiz's mind. Syndicalist sympathies by a company manager coexisted with firm Catholic beliefs. One brother of his father was then bishop of Malaga, and José María's elder brother had entered a priest seminary at a young age. Soon José María decided to follow his brother's footsteps, entering the priest seminary, just like his brother, in Malaga to be close to his uncle. Bishop Manuel González Garcia, however, repeatedly clashed with his superiors and, in the mid-1930s, was removed from the diocese of Malaga and relegated to the remote provincial town of Palencia on the barren high plains of Castilla-León. José María followed his uncle there, eventually receiving ordination at the hands of his nonconformist uncle in Palencia. But Bishop González Garcia had already recognized the intellectual talents of his nephew and had arranged for José María to enrol in the Faculty of Theology at the Pontifical Gregorian University in Rome. From the second half of the 1930s onwards, the Eternal City became a home away from home for González Ruiz, even though the stultifying atmosphere of Rome and the Vatican in the era of Mussolini and Pius XI did little to make José María feel comfortable there in the first period of his Roman education.[167]

THE APPRENTICESHIP YEARS OF GONZÁLEZ RUIZ

From 1945 to 1948, González Ruiz took up a post as parish priest in his native Seville, though in a part of town which was home to the vast army of disenfranchised, under- or unemployed *sevillanos* then barely recovering from

---

[166] José María González Ruiz, *Memorias de un cura. Antes de Franco, con Franco y despues de Franco* (Malaga: Miramar, 1995), p. 32.
[167] González Ruiz, *Memorias de un cura*, pp. 15–40.

the horrors of the civil war. 'I discovered something hitherto unknown to me: the nobility of the soul of the poor.'[168] A teaching stint at a church institution in Malaga followed; soon thereafter, however, he was able to arrange for an appointment as a researcher at an ecclesiastical institute in Rome. And this is where his life took yet another turn.[169]

'During my second stay in Rome [. . .] I observed a great change in Italian public life.'

> Roman bookstores were overflowing with inexpensive editions of Marxist clas-
> sics. I felt immediately attracted to this literature. I literally devoured several
> works of Marx, Engels, Lenin, and Stalin. I recall the enormous impact which *The
> German Ideology* and *The Holy Family* [early works by Karl Marx] had on me.
> But I read all this in secret or, better, all by myself for, though there was no formal
> prohibition to do so, no one would have understood what I was doing.

'I lay awake during many nights listening to the Spanish or Italian edition of Radio Moscow', González Ruiz added, though he also noted a characteristic feeling of unease. 'I confess that it produced in me the identical impression of monotony and affectation as did the programmes aired by Radio Vatican.' A feeling of great empathy coupled with dissatisfaction settled in. 'As I had already experienced the lack of adequate connection between "theory" and "practice" in my role as a Catholic, I began to suspect that, in the other "camp", something similar was going on.'[170]

From then on, José María González Ruiz was consumed with the idea of bridging the gap between Marxism and Catholicism, two traditions which, in his view, had much in common but which also suffered from a tremendous lack of mutual recognition and respect. Forever travelling between the two worlds of Italy and Spain—Italy a democracy with a vibrant Communist tradition, Spain suffocating under a ferocious right-wing dictatorship but with growing pockets of resistance champing at the bit—with Malaga, Madrid, and Rome serving as home bases, González Ruiz eventually became a leading intellectual in various associations aiming to break down the artificial barriers between (unorthodox) Marxism and (progressive) Catholicism, notably with-in the Internationale Paulusgesellschaft, animated in its heyday in the second half of the 1960s by the Austrian gadfly journalist, Günther Nenning.

High-level gatherings assembling leading intellectuals from Eastern and Western Europe were part of González Ruiz's calling, just as much as more intimate encounters between curious individuals hailing from both camps. González Ruiz's account of the meeting between José María Díez-Alegría, perhaps the second most prominent Spanish Left Catholic theologian after

---

[168] González Ruiz, *Memorias de un cura*, p. 53.
[169] González Ruiz, *Memorias de un cura*, p. 69.
[170] All citations are from González Ruiz, *Memorias de un cura*, p. 70.

González Ruiz himself, and the leading Spanish Communist Manuel Azcárate at a *trattoria* in Rome may speak for itself: 'I believe that this was the first time that the—at that time—illustrious professor at the Pontifical Gregorian University in Rome had contact with a flesh-and-blood Marxist from abroad […] During the meal, Alegría, despite his natural communication skills, at first behaved rather awkwardly; but, as soon as we began to feel the effect of the wine from the hills surrounding Rome, the conversation became animated and the friendship was sealed.'[171] Not only was José María Díez-Alegría a prominent faculty member at the Roman Catholic university, but two of his brothers were officers in Franco's military!

GONZÁLEZ RUIZ AS SCHOLAR

Yet José María González Ruiz was just as much devoted to his studies. Theory and practice were, to him, always merely two sides of the same coin. True belief, for González Ruiz, was never concerned solely with orthodoxy, a term derived from the ancient Greek denoting 'correct belief', but to an equal extent with orthopraxy (correct action).[172] In an interview published in 2001, four years before his death, the Spanish theologian, whose work has been translated into all the major languages of the western world, noted that he had never accepted the standard division of theology into dogmatic theology, focusing on the theoretical truths of faith, and pastoral theology, concentrating on the practical applications of these theoretical truths: 'I always felt that theology is a pastoral stance and that pastoral activity must in some way be theological.'[173]

Starting in 1954, González Ruiz began to publish theological articles (and, eventually, close to two dozen book-length works) which rapidly established his name as an authority in biblical studies. What from early on began to characterize the theological contributions by González Ruiz was not so much his fervent devotion to the necessity to develop a 'theology of the world', a trend receiving a welcome boost by Vatican II, but his ability to substantiate the tenets of such a theology by reference to biblical passages which, in his eyes but not only in his eyes, had pointed the way in the identical direction already several thousand years ago. Equally familiar with orthodox and

---

[171] Cited in Pedro Miguel Lamet, *Díez-Alegría. Un jesuita sin papeles* (Madrid: Temas de Hoy, 2005), p. 152.

[172] The side-by-side discussion of 'orthodoxy' and 'orthopraxy', in the wake of 1968 a standard feature of Left Catholic thought, was a constant in González Ruiz's vocabulary then; note, for instance, the brief but pithy discussion in José María González Ruiz, *Dios está en la base* (Barcelona: Estela, 1970), p. 19.

[173] 'González Ruiz, el teólogo "cheuá"', conversation with Rafael Gómez, *El ciervo* (607), October 2001, p. 21.

unorthodox schools of thought in the realm of Marxist philosophy and Catholic theology, González Ruiz understood how to employ authorities from Paul the Apostle to Jacques Maritain—and Friedrich Engels to Erich Fromm—to construct an argument which appeared to synthesize the ideas of the entire range of unorthodox Catholic thinkers briefly featured in earlier sections of this chapter.

The necessity for a historical approach to theological studies, the imperative need for the church to shun privilege and to cast its lot with the poor and oppressed, the emphasis on the prophetic and messianic tradition within Christian practice and Christian thought, the defence of the necessity for humanity to construct its own world—without losing sight of the presence of God beyond this world: these and other tenets of the emerging tradition of Western European 'liberation' theology found powerful and evocative expression in the theology of José María González Ruiz. In this concluding sub-chapter of Chapter 1, rather than developing one or several particular points of González Ruiz's theology, I instead wish to highlight several insightful and lively passages to present the overall flavour and context of his work.

In 1967, writing for the flagship opposition journal, *Cuadernos para el diálogo*, González Ruiz straightforwardly asserted that 'capitalism must be considered from a Christian moral perspective as intrinsically perverse',[174] a declaration of disgust which, every reader then knew, did not hark back to the supposed golden age of Catholic civilization in bygone centuries, but looked forward to a future age when humanity could develop freely without cumbersome, unwanted, and unnecessary hierarchies and inequalities blocking its path. 'The New Testament, above all Paul, distinguishes between "power" (exousía) and "strength" (dunamis). Power is a technique of command; strength is the creative capacity of an ideal. [. . .] The "strength" of the ecclesial community stands in inverse relationship to "power". If the church lets itself be dazzled by power, it automatically loses part of its strength.'[175] As the title of one of González Ruiz's more famous texts gives away, 'God is at the grassroots' (*Dios está en la base*). Correspondingly, there are many passages celebrating the messianic message of Christianity as, even and especially within the Catholic church, there was a need for the creative interaction between leadership and ranks. 'An ecclesiology which is constructed from below inevitably results in the revalorization of the charisma of prophecy.'[176] Yet such charismatic leaders were neither removed in spirit from their followers nor were they unconcerned with earthly concerns and the details of the here and now. 'Prophets, the religious leaders of the people, were in no way

---

[174] Cited in Javier Muñoz Soro, *Cuadernos para el diálogo (1963–1976). Una historia cultural del segundo franquismo* (Madrid: Marcial Pons, 2006), p. 101.
[175] González Ruiz, *Dios está en la base*, pp. 71–2.
[176] González Ruiz, *Dios está en la base*, p. 94.

men who fled from reality and who solely kept themselves busy with "spiritual matters" in the Hellenic sense of the expression. To the contrary! They were marvellously informed about the political and social conditions determining the life circumstances of their people, and they spoke a concrete language, direct and committed.'[177]

'About a century ago,' wrote González Ruiz in one of his most memorable phrases, 'Karl Marx proclaimed an authentic cultural revolution within the realm of philosophy when he declared in his Eleventh Thesis on Feuerbach: "Philosophers have hitherto only interpreted the world in various ways, the point is to change it." I believe', González Ruiz added, 'that within the realm of theology we must proclaim an equivalent cultural revolution: "Theologians have hitherto only interpreted the saving gesture of God; the point is to make it happen."'[178] Or, as he stated later on in a similar vein, 'it is not honest to speak about a "theology of revolution" if one has not previously carried out a "revolution of theology"'.[179] 'As a consequence of what has been said so far, it is logical that the unit of measurement which one must employ, when judging major thought systems which intend not only to interpret but also to transform the world, is their relationship to practice.'[180]

GONZÁLEZ RUIZ AS ACTIVIST

The frail scholar, who, from childhood onwards, battled a series of health problems, would have probably devoted his entire life to intellectual pursuits in the relative comfort of the study chamber, had he been born in a different time and place. As it was, however, José María González Ruiz lived his life in accordance with the message of his own teachings, and he lived a more than full life. After 1961, often spending time in his tiny apartment with little daylight in 20 Calle Galileo in the Arguëlles district in central Madrid, 'little by little, and with the help of some friends, the minuscule flat became converted into a mini-residence, crammed with books from top to bottom, and it also became a pilgrimage destination for a significant proportion of the "Spanish intelligentsia", and for young people fighting for democracy'.[181] In Malaga, González Ruiz likewise became a magnet for opposition activists, together with his older brother and the rather charismatic figure on the Christian Left,

---

[177] José María González Ruiz, *El Cristianismo no es un humanismo* (Barcelona: Península, 1973), p. 73, a work first published in 1966 and placing particular emphasis, amongst other topics, on the theological possibility and necessity of a Christian–Marxist dialogue.

[178] González Ruiz, *Dios está en la base*, p. 12.

[179] González Ruiz, *Dios está en la base*, p. 175.

[180] González Ruiz, *Dios está en la base*, p. 24.

[181] González Ruiz, *Memorias de un cura*, p. 140.

Alfonso Carlos Comín, who took up residence in the Andalusian port city in the early 1960s.[182] The underground trade union network, which eventually grew into a central challenge to the Francoist state, the Comisiones Obreras, constituted themselves in a slow and dangerous process at first within individual locations before going on to create a provincial and then a national umbrella. In 1966, the underground Comisiones Obreras of Malaga held their founding convention in the home of José María González Ruiz![183]

In the course of editorial work on an ecumenical edition of the New Testament in 1966, González Ruiz spent significant stretches of time in Barcelona. He used his presence in the Catalan capital also to give incendiary sermons in the parish church near where he was staying. González Ruiz soon began to coordinate a quickly growing group of dissident local priests. When news broke of a particularly horrendous act of torture of an activist student in the city, an unprecedented 100 priests gathered in the Barcelona cathedral, collectively reciting biblical passages and prayers before marching to the neighbouring prefect's office to deliver a protest message. When the demonstrators reached the building, their entry was blocked by riot police who proceeded to bludgeon and beat indiscriminately the stunned group of priests. Several of the protesters needed to be hospitalized, and the brutal repressive act made national and international news. Vicious repression of demonstrators was not at all unusual in this mainstay of the 'free world', but for a significant number of priests to become such victims was unprecedented.[184]

Finally, in the course of 1968, José María González Ruiz was prosecuted by the judiciary. A text he had first delivered as an oral presentation in Italian at the ecumenical retreat centre of Agape, run by Waldensians in the Italian Alps west of Turin, served as a pretext. The piece, entitled 'Christianity and Revolution', scheduled to be published in the February 1968 Catholic Action *Boletín de la HOAC*, contained a passage in which González Ruiz refused to disown legitimate acts of violent self-defence by victims of aggression, something which the Francoist state interpreted as a sanction of

---

[182] There are several book-length publications about this prominent and ubiquitous Catholic activist, whose political commitments included leading roles in the Spanish New Left, Far Left, and Old Left. Note, above all, Francisco Martínez Hoyos, *La cruz y el martillo. Alfonso Carlos Comín y los cristianos comunistas* (Barcelona: Rubeo, 2009), and José Antonio González Casanova, *Comín, mi amigo* (Barcelona: El Lector Universal, 2010).

[183] Carmen R. García Ruiz and Alberto Carrillo-Linares, 'Cobertura de la Iglesia a la oposición político-sindical al Franquismo. La colaboración con CC.OO. Los casos de Málaga y Sevilla', in José María Castells, José Hurtado, and Josep Maria Margenat (eds), *De la dictadura a la democracia. La acción de los Cristianos en España (1939–1975)* (Bilbao: Desclée de Brouwer, 2005), p. 41; Francisca Sauquillo Pérez del Arco, 'El Compromiso de una vida', in Castells, Hurtado, and Margenat (eds), *De la dictadura a la democracia*, p. 467; and Rafael Morales Ruiz and Antonio Miguel Bernal, 'Del Marco de Jerez al Congreso de Sevilla. Aproximación a la historia de las CC OO de Andalucía (1962–1978)', in David Ruiz (ed.), *Historia de Comisiones Obreras (1958–1988)* (Madrid: Siglo XXI, 1993), p. 238.

[184] González Ruiz, *Memorias de un cura*, pp. 119–21.

armed revolt. In a letter to a leading co-thinker and Catholic activist in Italy, Don Enzo Mazzi, spiritual leader of the flagship base community of the Isolotto in Florence, González Ruiz wrote that

> they are asking for three months of incarceration and a 100,000 lire fine. But, as the article in question was, earlier on, already published in the review *Surge*, a publication of spiritual reflections geared at priests, they are preparing for another court case for having published the article there as well. Yet another judicial procedure is under way: We sent a letter to the Minister of the Interior protesting against the use of torture. 1,500 signatures were collected—of which a good number of priests: the abbot of Montserrat and many others (a certain González Ruiz amongst them). I have no idea how they will manage to take 1,500 people at the same time to court.[185]

In the end, on 9 March 1969, González Ruiz was acquitted of all charges in the case of the contested article, as the judges found that the piece was not directed against the Spanish state but more properly belonged to 'the speculative terrain of Social Christian philosophy'. The *Boletín de la HOAC* including the incriminating 'speculations' by González Ruiz was nonetheless refused permission to be distributed, and all copies of the confiscated *Boletín* were destroyed.[186]

González Ruiz was certainly what Antonio Gramsci would have called an 'organic intellectual', even if hailing from the rival Catholic fold. It is instructive to compare the Andalusian theologian of world renown with the most famous second wave theologian of Italian descent, presented in the preceding subsection of this chapter. Ernesto Balducci never shied away from an uncompromising defence of Catholic dissent, but he rarely merged his own world view with that of the radical grassroots movements under attack. Despite his passionate advocacy of the disinherited within the Catholic church, Balducci ultimately stayed aloof from their day-to-day practices. Two veteran activists of the Isolotto base community, Urbano Cipriani and Sergio Gomiti, recently put it like this: 'Father Balducci was no parish priest. His [ultimate] target audience was reform theology and the enlightened bourgeoisie.' González Ruiz was also no parish priest, but in the frequent evocation of González Ruiz's interactions with the Isolotto community in conversations with this author forty-five years after the events, base community activists firmly and persistently point to González Ruiz as the *one* progressive theologian who stood closest to this beleaguered community even and especially at the darkest of all

---

[185] Letter (in Italian) by José María González Ruiz to Don Enzo Mazzi, 20 January 1969—Archivio storico della Comunità dell'Isolotto, Florence, Italy, LT 0531.

[186] For González Ruiz's own detailed account of this affair, see González Ruiz, *Memorias de un cura*, pp. 122–7. Even the library of the HOAC in Madrid today does not have a copy of this confiscated journal; see email communication from 'Noticias Obreras' to this author, 15 February 2013.

times. It is of more than symbolic value that, during his frequent visits to Florence, González Ruiz, even when on official church business, never even once stayed in housing provided by the Florentine hierarchy but always chose to be accommodated by families in the Isolotto.[187]

The title of González Ruiz's 1967 monograph, *Creer es comprometerse* (To Believe is to Get Involved), became a slogan taking on a life of its own in the rapidly burgeoning Left Catholic communities across Spain[188] and elsewhere. We will see in the following chapters how the theological messages portrayed in this opening chapter were translated into activism by a growing army of believers in Europe as a whole.

---

[187] Note the written confirmation of these observations, frequently evoked in the course of conversations during this author's two-week visit to Florence in late January and early February 2012, in a letter to the author by Urbano Cipriani and Sergio Gomiti on 18 February 2013.

[188] This, at any rate, is the claim by the historian of Catalan progressive Catholicism, Joan Castañas, in his *El progressisme Catòlic a Catalunya (1940–1980). Aproximació històrica* (Barcelona: La Llar des Llibre, 1988), p. 296.

2

Red Priests in Working-Class Blue

FRENCH FIRST WAVE WORKER PRIESTS

Perhaps the most stunning symbolic image of the first wave of Left Catholicism prior to Vatican II had been the activities carried out by no more than 100 French and a dozen Belgian priests in the 1940s and early 1950s, who voluntarily chose to become full-time blue-collar workers in the service of the missionary cause. Designed to reverse the tide of working-class de-Christianization by showcasing the commitment to working-class values by ordained priests exchanging their soutane for working-class blue, in fact this tiny number of worker priests in the end was far more adept at adopting the lifestyle and the political vision of their secular comrades than at attracting their co-workers to the Catholic fold. The radicalization of the worker priests, rather than the hoped-for conversion of blue-collar workers, became the headline news by the late 1940s and early 1950s. By 1954 (1955 in Belgium) the ecclesiastic hierarchy which, roughly ten years earlier, had sanctioned and encouraged the worker priest experience, cut short their authorization for ordained priests (and members of religious orders) to engage in full-time industrial and other forms of waged labour.

The shock of this command by the hierarchy was real, and all Belgian and roughly half of the French worker priests followed those orders. In fact, however, the impact was somewhat mitigated by the specifications stipulated in the admonition to quit full-time industrial labour. Part-time work up to three hours per day was still permitted, but of course this meant that the idea of priests sharing all trials and tribulations of their working-class comrades could no longer apply. Moreover, the new regulation also mandated that all trade union activities would henceforth have to cease, and the national coordinating body of worker priests, which in effect provided much concrete solace and support to them, would have to cease functioning. In fact, those priests submitting to the wishes of their superiors were effectively forced to quit their positions, thus cutting short contacts established by painstaking efforts over a period of quite some years.[1]

Virtually every single one of those fifty-four French worker priests who quit full-time posts by 1 March 1954 went back to work before long, though now restricted to part-time positions in, for the most part, small workshops. With certain bishops firmly on their side, all sorts of pretexts served to—slowly but surely—quietly subvert Roman instructions. Thus, Bernard Tiberghien, with the express permission of Cardinal Liénart, returned to work as a dock worker, as—in the words of Liénart—'there are not enough ships to unload every single day; there is not always enough work for everyone. Thus, quite loyally, I can make this fit, as it corresponds to the formula of three hours per day: $6 \times 3 = 18$. You will no doubt rarely work more than 18 hours per week. Thus, I allow you to go there. It is part-time work.'[2]

André Depierre received the explicit authorization of Cardinal Feltin to join the workforce constructing the gigantic UNESCO World Headquarters in Paris as a full-time labourer. When the 220 workers employed at the site went on strike to protest the subminimal working conditions at this non-union shop, André Depierre was chosen to be their spokesperson. Depierre asked his comrades to give him two hours' time to let him decide whether to accept this position of responsibility. He used this reprieve to seek out Cardinal Feltin, who immediately gave Depierre his permission to become the official negotiator for the UNESCO building site workforce. Management, after some difficult negotiations, agreed to the workers' demands, but under one condition: André Depierre would not be allowed back to continue work on the site. It took some diplomatic skill for André Depierre to convince his colleagues to give in to this demand. Depierre now went to the courts to obtain his rights, winning his case at the initial industrial tribunal and in the Court of Appeal.[3]

Thus, no strangers to controversy, the worker priests continued on their personal mission even after 1954, though under different overall conditions. In fact, Rome, having unilaterally imposed new restrictive standards, after 1 March 1954 took a passive approach. The warning shot having been fired, the curia was now content to tolerate the subsequent evolution of this experiment, turning a blind eye to the complicity of a number of bishops and even cardinals. Even those forty-odd worker priests who refused to heed the Roman command were never sanctioned *by Rome* for their continued defiance.[4] Even

---

[1] Of the wealth of sources describing the *Abwicklung* of the worker priest experience, perhaps one of the most concise analyses is Pierre Pierrard, *L'Église et les ouvriers en France. 1940–1990* (Paris: Hachette, 1991), pp. 271–95.

[2] Cited in the informative work by two second-generation worker priests, René Poterie and Louis Jeusselin, *Prêtres-ouvriers. 50 ans d'histoire et de combats* (Paris: Harmattan, 2001), p. 133.

[3] Poterie and Jeusselin, *Prêtres-ouvriers*, p. 134.

[4] Poterie and Jeusselin, *Prêtres-ouvriers*, p. 132.

the definitive absolute ending of the worker priest experience by Cardinal Pizzardo in the summer of 1959, now outlawing even part-time industrial labour, which confounded those Catholics who had believed in a rapid *aggiornamento* of their church after the death of Pius XII, changed little in the daily routine of the 'priests at work', *prêtres au travail*, as they were now officially called. Poterie and Jeusselin assert that 'the French episcopacy did not modify its chosen course. Neither the bishops, indirectly concerned, nor the worker priests, who had gone back to work, appeared very rattled by this regrettable intervention.'[5]

THE SECOND WAVE GETS UNDER WAY

In fact, in the years between 1954 and 1965, many other priests, over and above the first pre-1954 generation of worker priests, began to take up industrial employment, usually also in small workshops. By the mid-1960s, thus, the cumulative number of priests who had, at some point, exercised their profession as 'priests at work' approached the 600 mark, a remarkably quiet subversion of curial intent.[6] And the ex-worker priests undertook further offensives. In the run-up to Vatican II, five different trips to Rome assembled former worker priests, bishops, and theologians in an effort to convince the Vatican to reverse its 1954 decision. At one point even the future Pope Paul VI, Giovanni Battista Montini, then archbishop of Milan, went to Rome for conversations with the visiting French worker priests, though himself travelling incognito.[7] With Vatican II under way, the former worker priests decided on a permanent presence in Rome, adding to the ebullient off-Vatican atmosphere which characterized the cultural climate in the Eternal City between 1962 and 1965.

André Depierre became the central figure of this worker priest outpost in Rome, with other French and Belgian worker priests taking turns to assist his efforts. Bishops and cardinals from all over the world were targeted by their lobbying efforts, with the highpoint a private audience with Pope John XXIII, during which Roncalli assured his visitors of his support, adding that the Council 'and my successor will do what I cannot do myself'.[8] 'Without them

---

[5] Poterie and Jeusselin, *Prêtres-ouvriers*, p. 136. On the controversy surrounding Cardinal Pizzardo's hard-line document, see Gregor Siefer, *The Church and Industrial Society. A Survey of the Worker-Priest Movement and its Implications for the Christian Mission* (London: Dartman, Longman and Todd, 1964), pp. 91–104.

[6] Charles Suaud and Nathalie Viet-Depaule, *Prêtres et ouvriers. Une double fidélité mise à l'épreuve. 1944–1969* (Paris: Karthala, 2004), p. 12.

[7] Poterie and Jeusselin, *Prêtres-ouvriers*, p. 135.

[8] Poterie and Jeusselin, *Prêtres-ouvriers*, pp. 139–42, citation on p. 140.

[the worker priests pushing their cause in the antechambers of the Vatican] the miracle of 23 October 1965, when, in the closing moments of the Council, an extraordinary plenary assembly of French bishops unanimously approved the resumption of the "working priest" experience, would probably never have occurred.[9] Together with Cardinal Veuillot and a number of close supporters, the worker priests present in Rome that day gathered in a trattoria in Trastevere to celebrate this momentous decision.[10]

Nonetheless, this landmark reversal of the 1954 strictures was initially only a partial victory. The authorization of a second cohort of worker priests linked this decision to strict conditions. Candidates had to have a track record of links to the world of labour. They were strictly subordinated to their diocesan bishops in the cases of secular priests, to the superiors of their orders in the case of regular priests. No attempts at autonomous coordination amongst this new group of worker priests were permitted. They were, likewise, not permitted to take on positions of any responsibility within trade union structures. An initial trial period of three years was to test the consequences of this decision. All new priests at work had to integrate themselves into the structures provided by the Mission Ouvrière, a body set up by the French hierarchy in the second half of the 1950s to coordinate various missionary efforts then under way, targeting the world of industrial labour.[11]

With most first-wave worker priests belonging to the Mission de France, the bypassing of this traditional organizational 'home' of French worker priests to the exclusive benefit of the Mission Ouvrière, then under much tighter hierarchical control, was rightfully interpreted as a rebuff to the original cohort. From January 1966 onwards, the Episcopal Commission of the Mission Ouvrière began to select candidates, and when the first fifty-four priests were nominated, only one first-generation worker priest was amongst them. Thus, for three years, the fifty-four officially chosen to constitute the first team belonging to the new second-generational cohort coexisted with the pre-existing cohort of 'priests at work' without any official contact between them allowed.[12] In April 1966, when the second cohort was just beginning their assignments, an inventory of priests at work came up with the following

    [9] Pierrard, *L'Église et les ouvriers*, pp. 348–9.
    [10] Poterie and Jeusselin, *Prêtres-ouvriers*, pp. 143–4.
    [11] Suaud and Viet-Depaule, *Prêtres et ouvriers*, p. 14; on the genesis of the Mission Ouvrière, see Gerd-Rainer Horn, *Western European Liberation Theology. The First Wave, 1924–1959* (Oxford: Oxford University Press, 2008), pp. 287–8. On the difficult coexistence of Mission de France and Mission Ouvrière in the first few years after 1965, see Tangi Cavalin and Nathalie Viet-Depaule, *Une histoire de la Mission de France* (Paris: Karthala, 2007), pp. 206–10.
    [12] On the bad feeling expressed by the first-generation worker priests, who, unless age or illness prevented this, continued to work also, note Poterie and Jeusselin, *Prêtres-ouvriers*, p. 151; Suaud and Viet-Depaule, *Prêtres et ouvriers*, p. 14, likewise stress the uneasy parallel existence of multiple networks guiding a variety of cohorts of 'priests at work' between 1965 and 1968.

count. Of the 233 'priests at work', 125 worked part-time, 41 full-time, and another 67 full-time without authorization.[13]

THE IMPACT OF MAY '68

'May 1968 blew apart the restrictions imposed by the Mission Ouvrière.'[14] The entire range of 'priests at work' lived through a period of intense engagements at the side of their secular comrades, with many priests spontaneously assuming responsible positions in the course of the multiple conflicts breaking out in all corners of the land. About 1,000 additional priests, who had up to now stood aside from all forms of 'priesthood at work', were suddenly inspired to don the working-class blue, never bothering to seek authorization from their bishops or the Mission Ouvrière. By November 1968, the Episcopal Commission of the Mission Ouvrière deemed the three-year trial period of the first official cohort of fifty-four second-generation 'priests at work' a success and lifted the cap on the number of such engagements. Also in November 1968, the French Bishops' Conference added its stamp of approval, and henceforth the original term of 'worker priests' replaced the more cautionary utilization of 'priests at work' even in official parlance. The artificial distinction between the first and second generations of worker priests fell by the wayside, and the worker priests were given the green light to elect their own national leadership. The four chosen representatives, together with one additional elected delegate from each of four regions (Paris, the North, the South and Southeast, and the West), now effectively coordinated the worker priest collective as a self-governing enterprise, though each member still kept close ties with their respective bishops.[15]

'By 1970, the Mission Ouvrière had become a place for mutual encounters, research and experimentation in view of a prophetic Church, allowing a variety of experiments, and certainly providing ample opportunities for the bearing of witness of the Gospel within the working class. As such, it was henceforth seen as a positive factor by the worker priests.'[16] In 1972, the first regular national gathering of the post-Vatican II worker priests was held; from 1974 onwards, *Le Courrier P.O.* served as a crucial communication link between the bi- or triannual National Conventions. The second wave of the French worker priest experience was clearly engaged in a seemingly unstoppable

---

[13] Pierrard, *L'Église et les ouvriers*, p. 350.
[14] Suaud et Viet-Depaule, *Prêtres et ouvriers*, p. 15.
[15] Informative sources on the conjuncture of 1968 are, once again, Poterie and Jeusselin, *Prêtres-ouvriers*, pp. 158–9, and Suaud and Viet-Depaule, *Prêtres et ouvriers*, p. 15.
[16] Poterie and Jeusselin, *Prêtres-ouvriers*, p. 161.

ascent. Counting solely those worker priests with firm links to the Équipe Nationale, thus leaving unaccounted for the even larger number of unauthorized working priests, by January 1969 there were 82 members in 14 locations throughout France, by May 1969, 168 in 37 towns, by April 1970, 287 worker priests in 75 locations, in 1972, 521 and 756 by 1974.[17] By all accounts, the second wave of French worker priests far outdistanced in quantity their first-generation ancestors, some of the latter, of course, being included in this count.

Yet the quality of their commitment did not lag behind that of their pioneer predecessors. Not only May/June 1968, but many subsequent flagship labour struggles saw worker priests once again in the forefront of events. To mention but one particular case, the Dominican Jean Raguénès: born in 1932, ordained in 1966, he served from the autumn of 1967 onwards as student chaplain for University of Paris students enrolled in Economics and Law. His home base was then the Centre Saint-Yves in the rue Gay-Lussac, at the very centre of student unrest.[18] In September 1970, Jean Raguénès chose to become one of the legion of enthusiastic young worker priests, opting for Besançon as his home base. By May 1971, he became a full-time worker at the LIP watch factory which, two years later, happened to become the symbol par excellence in France, and Europe as a whole, for the sudden wave of experiments in workers' self-management.

Forced by management to go on the offensive, the workforce of LIP, to forestall the planned sacking of 480 production-line workers, occupied the premises, sequestered the then-current stock of 25,000 watches, resumed production under their own authority and supervision, and then built up a solidarity network throughout France and other European countries. One of the central figures in the brains trust coordinating these actions was none other than Jean Raguénès. In the words of one former LIP worker interviewed more than a quarter-century later, Bernard Girardot, Jean Raguénès 'was a prophet [...] Jean has truly left a mark on LIP, for he had put down deep roots there, he had physically married the cause of *les LIP*'. Jean Raguénès played crucial roles at each stage of the radicalization of this exemplary conflict which rendered LIP a household term across Europe for some years, no longer seen as a militant strike to defend employment but having taken on the clear contours of a major 'stepping stone towards emancipation'.[19]

[17] Pierrard, *L'Église et les ouvriers*, p. 353.
[18] For an empathetic and informative evocation of the Centre Saint-Yves as the nerve centre of the French Catholic 'May '68', see Grégory Barrau, *Le Mai 68 des catholiques* (Paris: Atelier, 1998), pp. 67–71.
[19] A marvellous autobiographical account of this remarkable figure is Jean Raguénès, *De Mai 68 à LIP. Un dominicain au cœur des luttes* (Paris: Karthala, 2008), with the centre section on his experiences at LIP on pp. 112–210. An evocative summary of the impact of Jean Raguénès on the community of *les LIP* is Jean Divo, *L'Affaire LIP et les catholiques de Franche-Comté* (Yens-sur-Morges: Cabédita, 2003), pp. 89–97, citations on pp. 92 and 96.

WORKER PRIESTS IN BELGIUM AFTER 1965

The first wave of worker priests had been limited, in terms of geography, to France and Belgium. And it was only logical that this common history forged close bonds between these two groups. Thus, an annual report of the national team of French worker priests in 1975 could mention prominently, almost as a matter of course: 'With our Belgian comrades we have shared what can almost be regarded as a common life history for the past thirty years.'[20] As in France, the 1970s saw the highpoint of the second wave of Belgian worker priests, though the absolute numbers were obviously much more reduced. Whereas the higher number of first wave Belgian worker priests ever operating at any one time was probably never higher than eight, the second wave saw many times that number. In France, the highpoint was reached towards the end of the 1970s, when more than 1,000 priests had donned working-class blue; in Belgium it was 1974, when fifty-one priests were engaged in full-time labour at the same time.[21]

First wave Belgian worker priests had been organized in two teams centred, respectively, on Charleroi and Liège. The Charleroi team disappeared in the wake of the 1955 decision to close down the Belgian worker priest experiment, just as French worker priests had received their curtain call in 1954. Also, just as in France, however, priests wishing to engage in manual labour could continue to do so with the benevolent acquiescence of the bishops of Tournai and Liège. As long as they shunned employment in high-visibility workplaces, first wave Belgian worker priests could continue to ply their trade as blue-collar operatives in small factories. 'To demonstrate good will to Rome and to follow, more or less, the pathway chosen by French bishops', two first wave worker priests were nonetheless asked to abandon their chosen labouring career to return to their original calling as parish priest.[22]

After the green light obtained in the wake of the French re-authorizations on the eve of the closing ceremony of Vatican II, between 1965 and 1980 the Liège worker priests were joined by new teams in both linguistic halves of the Belgian state, including two teams, one Flemish and the other franco-phone, in the capital city of Brussels. Thus, apart from the two groups in Brussels, Walloon worker priests operated in Liège, Brabant, and Namur. Flanders had active teams in Ghent, the first Flemish team to get off the ground, Antwerp, and Hasselt. By 1969 a National Council began to coordinate

---

[20] 'Compte-rendu de mandat de l'Équipe Nationale [Française] P.O.', p. 4—Archives des Prêtres-Ouvriers Belges (APOB) [Flémalle], Classeur 'Équipe Nationale'.

[21] See the graph included in the unnumbered pages between pp. 75 and 76 in Dominique de Greef, 'Les Prêtres-ouvriers en Belgique', Mémoire de license, 1985, Faculté de Théologie, Université de Louvain.

[22] André Marie Antoine, 'Les Prêtres ouvriers belges. Regard sociologique', n.d.—APOB.

country-wide efforts; from 1972 onwards a more firmly organized Équipe Nationale took over from the Council.[23]

A series of snapshots of the inner life and orientation of the Belgian teams, composed for their national gathering of late May 1977, allow a detailed picture to emerge which, in its basic outlines, would similarly apply to the French cohort. What becomes clear is that the nucleus of actual worker priests within each team often provided the infrastructure for a somewhat extended community of co-thinkers and activists who, in effect, formed a type of base community, without, however, using this particular term. The francophone Brussels team, for instance, consisted of a total of five men and three women, who worked in various sectors of the Brussels economy (two worked for large retail firms; two others for the Brussels public transport system; one as a social worker; one in the insurance industry; one as a full-time trade union official; and one as an electrician). All lived in working-class neighbourhoods, with some amongst them active in neighbourhood action committees over and above their full-time paid employment. One member of the group also served as a municipal councillor.[24]

The Flemish-language Brussels team of six consisted of an equal number of men and women, suggesting once again the important, but much overlooked, role of female activists in second wave Left Catholicism. What was somewhat unusual in the Flemish Brussels team was the high number of activists belonging to religious orders. One layperson (an ex-member of the Franciscan Sisters of the Annunciation order) and five active members of religious orders, amongst them two Jesuits, formed the team which met for reflections and deliberations three times per month. In their self-statement, the multiplicity of engagements and personal trajectories are described in an illuminating manner, once again suggesting a creative admixture of individual orientations as the basis for such experiments.

André, one of the Jesuits, is described as rather critical of the structure of the church, as having 'a rather global and Marxist view of social and political realities', and as focused on close contact with his co-workers; Cécile, belonging to the order of the Dames van Maria, where she exercised an active leadership role, had been a social worker and then a blue-collar worker in Brazil for some time and now worked as a cleaning woman in the building of the national headquarters of the banking giant Société Générale. 'Cécile regards the circumstances around her work situation and her neighbourhood activism as closely related, a reflection of the identical system of exploitation.' The other Jesuit on the team, Hugo, took an active role in the provincial leadership of his order, while 'emphasizing his engagement at work and in his

---

[23] De Greef, 'Les Prêtres-ouvriers en Belgique', p. 78.
[24] André Boxus, 'Équipe P.O. Bruxelles'—APOB, '27–29 mai 1977', III.

neighbourhood [. . .] Very active in pastoral work for the Flemish in his parish.'[25]

INDIVIDUAL MOTIVATIONS, COLLECTIVE DYNAMICS, POLITICAL EVOLUTIONS

The Liège team provided interesting detail as to the motivations to become a (Belgian) worker priest. Charles-André Sohier underscored, for instance, the central role which May 1968 played in his life. 'My participation in several actions and gatherings of students in Liège and a presentation by Paul Blanquart', one of the most visible and dynamic young radical French activists and philosophers, then a member of the Dominican order, 'allowed me to become conscious of the political dimension of working-class struggles for justice and against capitalist alienation'. An Italian member of the Liège team, Lucio Del Basso, exemplified the transnational dimension of the worker priest phenomenon, which benefited from Southern European migrations to the north and—when the wave of military takeovers began to cast a dark shadow over Latin American states—from Latin Americans seeking refuge in various European states, the latter forced emigrations paradoxically contributing to the mutual exchange of activist ideas and practices between South and Central America and Western Europe. 'At the age of twenty', Lucio Del Basso wrote, 'I worked as an employee for the Italian State Railway in Rome', experiencing alienation even worse than what he later experienced when working in the Liège region. An encounter with several priests belonging to the order of Oratorians, founded by Saint Filippo Neri, led the young Italian to join that order.

'The first book which opened my eyes to the experience of the worker priests was *En Mission Prolétarienne* by Jacques Loew', one of the pioneer French worker priests of the first generation. 'In conversations with the Genovese group around *Il Gallo*', a flagship journal of the Italian Catholic Left since 1946, 'we constantly discussed this issue, and it was there that I met an Italian worker priest who frequently came to the gatherings of that group. As it was then very difficult to launch a worker priest project in Italy, I emigrated to Belgium where I saw that it was easily feasible to do so.'[26]

---

[25] Two documents in APOB, '27–29 mai 1977', III, allow insight into the Flemish Brussels team, a four-page survey in French, 'Équipe Bruxelles Flamand', and an untitled Flemish version, of which only the first page is extant.

[26] Both personal accounts by Sohier and Del Basso are in 'Notes en vue de la rencontre de la Pentecôte '77', 6 May 1977—APOB, Classeur 'Équipe de Liège'—with Sohier's comments on p. 4 and Del Basso's reflections on p. 3.

The material on the Belgian worker priest experience also allows insights into the radicalizing dynamics affecting second wave priests. If they openly engaged in politics, first wave worker priests had mostly been attracted to the only game in town, the Old Left organizations dominating the French and Belgian Left in the late 1940s and the early 1950s, in France above all the French Communist Party (PCF). A September 1972 document penned by one of the first wave Belgian worker priests who continued to animate his comrades-in-arms for several decades after 1965, Louis Flagothier, not only underscores the crucial role for Belgians played by French politics, but at the same time highlights what it meant to be a Left Catholic rebel in the rapidly evolving post-May '68 atmosphere. Intimately familiar with French politics on account of his frequent trips to Paris which commenced in the late 1940s, Flagothier now wrote about the political preoccupations of the cohort of French worker priests active in the early 1970s:

> What then is *the* revolutionary line? Is it that of the Communist Party or the line of the PSU, the Parti Socialiste Unifié, the flagship organization of the French New Left, benefiting from a heavy presence of Left Catholics from its very origins, or of one of the groups composing the Far Left? Is it the line of the CGT or the CFDT? At the Easter gathering in Paris, more than one person present underlined the difficulties to sustain dialogue between worker priests of whom some are active in the CGT and others in the CFDT. Just recently I learned from *Le Monde* that a conflict in a certain factory became particularly bitter due to the fact that at the head of the local branch of the CFDT stood a worker priest who—of all things!—also happens to be a municipal councillor representing the PSU.[27]

Belgian first-generation worker priests had never been as closely associated with Moscow-oriented Communism as had been the case with some sections of their French equivalents in the early 1950s. Belgian second wave worker priests nonetheless struggled to redefine their political and organizational preferences and their spiritual quests in the wake of the turbulence of global 1968. The traditional Catholic Action groupings mandated to missionize the working-class milieux, above all the Jeunesse Ouvrière Chrétienne (JOC), traditionally viewed as an ally in Belgium as much as anywhere else, were now deemed to have become largely irrelevant. Most Belgian worker priests, two-thirds of them having been JOC chaplains before their decision to effect their move into industrial work, were now regarded with suspicion by the JOC, who felt left in the lurch. In turn, an official document of the francophone worker priests in Belgium had few good things to say about the JOC:

[27] Louis Flagothier, 'Seraing, 25 septembre 1972', p. 3—APOB, Classeur 'Équipe Nationale'. The Confédération Générale du Travail (CGT) was the major French trade union federation controlled by the PCF; the ex-Catholic Confédération Française Démocratique du Travail (CFDT) was then openly advocating workers' self-management and far more in tune with the anti-authoritarian French New Left than the hardline Communist CGT.

'The JOC is very totalitarian.' And the text continued: 'Within the blue-collar milieu, there are many young people, but not very many members of the JOC.' The same document later on also, once again, drew a parallel to France. There, the traditional Catholic Action organization geared towards work in adult working-class milieux, 'the Action Catholique Ouvrière (ACO), is likewise fundamentally under attack. The long, patient and selfless presence of activists within the working class', a trademark feature of the ACO, closer to the relatively moderate PCF than to the French New or Far Left, 'is no longer seen as adequate to the needed tasks!' Instead, young French worker priests were now clamouring: 'Let us build a revolutionary Church!'[28]

Belgian worker priests, of course, had to face at least one more problem than their French counterparts: a deep-going and deepening split between the two linguistic (and, increasingly, cultural) halves of Belgian society. A member of the Antwerp team, in late 1974, made an interesting observation, the potential implications of which cannot be adequately addressed in the context of this monograph, but which is worth citing nonetheless: 'Frans (Antwerp) high-lights a difference between the mentality of Walloon worker priests (trade union activism, active engagement in social movements) and the mentality of Flemish worker priests (prophetic world views, intensive dislike of structures).' Whatever element of insight may have been captured by this chance observa-tion, another speech at the 8 December 1974 gathering of the Équipe Natio-nale, by a member of one of the Brussels teams, certainly another speech the then-current status and the attendant difficulties facing Belgian worker priests in general. In fact, this one sentence well describes the functioning of the teams of worker priests (and other Left Catholic groupings!) anywhere in Europe at that time: 'We note major differences between teams: some are quite large, others minuscule—some gather frequently, others almost never—some have an action programme, others improvise—some operate in a democratic fash-ion, others follow a top-down model—etc.'[29]

FACTORY CHAPLAINS IN TURIN

The only other national association of worker priests with which the French 'mother organization' had established close contact by the mid-1970s was the Italian group.[30] The fraternal links between France and Italy benefited from

---

[28] 'Conclusions de la réunion des prêtres-ouvriers francophones des 1 et 2 mai 1971'; citations on pp. 1 and 4—APOB, '1971'.

[29] 'Équipe Nationale, 8 Décembre 74', p. 2—APOB, Classeur 'Équipe Nationale'.

[30] 'For three years now', wrote the French coordinating body in 1976, 'our ties with our Italian comrades have grown increasingly close'—'Compte-rendu de mandate de l'Équipe Nationale P.O.', [1976], APOB, Classeur 'Équipe Nationale', p. 4.

the fact that the nucleus of post-Vatican II Italian worker priests was located in Piedmont, traditionally the part of Italy most oriented towards its French neighbour. No doubt, the personal ties to French co-thinkers already established in the 1950s by the spiritual and organizational centrepiece of the subsequent community of Torinese worker priests, Carlo Carlevaris, had laid the groundwork for this link.

The very first Italian priest to take up industrial labour, however, was Sirio Politi, ordained in 1943 in Lucca, and then a parish priest in Bargecchia, a small community in the hills above the Tuscan industrial port of Viareggio. In early 1956, he decided to leave his rural parish, and he rode on his beloved Vespa into Viareggio, where he constructed a makeshift chapel in the immediate vicinity of the port, soon finding employment and comradeship. Forced to make a choice between his commitment to his blue-collar community and the church in 1959, Politi opted for continued association with the latter, but the first step had been taken. Sirio Politi remained the linchpin of the eventually emerging community of Italian worker priests, though himself subsequently employed primarily in artisanal workshops, particularly in the iron-working sector.[31] The actual launch of a bona fide Italian worker priest experience did not occur until 1968.

One preparatory stage was the important experiment, centred on Turin, of factory chaplains, priests whose 'parish', so to speak, became the workforce of the various—sometimes giant!—Torinese factories. There had been earlier trial runs but such factory chaplainships did not get permanently under way as an institution until the mid-1940s, and they then continued to operate throughout the 1950s and 1960s. The flagship enterprise of the Torinese industrial complex, FIAT, was then actively engaged in promoting such a partnership between the church and private enterprise, organizing under its auspices annual pilgrimages to Lourdes.[32] If the initial cohort of factory chaplains was often in tune with the design of the church hierarchy and FIAT management, in the course of the 1950s a number of such factory chaplains developed a rather critical attitude towards such collusions, misgivings which deepened in the course of the 1960s.

One such factory chaplain was the already mentioned Carlo Carlevaris, ordained in 1950, whose first assignment was as parish priest in the small community of Beinasco, about 15 km from Turin. Serving in that capacity from 1951 to 1954, Carlevaris often went to factory entrances in the industrial belt near Beinasco, talking to blue-collar workers and getting to know their

[31] M. Grazia Galimberti, 'Don Sirio Politi 1920–1988': <http://www.lottacomeamore.it/Biografia_sirio.asp> (8 July 2013).
[32] For the original Turin experience in the 1940s, see, above all, the pioneering study by Barbara Bertini and Stefano Casadio, *Clero e industria in Torino. Ricerca sui rapporti tra clero e masse operaie nella capitale dell'auto dal 1943 al 1948* (Milan: Franco Angeli, 1979), and Vito Vita, *Chiesa e mondo operaio. Torino 1943–1948* (Cantalupa: Effatà, 2003).

concerns, problems, and issues.[33] Coming from a rather conservative family background in the Cuneo region himself, these personal encounters caused Carlevaris for the first time to consider a working-class pastoral career. In the summer of 1954 he took the first steps. 'I took my motorcycle and I went on a trip to France, from Marseilles to Paris, to understand what the JOC and ACO were all about.'[34] His educational journey to the homeland of the working-class apostolate lasted an entire summer, followed by further exploratory voyages to the other side of the Alps, including Belgium, in subsequent years.[35]

Carlevaris soon joined the team of factory chaplains in the sprawling FIAT complex, but rapidly encountered hostility from and friction with FIAT management on account of his defence of blue-collar workers' concerns. By October 1959 this led to Carlevaris's removal as FIAT chaplain, though he continued in the same position in other companies, now firmly dedicated to the cause of rank-and-file workers' physical and spiritual welfare.[36] The whirlwind consequences of Vatican II and the nomination by Pope Paul VI of the nonconformist Michele Pellegrino as archbishop of Turin in 1965 eventually provided the context for a revitalization and renewal of the working-class apostolate in the industrial zones of Turin and Piedmont. Now began an extraordinary period of close cooperation between the head of the Turin Catholic church, Michele Pellegrino, and a fledgling team of rank-and-file factory chaplains, parish priests, seminarians, and lay activists, which led to the birth of the Italian worker priest movement as a collective enterprise.

THE GENESIS OF THE *PRETI OPERAI*

The twelve years (1965–77) of Pellegrino's presence at the head of the Torinese church during a period of momentous labour struggles in Italy's premier industrial city changed the parameters of what was possible for the rapidly growing team of radical grassroots activists devoted to the blue-collar apostolate. In the words of Carlo Carlevaris: 'The Church in Piedmont was [then] influenced more by Turin than by Rome.'[37] And it was undoubtedly the creative confluence of the designs of the intellectual Pellegrino—prior to his

---

[33] Conversation with Carlo Carlevaris, Turin, 1 December 2011.

[34] Interview GO Data creazione, 13 September 2000, manuscript version—Archivio Carlo Carlevaris (ACC) [Turin], GIOC, documenti.

[35] Conversation, 1 December 2011.

[36] An evocative portrayal of Carlevaris's engagement as factory chaplain can be consulted, for instance, in Carlo Carlevaris, 'Fàbbrica e Chiesa nella testimonianza di un prete operaio', *Nuovasocietà*, 15 January 1973—ACC, P.O. Italiani 3, 'Articoli'. All subsequent references to contemporaneous newspaper clippings on the history of the Italian worker priests stem from the same rich and indispensable source.

[37] Conversation, 1 December 2011.

appointing as archbishop a university professor in the literature department of the University of Turin—and the seemingly boundless energies provided by grassroots chaplains and priests—Carlo Carlevaris: 'I was never good at theology. I was at home in the factories'[38]—which created a laboratory of the radical working-class apostolate without parallel anywhere else in Italy and, probably, Europe as a whole.

The central role of Carlevaris within this team is attested to by a close intellectual friendship which soon developed between an unlikely duo of radical reformers. Carlevaris, for the duration of Pellegrino's position as archbishop, frequently received late night phone calls from the latter. Pellegrino, who habitually began those phone calls with the expression, 'Can you spare a moment for me?', in this manner sought the advice from Carlevaris on a whole range of issues central to the preoccupations of both. Symbolically, when Carlevaris went to obtain benediction from his spiritual guide three days before Pellegrino's death in October 1986, Carlevaris was fond of recalling years later, the cardinal—Pellegrino had become cardinal in June 1967— wanted to raise his right arm to bless Carlevaris but could not move his right arm. The nurse tending to Pellegrino then suggested he use his left arm instead, which, given the personalities involved, Carlevaris later reflected, was by no means inappropriate. The cardinal broke out in a smile and blessed Carlevaris with his raised left arm. In Carlevaris's words: 'It was his last smile. He fell into unconsciousness during the next two days, and he then died.'[39]

'On 18 February 1967, at the office of the Turin Centro Cappellani del Lavoro, the archbishop presided over an assembly of all factory chaplains within the diocese, in the course of which he announced his intention to transform this "Centre for Factory Chaplains" into a "Centre for the Evangelization of the World of Labour" in order to better respond to the pastoral needs of that sector.'[40] It is beyond the remit of this monograph to provide much further detail on the ensuing flurry of activity and initiatives.[41] Suffice it to say that the year 1968 once again proved to be decisive. It was in 1968 when three young seminarians, Giuseppe Trucco, Pasquale Busso, and Leo Paradiso, were authorized by Pellegrino to work full-time as part of their seminary

---

[38] Conversation with Carlo Carlevaris, 7 January 2011.

[39] Conversations with Carlo Carlevaris, 4 January 2011 and 1 December 2011.

[40] These are the opening lines of an extensive reportage, 'Il "Centro di Evangelizzazione del Mondo del Lavoro"', special reprint of an article which first appeared in the *Rivista diocesana*, no. 3, March 1967—ACC, 'C. Cappellani del Lavoro', c.b.11.

[41] The keynote document reflecting the ebullient atmosphere characterizing Turin's working-class apostolate in the late 1960s and early 1970s is the December 1971 pastoral letter by Michele Pellegrino, 'Camminare insieme', characteristically building upon earlier discussions in Pellegrino's brains trust of the Ufficio Diocesana di Pastorale di Lavoro, the former Centro di Evangelizzazione, notably an important early draft of the document by Carlo Carlevaris. See the materials included in the reprint of Michele Pellegrino, *Camminare insieme. Rilettura ed attualizzazione* (Fossano: Editrice Esperienze, 1993).

preparations for the priesthood. Even more importantly still, the veteran activist and long-time factory chaplain, Carlo Carlevaris, similarly received the authorization to engage in—in his case—permanent full-time labour, thus becoming the first of a rapidly growing cohort of worker priests benefiting from the opportunities provided by the atmosphere of global 1968 in general and the 1969 Italian Hot Autumn in particular.[42]

Since Sirio Politi was still regarded as the doyen of Italian worker priests, it only stood to reason that the letter of invitation convoking the very first national gathering of worker priests was penned by him and his closest co-worker, Don Rolando Menesini. Equally characteristically, Don Sirio and Don Rolando referred to a smaller gathering in Turin as the moment when the idea to call a national meeting was spawned: 'Dear friends, several days ago we met in Torino with Don Carlo Carlevaris, where we talked about an idea suggested by Don Luisito and Don Gianni from Alessandria with regard to the organization of an assembly of all priests and members of religious orders who have committed themselves to manual labour.'[43] From the afternoon of 6 December until the morning of 8 December 1969, twenty-three worker priests thus met for their first deliberations as a national group in Chiàvari on the Ligurian coast. A second national gathering quickly followed in Bologna on 25–6 April 1970, with about fifty in attendance.[44]

Yet it was not until the national assembly of 24–5 November 1973 in Baragallo (Reggio Emilia) that the Italian cohort began to set up a firm organizational structure. A National Secretariat henceforth operated as a coordinating body, animated by the energetic Angelo Piazza in Parma. Hitherto the Turin cohort had served as the de facto networking agency for Italian worker priests, but the geographic switch of the centre of coordinating activity from Turin to Parma denoted more than a mere administrative change of location. For with the growth of the movement—ninety worker priests attended the Baragallo event, representing a community that had now swollen to a total of 300—came the entry of a new generation of young priests, whose motivations often differed in some fundamental respects from those of the founding generation in Turin. Depending on location, moreover, some of

---

[42] Note the chronology provided by Carlo Demichelis, 'Cronologia. Tappe di un'evoluzione', in Gianni Fornero, 'I preti-operai', in Luigi Berzano et al., *Uomini di frontiera. 'Scelta di classe' e trasformazioni della coscienza Cristiana a Torino dal Concilio a oggi* (Turin: Cooperativa di cultura Lorenzo Milani, 1984), p. 275. A stimulating snapshot of the Turin worker priest ambience is provided by Sandro Magister, then in the early stages of his lifelong journalistic career, 'La scommessa dei preti-operai', *Sette giorni* 250 (26 March 1972), pp. 46–8.

[43] Letter by Don Sirio and Don Rolando, Viareggio, 5 November 1969—ACC, 'Preti operai italiani (1)'.

[44] Marco Scambruna, 'Dio nella fàbbrica. Storia dei preti operai in Italia', unpublished manuscript, p. 86—ACC Library.

them were forced to operate in semi-clandestinity, out of fear of reprisals by particularly hostile local representatives of the curia.

THE WINDS OF THE HOT AUTUMN

In a 1975 interview with the magazine *Famiglia cristiana*, Carlo Carlevaris put it like this: 'At first, we had priests as protagonists who were no longer young, myself included. We thought that going to work in a factory meant the organization of a presence by the Church within the working class. [...] In the last two or three years, most choosing factory employment are doing so for political reasons. The youngest are in fact convinced that the working class will change society in a radical fashion. And they assume an attitude of a clear distantiation vis-à-vis the Church.'[45] Angelo Piazza confirmed Carlevaris's assessment of a generational shift in the motivation to take up full-time industrial labour: 'At the beginning there was doubtless the referral to the experience of the French worker priests, allowed to continue their calling in 1965. [...] The ecclesiastical climate of those years was characterized by hope in the [Vatican II] Council [...] and the renovation of theological studies. But such stimuli coming from the ambience of the Church did not remain isolated from the cultural turbulences which left their mark on the student and workers' movements in 1968 and 1969.'[46]

The first three Piedmont seminarians who, after their one-year trial period, had been given the go-ahead by Michele Pellegrino in the autumn of 1969 to continue as permanent full-time worker priests, the aforementioned Trucco, Busso, and Paradiso, reflected on their own itinerary of radicalization from the vantage point of early 1972—and their recollections underscore that the turbulence caused by the explosion of Italian social movements after 1968 by no means bypassed Turin itself:

> At the beginning, we continuously asked ourselves: How can I best exercise my calling as a priest in today's circumstances? Today, by contrast, we are asking ourselves: What are we trying to say when stating that Jesus Christ saves and liberates? We embarked on our venture with the purpose of preaching and evangelizing. Then we began to understand that this was a pretentious idea. To preach means, in reality, to convey a message of liberation, i.e. once again to place

---

[45] Angelo Montonati, 'I preti-operai a una svolta', *Famiglia cristiana*, 23 February 1975, p. 42.

[46] Angelo Piazza, 'L'esperienza dei preti operai in Italia', special issue on the 1976 national convention of Italian worker priests, supplement to *Com Nuovi Tempi*, 2/1976. Elsewhere, Angelo Piazza said: 'For many of us, the labor struggles during the Hot Autumn provoked an identity crisis'; cited in Bruno Marolo, 'Quei preti mangiapreti', *Gazzetta del popolo*, 10 January 1975.

the worker inside a straitjacket. Fact is that the Gospel, as it is preached in the parish, within the institutionalized Church (and thus also by us, as we have internalized our tightly regulated education and training), has nothing in common with the Gospel as it should be announced to workers. Conclusion? We priests utilize a type of foreign language, which we still speak, but which has become nonsensical to continue to employ. The real problem is henceforth for us to work for the construction of a truer and freer world, where this language, which today comes across as totally odd, can become a language spoken and understood. Obviously after a radical and thorough revision.[47]

Carlo Carlevaris, in *Famiglia cristiana*, employed a catchy formula to characterize the changing attitude of worker priests: 'The time of *preti-operai* ["priests-workers", the standard expression for worker priests in Italian] is over. Tomorrow will be the time of *operai-preti*', a formula which reversed the emphasis in accordance with the post-1969 atmosphere current on Italian factory floors.

The recognition of an inherently positive message and content within working-class culture as such, coupled with a growing distance from the official structures of the church, almost inevitably led to a cycle of radicalization of the worker priest experience in Italy. The gulf separating the group of worker priests, counting roughly 300 men throughout the second half of the 1970s, from the church hierarchy came to the fore in unmistakable fashion on the occasion of two national assemblies which met in early January 1975 and early January 1976 in a small hamlet on the northern slopes of the Appenine, Serramazzoni, south of Modena. About 100 worker priests met there for the first time from 4 to 6 January 1975 to take stock of their experiences. Delegates from the French and Belgian worker priests were likewise present at Serramazzoni. The sole member of the ecclesiastical hierarchy who found his way to the remote Appenine village was the bishop of Ivrea, Luigi Bettazzi, who, however, attended solely in his personal capacity as an interested observer.

Bettazzi had been a one-time member of the team of the controversial archbishop of Bologna, Giacomo Lercaro, who had been removed from office by the Roman curia in early 1968 after delivering a fiery speech as a New Year's homily in the Bologna cathedral, where he had publicly denounced American policies in Vietnam. Bettazzi was thus one of the few Italian bishops openly sympathizing with the worker priests assembled in Serramazzoni. As reported by the correspondent for the Turin-based daily, *Gazzetta del popolo*, when Bettazzi first addressed the assembled crowd, he introduced himself, a member of the hierarchy himself, tongue in cheek as 'Luigi Bettazzi, enemy of

---

[47] Magister, 'Una scommessa', p. 47.

the working class', then expressing his hope that the church might still be capable of executing a serious internal reform: 'We witnessed several hopeful moments offered by the Council, even if in practice we have lived through many disappointments since then. That is why I am still a member of the Church. I, too, just like the encyclical *Pacem in Terris*, believe that the ascent of the workers' movement is a sign of the times.'[48]

The January 1975 assembly at Serramazzoni was the first time the worker priest movement received major news coverage in the national press. The Milan daily, *Il giorno*, in its opening paragraph prominently cited one of the assembled *preti-operai*: 'Many of us are delegates in factory councils, even members of the [Communist trade union federation] CGIL; many are active in political parties, within the Italian Communist Party [PCI] or within Il Manifesto [a leading organization of the colourful Italian Far Left]; some are parish priests.'[49] The aforementioned article in the *Gazzetta del popolo* noted the unusual ambience of this particular assembly of priests: 'In the intervals between the deliberations Anarchist songs are sung.'[50] Another featured article in the *Gazzetta del popolo* described the group at Serramazzoni in the following uncompromising terms: 'They have taken up active roles in neighbourhood associations; one finds them with red flags on the picket lines, at the gates of occupied factories. They are all affiliated to trade unions, some are also active members in political parties, many of them prefer the [Far Left] PDUP to the PCI.'[51]

One national daily, *La stampa*, quoted the Parma worker priest, Bruno Gandolfi, who assisted Angelo Piazza in running the National Secretariat, summarizing the three-day retreat: 'Now we can say that the Marxist utopia and the Christian utopia have encountered each other, and together we shall march united to join in the struggle.' Gandolfi later reminisced: 'We left to evangelize, and what happened was the opposite. We have become evangelized. We have found Christ there where we thought we would need him to be introduced: within the working class.' The journalist for *La stampa* noted the symbolic mixture of greeting styles which the worker priests employed to bid each other farewell when the assembly high up in the Appenine disbanded: 'They are leaving the *birreria* to return to the factory. Some clench their fists as a greeting, others give each other a hug and a kiss.'[52]

---

[48] Bruno Marolo, 'La società del futuro secondo i preti operai', *Gazzetta del popolo*, 6 January 1975.

[49] Raffaele Lazzari, 'Una scelta di vita, non esperienza di laboratorio', *Il giorno*, 6 January 1975.

[50] Marolo, 'Società del futuro'.

[51] Bruno Marolo, 'Quei preti mangiapreti', *Gazzetta del popolo*, 10 January 1975.

[52] Franco Santini, 'Preti operai—criticata la pastorale del lavoro', *La stampa*, 7 January 1975.

SERRAMAZZONI II

Precisely one year later, from 3 to 6 January 1976, 150 worker priests reassembled in Serramazzoni. Piedmont, Lombardy, the Veneto, and the Emilia Romagna had delegates from every single diocese present in the Appenine outpost. 'In Rome, Naples, the Marches, Tuscany and the Islands, the implantation is less complete but still considerable; by contrast the movement remains unorganized in the Basilicata, Puglia and Calabria.'[53] Several open-minded theologians had been invited to participate in the assembly, amongst them notably Enzo Bianchi, the founder of an ecumenical monastery near Turin, who in subsequent decades became one of the most well-known nonconformist theologians in all of Italy. The Turin Cardinal Pellegrino and the bishop of Ivrea were the sole members of the hierarchy officially invited to attend. Pellegrino was forced to decline the offer because of ill-health; Bettazzi chose to stay away, counselling the worker priests not to burn all bridges with the Italian church hierarchy.

And, in fact, in the run-up to the second Serramazzoni gathering, the festering conflict between the *operai-preti* and the Assembly of Italian Bishops (CEI) had come out into the open. Sandro Magister, now writing for the mass-market magazine *Espresso*, noted in a background article to the 1976 Serramazzoni gathering that the CEI had promoted a modus vivendi between the two camps more or less benevolently until late 1971. With the deepening of the ideological and theological gulf, mutual recriminations then became more heated. In late 1975 the CEI 'went onto the attack. On 20 December 1975 [the CEI delegate Bishop Cesare] Pagani met in secret with Angelo Piazza', Pagani offering an agreement between the CEI and the association of worker priests, in which the hierarchy offered to recognize them officially and to agree to a wide-ranging autonomy for the movement to continue its journey, in many respects a remarkable concession to 'the signs of the times'. Piazza was reported to have answered: 'Monsignore, you must not expect any sort of response from me. Only the collective has the power to decide.'[54]

Thus, the official interlocutor for the Assembly of Italian Bishops, Cesare Pagani, was forced to make the arduous journey to Serramazzoni by car. When he arrived, the bishop was greeted by the 150 worker priests ostentatiously singing the symbolic chant of the Chilean Popular Unity coalition, 'Venceremos'.[55] The assembly had chosen 'Venceremos' not solely for its obvious political connotations. 'Venceremos' was also the very song which

---

[53] Vittorio Monti, 'Requisitoria dei preti-operai contro i "peccati" della Chiesa', *Corriere della sera*, 7 January 1976.

[54] Sandro Magister, 'Preti operai? No: operai preti', *Espresso*, undated clipping, p. 23.

[55] Francesco Santini, 'Preti operai col pugno chiuso salutano l'inviato del Vaticano', *La stampa*, 6 January 1976.

the most famous songwriter of the Latin American Left in the long sixties, Victor Jara, had sung in the infamous football stadium of Santiago de Chile, converted into an open-air mass prison in the immediate period after the overthrow of the Chilean Socialist President, Salvador Allende. Having crushed all the fingers, hands, and ribs of the accomplished guitarist and singer, his torturers mockingly challenged the severely injured Victor Jara to play his guitar. Jara defiantly intonated 'Venceremos' in front of his torturers and fellow-prisoners. He was subsequently machine-gunned to death. The Chilean Catholic hierarchy famously had remained silent in the face of the military overthrow of the democratically elected Allende government in September 1973. The Serramazzoni gathering intonating 'Venceremos' thus warned Bishop Pagani that his mission would be tough. Photos of this more than symbolic and decidedly less than friendly 'welcome' ceremony made headline news across Italy.

The CEI's proposition of an 'organic accord' was hotly debated by the assembled priest-activists. Enzo Bianchi, himself no stranger to controversy, at one point intervened: 'We are very bold to talk badly about bishops, but are we in fact capable of constructing an alternative discourse? None of us support class collaborationist positions. None of us wish to remove ourselves from our commitment to tackle the social question. But we do not need Christ to engage in class struggle. We stand in solidarity with the workers' liberation movement until the end; but we must know that faith means more than that.'[56] Yet a majority of the assembled priests argued differently. The fear was prominently expressed that all the CEI had in mind was to reclaim for its own purposes 'the workers' movement in this particular political conjuncture lived by the country as a whole'. Why this sudden interest in forging links with blue-collar working-class communities by the hierarchy? In the name of the group of worker priests hailing from Lombardy, Mario Colnaghi, employed by the flagship enterprise Pirelli, turned to Bishop Pagani: 'We realize that, in this particular moment, you feel alone and isolated. It is the same sense of isolation which we have lived with for twenty years. You should do some penance yourself, in the name of your brother bishops.'[57]

In the end, a majority of 55 (against 31) worker priests voted against an accord with the CEI, asking the CEI instead to recommend to its bishops, if they truly 'believe in the necessity for a positive link with the world of labour', to establish such ties locally, within each diocese, where such a measure would be far more meaningful, rather than perfunctorily on a national level.[58] A majority of worker priests was clearly convinced that the future lay in the hands of the Italian working class rather than those of the Italian episcopacy,

[56] Bruno Marolo, 'Preti operai e vescovi. Dialogo difficile', undated and unidentified clipping, but referring to the second Serramazzoni gathering.

[57] Santini, 'Col pugno chiuso'. The last sentence went like this in the Italian original: 'Fai un pò di penitenza anche tu per i tuoi confratelli vescovi.'

[58] Magister, 'Preti operai?', p. 23.

and that this future would be 'red'. Or, in the words of one of the most actively engaged worker priests in the course of those heady years, Gianni Fornero: 'We experienced the 1970s under the sign and in the expectation of an imminent revolution. We had hoped for and believed in the proximate arrival of a grand historical catharsis. How many times did we not prefigure this new world which was bound to arrive?'[59] When Bishop Pagani left the gathering, the farewell gesture by the assembled worker priests was once again a musical interlude. The often-bearded worker priests then sang 'The International' while raising their clenched fists.

As it so happened, the seemingly unstoppable ascent of the Italian working class in the wake of the Hot Autumn came to an end precisely at the very moment when Italian worker priests definitively cast their lot in favour of the societal mission of blue-collar workers. After 1976 Italian workers began to encounter increasingly serious difficulties in obtaining their seemingly utopian goals, and a series of defeats cast a first range of dark clouds over their future societal trajectory. As we now know, the changing tide of 1976–7 was merely the beginning of an ignominious end to the role of Italian emancipatory working-class politics in Italian society in general. Fifteen years later the world witnessed the remarkable self-dissolution of the PCI, the western world's leading Communist Party, and the meteoric rise of media-tycoon–buffoon Silvio Berlusconi to pole position in national politics. For the worker priests, too, the tide change of 1976/7 meant the necessity to adjust their own course as well.

The next national convention after Serramazzoni II, a gathering from 22 to 25 April 1977 in Salsomaggiore (Parma), gradually began to reconsider the worker priests' partially self-imposed alienation from their church hierarchy, with the Piedmont delegates in the forefront of those favouring dialogue rather than continued confrontation.[60] At the Frascati gathering in March 1981, the 300 Italian worker priests voted to engage constructively in official channels of dialogue with the CEI, the near-split of 1976 having been successfully overcome.[61] As fate would have it, however, with the decline of the centrality of working-class struggles and working-class politics in Italian society in subsequent years, the mission of the worker priests lost part of its meaning as well. The cohort of Italian worker priests soon lost its inner cohesion and social influence as well, due to a series of minor internal squabbles but, above all, due

---

[59] Fornero, 'I preti-operai', p. 344. A 1971 movie by Elio Petri, *La classe operaia va in paradiso*, attempted to provide a filmic context for such aspirations, obtaining the *Grand Prix* at the 1972 Cannes Film Festival.

[60] Sambrune, 'Dio nella fàbbrica', p. 191.

[61] Lamberto Furno, 'Con un applauso 300 preti operai accettano il disgelo con la Chiesa', *La stampa*, 8 March 1981. The title of the piece reads like this in English: 'With a round of applause, the 300 worker priests accept the thaw with the Church.'

to 'the almost total absence of new recruits',[62] which alone would have revitalized a failing cause. The era of priests clad in working-class blue was drawing to a close.

THE PECULIARITIES OF THE NETHERLANDS

It is a sign of the particular vitality of second wave Left Catholicism that, parallel to the spread of a renewed worker priest apostolate in the wake of Vatican II, another vibrant experiment caught the imagination of progressive priests. Starting in the late autumn of 1968, suddenly, in country after country, associations of radical (largely parish) priests began to emerge which became the focus of media attention almost from day one. If the most visible and contentious symbol of first wave Left Catholicism had been the efforts of the first generation of worker priests in the late 1940s and early 1950s, second wave Left Catholicism produced an independent and powerful wave of radical parish priest associations from Portugal to Austria and from England to Italy. This movement, from its outset, managed to outstrip second wave worker priests in the degree of public attention bestowed upon their cause. As if by spontaneous generation, the calendar year of 1968 witnessed the unanticipated and unforeseen arrival of such rebel priests, independent of the worker priest phenomenon, as the new vectors of contestation within the priesthood as a whole. Though there was a certain degree of overlap with second wave worker priests, the newly emerging radical priests covered the entire range of vocations entered into by ordained priests, from parish priests to members of religious orders. In the early years of the phenomenon, perhaps the most central place in the kaleidoscope of national movements was taken by the Dutch contingent.

For several decades, starting in the 1960s, the Netherlands benefited from an international image as a country living under relaxed and permissive rules of social interaction and interpersonal relations. The title of a documentary produced at the tail end of several decades of Dutch exceptionalism, 'Sex, Drugs and Democracy',[63] nicely captured the socio-cultural and political circumstances which, from the 1960s onwards, had fashioned the Netherlands in general and Amsterdam in particular as the preferred travel destination for several generations of disaffected youth in Europe and North America. A number of sometimes unrelated factors were responsible for this development.

---

[62] Sambruna, 'Dio nella fàbbrica', p. 191.
[63] Jonathan Bland, 'Sex, Drugs and Democracy' (USA, 1994): <http://www.youtube.com/watch?v=5JWOVoHGMwE>.

It is beyond the purview of this monograph to engage in a discussion of these issues. May it suffice to point to several symbolic markers: the comet-like rise and fall of the ludic countercultural rebels captivating the Dutch and European public in the mid-1960s, the Dutch Provos, and the subsequent transformation of Amsterdam into the capital city of squatters and alternative cultural experiments in all walks of life. If already during the 1960s 'a climate of mild insanity' reigned in Amsterdam, by the early 1970s the city on the Amstel definitely appeared to march to a different beat.[64]

Incredibly enough, certain developments within the Dutch Catholic church had aided in the creation of an image—and a corresponding partial reality—of the Netherlands as a haven for progressive and libertarian experimentations in all walks of life. By the second half of the 1960s, Dutch Catholicism stood in the front lines of innovation emanating from Vatican II. The Dutch episcopacy was the sole national body of bishops anywhere in the world which stood solidly united behind the proverbial spirit of Vatican II. The 1966 Dutch Catechism, reflecting the new winds perceived to be blowing from Rome, became an international bestseller, was translated into countless languages, and raised a storm of controversies amongst what was initially regarded as a rearguard of Catholic conservatism.[65] Dutch Catholicism briefly moved centre stage in the Catholic world.

It had not always been that way. In fact, just as Dutch society up to the 1950s was rarely characterized by an unusual degree of permissiveness, so Dutch Catholicism hitherto had been by no means a haven for religious innovators. An astute observer of Dutch Catholic life once put it like this: 'By the beginning of the 1950s, Dutch Catholicism was the best organized, most conservative and observant of traditional Catholic laws, and least ecumenical Catholic population in industrial Europe.' And as late as 1954, Cardinal Alfrink, at Vatican II one of the mainstays of the reforming wing along with the Belgian Leo Suenens, still 'appealed to a linear, hierarchical, and one-way chain of command in the church, which saw bishops as agents of the pope, priests as agents of their bishops, and the laity as agents of the will of

---

[64] On the Provos, see, in English, Richard Kempton, *Provo: Amsterdam's Anarchist Revolt* (Brooklyn, NY: Autonomedia, 2007), but above all Niek Pas, *Imaazje! De verbeelding van Provo 1965–1967* (Amsterdam: Wereldbibliotheek, 2003), citation from the latter, p. 90. For an assessment of the Provos' place within the evolution from countercultural nonconformity to political contestation, see Gerd-Rainer Horn, *The Spirit of '68* (Oxford: Oxford University Press, 2007), pp. 38–42. On the transformation of Amsterdam into a laboratory of non-traditional modes of living and the creation of virtually libertarian zones within the most important city of the Netherlands, anticipating and prefiguring the subsequent emergence of some parts of West Berlin as islands of cultural and political experimentation, see Virginie Mamadouh, *De stad in eigen hand. Provo's, kabouters en krakers als stedelijke sociale beweging* (Amsterdam: Sua, 1992).

[65] *De nieuwe kathechismus. Geloofsverkondiging voor volwassenen* (Hilversum: Paul Brand, 1966).

priests and bishops'.[66] What happened in the late fifties and early sixties to turn Dutch Catholicism into the vanguard of radical change?

There are many explanations for this seeming miracle. One popular attempt to understand the almost 180-degree turnaround within Dutch Catholicism in the space of less than a dozen years refers to the very fact of the long survival of traditionalism as the dominant paradigm for Dutch Catholicism until the 1950s. Once, under the pressure of modernization and given an added impetus by Vatican II, new ideas began to circulate amongst the close-knit community of Dutch Catholic believers, they caught on like wildfire. Once the lid was lifted off the boiling kettle, steam started hissing out in entirely unanticipated directions. The presence of open-minded social scientists in influential positions within Dutch Catholicism in the 1950s, attuned to the latest trends in sociology and political science, is likewise adduced as a factor playing a distinctly progressive role. The emergence of a brilliant set of young theologians champing at the bit, amongst them the internationally renowned Belgian-born Edward Schillebeeckx, undoubtedly added to the explosive mix.

All of these factors doubtless exerted important pressures in the direction of progressive changes but, as John A. Coleman perspicaciously suggests, pressure from below alone cannot explain the Dutch miracle: 'A comparative cross-national perspective suggests evidence of shifts very similar to those registered for the Netherlands among the theologians, lower clergy, and lay elites in the late 1950s and early 1960s in almost every Western industrial country.'[67] But nowhere else did the respective national hierarchies eventually embrace these new trends. Only in the Netherlands did the episcopacy eventually embrace innovation and experimentation—and not just as a temporary concession or a ploy.

In the last analysis, Coleman claims, it was due to the personalities and intellectual calibre of the Dutch bishops that change could be effected so rapidly and effectively: 'The Dutch bishops are a different breed from many of their confreres in the world episcopacy.'[68] Given the hierarchical structures of the Catholic church, changes in the outlook at the apex of the pyramid could fundamentally alter the course of Catholicism. As was noted at the outset of Chapter 1, the election of Pope John XXIII engendered a host of entirely unforeseen consequences. A change in crucial personnel, entailing a sudden alteration in course, applied to some extent in the case of Dutch Catholicism as well. In the Dutch case, however, although one must note a series of new appointments and the creation of two new dioceses in 1956, older bishops, too, notably Cardinal Alfrink, proved to be intellectually agile and flexible enough to shift their own outlook from traditionalism to radical

---

[66] John A. Coleman, *The Evolution of Dutch Catholicism, 1958–1974* (Berkeley: University of California Press, 1978), citations on pp. 53–4 and p. 88.

[67] Coleman, *Dutch Catholicism*, p. 100.   [68] Coleman, *Dutch Catholicism*, p. 100.

reformism. The top-down structure of the church, designed to perpetuate tradition and conservatism, could on occasion produce the opposite effect.[69]

To be sure, several circumstantial elements aided the transformation of the Dutch Catholic church from the late 1950s. Traditionally a beleaguered minority in the Calvinist Dutch Low Countries, Dutch Catholicism had forged close ties amongst its adherents which led to the construction of a dense defensive network of Catholic institutions, which imparted an aura of stead-fastness in the presence of adversity. Yet this also meant that innovations were not immediately or automatically regarded as challenges to the status quo or as heresies. 'If there was ever a church which was strong enough to experiment with change, it was the Catholic church in the Netherlands. [...] If new people with new visions came to control the elaborate apparatus of school systems, unions, newspapers, and radio and television, the same resources which had once supported traditional Dutch Catholicism could be mobilized to provide a unique laboratory, a pilot church for post-Vatican II structures.'[70] And a pilot experiment it certainly became.

For at least a dozen crucial years, the Dutch Catholic church pioneered new approaches to the vexed question of how to retain the allegiance of the faithful in the age of modernity and secularization. With the parish of the University of Amsterdam often performing the role of vanguard within the vanguard,[71] new liturgical methods were tested which set new standards and soon became the norm across the Netherlands. Just as the international media sought out the smoke-filled 'anti-smoking' happenings of the Dutch Provos, investigative journalists from other parts of Europe visited Dutch parishes to report on a quiet revolution seemingly at work in the Low Countries.[72]

For in the Netherlands it was no longer entirely unusual for mass to be accompanied by Hammond organ, drums, and guitar, modern rhythms and modern songtexts. Priests, even bishops celebrating mass, frequently discarded traditional vestments in favour of simple Benedictine-style attire. 'There are no more assortments of little pieces of cloth and laced choir gowns, and the altar tools no longer include little golden spoons and plates.' Wine used in mass was poured out of regular carafes into regular goblets, the host

[69] No Dutch-language publication, in my estimation, comes close to the level of sophistication and analytic power on these issues displayed in John A. Coleman's work. Two important contributions by Dutch authors are, however, Richard Auwerda, *De kromstaf als wapen. Bisschopsbenoemingen in Nederland* (Baarn: Arbor, 1988), and the superior biography of the key player in the Dutch episcopacy in those years, Ton H. M. van Schaik, *Alfrink. Een biografie* (Amsterdam: Anthos, 1997).

[70] Coleman, *Dutch Catholicism*, p. 87.

[71] Coen Stuldreher, 'De Amsterdamse Studentenecclesia. Over de oorsprong van een conflict', in *Alternatieve groepen in de kerk* (Amersfoort: De Horstink, 1972), pp. 24–58.

[72] A fascinating book-length travelogue by two young French journalists visiting the hotspots of radical Catholicism, the Netherlands, and Spain, is Philippe Alfonsi and Patrick Pesnot, *L'Église contestée. Hollande/Espagne* (Paris: Calmann-Lévy, 1971).

consecrated in everyday breadbaskets. Taking turns, families belonging to the congregation assisted the priest in celebrating the Eucharist, rather than altar boys in frocks.

Dutch bishops were noted to have arrogated de facto certain powers normally reserved for Vatican administrators. Candidates for vacant episcopal positions were selected by the laity and clergy of the concerned diocese—and only then were the names of the chosen candidates forwarded to Rome. Ecumenical church services became commonplace, often presided over by pastors of one confession only. Divorced Catholics were quickly readmitted to receive the sacraments even if remarried, and even if they had initiated divorce proceedings. Moreover, 'in consistent recourse to what was essential about the priesthood, Dutch bishops made an effort to continue to employ married priests in other church-administered services, until such a time that they will have convinced Rome to allow married priests to exercise their calling'.[73]

THE LAUNCHING OF SEPTUAGINT

If there was one overarching issue which agitated priests in virtually every single European country, it was the issue of celibacy. In the wake of Vatican II, many observers were expecting a papal pronouncement which would liberalize this regime. Yet as months and then years went by without such a move from Rome, some priests decided to take matters into their own hands. Priests marrying and then seeking out a new profession, renouncing their status as priest, had been a phenomenon throughout history, just as had incidents of priests living in a free partnership with a lover, though the latter generally covertly. By the late 1960s, in a general atmosphere of experimentation and the assertion of new rights, the number of priests wishing to avoid recourse to hypocrisy and continual subterfuge grew exponentially. One of the very first to challenge frontally church dogma on this point was Jos Vrijburg, a student chaplain in the infamous Amsterdamse Studentenecclesia. A mainstay of that university parish since its founding in 1960, in November 1968 Jos Vrijburg publicly announced his intention to marry without giving up the soutane. His superiors in the liberal Dutch hierarchy expressed to him their understanding of his wish, but also unmistakably communicated to Vrijburg that they could not countenance such a unilateral move on his part. Jos Vrijburg's marriage

---

[73] A series of articles appearing in a leading West German daily newspaper, the *Süddeutsche Zeitung*, from mid-December 1968 to mid-January 1969 gave a sympathetic and lively succession of snapshots of everyday life in the Catholic Netherlands. The individual contributions were then republished as a special reprint: Hannes Burger, *Durch Reformen zu einer neuen Kirche. Vitaler Katholizismus in Holland* (Munich: SZ, 1969). I cite from the brochure I was able to consult in the Katholieke Documentatie Center (Nijmegen), Septuagint (LXX), fo. 205.

plans became the talk of the town and animated discussions across the Netherlands.[74]

Two young priests from the Haarlem diocese, Joep ter Linden and Pieter Jan Blankendaal, on the eve of their departure for Brazil, at this very moment visited a number of colleagues and friends to say their goodbyes, and it struck them how central the *casus* Vrijburg—the issue of celibacy—was in every single conversation with their colleagues. During their meeting with a young chaplain in Beverwijk, Jan Ruijter, the idea emerged to organize a gathering with other priests to discuss this in a larger setting with others present. Each of the three priests present in Ruijter's home promptly telephoned five colleagues, suggesting that each of the five call a further five fellow priests, and so on, with a view to a gathering in a few days' time.[75]

On 16 December 1966 seventy-three Dutch priests met in a large hall in the Amsterdam Hotel Américain to discuss the topic of celibacy, Jos Vrijburg's statement of intent, and what they could do about this situation. The small crowd present decided to draft a letter to the Dutch bishops, asking them to take a unilateral decision permitting the continued employment of married priests as priests, without waiting for prior approval of such a move from Rome. The names of the co-signers appeared at the bottom of the bold letter. Press and television journalists were present at the meeting in the Américain, ensuring that this gathering would find a public echo. Within days a flood of letters arrived at the contact mailbox of the Américain group, indicating support, written by both secular and regular priests all across the Netherlands, some taking the form of a collective letter signed by close to a dozen priests at a time.[76]

The Américain group soon changed its name to Septuagint, the name given to the legendary seventy Jewish scholars who translated the Hebrew Bible into Hellenistic Greek, the lingua franca of the Eastern Mediterranean for many centuries in antiquity. The French/American connotation of the original name was deemed to be too confusing, especially when international contacts multiplied.[77] A second meeting was convened on 14 February 1969 with double the number of priests in attendance. A coordinating committee was formed,

---

[74] An interesting short appreciation of Jos Vrijburg, complete with photos of the eventual 27 June 1969 wedding, can be read at <http://www.huubmous.nl/2009/02/28/prima-della-rivoluzione/>.

[75] Richard Auwerda, 'Vier jaren geschiedenis', *Conto* 6, no. 11 (November 1972), p. 4.

[76] Septuagintgroep (ed.), *Septuagint van Chur naar Rome. Dossier van de solidaire priestergroepen* (Amersfoort: Katholiek Archief, 1969), pp. 11 and 22, with the text of the letter reproduced on pp. 10–11. A copy of the original typewritten letter with the list of names at the bottom can be consulted in Katholiek Documentatie Centrum (KDC) [Nijmegen], Aktiegroep Septuagint (LXX), fo. 107. A collection of letters expressing support for this initiative can be found in KDC, LXX, fo. 15.

[77] 'Inleiding van J. Ruyter en verklaring van de bijeenkomst van Septuagint op 23 juni 1969 te Utrecht', in Septuagintgroep (ed.), *Van Chur naar Rome*, p. 22.

which then sat down to draft a letter to all Dutch Catholic priests, where issues far beyond the question of celibacy began to be addressed. The church—laity, priests, bishops, and the pope—was urgently asked to modernize its outlook, inner structure, and orientation.[78]

The coordinating committee consisted of 20–30 priests, who gathered most frequently in Utrecht, operating as the de facto leadership for the duration of Septuagint. A financial report for September 1969 lists the number of individuals who were then members of Septuagint as 605, including a not inconsiderable number of members of religious orders, including notably sixty-four nuns.[79] Septuagint quickly became an important player in Dutch public life, benefiting from the liberal atmosphere then prevalent within the Dutch Catholic church. From July 1969 onwards, lay activists began to join Septuagint as full members, though they remained, for the most part, in the shadows of the organization. By October 1969, according to one source, 1,300 Dutch Catholic priests had come out in solidarity with the goals of the organization. In May 1970 a group of sixty critical ministers belonging to one of the major denominations of Protestantism in the Netherlands, the Hervormde Kerk, joined Septuagint. Two months later, about 100 Jesuits, the Helvoirt Group, likewise joined forces with Septuagint. The wind was clearly in the sails of the insurgent forces challenging the authorities.[80]

The highpoint of Septuagint's influence was probably reached in the second half of 1970 around the time of the First World Congress of radical priest associations, which met in late September and early October in Amsterdam. The unofficial internal ten-page history of the group referred to in the previous paragraph suggests that at the point of maximum extension Septuagint counted 2,000 members. A significant proportion of this number—though never more than half—were lay members. Thus, at least about 1,000 Dutch priests were directly involved in this dynamic group. Given that the Netherlands at that time counted no more than 4,000 secular priests, this made Septuagint by far the most important such grouping in Europe in terms of its hold over a significant proportion of the national priesthood.[81]

---

[78] 'Inleiding van J. Ruyter', pp. 23–4. The text of the letter sent to all Dutch priests is reprinted in Septuagintgroep (ed.), *Van Chur naar Rome*, pp. 12–19.

[79] 'Septuagint—Kasoverzicht—18 September 1969'—KDC, LXX, fo. 200.

[80] Much of the information in this paragraph stems from an unsigned and undated ten-page synopsis of the history of Septuagint, written in or shortly after 1975: 'Septuagint'—KDC, LXX, fo. 1. The figure of 1,300 priests expressing their solidarity is mentioned by Herman Verbeek, 'Journaal van 14 dagen Rome', in Septuagintgroep (ed.), *Van Rome naar Utrecht* (Amersfoort: Katholiek Archief, n.d.), p. 34. The collective enrolment by the Helvoirtgroep is documented in Septuagintgroep (ed.), *Van Utrecht naar huis . . . ?* (Amersfoort: Archief van de kerken [1970]), pp. 35–7. Concrete figures for Protestant members of Septuagint are mentioned in an unsigned report, 'Bericht zur Lage der Nation—Nation: Niederlande', 'Beverwijk, mei 1970'—KDC, LXX, fo. 1.

[81] The guestimate of 'roughly 1,000' priests amongst the total membership of Septuagint is the informed opinion of its former spiritus rector, Jan Ruijter, expressed in a conversation with the

FROM AMSTERDAM TO CHUR

Given the unusually firm implantation of Dutch radical priests within the institutional structures of their reform-oriented church, it only stood to reason that Septuagint played a crucial role in the coordination of efforts to fashion an international network of like-minded priests. The second national gathering of Septuagint at the Hotel Américain on 14 February 1969 already counted representatives of German and French sister organizations amongst the close to 150 participants. The letter to all Dutch Catholic priests, referred to above, emanating from this assembly, ended with an action plan which notably focused on the necessity for an international assembly of some sort, to be held in Chur, Switzerland, in early-to-mid-July 1969. The occasion was a planned preparatory conference of European bishops in Switzerland's most ancient town, in order to organize for the coming extraordinary world synod of bishops in Rome in October 1969. 'Our Action Group, in collaboration with priests from other countries, intends to send representatives to Chur in order to closely follow the bishops' conference and to ensure that, via publications and documentation, an "extra-parliamentary" contribution to the event may be assured.'[82] The letter itself was the product of about a dozen successive, long-winded editorial meetings, and the drafters of the letter were exclusively Dutch.

While it is impossible to reconstruct which individual(s) may have first launched this action plan for Chur, it is curious to read in a documentary history of the French sister organization, Échanges et Dialogue, that supposedly one of the key personalities within Échanges et Dialogue, Jean-Marie Trillard, first proposed this particular event, and in a recent history of Échanges et Dialogue this claim is further inflated: 'The leadership of the French movement took the initiative to gather all the Western European groups in order to take a position at the bishops' assembly.'[83] Whatever the precise content of Trillard's intervention on this issue in the Hotel Américain may have been, it is clear beyond a shadow of a doubt that the organizational

---

author on 24 October 2013. The number of secular priests operating in the Netherlands is taken from Walter Goddijn, Jan Jacobs, and Gérard van Tillo, *Tot vrijheid geroepen. Katholieken in Nederland 1946–2000* (Baarn: Ten Have, 1999), p. 504. It is an approximation based on an informed interpretation of relatively detailed graphs. I thank Lodewijk Winkeler for this reference, together with his interpretation of the graphs, according to which 'in 1970 there were about 3,833 secular priests' in the Netherlands; see email by Lodewijk Winkeler to this author, 28 October 2013.

[82] Citation taken from a typescript of the letter, dated 'March 1969', 'Aktiegroup Priesters "Septuagint"', 'Aan alle priesters in Nederland'—KDC, LXX, fo. 1.

[83] For the claim of Trillard as creator of the idea to meet in Chur, see the editorial statement in Pierre Baligand et al. (eds), *Échanges et Dialogue ou la mort du clerc* (Paris: IDOC-France [1975]), p. 255. For the more far-reaching claim of French leadership of international coordination efforts in early 1969, see Sylvaine Guinle-Lorinet, *Libérer le prêtre de l'état clérical. Échanges et Dialogue (1968–1975)*, p. 83.

and intellectual preparation of the 'extra-parliamentary' assembly in Chur lay in the hands of the Dutch contingent, with considerable material assistance from their German colleagues.

The letter announcing the Chur action was finally sent in March 1969. A summary of that text was then sent to all of the approximately fifty sister groups of Septuagint in other European countries, once again authored (in French, the lingua franca for this milieu at that time) exclusively by the Dutch. Jan Ruijter, in his opening speech at the 23 June 1969 Septuagint assembly in Utrecht, reports on the response: 'In particular the idea we launched to be present in Chur triggered many reactions, above all outside of the Netherlands. We were asked how we intended to put this plan into action. What did we want to do in Chur? Was there housing available in Chur? How could they participate? A number of people came to the Netherlands to see what we had in mind.'[84] From all available documentation, it emerges that the West German group crucially assisted Septuagint in the logistics of the Chur event. 'Four men from Munich come to Beverwijk in the Netherlands to facilitate the organization of Chur. [Winfried] Seipolt, Ulrich, [Ludwig] Nieberle and [the Bad Reichenhall-based Ludwig] Prediger.'[85] More than forty years later, Jan Ruijter fondly recalls a most valuable contribution of the German group: they owned and operated a Gestetner mimeograph machine.[86] Efforts to ensure the success of what became the first international assembly of radical priests soon went into high gear.

What had propelled Chur into the position of a pre-eminent event for the fledgling group was not only the fact that this gathering of bishops was the most obvious target for intervention, as it constituted the most representative assembly of European bishops prior to the world synod in Rome. But, in addition, the explicit topic of this symposium of bishops happened to be 'The Priest in the World and the Church of Today'. It only stood to reason that Septuagint and related European groups felt that they should be present at this debate, ideally in order to influence the proceedings.

A meeting to finalize the plan took place on 12 June 1969 in Leuven, which soon emerged as the international administrative centre for the assembly of dissident priests. Invitations to this planning session had been sent to sympathizers in Germany, Austria, Belgium, France, Italy, and the Netherlands. In the end, twenty-two men gathered in Heverlee on the outskirts of Leuven, and they decided to send an open letter to the bishops of their respective dioceses. They noted their collective consternation that the planners of the symposium on the role and function of the priesthood had seen fit *not* to invite any priests

---

[84] 'Inleiding van J. Ruyter', p. 4.

[85] Jan Ruijter, 'Septuagint: Rückblick und Zukunftsschau', 14 March 1970, p. 4—KDC, LXX, fo. 1.

[86] Conversation with Jan Ruijter, 14 January 2012.

to their deliberations. 'Therefore we believe it is necessary for us to be present in Chur in order to discuss with representatives from various countries—amongst them the signatories of this letter—the very topics which you have placed on your agenda.'[87]

CHALLENGING THE CURIA AT CURIA

Chur played a double role for the emerging forces of radical priest associations. Though it shocked many participants to realize the seemingly unbridgeable gap which appeared to separate the European episcopacy from their grassroots priests, it also provided a first opportunity for dissident priests from various corners of Europe to get to know each other and to realize that their individual battles in their respective countries were part of a much larger continental campaign. About 100 radical priests assembled in Chur, arriving with guarded expectations, returning home simultaneously disappointed and yet re-energized.

The wider external circumstances of the European bishops' symposium were notably inauspicious for the handful of priests who had come to challenge authority. The official symposium took place in a seminary building on a hillside at the southeastern edge of the old town, a complex of buildings—the Hof—including the Dome. To this day, the Hof stands somewhat aloof and separate from the actual living centre of Switzerland's oldest town. The assembly of European priests took place in the lower town, in the austere, alcohol-free Rätisches Volkshaus. Journalists came to refer to the two gatherings as 'the Upper Assembly' and 'the Lower Assembly'.[88] During the opening ceremony of the official event, on the evening of 7 July 1969, between fifty and sixty policemen surrounded the Seminary where the bishops congregated. One of the assembled priests could not help but remark: 'Why are the bishops so afraid of their priests? Could it perhaps be that they have a bad conscience?' Another Dutch priest, Fred Keesen, pointedly remarked in a conference report on Chur: 'On top of everything else, the Latin term for Chur is *curia*.'[89] The dividing lines were clearly drawn.

---

[87] See 'Addresses de l'invitation pour le 12 juin [1969] à Louvain'—KDC, LXX, fo. 19; 'Liste des participants'—KDC, LXX, fo. 158; 'Brief van de op 12 juni in Leuven aanwezige priestergroepen aan hun respectivelijke bisschoppen', in Septuagintgroep (ed.), *Van Chur naar Rome*, pp. 20-1.

[88] The geography of the two assemblies is evoked in the report on Chur by Échanges et Dialogue: Jean-Marie Trillard, 'Assemblée Européenne des Prêtres. Coire. 5–10 juillet 1969', p. 2—KDC, LXX, fo. 185.

[89] The heavy police presence at the Upper Assembly is mentioned in the 'Erklärung von W[il] Jansen, Studentenpfarrer, Utrecht, Holland, im Namen der Gruppe Septuagint', p. 2—KDC,

The detailed account by Jean-Marie Trillard of the various attempts by the rank-and-file priests to secure a hearing from their bishops makes clear that the European priests were given the cold-shoulder treatment throughout the entire four-day conference of the Upper Assembly. A first meeting at 2 p.m. on 8 July between a delegation of the priests and the chief organizer of the official symposium went nowhere. Mgr Roger Etchegaray told them explicitly that they would not be welcome to participate in the Upper Assembly. In response, by 5 p.m. the entire assembly of grassroots priests went up the hill, asking to be heard. At 6:30 p.m., an emissary from the Upper Assembly told the priests that they would receive an official response from the Upper Assembly the following day. At 2:30 p.m. on 9 July, the answer arrived. Every single demand of the priests was rejected. Noticeably agitated by the complete refusal to hear the voice of priests on the issue of 'The Priest in the World and the Church of Today', the activist crowd continued to press for an opening. That evening, at 8:45, seven bishops met for a discussion with a significant number of the contentious priests. In what was mostly a face-saving gesture by the Upper Assembly, the seven bishops consistently had recourse to purposefully vague responses to the concrete questions raised by their interlocutors. Jean-Marie Trillard highlighted the ominous initial thirty-second silence of the seven bishops when asked about the instances of collusion between church and state in countries living under dictatorships, as in Portugal and Spain.[90] Jan Ruijter summarized the experience of the European bishops' symposium in Chur: 'For the bishops, for the most part, this gathering was either a pious retreat with some trivial chit-chat on the side or a folkloristic event in the Swiss Alps.' He added: 'We have never before encountered such a shocking experience as the meeting between the representatives of the groups of priests and the bishops.'[91]

Yet, as hinted at earlier, there were some positive outcomes from Chur. For one thing, Chur put the newly emerging groups of radical priests in the limelight of international media attention for the very first time. The press was present in Chur in significant force, with the number of journalists almost twice as many as the participants in the Upper Assembly.[92] Thus, 'Chur was a gift of God for the group of critical priests.' Richard Auwerda explains: 'The bishops met behind closed doors in a seminary building. Every so often they organized a press conference where they said very little in very many words. Reporters for the international media—though they had not come to Chur to follow closely the activists of the alternative gathering of priests—began to

LXX, fo. 185. The accidental linguistic reference to the Roman *curia* was noted by Fred Keesen, 'De gebeurtenissen in Chur. Een stroomversnelling', p. 1—KDC, LXX, fo. 185.

[90] See note 88.
[91] Jan Ruijter, 'Voorwoord', in Septuagintgroep (ed.), *Van Chur naar Rome*, p. 7.
[92] 'Persreacties op Chur', in Septuagintgroep (ed.), *Van Chur naar Rome*, p. 87.

frequent the Volkshaus to while away their time. And they would not have been proper journalists if they had not realized that the dusty halls, the endless discussions and the stacks of stencils exuded what one of them called the energy of the original Pentecost, combined with a minor miracle of tongues.'[93]

For the grassroots priests used their forced exclusion from the Upper Assembly to concentrate on each other, to discover that their worries and problems were shared by priests all over the world. They drafted and discussed position papers, passed resolutions, and engaged in ceaseless communications, which stood in stark contrast to the stasis of the Upper Assembly. 'The most significant result of this European meeting was certainly this: the opportunity for mutual encounters, the reciprocal listening to each other's inspirations and concerns, an understanding of the pastoral condition in the various countries. During the days of Chur, strong bonds of solidarity were forged between each other's often rather different concrete problems, but which all pertained to the issue of the priest in the world and the church of today.'[94]

There was one ray of hope in the Upper Assembly. The Belgian Cardinal Suenens had been designated to give the final address to the symposium. In this closing speech, delivered in an informal manner, 'almost gossipy, as if he were chatting over the pretty landscape surrounding Chur', Suenens included the text of a letter sent to him by Hans Küng who, though not present in Chur, shared the concerns of the priests gathered in the Lower Assembly. Suenens, reading Küng's letter aloud, urged his fellow bishops to take action. 'In this hour, five years after Vatican II, we do not need any more resolutions and explanations; we expect practical decisions.' Küng warned the European episcopacy—and Suenens introduced the following sentences with the words: 'And here comes the punchline!'—'The renewal of the Church will be carried out together with the bishops or without them and, as a result, against them. The second option would be unfortunate.' Küng's letter, read by Leo Cardinal Suenens, received scant applause from the assembled leadership of the European Catholic church.[95]

FROM CHUR TO ROME

Despite the generally upbeat atmosphere within the ranks of the priests composing the Lower Assembly, some differences between (and within) the

---

[93] Auwerda, 'Vier jaren geschiedenis', p. 7.

[94] Wim Al, 'Priesters contesteren rond bisschoppen-symposion te Chur', *Théologie en pastoraat* 3 (1969), p. 273—KDC, LXX, fo. 185.

[95] The text of Küng's letter, with Suenens' interjection, can be consulted in Septuagintgroep (ed.), *Van Chur naar Rome*, pp. 72–4, citations on p. 73. The atmosphere of this singular event at Chur is described in Keesen, 'De gebeurtenissen in Chur', p. 3.

various national delegations were already becoming visible at that time. Southern European delegations, on the whole, held a more negative view of their respective national hierarchies than Northern European delegates.

> Past disappointments, especially in the southern part of Europe, have led a number of priests to the point of not expecting anything any more from their bishops. The extreme example of complete lack of freedom is that of the Basque priests, who experience nothing but oppression even from the secular powers. On the other hand, the relatively favourable situation in the Netherlands, where a clear relationship of trust exists between bishops and priests, exerted a moderating influence on the frequently radical positions of some other groups. For the latter, used to coexisting in permanent tension with their superiors, the Netherlands constitutes a hitherto unknown alternative.

As a result, Richard Auwerda recalled: 'In Chur, the Dutch played first fiddle.'[96]

Following Chur, a more permanent institutional structure was created, the European Assembly of Priests, with an administrative centre in Brussels, with Robert Detry, student chaplain at the University of Leuven, responsible for the day-to-day operations. The European bishops' symposium of Chur having been a preparatory meeting for an extraordinary World Synod of Bishops in October 1969 in Rome, the European Assembly of Priests, fresh from their invigorating first encounter in Chur, soon began to prepare for their own intervention in the forthcoming Rome event. The World Synod was scheduled to begin on 11 October and to last for two-to-three weeks. Parallel sessions of the European Assembly of Priests were planned to run from 10 to 16 October. Added importance was given to the Roman encounter because, from 8 to 12 October, an international commission of theologians was meant to deliberate in Rome in conjunction with the World Synod.

The theme of the priests' assembly was chosen to be: 'To Liberate the Church in order to Liberate the World', in obvious allusion to the official title of the European bishops' assembly in Chur. Various workshops were to structure the 'Lower Assembly' in Rome, with specific national delegate groups responsible for the preparation and presentation of their respective working papers. The key local organizer responsible for logistics was Giuseppe Cappa, a Piedmont priest from Plello di Borgosesia, who had already been present at Chur. In the run-up to the synod, the differing strategies and tactics within the European priest delegations came to the fore again. In particular the French, reflecting their enforced position at the margins of the French church, urged a rather propagandistic approach: 'The French delegates propose a presence in Rome which should be a public manifestation of our belief and hope by means of significant gestures', reads a report on a preparatory meeting by the organizers. The document continues: 'The idea of "significant gestures" is an

---

[96] Auwerda, 'Vier jaren geschiedenis', p. 8.

interesting approach to ponder, but it must be reflected upon in more considerable detail. The majority [of the organizing committee] think, however, that, although one must surely talk about the problems of belief in Rome, one must seek out a synthesis between the mystical approach and the realist approach.'[97]

With all Catholic institutions in Rome closing their doors to the dissident priests, the Lower Assembly in Rome took place in the building of the theological faculty of the Waldensians, ten minutes on foot from the Vatican, near Piazza Cavour. The social centre of European Assembly members and sympathizers, however, became the Piazza Navona, less than ten minutes on foot from the Waldensian university, on the left bank of the Tiber. Already two days before the official opening of the Lower Assembly, a number of radical priests had arrived in Rome and begun to gravitate towards Piazza Navona. 'The conspirators of Chur here meet again. For hours they tell each other what has happened since in their respective home countries and what is to happen here in Rome in the upcoming days. Many members of the press corps frequent the Piazza Navona to get some initial information. The Dutch journalists alone take up all the chairs of one of the open-air cafés. As a matter of course, radio and television are here as well.'[98]

Attending the gathering were 127 delegates from Austria, Belgium, France, Germany, Italy, the Netherlands, Portugal, and Spain, with a further thirty-eight unofficial representatives of eight South and North American countries joining the crowd. 'In addition, many priests—and laypersons too—from Rome and elsewhere also stopped by, staying for one or several days.' As the theological commission partially preceded the actual World Synod, one of the first decisions of the radical priests was to seek out members of that commission for an exchange of opinion. The commission deliberated in the imposing, fortress-like Domus Mariae on Via Aurelia on the outskirts of Rome, and at first the consensus amongst the priests was that they would never be permitted to enter these hallowed halls. Packed into Giuseppe Cappa's car, Jan Ruijter and Joost Reuten nonetheless drove out to the nerve centre of Italian Catholic Action. Reuten, a leading activist in Septuagint, quickly succeeded in reaching the thirty-odd theologians while they were eating lunch in the dining hall. Reuten immediately targeted Karl Rahner. Rahner, already present in Chur at the official Upper Assembly, had been one of the few participants in the deliberations in the Hof at Chur to seek out the Lower Assembly priests for dialogue and communication. Rahner now told Reuten spontaneously that he

[97] 'Compte rendu de la réunion du Bureau de l'Assemblée Européenne des prêtres tenue à Bruxelles le 6-9-69'—KDC, LXX, fo. 159.
[98] The leading member of Septuagint, Herman Verbeek, penned a remarkable and highly detailed summary of his impressions, 'Journaal van 14 dagen Rome', already referred to in note 80; citation on p. 25 of this informative document.

would 'be immediately available, as long as he could first be permitted to eat his dessert'.[99]

At 8 p.m. that evening, Rahner, Yves Congar, and two other theologians met the executive committee of the European Priests Assembly in the International Documentation and Information Centre (IDOC) on Piazza Navona, the leading press agency providing an indispensable service to progressive Catholics, originally founded and financed by the Dutch Catholic church in the days of Vatican II. Congar, but even more so Rahner, presented himself as standing in solidarity with the basic demands of the priests. Rahner asserted that, in his view, 'the insurgent groups are theologically completely legitimate; Congar added, on the basis of his many years of experience with ecumenical questions, that renewal of the Church initially does not utilize official structures and institutions, but that it follows a dynamic path, via spontaneous local action. However,' Herman Verbeek continued, 'when we asked those theologians about their opinion with regard to specific concrete actions in the Church, they both hid behind long-winded theological arguments, betraying a distinct sense of paralysis. This attitude seriously disappointed us.' Still, for the most part, the spontaneous discussion with Rahner and Congar—the other two theologians apparently played little role in the exchange of opinions—was registered as a positive event, given the overall climate in October 1969 in Rome.[100]

The curious encounter between theologians and radical priests occurred on the eve of the official opening of the Lower Assembly in the Waldensian Faculty of Theology. From 10 to 16 October, then, the actual deliberations and workshops took place where the European priests sought to further define their positions. The Dutch contingent had produced position papers in the form of a brochure, which became infamously known as 'the little red book' due to the flashy red colour of the cover page. Fifteen hundred copies arrived hot off the press at Schiphol airport in Amsterdam moments before the Dutch delegation had to board the plane. Translated into French and German, it drew the attention of the European Assembly. A second text, 'Avoir—Pouvoir—Savoir' by Échanges et Dialogue, provided a partially alternative vision. In particular the German delegation criticized what they regarded as the radical fundamentalism of the French position paper, which of course—the German critics knew and understood very well—reflected the hostility of official church authorities towards grassroots efforts at much-needed reform in France. 'The meaning and the role of the Church', the Germans asserted, 'which the French text is meant to describe, is depicted in the entire document

---

[99] Verbeek, 'Journaal', citations on pp. 28 and 26.

[100] Herman Verbeek's published 'Journaal' recounts this episode in some detail, but an earlier unpublished summary of his impressions from Rome provides some additional critical detail: Herman Verbeek, 'Rome-brief 28 oktober 1969', citations on p. 3—KDC, LXX, fo. 189.

as mostly negative. All existing structures are rejected, without any attempt to lay out realistic and practicable indications on how a positive renewal of the Church could be carried through. One gets the impression', the German critics continued, 'that not only are the actually existing institutions severely criticized, but all organizations as such on principle.' And even the francophone Belgians present in the Waldensian Centre, themselves by no means belonging to the moderate camp, wondered aloud, when commenting on the French document, 'whether our assembly is not falling into the same trap which we note with regard to the World Synod: the tendency towards what is, in fact, a form of dictatorial dogmatism, the tendency towards a triumphalist stubbornness, towards the imposition of a European superstructure, which we attempt to enforce on each other, and which gives us no chance to seriously consider the multiple problems facing us. Let the assembly become a space where we can meet each other and where we can freely discuss those concerns which are on our mind.' Only the Romance-language delegations south of the Franco-Belgian border unequivocally supported the French position, though Septuagint recorded its approval as well. Interestingly enough, at the same time Herman Verbeek noted: 'Everyone supported the little red book, except for the Belgians and Portugal.'[101]

And, although the various disputes on the strategy and tactics of the movement did not lead to serious differences amongst the mass of delegates, the mood at Rome did differ from Chur. Herman Verbeek's observations once again hit the spot: 'In Chur we all enthusiastically embraced each other. The group was relatively small, the atmosphere rather intimate, the ambience of solidarity could more easily be established—though this also rendered it more superficial. Now the delegations are bigger, there is more to discuss, the expectations are more urgent, and the press follows us much more closely.' As Richard Auwerda remarked, 'Chur raised expectations which Rome could not deliver'. But the Dutch journalist and Catholic activist immediately followed up this remark by stating: 'Nonetheless! Those who were present in the building of the Waldensians for those ten days [. . .] know that the Holy Ghost was very busy.' At 8 p.m. on Thursday, 16 October, the delegations gathered for one last simple dinner all together in a neighbourhood trattoria.

---

[101] A copy of 'the little red book'—its bilingual French and German title read 'Une église à libérer pour le monde | Die Kirche befreien um die Welt zu befreien'; and the flashy red cover was consciously chosen as a partly whimsical reference to the other 'little red book' then much in vogue, the so-called Mao Bible—can be consulted in KDC, LXX, fo. 189, as can the French 'Avoir—Pouvoir—Savoir' and the German declaration in opposition to the French text, 'Erklärung der deutschen und österreichischen Delegation zum Text "Avoir—Pouvoir—Savoir"'. The Belgian position is paraphrased in Verbeek, 'Journaal', pp. 57–8. The attitude of the national delegations with regard to the little red book was likewise noted in Verbeek, 'Journaal', p. 60. The fact that Septuagint also supported the French position once again suggests that the Dutch group served an important function as a mediator between the various opinions within the European Assembly of Priests.

'One bottle of wine per table, the piano played by [Giuseppe] Cappa, the flute played by Frank [Leeuwenberg], and the plans for the future were becoming increasingly concrete.'[102]

If, on balance, the European priests regarded Rome as a positive event, much no doubt had to do with the recognition of a certain move by sections of the church hierarchy towards engagement in some sort of dialogue with the dissident priests. Two Dutch members of Septuagint from Breda noted in their evaluation of what had become, in effect, the second international gathering of radical priests that, amongst 'a growing number' of bishops, the priests were beginning to be taken seriously. 'A good indicator of this trend is the greater ease with which meetings with individual cardinals and bishops could be arranged', a noteworthy feature of Rome which, in turn, was also in part the result of a different approach to the World Synod by the radical priests, compared to that at Chur. 'The assembly called forth much good will by the calm and quiet manner in which it approached the event. Thus, it had been decided in advance that one would make no efforts to be included in the sessions of the bishops' synod, in clear contrast to Chur where one attempted in vain to make contact with the participants in the symposium. There was also more emphasis placed on small details which, nonetheless, on occasion can make a major difference. Thus, we consciously addressed a letter to the Pope not, as in Chur, to "our brother Paulus", but to "His Holiness the Pope".' As a result, Jac Broeders and Jan Zuidgeest pointed out, even a centrist Italian daily newspaper such as the Milanese *Il giorno* could conclude their assessment of the 'Lower Assembly' in Rome in approving terms: 'The European Assembly of Priests in this manner refutes the false image which portrays them as easy prey to anarchist rantings, and it offers proof of their capacity for self-control and a keen sense of responsibility.'[103]

Not only did the activist priests manage to establish constructive dialogue with some of the Catholic world's most influential theologians, but they also learned from Roberto Tucci, the well-connected Jesuit and player behind the scenes in Rome, that Pope Paul VI, upon receipt of the letter sent to him by the European Assembly at the beginning of their deliberations, expressed his regret that, against his instinctive wishes, he could not arrange for an audience with the rebel priests. 'Given the fact that there exist tensions between some of us'—in the words of a subsequent report of the meeting between the priests and Tucci written from memory—'and our bishops, the Pope explains his decision by pointing out that he would create a conflict with his brother

---

[102] Verbeek, 'Journaal', p. 42; Auwerda, 'Vier jaren geschiedenis', p. 9. The description of the parting meal and impromptu concert is, again, taken from Verbeek, 'Journaal', p. 64.

[103] Jac Broeders and Jan Zuidgeest, 'Evaluatie van de europese priesterassemblee (Rome, 10–16 oktober 1969)'—KDC, LXX, fo. 189.

bishops, if he should receive us without asking them first. [...] To receive us would immediately be interpreted by some as an approval of our movement with all its specific claims.' Although Montini also underscored in his response that the position papers of the European priests do not meet his approval, the secretariat of the Lower Assembly concluded: 'The Pope has not taken a principled position against the fait accompli of our assembly. On the contrary, we may well conclude that, in a certain way, he acknowledges our gathering.'[104]

Despite this, when all was said and done, the European Assembly was a mixed success. It raised hopes for an eventual change of direction from above, but also emphasized some fundamental differences within the rapidly grow-ing groups of priests. Jan van den Dool put it like this: 'A kaleidoscope of viewpoints. The synod of bishops was unconcerned with it. The gathering of priests almost suffered shipwreck because of it.' The chaplain from Rijswijk then noted, in a no doubt purposefully exaggerated reading of accurate characteristics, 'that it was impossible to chat with the Germans, as they always wanted to do everything so dreadfully *gründlich* [= thoroughly]. That it was impossible to work with the French, as they wanted to do nothing else but bear witness to things which did not even feature on our agenda. That the Spanish had obviously sent us a set of old fuddy-duddies [*een stel kneusjes*] who kept themselves so busy with their own problems that it was impossible to engage in meaningful dialogue with them. We later learned that we, the Dutch, were seen as a bunch of obstinate fellows who wanted to push through at any cost whatever was on our mind.' The miracle of tongues, much vaunted at Chur, was beginning to be torn apart. Worse still, as the German theologian and activist, Michael Raschke, pointed out: 'How much time, energy and persuasive powers did we waste on issues related to our internal quarrels, in which, under the pretence of discussing formalities, what was really at stake was the influence and prestige of individual groups.' Jan van den Dool, however, was quick to point to the saving grace of the assembly at Rome: 'The gathering of priests could easily have foundered on this multipli-city of views. And this would doubtless have occurred if, alongside the official gathering, there had not been space for all sorts of informal exchanges, where theory was not uppermost in our minds, but rather the daily practice of our lives.'[105]

---

[104] 'Nota van het sekretariat' of 13 October 1969, and 'Stellungnahme des Sekretariats der europäischen Priestergruppen zur Antwort des Papstes auf unseren Brief vom 11. Oktober'—KDC, LXX, fo. 189.

[105] Jan van den Dool, 'Een pluriforme kerk begint bij het respekt voor ieders eigenheid'—KDC, LXX, fo. 189, and Michael Raschke, 'An die Mitglieder des Sekretariats der A.E.P.', 22 October 1969—KDC, LXX, fo. 84.

AMSTERDAM: THE DISCOVERY
OF THE THIRD WORLD

Thus, still in the upswing of the mobilization cycle begun just one year earlier, the European Assembly of Priests continued to expand and to make waves. In part because of the mediating position of Septuagint between the more cautious reformers of the Germanic states and the more overtly revolutionary sentiments of many Romance-language groups,[106] the Netherlands was chosen to host the next international conference. Hitherto, all international gatherings had been, in a way, reactions to official conventions organized by the hierarchy for the hierarchy. The forthcoming conference in the Netherlands was, thus, the first convention of radical priest groups which could meet and deliberate unconcerned with parallel manoeuvres by their superiors. For that reason, the 1970 Amsterdam Congress is sometimes referred to in contemporary documents as the First World Congress of the movement. Initially planned for the spring of 1970, the Assembly eventually took place from 28 September to 3 October 1970. One of the reasons for the delay was, no doubt, the need to consolidate the various fledgling national groups.

Not only was Amsterdam by far the largest assembly of radical priests up to that point, it also became the first true *world* gathering of this movement, notably including a significant delegation of Latin American activists. A total of 372 delegates officially registered for the proceedings in the Van Nispelhuis, with one entire afternoon and evening, Wednesday, 30 September 1970, devoted to Latin American Affairs. In fact, it was the Latin American contingent which largely stole the show at Amsterdam. A post-conference assessment by some Rotterdam sympathizers of Septuagint captures the sentiment

---

[106] This division between moderate 'North' and radical 'South', however, should be regarded, above all else, as a heuristic device, and it does not do justice to the multiplicity of viewpoints within each national group of the European Assembly. The case of the German Arbeitsgemeinschaft der Priester- und Solidaritätsgruppen in Deutschland (AGP), which, in a May 1971 document listing the membership of all European groups, emerged as the largest group of all in terms of absolute numbers, with 1,500 members, is a good case in point. (Incidentally, the Netherlands came second with 1,250, France third with 1,000 members, and Belgium fourth with 700 members—subdivided into 400 Walloon and 300 Flemish.) Anton Bühler, a Swiss activist in the European Assembly, points out in his 1975 monograph—a cogent comparative analysis of the German, Dutch, and French detachments—that the important local groups operating in the Munich area and the Trier region rather differed from the general penchant amongst AGP members for—relative!—moderation. See Anton Bühler, *L'Innovation dans l'institution religieuse. Une analyse sociologique de trois groups de prêtres contestataires: France, Allemagne, Hollande* (Leuven: Faculté des Sciences Économiques, Sociales et Politiques, 1975), p. 169. The German group, it should be pointed out, appears to be the sole group of the original constellation of radical forces amongst European priests which survives until today. For a recent history of the AGP, see Edgar Utsch and Carl-Peter Klusman (eds), *Dem Konzil verpflichtet—verantwortlich in Kirche und Welt. Priester- und Solidaritätsgruppen in Deutschland (AGP) 1969–2010: eine Bilanz nach 40 Jahren* (Münster: LIT, 2010). The document listing membership figures is 'Situation financière de l'A.I.C.S. au 27 mai 1971'—KDC, LXX, fo. 85.

which emerged from other accounts as well. Introductory keynote speeches 'contributed little to the course of the Congress. Especially the presentation by Albert van den Heuvel [from the ecumenical Geneva World Council of Churches] on the topic of ecumenical Christianity struck barely a chord. The Congress only really got going when the topic of the Third World began to be addressed.'[107]

Even five years later, an internal document providing a synopsis of the overall evolution of Septuagint highlighted that 'especially the contribution of the Mexican delegation was of great importance for Septuagint' and also what became of Septuagint. 'The theology which was introduced to the Amsterdam Congress by the Mexican delegation consisted of two points: exodus and solidarity.' Solidarity referred to the urgent need to combat relations of exploitation which dominate the world. 'We must analyse and document the various mechanisms of national and international exploitation. As prophets we must confront this sinful and unjust condition.' 'Exodus' meant 'that a community of believers should never rest, but should always attempt to be on the move, to depart', aiming to replace the deficient present with a 'more humane and more just future. The other world, a possible and desirable world, functions as a sort of mirror, in which present conditions are reflected as comparatively less free and less ideal.'[108]

The Amsterdam assembly occurred precisely at a moment when European activists, initially motivated by efforts to reform—if not revolutionize—the church, began to shift their attention to the critique of society as a whole. The particularly dire circumstances of Spanish and Portuguese activists had already primed attentive observers from other European states, certainly the radical priests who had listened to the horror stories of their Spanish and Portuguese colleagues at international gatherings, to acknowledge the deep gulf between their own relatively privileged societies and the socio-political circumstances of Iberia. The discovery of the Third World magnified this recognition of the fundamental flaws underpinning modern societies. It was a process which equally affected other activist milieux at this particular con-juncture, not just Left Catholics. The issue which prompted European (and North American) activists in the late 1960s and at the very beginning of the 1970s to begin to formulate an increasingly scathing critique of the world around them was precisely the topic of global inequalities in the form of the

[107] 'Liste des participants', 'Assemblée Internationale des Chrétiens Solidaires', 'Van Nispel-huis, Amsterdam, du 28 septembre au 3 octobre 1970'—KDC, LXX, fo. 215; the special session devoted to Latin America can be verified in the detailed conference programme, 'Communiqué de l'équipe d'organisation aux participants', p. 4—KDC, LXX, fo. 150; the astute assessment of the momentous impact of Latin American participants is taken from 'Samenvatting van het gesprek van enkele sympatisanten van LXX uit Rotterdam en omgeving, gehouden op 13-10, '70 te 20.00 uur in de Thomas Morus school', citation on p. 1—KDC, LXX, fo. 5.
[108] 'Septuagint', n.a., n.d., pp. 7–8—KDC, LXX, fo. 1.

exploitation and oppression of the Third World. Via the prism of Third World oppression, European activists quickly became ardent supporters of Third World liberation movements and tireless solidarity activists. Left Catholics mutated from reformers and revolutionaries within the church to radical critics of uneven development and the contemporary world system underpinning this vicious cycle. This process affected not just the European Assembly of Priests but the entire kaleidoscope of Left Catholic activists, notably including virtually every single branch of specialized Catholic Action, at roughly the same time.

For the priests, as for others, the learning process proceeded at a remarkable pace. Septuagint had begun its journey with a critique of celibacy. It quickly began to attack what they regarded as the generally deplorable state of church affairs in general, though initially focusing on their roles as priests. The official motto of the European symposium of bishops in Chur, 'The Priest in the World and the Church of Today', triggered the first international assembly of critical priests precisely because the subject centrally occupied their hearts and minds. In October 1969, the emphasis had already begun to shift slightly: 'To Liberate the Church in Order to Liberate the World'. The Amsterdam assembly had adopted the unifying slogan: 'The Church in Society'. Never again would church affairs be so central for this fronde of rebellious priests.

OPERATION SYNOD

There was one more step in the learning process which the Christian Solidarity International Congress, as the European Assembly had begun to be called since Amsterdam, had to complete. Amsterdam, for all practical purposes, was the first and last international congress of what was called, until the eve of the conference, the Assembly of European Priests. The Amsterdam event itself, with a noticeable contingent of extra-Europeans—not just Latin Americans— in attendance, was called the International Congress of Solidarity Groups. The next (and last) major international effort was a mobilization for the Second World Synod of the Catholic church, scheduled to begin its deliberations in the Eternal City on 30 September 1971. The topics for consideration at the Synod were 'The Danger of a Fundamental Law other than the Gospel', 'Justice in the World', and once again 'The Priestly Ministry in the Church of Tomorrow'. Unlike what happened in October 1969, the radical priests were no longer keen to mobilize their troops for an international show of force in Rome. Actions of varying sorts were, however, to occur in a decentralized manner around the world. In practice, or so it seems, much of the ensuing action was coordinated from Western Europe. It was an impressive organizational challenge. Except for a handful of activists sent to Rome, working in coordination with the ever-present and tireless head of the IDOC, the

Dutchman Leo Alting von Geusau, all essential activities were to occur on location in each individual country, including the Philippines, South Korea, Jordan, Japan, Peru, the Congo, and Colombia.[109]

Little was to be left to chance. Perhaps unconsciously mirroring time-worn national stereotypes, the organizers devised an ingenious division of labour. 'The coordination of *technical* activity of Operation Synod will be given to the centre at Frankfurt.' 'The coordination of the *intellectual* activity of the Operation will be given to the centre at Paris.' 'The coordination of *financial* activity of the Operation will be given to the centre at Zurich.' Leuven was earmarked to continue its function as the general coordinating centre and, perhaps because of their reputation as mediators, the Dutch were entrusted to assist with the launching and strengthening of the various regional centres. 'Amsterdam will establish a harmonious development between the different world participants.'[110]

Meetings, public relations efforts, and special church services were to alert Catholics around the world to what was at stake in Rome. IDOC would strive to publish all relevant documentation emerging from the Synod and related events in Rome. Equally, IDOC would endeavour to filter back into Rome significant statements emanating from the rest of the world. 'This means that Operation Synod in Rome could relay to the Synod and the mass media present in Rome the reactions from other parts of the world, which IDOC will receive from their regional centres via telephone, within one or two days after important Synod documents have been sent around the world.'[111] To all intents and purposes, it was a massive, last-ditch international coordinating effort to change the course of the Catholic church.

To no avail. No noticeable changes of direction were recorded by the World Synod in Rome. The tender shoots of hope that were prominently registered during the October 1969 Extraordinary Synod vanished into thin air. Most importantly, an overwhelming majority of the Synod firmly rejected the priests' demand for the abandonment of celibacy rules.[112] The 1971 Synod did adopt a text on 'Justice in the World' which remains a reference point in church doctrine until today because of its adoption of some elements from the language repertoire of liberation theology. But the final version of this document came across as a disappointment to grassroots activists after all. As Henry ter Kortenaar commented at the time: 'Its theology is a good deal more

---

[109] Informational materials on what came to be called 'Operation Synod' can be consulted in KDC, LXX, fo. 162 (preparatory meeting in Leuven, 12–13 March 1971), fo. 195 (preparatory meeting in Turin, 4–5 September 1971), and fo. 132 (including a detailed outline of the organigrame for the Operation).

[110] 'J. R. and L. N.', 'Operation Synode '71', pp. 465—KDC, LXX, fo. 132.

[111] 'Operation Synode, Amsterdam—Rome, 3-9-71'—KDC, LXX, fo. 132.

[112] A cogent discussion of the Second World Synod in this respect is given in Denis Pelletier, *La Crise catholique* (Paris: Payot, 2002), pp. 221–6.

challenging than that on the priesthood; some of its practical conclusions, on international and ecumenical cooperation, for development, etc., are excellent; it also denounces some of the major ills of the modern world (armaments, pollution, discrimination, etc.); yet it does not name any concrete situations of injustice, as several bishops had asked. Among the reasons given for this silence were the impossibility of naming them all, the difficulty of determining where concrete injustice lies, and the danger that some bishops might get in trouble.'[113] For the members of the Christian Solidarity International Congress it was too little, too late.

THE IMPLOSION OF THE CHRISTIAN SOLIDARITY INTERNATIONAL CONGRESS

The various national sections predictably reacted in widely divergent ways. Septuagint, benefiting from optimal relations with regard to their Dutch superiors, carried out perhaps the most astounding change in orientation. Jan Ruijter drew his conclusions on 21 October 1971: 'But after the Synod, there is no point in any further attempt to influence the hierarchy, even within the Netherlands. The Church, as it presented itself at the Synod, is busy paralysing itself. What we may have to decide rather soon is whether to abandon Septuagint in its old form. At any rate, there is a need for a change of course. All of us will have to face this issue.'[114] Septuagint decided to desist from any further propaganda actions for a while and to concentrate on a collective reflection on which way to move forward. A kind of 'retreat' was on the agenda which was to become a stocktaking of accomplishments, of hopes, but also of failures.

'We asked ourselves whether it was not advisable to abandon fighting against the hierarchy and to begin instead to focus our energies on serving the grassroots in the form of local or regional groups, communities or parishes. [. . .] After several months of intensive consultations and a meeting on 11–13 May [1972], we decided to seek out a new path', and the same document then summarized the new orientation in the following words: 'We wish to coach and strengthen politically oriented groups within and outside the Church by helping to create brand new associations or by helping to develop already existing groups.' In short, Septuagint began to reorient itself from a movement of dissident priests towards a movement to promote what

---

[113] Henry ter Kortenaar, 'Go, and Synod No More', *Commonweal*, 26 November 1971, p. 197. For 'Justice and the World' itself, see <http://www.shc.edu/theolibrary/resources/synodjw.htm>.

[114] Jan Ruijter, 'Zaandam, 21-10-71'—KDC, LXX, fo. 2.

came to be called, in the Dutch context, 'critical communities'.[115] Septuagint began to see itself as a coordinating body of emerging base communities in the Netherlands. This is where the future appeared to lie, rather than in fruitless and energy-consuming efforts to lobby the hierarchy.

In March 1973, Septuagint addressed an interim report to its membership, in which the reorientation effected in 1971/2 was reconfirmed and where Third World solidarity efforts, but also a growing desire to link up with dynamic, non-traditional labour struggles in the Netherlands itself, received prominent mention. 'This report, called an interim report by Septuagint, was at the same time the last public statement of the movement. Septuagint is no longer referred to as a movement in subsequent documents', though it was never officially dissolved. Almost forty years later, Jan Ruijter insisted on the fact that Septuagint simply continued as a constituent part of the rapidly growing movement of Dutch base communities. Nevertheless, after March 1973, Septuagint had ceased to exist as an independent group assembling critical priests.[116]

Échanges et Dialogue had never enjoyed positive relations with the French hierarchy, even though the French episcopacy was less hostile than, say, its Italian counterparts or, worse yet, the Portuguese or Spanish hierarchy vis-à-vis its insurgent priests. From the start, Échanges et Dialogue had focused on what they called the 'declericalization' of the priesthood, the necessity for priests to lead lives similar to those of their parishioners. The right to take up paid employment, to become activists within their unions, and to marry like everyone else were initially merely demanded but subsequently arrogated by priests belonging to the movement. Marriages by priests belonging to Échanges et Dialogue—as, indeed, by priests active in some other national sections of the Christian Solidarity International Congress—became less and less unusual as time went by. Échanges et Dialogue, moreover, stood out for the high number of their members who, within the space of very few years, chose to become worker priests. Échanges et Dialogue, nonetheless, claimed a special role for its members as prophets of a better future within their congregations, and it remained the sole organization of the Christian Solidarity movement to restrict membership to priests only.[117]

---

[115] '"Vertaling" van Bericht van Septuagint', June 1972, citations on pp. 1, 5, and 6—KDC, LXX, fo. 1.

[116] I consulted the March 1973 interim report in a German translation, 'Ein Zwischenbericht an die Basis'. The citation is from a document already repeatedly referred to, written in or shortly after 1975, entitled 'Septuagint'—both items are in KDC, LXX, fo. 1. Jan Ruijter's comment that Septuagint never dissolved itself but organically merged with the welter of base communities was made during a conversation with the author on 14 January 2012.

[117] Guinle-Lorinet, *Échanges et Dialogue*, pp. 200–5, highlights the strategy of declericalization. For a snapshot of the concrete consequences of the French group's programmatic outlook, note, for instance, the situation report of March 1971: 'Échanges et Dialogue organizes about 1,000 priests. In addition, there exist many groups of sympathizers. More than half of the 1,000

The October 1971 Synod thus had less of a shock effect on Échanges et Dialogue than on Septuagint, and the former continued undaunted to pursue their chosen path. With Septuagint withdrawing from the front-line ranks, henceforth Échanges et Dialogue became the de facto international organizing centre.

Coincidentally, at this very same time, a shift began to be noticed in the intellectual and activist trajectory of the Catholic Left, affecting radical priest groups as much as all other Left Catholic milieux, notably Specialized Catholic Action. Intensely politicized in the course of Third World solidarity work which alerted them to the structural injustices in the contemporary world, activists now began to shift their attention to domestic politics. Realizing that Third World poverty and social injustice were products of a globally operating world system of imperialist exploitation, Third World solidarity activists turned into European revolutionaries. By targeting the home base of imperialist power and arrogance, the First and the Third World could, they argued, be liberated in one fell swoop. A cycle of radicalization was now reaching its apex. Initially politicized by authoritarian attitudes of traditional church hierarchies, progressive Catholics had gradually become aware of the democratic deficits of society and politics in their respective native lands. Their eyes were then further opened by encounters with Third World conditions via personal contacts and intense study of relevant texts. Soon, radical, if not outright revolutionary, solutions appeared to be the sole appropriate answers to the problems at hand. It was now merely one small further step to apply the same messianic tools for liberation, initially earmarked for Third World countries, to the situations on their own doorstep in First World contexts back home.

As far as the Christian Solidarity International Congress was concerned, after three international gatherings in the space of less than fifteen months—Chur, July 1969; Rome, October 1969; Amsterdam, September/October 1970—and one decentralized but internationally coordinated global effort (Operation Synod in October 1971), it took more than two years for the next international show of force to be organized. About 1,000 persons assembled on 17–18 November 1973 for the—note the characteristically maximalist name change!—International Assembly of Christians for the Revolution, at first sight a threefold increase in attendance, compared to the previous highpoint, the Amsterdam convention, and thus a seemingly unqualified success. But, as Denis Pelletier had already astutely remarked: 'Lyon, which should have

members are engaged in full-time professional work. About one hundred of them carry out political work inside their unions. About two hundred are married'—'Réunion des délégués à Louvain les 12 et 13 mars 1971 en vue des événements de Genève (avril) et Rome (octobre)', p. 4—KDC, LXX, fo. 162.

allowed a unification of struggles, to the contrary initiated a process of implosion.'[118] How could that be?

In fact, as Pelletier makes clear, though the international network of the Christian Solidarity International Congress was crucially involved in the planning for Lyon, the Lyon Assembly served simultaneously as a focal point for a whole range of Left Catholic organizations and movements in France, many of them having undergone a radicalization process just like Échanges et Dialogue. Rather than primarily a convention of the Christian Solidarity network, Lyon took on the characteristics of an assembly of the Left Catholic battalions within the French Far Left. Robert Detry, already for several years the administrative coordinator of the ex-European Assembly of Priests, on New Year's Eve 1973 penned a scathing report to the organizing bureau responsible for the Lyon Assembly in which he highlighted that, 'as far as the international dimension is concerned, Lyon seriously lags behind Amsterdam (32 countries) and the Operation Synod (38 countries). The main absentees at Lyon were the English, the Americans, the Poles, the Angolans, the Palestinians, but also the Germans and the Italian Swiss, the Flemings and the Spaniards apart from the Basques and Catalans. At Amsterdam three-quarters were non-Dutch, at Lyon less than a third were non-French (even in absolute numbers, there were fewer foreigners here than in Amsterdam!). Moreover, how can one pretend to be international and to send out invitations solely in French to our English, American, and other friends? Why should we be surprised that they did not come? The invitations for Amsterdam were drafted in four languages. How can one call oneself international by handing all the texts to participants exclusively in French? At Rome texts were in German and French, and at Amsterdam in English and French.'[119]

Yet there was another element at play which facilitated the effective disintegration of the erstwhile Christian Solidarity International Congress. Robert Detry highlights the existence of 'the classic gap between revolutionaries and reformists', though Detry was quick to add that 'this does not correspond to the North–South division; it is a difference of opinion which exists within each individual country'.[120] Moreover, within the French contingent assembled at

---

[118] A selection of important documents from the Lyon Assembly can be consulted in Baligand et al., *Échanges et Dialogue*, pp. 318–41, but should be supplemented by the documentation in the rich collection of materials by their Italian co-thinkers: Archivio Storico della Camera dei Diputati (Rome) [ASC], Sette Novembre (7N), B 18 F 1–3. On the eve of Lyon, the Italian co-organizers published a book-length interim report on international coordination efforts and a series of country studies: Commissione Culturale del Movimento '7 Novembre 1971' (ed.), *Le organizzazioni rivoluzionarie nelle chiese europee* (n.p.: Ora Sesta Edizioni, 1973). Denis Pelletier's relevant comments on Lyon are in his *Crise catholique*, pp. 171–7.

[119] Letter by Robert Detry to the 'executive committee responsible for Lyon 73', 31 December 1973, p. 2. This important document is extant in KDC, LXX, fo. 183, and in the ASC, 7N, B 24 F 4.

[120] Letter by Detry, 31 December 1973, p. 2.

Lyon, for instance, a notable point of discord—despite an overall agreement for priorities to be placed on pressures for societal changes at the expense of exclusive church concerns—was a tactical dispute. One tendency pushed for an institutional rupture with the church, the other wished to carry on the struggle within the structures of the church.[121] Having increasingly moved away from a primary orientation towards the radical reform and/or revolution of the church, Échanges et Dialogue—and significant elements within the French Catholic Left as a whole—began to reproduce and copy oftentimes acrimonious debates, disputes and attitudes characteristic of the radical Left as a whole.

There was one—at first sight astounding—apparent counterpart to the gradual implosion of the Christian Solidarity International Congress. There had been Italian representatives present at all international gatherings starting with Chur. But, unlike other national groupings, the Italian sympathizers acted in a personal capacity or as members of a local circle of activists, by no means all of them priests. In a curious dialectic, Operation Synod, which served to deflate the energies of a number of prominent sections, notably Septuagint, in Italy itself called forth the opposite reaction. The Second World Synod had lasted from 30 September to 6 November 1971. The Italian supporters of the Christian Solidarity movement now decided to launch a national association. In direct reference to what they regarded as a failed synod, they named their movement 'Movimento 7 Novembre 1971', 'with the explicit intention of proclaiming that the reform of the priesthood— hitherto expected to emerge from an initiative by the hierarchy, which turned out to have been a groundless hope—would henceforth be pushed from the bottom up'.[122] This daring initiative from below quickly attracted hundreds of enthusiastic responses and the movement was officially launched on 25 April 1972 in Rome.

Yet, in Italy, near-identical divisions to those that were beginning to complicate the inner life of Échanges et Dialogue soon led to the implosion of a project that briefly captured the imagination of the entire Italian Catholic Left. The comet-like rise of Sette Novembre came to an abrupt end within two years of its triumphant take-off in Rome. By early 1974, Sette Novembre experienced faction fights all-too-familiar to participant-observers of the contemporary radical Left, complete with massive attempts to influence the outcome of important votes by packing meetings with large numbers of new members specifically recruited for the occasion. The precise line-up of factions differed somewhat from the internal wranglings of Échanges et Dialogue, though the noxious effects were depressingly similar. In the case of Sette

[121] Pelletier, *Crise catholique*, p. 174.

[122] Carlo Crocella, 'Una singolare espressione del dissenso cattolico negli anni Settanta. Il Movimento "7 novembre 1971"', in Carlo Brezzi et al. (eds), *Democrazia e cultura religiosa* (Bologna: Il Mulino, 2001), pp. 447–8.

Novembre, one faction stood 'close to the experience of base communities and the extraparliamentary groupings of the Left, the other strove to retain links to the episcopacy and stood close to the Communist Party'.[123] By the mid-1970s, the history of the Christian Solidarity International Congress had become, for practical purposes, a subchapter within the colourful and ultimately tragic history of the European Radical Left.[124]

---

[123] Crocella, 'Il movimento "7 novembre 1971"', pp. 447–77, remains the sole published history of this remarkable Italian group, whose archives remain unsorted in the Historical Archive of the Italian Parliament; citation on p. 452.

[124] Échanges et Dialogue officially announced its dissolution on 16 February 1975, to become effective on 1 March 1975 (Guinle-Lorinet, *Échanges et Dialogue*, pp. 136–51). Échanges et Dialogue decided to concentrate its energies on one of the emerging—but ultimately short-lived—factions within the larger network of the radical Catholic Left in France, the Chrétiens Critiques. A successor organization to the Italian Sette Novembre, Rinnovamento Conciliare, publicly proclaimed on 9 December 1974, turned out to be an ephemeral grouping as well. Carlo Crocella reports: 'No new leadership emerged, and within a few months it became obvious that the project was stillborn' (Crocella, 'Il movimento "7 novembre 1971"', pp. 475–6, citation on p. 476). Handwritten minutes testify to various efforts at international coordination of Chrétiens Critiques and Rinnovamento Conciliare (ASC, 7N, B 24 F 9), with Herbert Sibbe and Herman Verbeek of, respectively, the German AGP and Septuagint, also attending. A firm international link never materialized. Certain key personalities of the former Sette Novembre and Échanges et Dialogue, notably Fernando Cavadini and Robert Davezies, remained in touch, and the archives record on–off plans for further attempts at international coordination between 1977 and 1980, none of them destined for any measurable modicum of success (ASC, 7N, B 15 F 1).

3

Spontaneous Ecclesial Communities

COMUNITÀ DI BASE

The official report on the 1970 Amsterdam Congress by the French-language periodical produced in Leuven, *Savez-vous que*, began with a raving account of the way the Dutch organizers had solved the problem of housing the nearly 400 delegates. 'In Amsterdam we were living for six days in one of those "base communities" which are at the moment the talk of the town. The roughly 400 participants were not accommodated in hotels, but they were all placed within families. The friendly reception by the latter, their open-minded viewpoints on all sorts of subjects of interest to human interaction and religion, their passionate interest in the problems of contemporary Christianity will remain, for the participants, an extraordinary memory.'[1] The preparatory conference immediately preceding Operation Synod in Rome, organized in Turin from 4 to 5 September 1971, was in fact logistically in the hands of one of the earliest—and most notorious—base communities in all of Italy, the Comunità del Vandalino (about which more below).[2] Operation Synod itself was, one may recall, facilitated on location by a mere handful of individuals hailing from the Christian Solidarity movement. The key person animating the Roman IDOC, Leo Alting von Geusau, noted several weeks in advance of the Synod: 'Independent or "spontaneous" base communities around the entire world have increasingly devoted their attention to the Synod.'[3] In the planning for Operation Synod in Rome itself, base communities likewise performed valuable services. Given the minimal presence of organizers sent by the Christian Solidarity International Congress, the organizing committee

---

[1] 'L'Assemblée Internationale des Chrétiens Solidaires', *Savez-vous que* 2, no. 1 (November 1970), p. 1—Katholiek Documentatie Centrum (KDC) [Nijmegen], Aktiegroep Septuagint (LXX), fo. 150.
[2] See the relevant documentation surrounding the September 1971 Turin meeting in KDC, LXX, fo. 195.
[3] Leo Alting von Geusau, 'Specificiteit en verwachtingen van de synode in Rome in 1971', 8 September 1971, p. 2—KDC, LXX, fo. 132.

noted: 'Roman base communities will have to play an important role.'[4] One faction of Sette Novembre, readers may recall, decided to cast their lot with the future of Italian base communities. And the stunningly successful Dutch section of the Christian Solidarity Movement, Septuagint, transformed itself into a motor force within the burgeoning Dutch base communities with which, in effect, Septuagint eventually merged. What were these base communities which seemed to have become all the rage, and where did they come from?

In this chapter, attention will be exclusively directed towards base communities in Italy, for Italy—apart from Spain, starting in the late 1960s—saw the most vibrant development of such informal associations oftentimes combining ecclesial and social action outside of the regular channels of the church. Unlike Spain, however, where few paper trails remain with regard to the early history of base communities during the final paroxysms of the Francoist dictatorship, the Italian *comunità di base* can be reconstructed in all their vibrant kaleidoscope of incarnations and colourful detail. This, however, was no easy task. Thriving on informality and decentralization, the various pieces of the puzzle have to be put together in often difficult forensic work, as there is to date no central archive of the movement which, like its Spanish counterpart, continues to operate until today.[5]

In Italy, the highpoint of this veritable rage can be pinpointed to the mid-1970s, perhaps more specifically to their 25–7 April 1975 Third National Congress in the Florentine Palazzo dei Congressi, with 2,000 individuals representing more than 200 local communities from all over Italy in attendance. At any rate, the Italian network of base communities usually traces its point of origin to the first such national gathering in Rome in October 1971.[6] In this chapter, however, I have chosen to concentrate on what I regard as the formative period of Italian base communities, the 1960s and the very beginning of the 1970s. For it was precisely in this gestation period of base communities where the multiplicity of varieties can be best studied in almost laboratory conditions. The honeymoon period of second wave Left Catholicism, running from the end of Vatican II to 1968/9, provided a free-flowing favourable

---

[4] 'Réunion des délégués à Louvain les 12 et 13 mars 1971 en vue des événements à Genève (avril) et Rome (octobre)', p. 11—KDC, LXX, fo. 162.

[5] Information on the Italian base communities today can be obtained on their informative website: <http://www.cdbitalia.it/>. The equivalent website of the Spanish *Comunidades cristianas populares* is: <http://www.ccp.org.es/>.

[6] A list of national gatherings, starting with the October 1971 convention, can be found in the most comprehensive history of Italian base communities to date: Mario Campli and Marcello Vigli, *Coltivare speranza. Una chiesa per un altro mondo possible* (Pescara: Tracce, 2009), pp. 196–201. The same team of authors also underlines the singularity of the 1975 Florence *convegno* on pp. 65–8. As we will discover in subsequent pages of this chapter, there were, of course, earlier national gatherings of Italian base communities, but the official count most frequently begins with the October 1971 Roman gathering, which indeed ushered in a period of organizational consolidation after an earlier turbulent gestation period.

context to the testing of new waters in all sorts of imaginative ways, giving rise to an astounding range of experiments in virtually all walks of life. Alessandro Santagata has recently pointed to this brief interlude full of apparent hopes and promises as the decisive moment in the evolution of post-conciliar Italian Catholicism;[7] and it was indeed precisely then that base communities emerged into a visible and audible social force within church and society.

Readers somewhat familiar with Italian *comunità di base* will no doubt remark that the term 'base community' was not yet commonly—if at all—employed in the second half of the 1960s when, instead, terms like 'ecclesial groups' or 'spontaneous groups' were frequently chosen to denote such phenomena. The following pages will hopefully make clear that, regardless of the labels affixed, the informal groups arising outside of the regular channels of the church prior to the Roman National Conference of October 1971 belong to the same *genus* of 'base communities' as their more numerous and nationally organized successor organizations.

Apart from isolated precursors, loose organizations which, in retrospect, could easily be classified as base communities did not get seriously off the ground until the first half of the 1960s. To be sure, Christian 'autonomous groups, with a critical attitude vis-à-vis the official positions of the "Catholic world" existed also in the 1950s'.[8] But circumstantial evidence suggests that it was the years of Vatican II (1962–5) when things began to truly stir. 'Thus emerged groups exclusively composed of Catholics, some via the initiative of this or that priest, and under his guidance', but more often 'at the instigation of lay activists and with lay people in position of responsibility, with priests in the role of sympathetic assistants. In these groups the experience lived by clergy and laity freely mixed and merged. And there likewise emerged groups, initiated or co-led by Catholics, in which believers and non-believers jointly considered issues and topics' in the areas of culture and/or politics which had been central preoccupations of Catholic dissidence for quite some time. Nando Fabro, one of the few intellectuals to play a role in both the first and second wave of Italian Catholic dissent, placed his finger on the particularly crucial year when Vatican II came to a close: 'It was in the course of 1965 when ideas and individuals began to circulate with greater speed. Even when geographically separated by a certain distance, the groups organized debates,

---

[7] Alessandro Santagata, 'Dal Concilio al "dissenso"', in Vincenzo Schirripa (ed.), *L'Italia del Vaticano II* (Rome: Aracne, 2012), p. 57. See also his Ph.D. thesis: 'Il post-concilio. Cattolicesimo e politica in Italia dal Vaticano II al dissenso (1966–1969)', Facoltà di lettere e filosofia, Università di Roma 'Tor Vergata', 2011–12.

[8] Mario Cuminetti, 'Una lettura storica del "dissenso" dal '65 al '78', in *Massa e meriba. Itinerari di fede nella storia delle comunità di base* (Turin: Claudiana, 1980), p. 31. Ernesto Balducci's *Il Cenacolo* may well have been one of the first.

raised questions and began to propose manifestations of dissent or protest.'[9] What precisely happened within these early groups?

One of the most insightful participant-observers of Italian base communities, Mario Cuminetti, described their mode of functioning as such:

> In the beginning, when they were not yet called spontaneous groups, their thematic orientation was, for the most part, explicitly ecclesial or ecclesiastic: an insistence on the necessity for the church to become less anonymous, to be experienced via small groups; rethinking of the role of bishops and priests within the larger process of the declericalization of the life of the church; demands for a new liturgy; an ecumenism manifesting itself not solely via high-level exchanges at the apex of the respective hierarchies and an adjustment of nominal positions; rediscovery of the obligation to act within the secular sphere in a critically constructive manner and more closely linked to an analysis of societal changes; a church of the poor; a church no longer engaging in proselytism. The discourse of such groups was then still focused on the inner life of the church.[10]

TURIN: AN EXEMPLARY MICROCOSM

Perhaps one of the best ways to begin to portray the colourful and multifaceted kaleidoscope of base communities in Italy is via the prism of one particular location. The various organizational strands which ultimately found a new home within the fledgling autonomous groups can thus be discerned on an accessible micro-level, as may be their intellectual and ecclesial preferences. A congenial point of entry is provided by the industrial city of Turin. Far removed from the strongholds of Italian Catholicism in Italy's northeast, Turin became a landmark of social movement activism in the long sixties second to none. With a forceful presence of secular movements, Catholics in Turin had been on the defensive for some time. As was noted in Chapter 2, the central position of Turin at the intersection of secularization and industrialization led to early innovations in the working-class apostolate, notably the birth of the Italian worker priest experiment. By the second half of the 1960s, a vibrant student movement arose side-by-side with Turin's long-standing labour movement tradition. From September 1965 onwards, Turin's Catholic

[9] Nando Fabro, *I cattolici e la contestazione in Italia* (Fossano: Esperienze, 1970), p. 53. On Nando Fabro and the journal for which he edited, see now Paolo Zanini, *La rivista 'Il gallo'. Dalla tradizione al dialogo (1946–1965)* (Milan: Biblioteca Francescana, 2012). An earlier publication covers the intellectual itinerary of *Il gallo* all the way up to the early 1970s: Chito Guala and Romano Severini, 'Dialogo, Obbedienza "critica" e dissenso nel "Gallo". Momenti di una lunga presenza', in Sergio Ristuccia (ed.), *Intellettuali cattolici tra riformismo e dissenso* (Milan: Comunità, 1975), pp. 99–164.
[10] Cuminetti, 'Una lettura', p. 31.

activists in addition benefited from the appointment of the open-minded innovator, Michele Pellegrino, as archbishop. Pellegrino's presence at the head of the Torinese Catholic church from September 1965 to July 1977 meant that the city experiencing the highest degree of experimentation in the areas of both old and new social movements in all of Italy in the long sixties would witness an unusually high share of innovative Catholic experiments over and above a rich panoply of non-confessional dissident groups.

In late 1971, *Testimonianze*, a flagship journal of the Italian Catholic Left, animated by Ernesto Balducci, reprinted an article by a leading Torinese dissident Catholic monthly publication, *Il foglio*, on the history of Catholic dissent in Turin since the closure of Vatican II. The brains trust of individuals behind the launching of *Il foglio* noted towards the beginning of their account: 'The communitarian discourse was reinvigorated around 1962–3, above all inside the GIAC and GS.' The Gioventù Italiana di Azione Cattolica (GIAC) and Gioventù Studentesca (GS) were crucial points of entry of progressive Catholic ideas and practices into the generally rather staid and immobile structures of the Catholic universe all across the Italian state in the long sixties. *Il foglio* continued: 'The FUCI likewise—taken over by persons coming out of GS—embarked upon a similar road, notwithstanding some hesitations.'[11] The Federazione Universitaria Cattolica Italiana (FUCI), founded in 1896, was the classic organization assembling Catholic university students. What emerges very clearly then is that the original impetus for the rise of the phenomenon of base communities in Torino (as elsewhere) arose in a quasi-organic fashion out of the welter of pre-existing Catholic organizations in Italy. The Turin monthly *Il foglio* then underscored that, as happened elsewhere in Italy, the years 1965–6 in Turin witnessed an astounding

> multiplication of initiatives wishing to study, to deepen and to translate into practice the teachings of Vatican II. This sudden burst of activity led to the formation of many such groups in all walks of life, some of them independently from all other organizations, some within pre-existing associations, some even within parishes. The themes discussed or, before long, acted upon focused on liturgical innovations (at this very moment occurred the first practical experiments in Italy), on the study of the word of God (this was the moment when groups studying the Bible multiplied), or on conciliar texts. Likewise, conversations rapidly became very concrete about the necessity of a communitarian life shared amongst Christian believers. These groups arose in a disorganized and random fashion, with little overall coordination, acutely suffering from a lack of cultural preparation and the absence of any similar earlier reflections on these topics.[12]

---

[11] 'Cinque anni di dopo-concilio a Torino. I gruppi del dissenso', *Testimonianze* 14 (nos 139–40), November–December 1971, p. 830.
[12] 'Cinque anni', pp. 831–2.

One more lengthy citation from this pioneering editorial group, *Il foglio*, which continues to publish its monthly newsletter until today, may further underscore the beehive of activity and the exceedingly amorphous nature of these early discussion groups in Turin, but of course not only in Turin: 'Probably for these very reasons, the lifespan of many groups was rather brief. The majority of them in fact did not survive for more than a year. For practical purposes, it is safe to say that the only groups outlasting their peers were those who found a way to give concrete expression to the ideas on which they had reflected for some time. In or about 1966, in fact, commenced the experience of the Vandalino and, in the same period, the ideas began to take concrete shape which led the group, which met in the Via Piave, to form the community of Magnano.'[13] We will return to what became of the Comunità del Vandalino and the Comunità di Magnano later on in this chapter. For the moment, it will be instructive to cast a glance at one particular history of one of the welter of Torinese communities, in this case penned by the group in question itself. The second half of this self-statement points to events and processes in the late 1960s and early 1970s when, as we will see, a whole host of new issues tended to confront the wave of fledgling base communities. But the case of the Gruppo Fraternità Emmaus is instructive in part precisely because of the unusual longevity of the group:

> We are an ecclesial community of persons, some of us living together fraternally and others within their respective families, all of us searching for a new way of existence within the church and within society via new forms of immersion and participation within the lives—and facing the problems—of the poor and the disadvantaged working classes. After some years of social assistance-type work in an urban setting, trying to find solutions to the most urgent and desperate individual cases (1962–64) and then more particularly in the area of prostitution (1964–68), we developed an intense activity amongst young people, trying to establish relationships of friendship and trust, at the same time that we engaged in Third World solidarity work (1966–67). In 1969, we made a firm choice to concentrate on the working-class neighbourhood of Barriera di Milano in order to familiarize ourselves with the problems experienced by a specific social class. This allowed us to obtain an up-front and well-grounded awareness of the state of oppression experienced by the proletariat. In 1971, after two years in the Barriera di Milano neighbourhood, arose the need to establish a community facilitating reflection and a comparison of our experiences, and we thus transferred to Pino d'Asti, a small village in the hills to the east of Turin, about 20 km from the city.

The text, penned in 1972, then adds:

> Here we still live today, carrying out research and development of socio-political-ecclesial problems via documentation and continuous discussion amongst

---

[13] 'Cinque anni', p. 832.

ourselves and with others we have invited—individuals, groups, communities—
or by further deepening our ideas in various other settings, such as retreats, study
days, etc. Since 1971 we have established a kind of agricultural commune in
Carezzano near Tortona [in the foothills of the Piedmont Appenine] in order to
partake in the experiences of rural life and to facilitate an alternative way of living
for this disadvantaged social sector outside of the parameters of industrial society
built on oppression and the exploitation of human beings.[14]

The itinerary of the Gruppo Fraternità Emmaus is instructive in several
regards. It showcases the great variety of stages undergone in the collective
evolution of this community of believers in the space of no more than one
decade. Perhaps unusual in its early orientation towards social service work,
the longevity of the group confirms *Il foglio*'s comment on the necessity of
practical projects to ensure that a community would not disappear as quickly
as it had constituted itself. The sequence of primarily activist phases followed
by a period of reflection and stock-taking is another standard feature of base
communities. As we will see, the 'discovery' of the working class precisely in
the late 1960s and early 1970s is a further trope of base communities up and
down the Italian boot.

Most base communities up to, roughly, 1967 focused on ecclesial topics,
with many of them leading an ephemeral life, rarely leaving a paper trail.
Other than a conscious decision to engage in hands-on social service or
community work, the other mechanism that installed potential structure,
thus raising the survival chances of such groups, was the more or less irregular
production of written material reaching a wider audience or, conversely, the
organization of study sessions and the common reading of relevant journals of
national and international repute. Thus, the school teacher and Left Catholic
journalist, Ettore De Giorgis, reminisced about the early 1960s in the following
terms:

At the beginning of the sixties, the cultural ambience of Turin Catholics was one
of the most depressing in all of Italy. Nonetheless, there were certain islands of
restlessness. The most notable exception was perhaps the presence of a discrete
group called Amici di 'Adesso', named after the fortnightly journal founded by
Don Mazzolari and then directed by Mario Rossi. In these milieux a notable
influence was exerted by certain role models of French Catholicism which found
journalistic expression above all via the publications *Témoignage Chrétien* and

---

[14] 'Gruppo Fraternità Emmaus', in 'Assemblea delle Comunità Ecclesiali di Torino' [1972],
p. 6—Fondo Gianni Vizio, Fondazione Vera Nocentini (FVN) [Turin], faldone 2, fascicolo 'g'.
The experiment in developing an agricultural collective was soon shifted to other locations but
has continued until today, now located again in the hills east of Turin: <http://www.terraegente.it>.
Today, the former Gruppo Fraternità Emmaus is located in Albugnano and, in addition to
operating its agricultural commune, edits an influential journal of the Italian Catholic Left:
<http://www.tempidifraternita.it/>; information obtained in email communications by Franco
Fischetti on 18 November and 22 November 2013.

Esprit. [...] A group operating along similar lines, even if on a more intellectual level, was run by former activists in Democrazia Cristiana (DC) and the GIAC, giving birth to the Circolo Emmanuel Mounier, inspired above all else by Don Mazzolari and the founder of *Esprit* [...].[15]

The strong influence of French *nouvelle théologie* and the pioneering vanguard role of Don Primo Mazzolari is a notable feature of Left Catholic life at the margins of Italian Catholicism at the very beginning of the 1960s, as is the recourse to journals as an organizational backbone to embryonic efforts to construct a Catholic Left. In fact, reading clubs such as the Circolo Emmanuel Mounier should be regarded as the first wave of base communities, preceding and in fact preparing the terrain for a favourable reception of Vatican II.

When Vatican II got under way, such efforts to form autonomous groups spread beyond the limits of the sprawling megalopolis of Turin. 'One of them was Il Tamburino, animated by a number of young people from Rivoli who expressed themselves by means of a mimeographed sheet. This was an effort aiming for a space within the Catholic pillar. In fact, the members were activists within the left wing of DC, within the CISL and the ACLI [...].' In Pinerolo, a working-class town with a strong military presence literally at the base of the foothills of the Alps, De Giorgis pointed out, a progressive Catholic journal, *La fornace*, made waves, 'modelled after *Esprit* and run by Catholics, who for the most part operated within the DC Left, but which also counted on the support of Waldensians and secular activists'.[16] As already noted, from 1965 onwards informal and autonomous study and reflection groups suddenly began to multiply, though usually still focusing on ecclesial or ecclesiastic themes. 'From 1967 to 1969, the situation within the Torinese church—hitherto rather erratic [with regard to the embryonic Catholic Left]—began to stabilize and evolve towards progressively more radical positions';[17] a characterization appropriate to similar milieux elsewhere in Northern Italy as well.

A brief synopsis of the history of yet another one in this rapidly growing number of Turin base communities, the Comunità di Lucento, in a working-class neighbourhood about 4 km northwest of the city centre, provides some further interesting detail.

The group of young people from Lucento began to form about seven or eight years ago [i.e. about 1968/9] and initially engaged primarily in youth work within the parish under the guidance and coordination of a priest. As a result of the

---

[15] Ettore De Giorgis, 'Genesi dell'esperienza comunitaria', unpublished typescript, n.d., p. 1—Fondo Ettore De Giorgis, Biblioteca Civica, Lanzo Torinese—Scritti e materiali di lavoro: doc. 294.

[16] De Giorgis, 'Genesi dell'esperienza comunitaria', pp. 1–2. On the Confederazione Italiana Sindacato Lavoratori (CISL) and the Associazioni Cristiane Lavoratori Italiani (ACLI), see Chapter 5.

[17] 'Cinque anni', p. 833.

'politicization'—by which is meant the desire to question and to better under-stand the relationship between the profession of faith and social responsibility within the realm of politics—of several members of the group, some conflict-ridden situations arose precisely on those issues. Attempts were made to have the group reorient towards new topics and tasks, such as the setting up of a course on the Introduction to Politics and an effort to popularize a materialist reading of the Bible.[18]

The rapid evolution of the Comunità di Lucento from ecclesial youth group towards an activist group increasingly oriented in the direction of radical political action in the conjuncture of 1968/9 was, of course, a sign of the times. 'If the years from 1965 to 1967 were dominated by religious themes, now politics is in the ascendancy.'[19]

Nothing better symbolizes this sudden paradigm shift than some character-istic changes in the (self-)labelling of these groups. Groups founded between 1960 and 1965 adopted 'the names of Maritain, Emmanuel Mounier, of *Esprit*', indicating their spiritual and political orientation in no uncertain terms. But less than two years later, the chosen symbols suddenly change. 'The groups then emerging adopt the names of Camillo Torres, Fidel Castro, Che Guevara, Don Milani. The spiritual and reflective component is not discarded. But they no longer suffice. The correct yardstick is now intimately associated with "doing things", with the achievement of concrete, verifiable and palpable facts. Faith and deeds now count equally.'[20] It was a paradigm shift with lasting consequences. For one thing, as Danilo Zolo noted in April 1968 in an editorial in *Testimonianze*, Catholic dissent 'today no longer finds its expression and political outlet in that particular fringe within official Catholicism—the DC Left—which, at some point, collected and channelled the desire for renewal on the part of Catholic elites—which then considered themselves the vanguard—in the direction of a confused mixture of political and religious opposition within the confines of DC. What there remains today of the DC Left showcases itself—in the unanimous assessment of these groups—as standing in perfect alignment with the moderate line of the majority within DC.'[21]

DEFINING BASE COMMUNITIES

It is time to take stock and to address the varieties of ways in which base communities could manifest themselves in the years under consideration. As

---

[18] Comunità di Lucento, 'Storia della Comunità di Lucento', p. 1—Archivio Privato di Giovanni Baratta, Turin.
[19] Cuminetti, 'Una lettura', p. 33.   [20] Fabro, *I cattolici*, p. 55.
[21] Danilo Zolo, 'Editoriale', *Testimonianze* 11 (no. 103), April 1968, p. 195.

in other parts of the world where they emerged at roughly the same time, religious base communities were autonomous informal associations of individuals who, in whole or in part, focused on aspects of ecclesial life outside the regular structures of the—in this case Catholic—church. Individuals may have simultaneously been members of more traditional associations of Catholic life, such as Catholic Action, in particular Specialized Catholic Action, or members of Catholic (or Catholic-dominated) trade unions or political parties. But for an informal association of individuals to be considered a base community, the latter would have to operate largely independently of the traditional structures belonging to the Catholic official pillar. Members of base communities could (and did!) hail from all walks of life. Members of the clergy could (and did) fulfil important roles within such base communities—although usually priests performed such functions over and above their primary roles as spiritual guides of a parish. In fact, part of the characteristic of base communities was precisely its role separate and distinct from regular parish life. Though sometimes first emerging within one specific parish as a natural extension of habitual sociabilities, base communities most frequently included individuals who hailed from any number of distinct parishes. There were, however, some examples of base communities which evolved out of traditional parishes, including cases where in effect a specific parish evolved into a base community lock, stock, and barrel. In such relatively rare cases, however, in most instances certain innovative practices had led to tensions with the local hierarchy which in turn led a specific parish to pursue a pathway in open conflict with their superiors. Certainly in the Italian case, most base communities evolved out of any number of activities originally performed as part of regular parish life, most frequently within youth groups which first had met and carried out common activities as part of a parish-based effort.

In most cases, members of base communities did not practise communal forms of living, although sometimes communal living arrangements evolved in the process of ongoing common activities—by all or part of the group. Most frequently, base communities consisted of individuals who lived in nuclear families or on their own. Even less frequent than common living situations were communal work projects as (common) sources of income. Sociologically, most individual communities tended to have a distinct profile, in common with the specific group's outlook and goals, though cases of cross-class membership were by no means unusual and often warmly welcomed. Women were frequent participants in base communities, though almost always seriously underrepresented at the leadership level of such groups.

Informal associations of individuals were, of course, all the rage in the years under consideration—and not just in Italy. To be considered a Christian base community, however, a portion of their activities had to be geared towards ecclesial action. Many groups combined their characteristic ecclesial orientation with action programmes derived from their often prominently developed sense of social responsibility. This often took the form of social assistance to disadvantaged social strata or occupational categories (migrants, prostitutes, unskilled workers, etc.) or volunteer work in disadvantaged neighbourhoods or activities geared towards the workforce of a targeted enterprise. What characterizes many groups' evolution over time was a frequent shift in the axis of their concerns, i.e. from an exclusive focus on ecclesially oriented activities towards a significant commitment to social services or political work, then shifting back again towards a period when spiritual and intellectual reflection dominated their practices. Still, in the course of the 1960s, a certain evolution in their inner orientations can be traced over time. Towards the beginning of the decade, membership in (the left wing of) DC was quite common, as was membership in any number of associations of Catholic life, such as the CISL, the ACLI, the FUCI, GIAC, or, where it existed, GS. Likewise, at the very beginning of the 1960s, it seems that study groups with a distinct intellectual remit and pre-requirements were far more common than towards the end of the decade. Also, the role of priests as spiritual—and frequently organizational—linchpins of such nascent base communities was rather prominent then. Yet DC membership of individuals partaking in base communities became increasingly rare as the decade progressed. And a similar assessment pertains to membership in most Catholic Action groups or, a case apart, GS. '1968 definitely witnessed the crumbling of traditional organizations, such as Catholic Action, or the movement of GS.'[22]

Before setting out to cast some light on the capstone experience of the Italian *sessantotto*, ushering in a new period, it may be expedient to further highlight the varieties of base communities in Italy as a whole by one more concentrated look at the world of base communities in the capital city of Piedmont. For, as Enzo Bianchi, whom we first met in the pages of this book at the turbulent gathering of Italian worker priests in Serramazzoni in early 1976 and who in later decades evolved into one of Italy's premier media personalities, remarked at the onset of his 1970 survey of base communities in his native Piedmont:

> The phenomenon of ecclesial groups has thus far proven to be truly complex. Often one is confronted with facts as part of supposed evaluations which, for those living within these groups, have nothing or very little to do with reality. It is also not very easy to orient oneself within the lifeworld of these groups, and this for several reasons: the pluralism of motivations for their emergence; the diversity of ecclesial situations within which they operate; the rapidly changing attitude vis-à-vis political and ecclesial action; the high turnover of the membership; and the facility with which new groups see the light of day with an all-too-short lifespan.[23]

---

[22] Mario Cuminetti, 'Base ecclesiale e lotte di liberazione', *Idoc-internazionale* 20 (30 November 1973), p. 37.
[23] Enzo Bianchi, 'Una valutazione globale del fenomeno dei gruppi ecclesiali in Piemonte', *Testimonianze* 13 (no. 130), December 1970, p. 909.

COMUNITÀ DEL VANDALINO

From about 1969 to 1972, the most (in)famous base community in Northern Italy was a group operating in Turin, which had formed in 1966. Characteristically, its origins can be traced to two component parts, a group of friends who knew each other socially and had formed a biblical study group, and a circle of activists coming out of GS, of whom Vittorino Merinas, the spiritual dynamo of the group, had been the chaplain.[24] An early self-statement of the group provided an excellent snapshot of this circle in early 1967:

> The group consists mainly of young people, many of whom are still in search of their chosen path within society and within the Church (choice of occupation, family, sacerdotal and religious life). The group, however, also includes several persons (the priest and several married couples) who have already chosen their career. These individuals provide stability; they are serving as permanent reference points, inasmuch as they guarantee a certain kind of continuity to the entire group and, most importantly, a human and Christian equilibrium. As far as professional and social choices are concerned, the group includes university students, young blue-collar workers, teachers, white-collar employees and professionals.[25]

A report penned two years later points out that the core of the group then consisted of 'about twenty individuals, most of them young married couples, who live in adjoining apartments in a working-class district on the western edge of Turin'.[26]

A long article in the flagship Italian national daily, *Corriere della sera*, in November 1968, brought the Comunità del Vandalino into the national limelight, focusing on the colourful figure of Vittorino Merinas, the priest who guided the Comunità del Vandalino throughout the half-dozen years of its existence. Along with other Torinese dissidents, Vittorino Merinas had already been present at the first international assembly of rebel priests in Chur in July 1969.[27] 'Don Merinas represents the vanguard of those who wish for a deep-going renewal of the Church in Piedmont', wrote Alfredo Pieroni, who had paid a visit to Don Merinas's home. 'He speaks, sitting at the table in his room, wearing regular trousers and a jacket, and what he says he tells as a

---

[24] Information provided by Dario Oitana, a member of the Comunità del Vandalino, during an interview on 30 November 2011. Dario Oitana had been the President of the University of Turin's FUCI in 1957–8. He has also been a member of the editorial board of *Il foglio* from its very beginnings until today.

[25] Taken from a letter fragment, addressed to 'Reverendissimo Padre', dated 19 January 1967, p. 1—Archivio Privato Dario Oitana, Turin. All subsequent information on the Comunità del Vandalino, including newspaper sources, stems from this precious collection of data.

[26] Raffaele Guiglia, 'Una "nuova comunità" a Torino', *Il regno* 14 (no. 172), 1 January 1969, p. 12.

[27] 'Teilnehmerliste'—KDC, LXX, fo. 158.

member of his community, as his words are the convictions of all members of the group. The walls are covered with posters and proclamations reflecting an open mind: an artistic rendering of Mao next to another one of Che Guevara— or is it Castro?—next to a cartoon betraying the absence of much sympathy for Paul VI.' This relatively neutral portrayal of Merinas and the Comunità del Vandalino in Italy's premier daily newspaper was entitled in bold letters: 'A Portrait of Mao in the Home of a Priest'. At that point, relations with the rather tolerant Archbishop Pellegrino were still relatively neutral, and Pellegrino, also interviewed by the journalist, was likely thinking of the Comunità del Vandalino 'when he said, jokingly, and expressing a tolerant attitude: "This diocese is difficult to govern. Some are firmly behind Vatican I; others have already arrived at Vatican III. There are only very few here who subscribe to the positions of Vatican II." '[28]

One national publication which no doubt felt affinities with Vatican I was *Il borghese*, which ran an article in January 1969, entitled 'The Super Christ of Priest Merinas'. Piero Capello, reporting for *Il borghese*, had also visited Don Merinas in his third floor apartment at Via Vandalino 40. As was the case with the journalist for the mainstream conservative Milan daily, *Corriere della sera*, Capella focused on some exterior trappings to get the point across to his readers that base communities, certainly the Comunità del Vandalino, constituted an entirely unprecedented and unusual phenomenon: 'A workshop is located in front of his home, with two sheds attached. The priest has rented one of these garages, filled it with chairs, put a table in the middle of the open space and put a modern crucifix on the table, fastened with two iron ropes attached to the ceiling. It is impossible to say whether the crucifix is made of tin-glazed pottery or painted wood. On the crucifix one can discern the face of Christ, chequered and dark, as if shrouded in fog.' Clearly, the journalist for *Il borghese* disapproved. 'On the walls of the church a manifesto was prominently affixed, on which one can read these foolish lines: "Mao: yellow prophet; Luther King: black prophet; Christ: more than a prophet. All of them have been active in protest movements. We protest against a Christmas of consumption. We want a Christmas of struggle [*Vogliamo un Natale contestatario*]." ' The host, used in the Eucharist, to the journalist's great horror, appeared to be made of the same ingredients as ice cream cones and tasted like it. Piero Capello summed up his visit: 'This is the "church" in which the priest, who does not see himself as a priest and who regards a church service as a type of happening, sees fit to receive his handful of faithful believers.'[29]

The sentiments and interpretations of *Il borghese* aside, most observations appeared to conform to the factual truth. Except for one assertion. The

---

[28] Alfredo Pieroni, 'Il Ritratto di Mao in Canònica', *Corriere della sera*, 20 November 1968, p. 3.

[29] Piero Capello, 'Il Super Cristo del prete Merinas', *Il borghese*, 23 January 1969, p. 205.

Comunità del Vandalino was attracting far more than a handful of disaffected parishioners. By all less biased accounts, the church services in the former workshop of the Via Vandalino became a rousing success. For several years, Sunday Mass held by Vittorino Merinas normally attracted close to 100 participants, on special occasions up to several hundred at a time, the overflow crowd gathering on the street in front of the large shed. Sermons often addressed topical issues of interest to the crowd, those present in the church being invited to share in the joint discussion of ideas. An atmosphere of great informality bestowed a special imprint on the proceedings, no doubt accounting for part of its popularity. Smoking was allowed in the church, and the throng often stayed for at least two hours. When, after three hours, people were still not ready to leave, Vittorino Merinas literally had to chase people away. The mass in the garage of the Via Vandalino became an event. Curious adolescents from all over the city came to partake in the non-traditional ritual, even and especially if they were not necessarily particularly religiously inclined.[30]

Core members of the Comunità del Vandalino engaged in various sorts of concrete community projects, such as work with the mentally handicapped, or work with migrant labourers housed in substandard barracks on the outskirts of Turin. And in this context it is important to underline that the Comunità del Vandalino did not see itself in the time-honoured and time-worn tradition of charitable works performed by church members for many centuries. 'Rather than carrying out the regular work of social workers, they aim at the empowerment of the various families to reject the status quo and, instead, to seek humane solutions' on their own in interaction with other families, public officials, and relevant agencies.[31]

A MARRIAGE CEREMONY OF A SPECIAL KIND

What truly propelled the Comunità del Vandalino to national fame was an— certainly for Italy—unprecedented event on 6 September 1970. On that day, during regular Sunday Mass, Vittorino Merinas, in front of a crowd of more than 200 onlookers, presided over the wedding ceremonies of two couples.

---

[30] *Il regno*, in the article cited in note 26, suggests, for instance, 'at least more than eighty persons' as being in attendance at the Mass the journalist witnessed. The atmospherics of Holy Mass in the Via Vandalino can also be ascertained by some of the photographic evidence in the newsclipping collection held by Dario Oitana. In my 30 November 2011 interview, Oitana furnished many of the colourful details included in this paragraph. And it so happens that the proprietor of the bed and breakfast where this author stayed for several of his archival visits to Turin, recounted her surreptitious outings on Sunday morning to the Via Vandalino as a curious 16-year-old teenager in or around 1970.
[31] Guiglia, 'Una "nuova comunità"', p. 12.

What was unusual was that both bridegrooms were priests, moreover priests refusing to renounce their ordination. To further scandalize published opinion, one of the brides was a former nun. After Don Merinas had performed the sacred rites, the two newly wedded priests celebrated the Eucharist with the enthusiastic crowd. To avoid unwanted attention by paparazzi, at the end of the church service a car entered the garage serving as their church, the two newly wed couples stepped inside, and then left for their homes. The article in Turin's premier mass-market evening paper, *Stampa sera*, ended by drawing attention to another wedding performed on that very same day in another church in Turin. In Turin's Chiesa della Visitazione another priest—a member of a religious order who, however, had relinquished his soutane—took the marriage vow. What raised eyebrows in this case was the provocative fact that the ceremony was openly presided over by the bridegroom's former provincial superior.[32]

For Cardinal Pellegrino, the progressive head of the Torinese church, the situation had become intolerable. Similar to the Dutch hierarchy, Pellegrino sympathized with many of the demands of his rebellious flock; but a priest, Don Vittorino Merinas, marrying two other priests, one of them to a former nun, was too much to ignore. Having warned Merinas in advance that such an act would entail grave consequences, Pellegrino pronounced the suspension *a divinis* of the spiritual leader of the Comunità del Vandalino. As was not difficult to predict, this official condemnation only served to further heat up the atmosphere.[33]

During the controversial church service itself, the assembled overflow crowd, dressed in their Sunday finest, aware of the potential consequences of the ceremony they were witnessing, behaved in a joyous and exuberant manner. Photos showcase a multitude of smiling faces, cheerfully communicating with each other, some waving their hands in the direction of the photographer, others playfully engaging in gestures of defiance vis-à-vis the representatives of the media. When Archbishop Pellegrino proclaimed the destitution of Don Merinas, the latter, expressing the collective will of the community, not only refused to make any accommodating gestures of good will, but motivated his performance as a conscious act of defiance of 'clerical power'. The following Saturday, a general assembly of the Comunità del Vandalino in their makeshift church, with both newly wed couples in attendance as well, unanimously approved a resolution in which they accused the official church of the will 'to suffocate all instances of free and collective exploration of faith' and to stifle all efforts 'to bring about justice on earth'; traditionalist church dogma was judged to be without any meaning for human beings living in the contemporary world; the moral teachings of the church

---

[32] 'Nozze religiose di due preti senza permesso del vescovo', *Stampa sera*, 7 September 1970.
[33] 'Il Vandalino ha rotto con la Chiesa ufficiale', *Stampa sera*, 14 September 1970.

were labelled 'unconnected to reality'; and official church liturgy was judged to be designed to pacify parishioners and to keep them from engaging in meaningful activity to change the world. Moreover, 'the clerical understanding of the relationship between the hierarchy and the faithful is transposed onto civilian life, giving sacred approval to all sorts of civilian authorities in their dealings with their underlings'. Faced with the injunction not to celebrate the Eucharist as a result of the event of Sunday, 6 September, the Comunità del Vandalino retorted: 'Why is no one scandalized within our Church to see at the same table the poor and the rich, oppressed and oppressors, without any apparent effort undertaken to seek true justice and fraternity?'[34]

It so happened that, just a few weeks later, the Christian Solidarity International Congress in Amsterdam gathered for its historic deliberations, and the Italian delegation included three members of the Comunità del Vandalino. A resolution of solidarity with their act of defiance was passed by the Amsterdam assembly in the form of an Open Letter to the Community of Vandalino, propelling the Torinese base community to international fame.[35] From now on Vandalino became a household term in radical Christian circles not only in Italy but in Europe as a whole. Thus, it came as no surprise that the major international planning conference for the October 1971 Operation Synod was organized and hosted by the tireless activists of the Comunità del Vandalino.[36] In the end, however, the intensity and turbulence of activities undertaken by the flagship base community took its toll. As happened with many other such innovative and contentious associations, in January 1973 the members of the Comunità del Vandalino unanimously decided to put an end to their formative experience. Dario Oitana recalls that they felt 'exhausted' and uncertain about which further steps to take.[37] An exemplary chapter in the history of Catholic dissent in Turin and in Italy as a whole came to a quiet end.

COMUNITÀ DI BOSE

Not all Torinese base communities, however, chose a similarly conflictual and provocative route as did the youthful activists of the Via Vandalino and the

---

[34] 'Il Vandalino ha rotto con la Chiesa ufficiale'.

[35] Reproduced as 'Open Brief aan de gemeente van Vandalino', in Septuagint (ed.), *Solidariteit gezocht. Internationale informatie rond het kongres te Amsterdam, 28 september–4 oktober 1970* (Hilversum: Gooi en sticht, 1971), pp. 115–16. For the names and affiliations of Italian delegates, see 'Liste des participants'—KDC, LXX, fo. 215.

[36] Delegates from all participating European countries arrived in Torino for the gathering in the Via Arnaz, where the logistic centre of the group had moved to in the meantime from its former headquarters in the Via Vandalino, on 4–5 September 1971. See relevant documentation in KDC, LXX, fo. 195.

[37] Conversation with Dario Oitana, 19 November 2013.

Via Arnaz. An earlier group, based in Torino's Via Piave, at the edge of the city centre, took a rather different turn. A group of mostly Torinese university students regularly gathered—after initially utilizing the facilities of a former seminary building on Via XX Settembre—in Via Piave 8. On Monday evenings, this assembly included a mixture of Catholics, Waldensians, and Baptists meeting together for Bible study. Thursday evenings saw a heavy preponderance of Catholics and were devoted to project discussions and the study of conciliar documents.[38] 'This group was one of the first ecclesial spontaneous groups [*gruppi spontanei ecclesiali*] in all of Italy and no doubt served as inspiration and role model for other regional spontaneous groups.' After some time the members began to get restless. 'With the end of university studies approaching, amongst a number of participants the idea matured and took on precise contours to change orientation.'[39]

The desire to form a more permanent community spawned the search for a suitable location, and eventually they focused on an abandoned set of houses in Magnano, beautifully located in the softly undulating foothills of the Alps between Ivrea and Biella, about 65 km to the north of Turin. To the abandoned hamlet belonged the ruins of a Romanesque church, and the entire setting was visually dominated by the Monte Rosa mountain range further to the north. From late 1965 onwards, members of the Comunità di Via Piave regularly visited the site to begin the renovation works. Enzo Bianchi himself moved to Bose—and then lived there by himself for some time—on 8 December 1965, the very day of the closing ceremony of Vatican II.[40] In September 1966 a work camp was set up on location in order to repair the church. On 6 August 1968 the ecumenical community of Bose was officially founded, composed of Catholics and Protestants, soon including women side-by-side with men.[41]

The key source of spiritual and organizational energies of the Comunità di Bose was and remains until today Enzo Bianchi. Born in 1943 into an impoverished family, Enzo Bianchi was exposed to a mélange of potentially conflicting ideologies from early on, his mother being a devout Catholic and his father a Communist. After high school, Enzo Bianchi studied Economics and Business Administration at Turin University and, as a brilliant

---

[38] Enzo Bianchi, 'Preghiera comune. Esperienza di una comunità', *Rivista liturgica* 3 (1975), pp. 72–3.

[39] Enzo Bianchi, 'Una comunità interconfessionale in Italia. Bose', *Concilium* 9, no. 9 (1973), p. 135.

[40] Mario Torciva, *Il segno di Bose* (Casale Monferrato: Piemme, 2003), p. 26. This short monograph is perhaps the most accessible and comprehensive survey of the *Comunità ecumenica di Bose*.

[41] A brief synopsis of the history and development of what has since become known as one of the most dynamic new monastic projects in all of Italy is readily accessible in the special dossier devoted to 'Bose. I monaci dell'età secolare', *Jesus* 33, no. 9 (September 2011), pp. 41–73.

conversationalist, he appeared predestined for a stellar career either within DC or as an academic.[42] Yet, like so many others of his generation who came of age in the turbulent 1960s, Enzo Bianchi chose a fundamentally different path. At Bose, the members of the Comunità chose to live a common life in poverty and simplicity, earning income in various paid positions as teachers, psycho-analysts, and other salaried or waged work in Ivrea, Biella, or Turin, but with all such money earned placed into a common fund.[43]

Within Bose all work was carried out on an equal basis. In particular all manual work was shared in equal measure. 'Men and women are therefore enjoined to take turns at all tasks, in order to avoid the submission of women to men so common in secular reality, with these egalitarian guidelines likewise applying to religious life. [...] Last but not least, the community operates without hierarchies. No one is father, no one is mother, or director. Decisions are taken in weekly councils' with the chairperson mandated to ensure compliance with adopted decisions. Such coordinators, however, 'have no power or legislative authority'.[44] Apart from the manual labour of reconstruc-tion and maintenance, an increasing proportion of time and effort by mem-bers of the Comunità di Bose was spent on hosting an ever-larger flow of curious visitors. With a preponderance of young people, a steady trickle—then a stream—of individuals in search of 'authenticity' and 'spirituality' arrived in the foothills of the Alps.[45]

The combination of religious and political challenges to authority being a hallmark of many base communities, Bose likewise served both spiritual and societal needs, usually in close combination. 'For the members of the Comu-nità di Bose, a commitment to the world was never a choice and even less an effort'; it was a matter of course. 'To facilitate this engagement in worldly affairs, non-religious individuals frequent the Comunità in large numbers, and relations with them are based on common research and dialogue pertaining to today's most pressing political issues. At Bose, members of the *Movimento Studentesco* and individuals active in political parties meet, discussing the Chinese Cultural Revolution or working-class struggles, etc.'[46]

---

[42] A brief biographical sketch can be consulted in Robert Masson, *Bose: la radicalité de l'Évangile. Entretiens avec Enzo Bianchi et la communauté* (Paris: Parole et Silence, 2006), pp. 14–16, and in an informative newspaper article in Turin's mass-market *La stampa*: 'I quindici monaci in "blue jeans"', n.d. but written in 1978—Archivio Storico della Comunità di Bose, Magnano, 'Cartella articoli su Bose', no. 36.

[43] Enzo Bianchi, 'Una comunità ecumenica in Piemonte', *Servitium* 3, no. 11 (1969), p. 680.

[44] Bianchi, 'Una comunità interconfessionale', p. 140.

[45] 'Intervista con Enzo Bianchi. "Bose e i giovani"', in Bartolino Bartolini and Riccardo Tonelli (eds), *I giovani cercano la preghiera. Bose: una comunità che li provoca* (Turin: Elle Di Ci, 1972), citation on pp. 27–8.

[46] Bianchi, 'Una comunità ecumenica', p. 681. A virtually identical statement professing an equal interest in the promotion of profound changes in religious and in social spheres can be consulted in the editorial statement of the newssheet published by the Comunità: I fratelli e le sorelle di Bose, 'Lettera agli amici', *Qiqajon di Bose* 3 (Christmas 1973).

The growing wave of visitors soon taxed the capacity for hospitality by the Comunità di Bose. In 1972 alone, more than 8,000 visitors made the pilgrimage to the hillsite base community, most just day visitors but some staying up to a week, especially during the summer.[47] In late 1973, the communitarians felt compelled to put a limit on the number of guests, deciding 'to no longer accept more than a certain number of people in order to facilitate an authentic interaction with the community, so that it would not become a crowd phenomenon. Bose is not meant to become a Christian Woodstock!'[48] Yet by late 1973, the Comunità di Bose had already begun to mutate into something larger and distinct from an informal association of like-minded individuals in search of a common ecclesial and social project.

At Easter 1973 the first group of individuals living at Bose took vows of celibacy and the pursuit of a common life as faithful members of what could now be described as a fledgling monastic order. Already in August 1971, a set of rules governing the community had been adopted by the community council. But the Easter 1973 ceremony provided the point of no return.[49] The ecumenical monastery of Bose, operating on principles of gender equality, had come into its own.[50] In the more than forty years since that memorable early morning ritual, the monastery has undergone further changes. Originally referred to as the 'monks in blue jeans', with the bearded and long-haired Enzo Bianchi visually underscoring the countercultural and rebellious atmosphere out of which the Comunità di Bose emerged,[51] over time the communitarians exchanged street clothes for simple Benedictine-style habits. This Italian Taizé, perhaps the most dynamic monastic order operating in Italy today, at the point of origin and for the first half-dozen years of their existence, however, shared a common origin with the rebels of the Comunità del Vandalino as a fledgling base community reflecting the insurgent spirit of the long sixties.

GRUPPO ABELE

Yet another organization which has since become a household term throughout Italy, the Gruppo Abele, traces back its origins to another base community

---

[47] 'Intervista con Enzo Bianchi', p. 25.

[48] 'Lettera agli amici', Christmas 1973.

[49] Enzo, 'Lettera agli amici', *Qiqajon di Bose* 1 (Christmas 1972), announcing the intention of the group to mark the passage onto a new stage. The unsigned 'Lettera agli amici', *Qiqajon di Bose* 2, Easter 1973, provides ample detail of the ceremony at sunrise on 22 April 1973.

[50] Information on Bose can be gleaned most conveniently from its website: <http://www.monasterodibose.it>.

[51] The photograph accompanying the 1978 newspaper article, referred to in note 42, shows the young community members still in street clothes.

in the mean streets of 1960s Turin.[52] What is today perhaps best known as an organization actively promoting self-help-oriented social cooperatives and as a mainstay of Italy's anti-Mafia networks began as a loose association of young, mostly working-class activists in a Catholic Action youth group in a proletarian district southwest of the city centre. During the Christmas holidays in late 1965, a half-dozen of them decided to take to heart their Christian beliefs and to engage on behalf of the large numbers of socially disenfranchised Torinese. At first orienting their outreach work towards the homeless, in the course of 1966 they shifted their attention towards work amongst young gangs and other young people in difficulties. Adopting the name Gioventù Impegnata (Engaged Youth), they pioneered a number of initiatives targeting marginalized young people in Turin, one of the most successful ones being a sports club which served as an informal point of initial attraction for many individuals in their target group.[53]

From early on, this informal group diverged from standard practices within Catholic Action and soon embarked upon a distinct path of its own. In an insightful historical reflection on what became the Gruppo Abele, the group's organizational and spiritual centrepiece, Luigi Ciotti, wrote in 1980: 'Gioventù Impegnata emerged outside the structures of the parish and developed as an alternative to Catholic Action.' To be sure, this initially tiny group defined its identity in straightforwardly religious terms but—Luigi Ciotti continued—it 'presented itself, I believe it is fair to say, in innovative ways compared to the then-current tradition within Catholic groups. For one thing, we abolished the rigid gender division' which was then the norm within Catholic Action. From early on, Gioventù Impegnata linked their fundamental orientation towards religious values with social engagement, although the latter was initially seen as a matter of individual choice with no immediate political consequences.[54]

In late 1968, Gioventù Impegnata changed its name to Gruppo Abele, named after the biblical Abel. Luigi Ciotti noted: 'Gioventù Impegnata underscored the obligation of individual responsibility in the face of social reality. Gruppo Abele was a programmatic choice to indicate personal responsibility by all members in their common interactions with others in society.' The

---

[52] <http://www.gruppoabele.org>.

[53] Data taken from Maurizio Dematteis (ed.), 'Traccia cronologica dei principali avvenimenti lungo la storia dei 35 anni del Gruppo Abele con elenco del materiale cartaceo in archivio (1965–2001)', in Archivio Storico del Gruppo Abele (ASGA) [Turin], 'Eventi principali', fascicolo 3.

[54] This important document, a typescript serving as text for Luigi Ciotti's intervention at a summer retreat in 1980, can be consulted in ASGA, 'Campo Scuola', fasc. 13. The text passages cited are on the first two pages of the unpaginated text. In fact, handwritten letters 'A' to 'F' were later added to the text, with each letter denoting a sequence of two pages; thus, pp. 1–2 of the letter being 'A', etc. Part I of this document ends with 'F', Part II begins with a new numbering system of '1' to '7'. However, a central section between the end of Part I and the beginning of Part II is missing from the sole extant version of this precious document.

capstone year of 1968, which saw Turin as a national hotspot of radical political action, 'certainly helped the group to become more focused. At the beginning of 1969 or in late 1968, the group rented its first headquarters in Via Po 11 to serve as an anchor for the Gruppo Abele and its friends.'[55] In 1971, the Gruppo Abele was able to provide a separate home for underage adolescents in trouble, and in the course of the 1970s the infrastructure further diversified.[56]

At the very beginning of the 1970s, the delayed effects of the political upheavals of 1968–9 began to directly affect the Gruppo Abele. It was 1971, in Luigi Ciotti's words, which saw 'the arrival of politics within the action repertoire of the Gruppo Abele. Hands-on politics entered with a vengeance into this group which had been maturing steadily. The group which then counted about fifty persons discovered that it was insufficient to solely rely on direct personal interactions within the chosen domain of work.' A political action committee saw the light of day, and contacts were now established with political organizations and other social forces. Already in 1970, at the group's first annual summer camp in the Valtellina in Bormio, four participants hailing from the university milieu agitated for the abandonment of the Christian orientation by the Gruppo Abele, separating from the group when this call was not heeded. A reorientation towards public political and social action was then powerfully reinforced by the 8 December 1971 pastoral letter by Turin's progressive Archbishop Cardinal Michele Pellegrino, 'Camminare insieme'.[57]

By now, however, the concrete work with teenage problem youth had given rise to a diversification of the group's field of action. Soon prison reform and drug laws became additional central preoccupations of the Gruppo Abele. And the core membership rapidly increased in numbers. By 1972, it counted about 100 individuals, by 1973 more than 220. Trained psychologists and medical specialists had now joined the team, and by mid-decade a spectacular protest action against Italy's repressive drug laws definitely catapulted the Gruppo Abele into the national limelight. A makeshift tent city converted Turin's

---

[55] Luigi Ciotti, 'Campo Scuola', Part I, pp. 'C' and 'D'. Dematteis, 'Traccia cronologica', by contrast lists 1968 as the year when Via Po 11 became the group's home base. And veteran members of the Gruppo Abele have recently confirmed that the Via Po became their organizational centre in late 1968; email communication by Sara Donini to Gerd-Rainer Horn, 22 November 2013. Sara Donini, the archivist of the Gruppo Abele, reported this information after consulting several long-standing members in response to this author's query.

[56] An undated two-page document, entitled 'Comunità di Via Bligny', probably written in the early 1980s, lists May 1970 as the founding moment of their youth shelter in the Via Bligny—ASGA, 'Gli inizi', fasc. 16.4. But, according to veteran members consulted by Sara Donini, it was in 1971 that Via Bligny got off the ground as a runaway shelter for male adolescents, with a similar facility serving runaway girls in the Via Valdieri; email communication by Sara Donini to Gerd-Rainer Horn, 22 November 2013.

[57] Information, including the citation, taken from Luigi Ciotti's 1980 typescript, 'Campo Scuola', pp. 'D'.

central Piazza Solferino into the campaign headquarters of activists clamouring for the reform of Italy's antiquated drug laws, and from 28 June to 10 July 1975 a highly publicized hunger strike underscored the determination of the activists. On 25 July the Italian Senate approved a substantially liberalized law on drugs, finally becoming law on 22 December 1975.[58] Obviously, the reform package was by no means solely the result of the action by the Turin group, but the tent city on Piazza Solferino was the most significant symbolic action on this issue in the course of 1975. Amongst the supportive visitors to the Piazza Solferino were not only the ever-present Cardinal Pellegrino but also personalities of national renown, such as Europe's then most popular living playwright, Dario Fo.

Already some years earlier, clearly, the Gruppo Abele had changed its nature from a classic base community of religiously motivated social activists to something much larger. Nowadays, the Gruppo Abele oversees roughly sixty different projects, some receiving government funding, headquartered in a large former auto parts plant on the northern side of central Turin. Its social cooperatives alone provide employment to 700 individuals, about 300 of them physically or mentally handicapped. Luigi Ciotti, however, remains the head of the Gruppo Abele up to today. In November 1972 he was appointed as priest, with Cardinal Pellegrino ordaining the founding member of Gioventù Impegnata with the words: 'The street will be your parish.'[59] The Gruppo Abele is yet another example of a former base community making it big.

COMUNITÀ DI SANT'EGIDIO

It would go too far to provide many further synopses of the ecclesial and political itineraries of additional Italian base communities which eventually entered the national vocabulary, even if in an incarnation which went beyond their initial calling as a base community. Brief mention, however, must be made of one such community whose transformation made it into one of the Catholic world's most well-known organizations. The Comunità di Sant'-Egidio today claims a worldwide membership of roughly 50,000 members in more than seventy countries. And for some decades now, the Comunità di Sant'Egidio, involved in a range of activities including high-profile

---

[58] Luigi Ciotti, 'Campo Scuola'; Dematteis (ed.), 'Traccia cronologica'; and a special edition of mimeographed documents surrounding the hunger strike and tent city, 'La tenda di Piazza Solferino. Sciopero della fame per una nuova legge sulle droghe', available in the library of the Gruppo Abele.

[59] Dematteis (ed.), 'Traccia cronologica' cites from Pellegrino's speech: 'la strada sarà la tua parrochia'.

international peace initiatives, has been officially recognized by the Catholic church as a 'Catholic public lay association'. It had not always been like this.

The core group at the origin of what later became known as the Comunità di Sant'Egidio, a group of students in a Roman high school, the Liceo Virgilio, first constituted itself as a community in February 1968. The indisputably key personality behind this project was from the very beginning Andrea Riccardi. Already a member of Gioventù Studentesca in Rimini where his family lived until he was 16, Riccardi spent the last two years of high school in the Liceo Virgilio. As were so many other young people who came of age in the late 1960s, Andrea Riccardi was deeply influenced by the Italian *sessantotto* which, one should recall, in Italy had already commenced one year earlier at the very least. In a remarkable series of interviews, Riccardi reminisced: 'I was above all convinced that the world needed to change, that one must play an active role in shaping the future, that one must think about the way in which to effect this change, that one must change the rules of the game, and that one should outline the overall parameters of the developments to come.' Andrea Riccardi further recalled: 'The Church appeared to me rather distant. I did not like the parish very much, nor Catholic Action.' And so he began to organize his high school classmates in the relatively upscale Liceo Virgilio.[60]

For a generation enthusiastically embarking to conquer and change the world, the first serious question was to determine the first target of their interventions. In Rome, secular and Catholic young people on the move almost automatically gravitated towards the sprawling complex of shanty towns circling the Eternal City, products of the desperation of poor Italians fleeing from their native villages and towns in the more underdeveloped parts of Italy, seeking survival and perhaps even fortune in Italy's premier city. A journalist in a Catholic monthly explained in 1980: 'Many more or less politicized groups in those days took an interest' in the life and fate of Roman shanty-town dwellers. Groups hailing from the small universe of Italian New and Far Left milieux flocked to the makeshift working-class suburbs on the outskirts of Rome.[61] So did the young activists from the rather bourgeois Liceo Virgilio.

In Rome as elsewhere in Italy (and Europe), 1968 was 'a year in which various New and Far Left groupings, and their Catholic versions, small communities of believers, sprang up like mushrooms in the rain. Most led a brief and ephemeral life.' As was noted earlier in this chapter, groups which focused on a specific concrete project had a much better chance of surviving.

---

[60] Jean-Dominique Durand and Régis Ladous, *Andrea Riccardi, Sant'Egidio, Rome et le monde* (Paris: Beauchesne, 1996), citations on pp. 6 and 9. Riccardi's GS membership in Rimini was reported by Roberto Morozzo in a conversation with the author on 16 April 2012. I also thank Roberto Morozzo for furnishing me with the relevant documentation referred to in the subsequent pages.

[61] Giulio Cattozzo, 'A S. Egidio continua a fiorire la speranza', *Messaggero di Sant'Antonio* (June 1980), p. 67.

And for the high school rebels of the Liceo Virgilio, to improve the life of the *borgatari* became the anchor which allowed this group to prosper and persevere.[62] It was a worker priest who introduced Andrea Riccardi to the Quartiere Ostiense, and with the able assistance of this priest Andrea Riccardi embarked upon an intense crash course in Catholic theology—but of a certain kind. 'I began to read Congar, Chenu, de Lubac, Rahner, a bit of post-conciliar theology. The moment had come for me to discover what Vatican II had been all about.' Aided by another non-traditional priest, the group began to experiment with new forms of liturgy, though for the moment no priest became an actual member of their group.[63]

Eventually, the former high school activists, many of them commencing university studies, began to construct communities in a number of shanty towns on the outskirts of Rome, with blue-collar workers, women, and the unemployed of these *borgate* playing central roles. These communities provided the organizational and spiritual infrastructure for common liturgical reflections side-by-side with cultural and social functions. 'Thus were born self-managed social assistance centres to serve the needs of the neighbourhood. There emerged social clubs for the elderly, where pensioners could meet to read newspapers, to chat, to pursue their hobbies, play cards or to read the Gospel.'[64] Children and adolescents were aided in the provision of a whole range of activities, including after-school coaching sessions for students, many of them with preciously few chances of succeeding in the traditional school system.

As Mario Marazziti highlights in a short survey of the Comunità di Sant'-Egidio published in 1988: 'Initially, the group was characterized by the presence of young people from varying backgrounds, lay activists reflecting simultaneously the variegated and quickly evolving nature of the Church and the general outlines of youth culture characteristic of those years, without any real contact with classical Catholic associations or ecclesiastic institutions.'[65] The first priest to join the movement (in 1972), Vincenzo Paglia, put it like this in 1976: 'Our communitarian project developed and matured therefore at the margins of the traditional forms of intervention by the Church amongst young people, and it evolved in the cultural climate typical of that milieu in recent years.'[66] Andrea Riccardi further specified the political and

[62] Jean-Pierre Magnigne, 'Sant'Egidio. L'Évangile vécu au cœur de la ville', *L'Actualité réligieuse* 8 (15 January 1984), p. 10.

[63] Durand and Ladous, *Andrea Riccardi*, pp. 10–11.

[64] Cattozzo, 'Fiorire la speranza', p. 68. The concentrated efforts on the part of the Comunità to develop an apostolate geared specifically towards these impoverished shanty-town dwellers can be consulted in Comunità di Sant'Egidio, *Vangelo in periferia* (Brescia: Morcelliana, 1987).

[65] Mario Marazziti, 'Sant'Egidio', in Guerrino Pellicia and Giancarlo Rocca (eds), *Dizionario degli istituti di perfezione*, Vol. VIII: *Saba—Spiritualii* (Rome: Paoline, 1988), p. 776.

[66] Vincenzo Praglia, 'La comunità di S. Egidio: dalla contestazione alla teologia della città', *Communio* (1976), p. 70.

ecclesial context of their project: 'In those years much attention was devoted to the problem of the shanty towns, especially amongst young people, in contrast to the distinct lack of serious attention to such issues by mainstream Catholic milieux. This movement brought with it, even if in an imprecise manner, the demand for a different Church, with firm roots amongst the poor. To attempt to make this different role of the Church a reality, to construct it along the lines of the ideas which we developed out of our own responsibility, those were the most prominent goals emerging during that period.'[67]

In the first years of the development of what eventually became the Comunità di Sant'Egidio, when the loose association was named either after the specific shanty town in which it operated, or just 'Comunità' for short, it wholly conformed to the broad outlines of other such communities in Rome and elsewhere. They were 'small communities, of recent vintage, in general animated by lay activists; almost always the actual founders of the small communitarian nucleus emerging in various specific contexts of sociability (a school, a working class neighbourhood, etc.). With the increase in the number of such communitarian nuclei, the ties of friendship and spiritual affinity were supplemented by more articulated and stable frameworks, periodic gatherings that took the form of assemblies and councils.'[68]

In 1973, as the community had undergone a significant expansion, present in ten different *borgate*, the need for a central headquarters became increasingly evident. Several earlier attempts to establish such a social centre had failed, but then in 1973 the offer arrived to use an abandoned convent in a working-class neighbourhood in central Rome, Trastevere. The former convent and church of Sant'Egidio quickly bestowed its name on the group as a whole. 'Many of our members did not live in that neighbourhood. But the central building there facilitated a sort of synthesis—not a showcase, at least that is what I hope—i.e. a location serving as a unifying mechanism and a place for interaction for that archipelago of individual groups dispersed throughout the city. At the beginning, Trastevere served us as an address of convenience.' Only in subsequent years did the Comunità di Sant'Egidio develop firm roots in that neighbourhood, to the point where it has since become almost identified with the church of Sant'Egidio and Trastevere.[69]

The year 1973 also served as another landmark in the eventual growth and spread of the Comunità di Sant'Egidio. A cholera outbreak in Naples led to the dispatch of five members to the metropolis in Italy's south, leading to the first

---

[67] Durand and Ladous, *Andrea Riccardi*, p. 18.
[68] Marazziti, 'Sant'Egidio', p. 778.
[69] Andrea Riccardi, in Durand and Ladous, *Andrea Riccardi*, pp. 23–30, describes the gradual and initially circumstantial establishment of links between the Comunità and the neighbourhood, Trastevere; citation on p. 26.

de facto founding of a community outside Rome.[70] Only some years later did
this rather accidental diffusion of the Comunità's activity to Naples lead to a
more concentrated and willed effort to expand its geographical reach. With its
phenomenal success arrived the need for further structure. By 1979 non-
binding rules of conduct were compiled into the 'Orientamenti della vita
commune'. And in the course of the 1980s, serious efforts were under way
to obtain official recognition on the part of the Catholic church.[71] The
Comunità di Sant'Egidio, having arisen entirely outside the network of pre-
existing church organizations, was quickly becoming part of the church,
though retaining essential autonomy over its internal life and external operations. A former grassroots base community had, once again, made it big.

A SOCIOLOGICAL STUDY WITHOUT PARALLEL

Earlier on in this chapter, the initial development of base communities in
Italy—even if they did not yet regularly employ this particular designation—
was brought up to the late sixties. It was the flashpoint year of 1968 which saw
the first serious efforts under way to provide a national framework to this
ebullient movement of grassroots activists outside of the traditional structures
of the church—and the organized Left! The term most frequently employed
in 1967–8 to describe this welter of local initiatives was *gruppi spontanei*. As
a category of analysis, strictly speaking, it incorporated Catholic *and*
secular groups, as well as any number of possible combinations of Catholic
and secular (mostly Marxist) activists working within one and the same
spontaneous group.

   An extraordinary, scholarly assessment of this bewildering wealth of youthful activists attempting to stake out their own path in life in the course of 1968
can be gleaned in a sociological research project, funded by the Left Catholic
Fondazione Olivetti, in which a number of young activist academics cut their
teeth, who later emerged as leading historians, journalists, and sociologists in
their own right, such as Guido Romagnoli, Bruno Manghi, Lidia Menapace,
Ettore Rotelli, and Franco Rositi. In an uncanny coincidence of timing, this
team of researchers associated with the journal *Questitalia* decided in late 1967
to engage in a social scientific study of this milieu of *gruppi spontanei*, which
was then quickly becoming the talk of the town throughout Italy. They first
drew up a list of *gruppi spontanei* throughout the entire country. In the end,
they selected 312 individual groups for further study by means of a series

---

[70] Jacques Dupont, 'Les Communautés de Sant'Egidio', *Lettre de Clerlande* 15 (September
1987), p. 8.
[71] Marazziti, 'Sant'Egidio', pp. 778–9.

of detailed questionnaires. The bulk of their case studies were carried out between April and October 1968. Then a smaller sample of fifty of these groups was selected for yet more detailed investigations, including lengthy interview sessions with members of this smaller set of groups. The product is a unique and highly unusual snapshot of a vibrant and constantly shifting array of grassroots organizations precisely during a time of near-constant and hectic activism.[72]

The sociologists had early on decided to solely focus on those groups which had sprung up independently of mainstream political parties or the network of official church associations, such as Catholic Action. As the political dimension of their activities was central to the concerns of the researchers, communities which exclusively focused on ecclesial reform were excluded from their sample, but so were, for instance, groupings belonging to the sprawling network of Far Left groups, which often had emerged out of this magma of *gruppi spontanei* just months before the sociologists' research efforts got under way. To ensure the focus on the organizational independence and autonomy of each studied group, local chapters of the loose association of activists forming the influential Movimento Studentesco were removed from their sample as well. The idea was to cast a light on the inner life and the political orientation exclusively of such associations as were truly without ties to any larger organization. And the team of authors noted that, given the fluid period of transition during which the research happened to be carried out, by the time the book was written—the foreword is dated May 1970—many of the groups no longer existed or had changed character, which would no longer have warranted some of the groups being included in their sample, had the research commenced only then. In essence, all groups targeted carried out political work, most also devoted significant chunks of time to ecclesial issues, but none of them were exclusively oriented towards ecclesial issues only.

This extraordinary still photo of an activist world in motion provides rich data for a whole range of observations going far beyond the fledgling Catholic base communities. Thus, as the extremely fluid peculiarities of this phase in the genesis of the Italian Far Left would have it, while the Movimento Studentesco, itself thriving on its plurality of represented views and an often-times extremely decentralized organizational structure, was excluded, the first shoots of what eventually became Avanguardia Operaia or Potere Operaio, later on mainstays of the Italian Far Left, were then still included. But what makes the research of the Fondazione Olivetti particularly fruitful for a glimpse at Catholic grassroots communities in 1968 is the fact that a significant majority of the 312 groups studied belonged to the Catholic fold. Of all

---

[72] All references in this subchapter originated in the book-length study by Franco Ferraresi et al., *La politica dei gruppi. Aspetti dell'associazionismo politico di base in Italia dal 1967 al 1969* (Milan: Comunità, 1970).

surveyed groups 44.5 per cent were Catholic, a further 15.1 per cent consisted
of Catholics and non-Catholic Marxists, leaving a mere 17.7 per cent of non-
Catholic 'pure' Marxist groups and a further 3.5 per cent non-Marxist secular
groups. In 17.3 per cent of the case studies, the ideological origins of the
group were listed as imprecise. In short, the bulk of the sample consisted of
Catholic local autonomous groups, i.e. precisely the milieu which would—in
hindsight—be best described as Christian—or mixed Christian and secular—
base communities.

What emerges from the fascinating observations is a teeming world of
largely Catholic activists who were then attempting to change their world,
trying to seize the day, often in open or latent conflict with the local or regional
church hierarchies, but frequently aided by the lowest rung of the clerical
hierarchy, parish priests. By virtue of inclusion in the samples studied, all
Catholic groups engaged in a mixture of ecclesial *and* political or social action.
As the range of such activities has been amply described in preceding pages,
I will merely concentrate on that aspect of the sociologists' findings, where an
effort was made to compare and contrast Catholic and non-Catholic (usually
secular Marxist) groups. And it is here where the most interesting and
astounding conclusions came to the fore.

Though the activities of both secular and religious groups increasingly
tended to converge over time—obviously leaving aside explicitly ecclesial
work carried out by the Catholic groups—Catholic groups in the sample
consistently exhibited certain features distinct from their secular Marxist
cohort. Catholic associations showcased a much lower level of internal strati-
fication, with few attempts at a formalization of internal group functions, a
division of labour, or the elaboration of statutes. Catholic groups had a far
more pronounced penchant for the reliance on mechanisms of participatory
democracy, whereas secular groups relied far more frequently on elements
deriving from the tradition of democratic centralism—to be sure, the latter in
the original format of its non-totalitarian heritage. For Catholics, concrete
engagements in practical work played a much more central role than for the
secular Marxist groups. For Catholics, the elaboration of a political line was
usually a logical consequence of their empirical commitments; for the secular
cohort, the relationship between theory and practice was often the reverse.
Within Catholic groups, friendship networks and related networks of quotid-
ian sociabilities played a much more prominent role as a common glue than in
the non-Catholic sample. Last but not least, voluntarism was a key factor of
Catholic groups in this sample, with personal and subjective responsibility the
central motivator for the concrete involvement in their chosen practical tasks.

Any number of important conclusions may be drawn from the rich accu-
mulation of data assembled by the Olivetti team. In the context of this chapter,
I merely wish to underscore the elementary egalitarian impulse provided by

this mass of youthful enthusiasts emerging out of the Catholic universe, which then obviously still exerted a powerful pull in Italy. The sociologists did note that the *gruppi spontanei* in northern metropolitan areas tended to see a disproportionate—given the relationship of forces in Italy as a whole— preponderance of non-Catholic informal communities of activists, which is highly evocative and relevant for the subsequent development of the post-1968 Italian Far Left. But the consequences of this 'ominous' evolution in the metropolitan centres of the Italian North will have to await elaboration in a future study of the Italian (and European) Far Left I aim to carry out. For the moment, having strongly underlined the social relevance of Catholic base communities in 1968, it is incumbent to draw a brief sketch of the first wave of serious attempts to construct a national network of such groups.

GRUPPI SPONTANEI

Initially, in tandem with the spirit of those years, such endeavours at providing a framework for mutual exchange of experience and opinion included both Catholic-dominated and secular *gruppi spontanei*. In fact, some important early efforts at the establishment of a national fabric for such groups to flourish were actually carried out—or at least initiated—by several amongst the astounding range of prolific Catholic reviews and journals operating in Italy at that time.[73] Earlier on in this chapter, we have seen that reading groups of some of the publications in the early sixties often constituted one of the very first of the loose associations of like-minded curious minds which must, in hindsight, be regarded as, in effect, some of the earliest Italian base communities. In fact, the editorial teams of such newsletters or reviews themselves often acted and operated as base communities, as was noted by Ettore Rotelli with regard to *Questitalia*. 'In effect, the Milan editorial board of *Questitalia* not only functioned as a *gruppo spontaneo* and was a protagonist of efforts to coordinate these groups, but it also aided in making them the object of a state-of-the-art sociological study.'[74]

The first noteworthy meeting in a slowly emerging movement to federate the ebullient but often evanescent *gruppi spontanei* occurred in Bologna on 15–16 October 1966, when representatives from several leading Left Catholic journals met for deliberations, including *Questitalia* (Milan) and *Il gallo*

---

[73] Two book-length studies may serve as useful introductions to the kaleidoscope of progressive Catholic newsletters, monthlies, journals, and reviews: Ristuccia (ed.), *Intellettuali cattolici*, and the recent monograph by Daniela Saresella, *Dal Concilio alla contestazione. Riviste cattoliche negli anni del cambiamento (1958–1968)* (Brescia: Morcelliana, 2005).

[74] Ettore Rotelli, 'I gruppi spontanei del '68', in Lorenzo Bedeschi et al., *I cristiani nella sinistra. Dalla Resistenza a oggi* (Rome: Coines, 1976), p. 186.

(Genoa). This effort picked up speed in the course of 1967 when, on 1 August, the progressive editor of the premier Italian Catholic daily, *L'avvenire*, Raniero La Valle, was forced to relinquish his post. A Bologna base community, the Associazione Culturale 'Presenza', on this occasion published a protest manifesto which, within a few days, obtained further signatures from forty-five additional groups, 'with a growing number of declarations of support arriving in subsequent days'.[75] The Bologna group Presenza, riding the wave of popularity within the milieu of Italian Left Catholicism in the wake of its popularization of the *Avvenire* affair, now called for a gathering of *gruppi spontanei* who had signed the petition in order to facilitate mutual interaction and to establish personal contacts and exchange experiences. The key item on the agenda of the meeting in the Bologna Philharmonic Academy's Mozart Hall was the launch of a newsletter which would provide a link between the far-flung and often isolated groups.[76] On 14 January 1968, representatives of forty-six different groups from Palermo to Udine met for the first national gathering of *gruppi spontanei*. The minutes of the event make clear that, other than the plans for a national newsletter, the major function of the conference was the mutual cognizance of each other's existence, and the recognition that one's local enterprise was part of a much vaster national trend.[77] The newsletter project soon saw the light of day with the regular publication of the *Collegamenti* for the rest of 1968.[78]

Six weeks later, Bologna hosted yet another convention of *gruppi spontanei*, this one organized by the editorial group of *Questitalia*. Already on 25–6 November 1967, *Questitalia*'s tireless editor, Wladimiro Dorigo, had organized a conference meant to launch an effort at coordinating the emerging *gruppi spontanei*, but in effect the event was rather top-heavy, with key roles reserved for the interventions by national figureheads of dissident socialists— Luigi Anderlini and Franco Boiardi would soon be elected on tickets of the New Left PSIUP—and the head of the press and propaganda section of the PCI, Achille Ochetto. Consequently, the November 1967 Rimini conference mostly debated the choices for 'Catholics' in the upcoming elections.[79]

[75] Fabro, *I cattolici*, p. 57.

[76] A copy of the letter by the Associazione Culturale 'Presenza', 'A tutti i gruppi spontanei d'Italia', written on 5 December 1967, calling for this meeting, can be consulted in the Fondo Domenico Sereno Regis, Fondazione Vera Nocentini (FVN) [Turin], faldone 2, fascicolo B. Fabro, *I cattolici*, p. 62, provides some additional contextual information.

[77] One of the chief promoters of the 14 January 1968 gathering in the Sala Mozart, the monthly journal *Il gallo*, carried a report, 'Un incontro di "gruppi spontanei" a Bologna, nella Sala Mozart, il 14 gennaio 1968', in its February 1968 issue, p. 14. A copy of the forty-nine-page-long proceedings of the gathering can be consulted in Fondo Gianni Vizio, FVN, faldone 3b.

[78] Fabro, *I cattolici*, p. 63 note 2.

[79] On the 4–5 November 1967 Rimini *convegno*, see 'Introduzione' to Assemblea dei Gruppi Spontanei di Impegno Politico-Culturale per una Nuova Sinistra, *I gruppi spontanei e il ruolo politico della contestazione* (Milan: Feltrinelli, 1969), p. 5. On *Questitalia*, see Francesco Sidotti,

The 25 February 1968 Convegno Nazionale dei Circoli e Gruppi Spontanei d'Impegno Politica-Culturale thus became the first occasion for the initiative undertaken by the Catholic journal *Questitalia* to bring together in one hall members of base communities from all across Italy. The conference call was co-signed by sixteen local associations from Messina to Torino. From November 1967 onwards, a series of regional gatherings across Italy had prepared for Bologna. According to the organizers, the preliminary gatherings assembled a total of 2,000 participants, representing about 150 individual local groups. The 25 February 1968 convention assembled in the Sala del Trecento in Bologna's city centre landmark, the Palazzo di Re Enzo. The more than fifty local groups represented in the Palazzo constituted themselves as the Assemblea Nazionale di Collegamenti of the movement. Two subsequent gatherings were devoted to the drafting of a programmatic document. The 21 April 1968 gathering, with fifty-six groups represented, adopted a common platform giving rise to the 'Assembly of Spontaneous Groups with a Political and Cultural Commitment in View of a New Left'.[80]

The key difference between the two initiatives, which were not meant to be competitive but rather complementary efforts, was the more openly political focus of the 25 February Bologna convention in the Sala del Trecento. The 14 January 1968 Mozart Hall gathering was clearly focused on the inner life of the *gruppi spontanei* themselves, and the resulting bulletin, *Collegamenti*, became its logical organizational expression. Yet it would be wrong to ascribe to the crowd in the Sala Mozart a primarily ecclesial orientation and to view the participants in the Sala Trecento as primarily politically motivated. In both gatherings, though dominated by Catholic spontaneous groups, groups composed of non-religious activists were present as well. The January gathering also declared its intent to carry out urgently necessary interventions in public life. And, in fact, a number of the groups present in January also signed the conference call for the convention in the Palazzo di Re Enzo. The simultaneity of similar efforts was a symbolic expression of the sudden realization of the necessity for the countless local initiatives to construct networks. The fact that the student movement in Italy had entered the hot phase with a cycle

---

' "Questitalia" e la polemica sui temi dell'organizzazione e politica dei cattolici', in Ristuccia (ed.), *Intellettuali cattolici*, pp. 165–227, and Marcello Vigli, ' "Questitalia". Una via cattolica alla laicità', in Lucia Ceci and Laura Demofonti (eds), *Chiesa, laicità e vita civile* (Rome: Carocci, 2005), pp. 419–34.

[80] The conference call, signed by sixteen groups, can be consulted in the Fondo Domenico Sereno Regis, FVN, faldone 2, fascicolo B. On the series of preparatory meetings and the 25 February *convegno* in the Palazzo di Re Enzo, see 'Bologna. Prima tappa dell'associazionismo spontaneo per una "nuova sinistra"', *Questitalia* 11 (nos 118–19), January–February 1968, pp. 14–20. On the 25 February and 21 April 1968 gatherings in Bologna, see 'L'Assemblea dei gruppi spontanei', *Questitalia* 11 (nos 120–2), March–May 1968, pp. 16–19; and Nando Fabro, 'I gruppi spontanei in Italia', *Il gallo* 22 (no. 6), June 1968, p. 10.

of ever-spreading university occupations, starting in November 1967 with the Catholic University of Milan (see Chapter 4), contributed its own fair share to the growing politicization of spontaneous groups, Catholics and non-Catholics alike.

SPONTANEOUS GROUPS CLOSE RANKS

By the spring of 1968, however, yet another—a third!—initiative had got under way to bundle the energies of an entire generation of young people in motion. After the Battle of Valle Giulia on 1 March 1968, the month of March witnessed literally every single institution of higher education from Sicily to Südtirol engaging in highly charged protest actions, with many high schools showcasing clear signs of infection by this spirit of revolt. Corrado Corghi, a former regional secretary for DC in the Emilia Romagna, on 23 March 1968 announced the launch of a project to build regional 'Assemblies for Political Work' to channel the multiform and disparate but powerful enthusiasms in what he regarded as constructive directions. Four different preparatory work-shops met between late June and mid-September. At the 29 June 1968 meeting in Bologna, Corghi assembled a panoply of forces to the left of the traditional political parties, including a spokesperson from the Bologna Gruppo Presenza, responsible for the 14 January 1968 Sala Mozart conference, as well as the ever-present Nando Fabro of *Il gallo*, who thus participated in all three parallel efforts now under way to give coherence to the extraparliamentary forces of the anti-authoritarian Left, composed to a significant extent of Catholics.[81]

Questitalia had not been invited to the 29 June 1968 event, nor had the *gruppi spontanei* themselves. And *Questitalia* astutely pointed its finger at Corghi's initiative as an endeavour to recuperate the energies of grassroots social movements to bolster support for traditional electoral politics, with central roles reserved for the PCI. Dorigo, having invested all his efforts since late 1967 precisely to avoid such a constellation by creating a new political force beyond PCI and even the New Left PSIUP, penned a scathing critique of Corghi's project, which in effect would have sidelined the premier new political forces on the increasingly colourful scene of Italian left-wing politics, the *gruppi spontanei*, in favour of traditional political and electoral manoeuvres.[82]

---

[81] Fabro, *I cattolici*, pp. 67–8. The presence of Fabro, the Gruppo Presenza, and other like-minded forces at the first of these meetings organized by Corrado Corghi on 29 June 1968 is prominently mentioned in 'Reggio Emilia: "Felix Culpa"', *Questitalia* 11 (nos 125–6), August–September 1968, p. 115.

[82] 'Felix culpa', pp. 115–17.

As it happened, the whirlwind events of 1968 in general, amongst them the French May, the latter powerfully reinforcing the radical instincts of the Italian anti-authoritarian Left, undermined Corrado Corghi's best-laid plans. The national convention of the Assemblea dei Gruppi di Lavoro Politico, the fruit of Corghi's valiant efforts since March, did gather on 29 September 1968 in Reggio Emilia in the Sala Tricolore of the City Hall. More than 200 participants assembled, representing approximately fifty local groups. And at the outset of the historic gathering, it looked like the plans for electoral alliances would indeed dominate the proceedings. But then something happened! A spokesperson for the base community in Parma which had been responsible for the spectacular occupation of Parma Cathedral on 14 September (see Chapter 4) took the microphone, and the meeting began to change character. Forcefully present at Reggio, one after another of the representatives of various *gruppi spontanei* took to the floor after their comrade from Parma had blazed the trail to point out the gulf 'which separated the promoters of the initiative from those who the former had imagined' as the faithful footsoldiers of the former's electoral plans. The *gruppi spontanei* made a powerful plea for an independent course of action, against the recuperation of their energies for electoral purposes. Reggio Emilia became a declaration of independence of the new star on the Italian cultural and political horizon, the spontaneous groups, many of them hailing from the Left Catholic milieu.[83]

Yet there was trouble in paradise. The ubiquitous Nando Fabro, present at all assemblies in the course of 1968 and a committed and far-sighted chronicler of events, spent much of his lengthy and detailed conference report criticizing a feature of the post-May 1968 New and (especially) Far Left which would continuously haunt left-wing politics in the ensuing half-dozen or so decisive years of Europe-wide (and not only Italian) contestations. Fabro presciently took exception to the style and the proceedings of the convention at Reggio which, after the initial presentation of documents prepared in the course of the summer, proceeded along disorganized, tumultuous, and ultimately counterproductive lines. 'I was flabbergasted to realize that for practical purposes only those who were gifted public speakers and who displayed a penchant for vehement populism wound up being most attentively listened to, and they generated a consensus which manifested itself in the most traditional forms of audience applause, thus channelling and directing the assembly towards certain conclusions.'[84] Having narrowly avoided the fate of becoming pawns in traditional parliamentary politics, spontaneous groups manoeuvred

---

[83] 'Felix culpa', p. 117; see also Fabro, *I cattolici*, p. 78.

[84] Nando Fabro, 'Reggio Emilia, 29 settembre 1968. La prima "Assemblea dei 'gruppi di lavoro politico'"', *Il gallo* 22 (no. 11), November 1968, p. 17.

themselves into a corner by falling for an authoritarianism of a different, but similarly pernicious, kind.

Next in this hectic succession of closely related conferences and initiatives came the second national assembly of the forces behind the very first of these ventures, the 14 January 1968 Bologna convention which had given rise to the monthly newsletter *Collegamenti*. On 13 October 1968, again in Bologna, representatives of forty-six *gruppi spontanei* assembled, and it was proudly announced that *Collegamenti*, which had already published ten issues by September, had managed to obtain by then more than 500 subscriptions, the targeted threshold for economic and financial independence of the enterprise. Yet the same mixture of debilitating disorganization, coupled with pseudo-anti-authoritarian grandstanding, which had reared its ugly head on 29 September in Reggio Emilia, was now beginning to make a forceful presence amongst the supporters of *Collegamenti*. In addition, however, a further debate was now beginning to be aired. The October Assembly in Bologna brought into the open a sentiment that had been simmering subterraneously within the community of *gruppi spontanei* for quite some time.[85]

'Two distinct tendencies clearly saw the light of day. One expressed the need for a more decisively "political" orientation of the groups, thereby providing a distinct inflection to their work and to their commitments—as well as to their journalistic product: *Collegamenti*. [. . .] The other tendency expressed in equally decisive terms the need for a reorientation of the group towards ecclesial work, and a corresponding commitment of the groups to engage in activities on ecclesial issues.' Yet Nando Fabro, the most perceptive of all participant-observers with regard to the inner life of the *gruppi spontanei* in the all-important capstone year of 1968, immediately added: 'One cannot speak of any sort of polemical exchange between those two tendencies.' The importance of both ecclesial and political work was recognized by all. At the same time, both tendencies were acutely aware of 'the necessity to make a choice as far as the basic—or at least pre-eminent—commitment was concerned. In part this derived from the realization that it would be difficult to find the necessary time to engage in serious work simultaneously in both spheres—civic and ecclesial life—without falling into the habit of engaging in unfocused and hit-and-miss protest activities.' The conference for the moment resolved this discussion by deciding to give a more openly political inflection to *Collegamenti*, but to begin to publish, parallel to *Collegamenti*, a supplementary bulletin—*bollettino-supplemento*—geared towards the needs of groups more specifically oriented towards ecclesial work.

---

[85] The information in this and the following paragraphs is taken from 'Bologna, 13 ottobre 1968. Il 2° Incontro di "Collegamenti"', *Il gallo* 22 (12), December 1968, pp. 16–17.

THE QUESTION OF LANGUAGE

Already in his reflections on Reggio Emilia, Nando Fabro had taken exception not only to the tyranny of structurelessness characterizing the proceedings, but likewise the highly intellectualized, excessively abstract and, as a result, frequently confusing and incomprehensible nature of many of the interventions in the Sala Tricolore. Fabro pointed out the irony of many speakers in Reggio consistently making almost mandatory, incantatory references to Marx and Mao as authorities and role models, given that both Mao and Marx were known to have been sharply attuned to the necessity 'to express themselves in an extremely uncomplicated and straightforward language easily comprehensible by grassroots activists. This had certainly been the case whenever they had wanted their ideas to promote reflection and reconsideration and, especially, moves towards action by the ranks.'[86] The promoters of the primacy of politics at Bologna on 13 October 1968, Fabro asserted, suffered from the identical syndrome he had already detected in Reggio.

From 1 to 4 November 1968 the largest and longest of all such gatherings of *gruppi spontanei* took place in Rimini, organized by the Rimini Circolo Maritain. Three days, billed as a study session, assembled 200 participants representing 68 local groups. The fourth and final day of the gathering was slated as the 'Fourth National Assembly of Spontaneous Groups with a Political and Cultural Commitment in View of a New Left', with 600 activists in attendance. Organizationally, it stood in a line of continuity with the 25 February 1968 Bologna Assembly promoted by *Questitalia*. Two further national meetings in Bologna and Modena had taken place since February. By the time of the Rimini conference, however, *Questitalia* had begun to distance itself from this exuberant crowd which the editorial group of the journal had helped to create but which was now on a path leading in a rather different direction from Dorigo's original designs.[87] Both original sins at this particular moment of transition from the New to the Far Left—the fascination with the absence of structure in large and unwieldy assemblies, and the penchant for theoretical ruminations of almost metaphysical dimensions—were forcefully present at this culmination of a year-long effort to fashion the *gruppi spontanei* into a novel and dynamic national force for radical change in the seaside resort on the Adriatic.

---

[86] Fabro, 'Reggio Emilia', p. 19.

[87] On Rimini, Nando Fabro's accounts of the proceedings are, again, an intelligent and indispensable resource: Nando Fabro, 'Rimini, 1–4 novembre 1968', *Il gallo* 22 (no. 12), December 1968, pp. 17–18. On *Questitalia*'s growing alienation from the rapidly evolving movement they had helped to spawn, see Sidotti, 'Questitalia', pp. 210–15. Some information on the preceding gatherings in this cycle opened on 25 February can be found in Rotelli, 'I gruppi spontanei', p. 195, who provides solid confirmation of the intervening process of radicalization parallel to the growth of Italy's Movimento Studentesco and the French May '68 events.

Nando Fabro took perverse pleasure in reprinting the official communiqué emerging from the Fourth Assembly. He then noted: 'I have given this text to a cross-section of people—executive staff members, white-collar employees and blue-collar workers—who are all currently engaged in politics. None of them found it easy to comprehend. And one should note that this document is less encoded than the majority of presentations and speeches in the Study Session and the Assembly.'[88] Fabro also noted the slow crystallization of two distinct orientations vis-à-vis national politics within the welter of *gruppi spontanei*. 'One places all its bets on a more clear-cut and decisive intransigence vis-à-vis actually existing political parties, including the organization of the political "Left". The other calls such an intransigence political "infantilism". The latter propose as one of the key problems the study of realistic ways and means in which one may obtain agreements with those political forces agitating in favour of a politics "of the Left" for the better part of a century, while carefully avoiding any possible instrumentalization by these potential allies.' Fabro regretfully added that 'at Rimini the intransigent tendency carried the day', with spontaneous groups thus further setting sail in the direction of an increasingly worrisome marginalization and self-imposed isolation. If Corrado Corghi's spring and summer initiative, culminating in the 29 September 1968 Reggio convention, was a thinly veiled attempt at recuperation of the energies of spontaneous groups for mainstream politics, the welcome course correction introduced at Reggio was beginning to spin out of control.

The highpoint of the organizational life of these spontaneous groups, the four-day gathering in early November with 600 activists from all over Italy in attendance was also the endpoint of this simultaneously promising and frustrating experience. No further similar concentrated and united expressions of their vitality and confusion, trying to blaze a trail towards liberation in a moment of rapid societal and political changes, took place in the aftermath of the November 1968 Rimini conference. The two tendencies discerned by Fabro at Rimini henceforth tended to take divergent paths, with the intransigents oriented towards the sprawling network of the emerging Italian Far Left.

---

[88] Any attempt at translation would not do justice to the full impact of the original text. For readers familiar with the Italian language, points 2 and 6 of the seven-point communiqué may suffice to convey the flavour of the proceedings: '2. Confermano come atteggiamento di base il ritiro della delega agli strumenti istituzionali di espressione politica, proponendo invece la formazione autonoma e la gestione diretta, da parte della base, della domanda politica. 6. Tali movimenti di lotta autonoma richiedono un metodo ("induttivo") che si fonda sulla mobilitazione su particolari situazioni di sfruttamento direttamente vissute dai cittadini, per generalizzare progressivamente sui modi di tale sfruttamento.'

CHRISTIAN BASE COMMUNITIES

Gruppi spontanei, it should be recalled, almost always and nearly everywhere consisted of secular and Catholic circles, with Catholics heavily represented. It is for this very reason that much attention has been devoted in preceding pages to their course of action during the capstone year of 1968. The energies propelling members of *gruppi spontanei* to engage in radical social and political action were largely fuelled by Catholic activists in search of fields of engagement. Embracing the spirit of the times, Catholic activists underwent often in the space of very little time—and in 1968 time seemed to run more quickly than at most other historical moments—a learning process of extra-ordinary dimensions. Some of them eventually abandoned not only the Catholic church but religion altogether. Most, however, at least for some time, kept battling with the choices which Nando Fabro had identified as the crucial question raised in Bologna in October 1968. Should ecclesial or political work gain priority? Another contemporaneous sociological study of Italian *gruppi spontanei*, this one exclusively targeting those who set out to combine social *and* religious action, repeatedly highlighted the push and pull of both arguments. 'In many cases, these groups and individual members of these groups continually oscillated between one and the other option.'[89]

Apart from the debate over the degree of emphasis of political and ecclesial work, the other substantive discussion raged over the crucial topic diagnosed by Fabro at Rimini in November. Virtually all groups wishing to strengthen ecclesial work were in agreement that political work could and should not be ignored. But what sorts of politics would promise the most success? The emancipation from mainstream politics was felt by almost all such groups to be a blessing, but the ever-increasing stridency and intransigence of nascent Far Left politics, making massive inroads into the milieu of *gruppi spontanei* from the summer of 1968 onwards, was beginning to render the autonomy gained in the course of the spring and summer as a blessing in disguise. A cycle of radicalization ensued which gained majority support in the conjuncture of the moment, but which soon began to leave behind an important element of its troops. The primacy of revolutionary politics brought about a fateful split in one of the most visible and prominent detachments favouring radical social engagements in the course of 1968: the *gruppi spontanei*. As the momentary dynamic favoured the spiral towards politicization and concomitant radical-ization, those activists not wishing to relegate ecclesial work to the sidelines soon began to pull back. A certain revalidation of ecclesial work began to be

---

[89] Chiara Saraceno, 'Tra profezia e politica (Gruppi del dissenso)', in Gian Enrico Rusconi and Chiara Saraceno, *Ideologia religiosa e conflitto sociale* (Bari: De Donato, 1970), p. 219; this work equals the study financed by the Olivetti Foundation in rich empirical detail and analytic precision.

The Spirit of Vatican II

regarded as a solution to the impasse encountered consecutively in Reggio (September), Bologna (October), and Rimini (November). The path of the most intransigent groups began to separate from the path of the more ecclesially oriented circles. A multiform and energetic movement began to fray.

The more ecclesially oriented groups soon felt the need for a gathering of their own. A first regional meeting of the minds was organized in early January 1969 in Florence, promoted by *Testimonianze*, the house journal of Ernesto Balducci, which, already in an April 1968 editorial addressing the phenom- enon of *gruppi spontanei*, had expressed its doubts with regard to 'their political maturity and the secular orientation of their discourse'.[90] On 26 January 1969 a larger meeting along similar lines assembled yet again in Bologna. Out of this gathering emerged the plan to amend the October 1968 idea for a two-pronged journalistic offensive. Rather than publish a bulletin oriented towards ecclesial action as a supplement to the more straightfor- wardly political *Collegamenti*, participants agreed to create a journal organ- izationally separate from *Collegamenti*. Thus was born the *Bolletino di collegamenti fra comunità cristiane di Italia*, whose first issue was distributed in May 1969 and which operated on a regular schedule until 1973, when other periodicals took over the task of providing a national information network for what, by then, were increasingly identified as base communities (*comunità di base*).[91]

Collegamenti continued its separate publication throughout 1969 but was eventually absorbed by the *Bolletino di collegamenti*.[92] And it must be under- scored that the substitution of *Collegamenti* by the *Bolletino* was not meant to suggest a split between the two wings of the grassroots community of activists hailing from the former *gruppi spontanei*, who now increasingly referred to themselves as Christian communities—hence the full name of the *Bolletino*! The makers of the *Bolletino* never tired of underscoring 'that the choice for an ecclesial orientation was by no means intended to underestimate or to put in second place the choice for more openly political work'.[93] If there were any doubts that the more ecclesially oriented groups around the *Bolletino* con- tinued to be committed to a double-track approach, the First National

---

[90] For the editorial comment, see the untitled editorial by Danilo Zolo in *Testimonianze* 11 (no. 103), April 1968, p. 197. On the 4 January 1969 meeting in Florence, see 'Dove va il movimento di base?', *Bolletino di collegamenti* 5/1 (no. 29), January 1973, p. 7.

[91] On the 26 January 1969 Bologna gathering, see Fabro, *I cattolici*, pp. 99–100; on the publication history of the *Bolletino di collegamenti* and its subsequent avatars, see Pasquale Colella, 'Le comunità di base (centro-nord)', in Alberto Abelli et al., *Chiesa in Italia: 1975–1978* (Brescia: Queriniana, 1978), p. 159, n. 2.

[92] Mario Cuminetti, *Il dissenso cattolico in Italia* (Milan: Rizzoli, 1983), p. 129, implies that *Collegamenti* was immediately folded into the *Bolletino*, but Nando Fabro cites issues of *Collegamenti* dating to as late as September 1969 in *I cattolici*, p. 95, n. 5.

[93] Fabro, *I cattolici*, p. 100.

Assembly of Christian Communities gathering—how could it be any different?—once again in Bologna from 26 to 28 September 1969 put such worries to rest. The religious orientation of this gathering of 403 registered participants was underscored by the fact that 66 out of the 403 were ordained priests.[94]

Luciano Martini, one of the more prominent students of Ernesto Balducci, himself soon to take over editorship of *Testimonianze*, reported on the assembly.

> Notwithstanding the cautionary remarks which accompanied their intervention in the proceedings, in fact very many speakers identified an openly revolutionary engagement as the most effective method available today to express the brotherly love without which there can be no love of God. [...] Not everyone in Bologna shared such views, but I often had the impression, certainly when listening to the speakers addressing the crowd, that this reflected the dominant mood and that anyone raising objections to this line of thought was put on the defensive without adequate arguments at his disposal to propose a convincing alternative.[95]

In January 1973, in an unsigned thinkpiece on the history of base communities in the *Bolletino di collegamenti*, the anonymous author offered a similar assessment of the September 1969 Bologna convention: 'The assembly took place under the sign of the most unrestrained spontaneity. [...] In Bologna boundless enthusiasm, chaotic illusions and spontaneist intoxication celebrated their small Olympics.'[96] Was there no end in sight to the rapidly quickening cycle of radicalization affecting all segments of Italian society, especially with respect to its Catholic component? After the separation of ecclesially oriented groups from their most politicized comrades in late 1968, did history begin to repeat itself? As it so happened, from the point of view of mainstream conservative Catholics, in some very concrete ways the worst was yet to come. And it happened in Florence.

FLORENTINE EXCEPTIONALISMS

Florence is most famous throughout the world for its central role in the Italian Renaissance and the associated rich architecture and cultural heritage. Less well known outside Italy is its peculiar role within Italy's modern history.

---

[94] General information on the First National Assembly of Christian Communities can be found in 'L'Assemblea nazionale delle comunità cristiane', *Testimonianze* 12 (no. 117), September 1969, p. 617.

[95] Luciano Martini, 'Verso un nuovo messianismo?', *Testimonianze* 12 (no. 117), September 1969, p. 629.

[96] 'Dove va il movimento di base?', p. 9.

Focusing merely on Florentine history since World War II, one must note the vanguard role of Florence in the closing months of the Nazi occupation, the first instance in the long march of Allied troops from Sicily to Südtirol when the Anglo-American forces, upon entering a major city, discovered a fully functioning city administration already in full control of operations. The Tuscan National Liberation Committee (CTLN), the force behind the self-administration of Florence which puzzled Allied strategists, was heavily influenced by the presence of leading intellectuals and activists of the radical democratic Partito d'Azione, and it was little surprise that the most concerted effort by post-liberation civil authorities to give a prominent place to the network of National Liberation Committees within the structures of post-liberation Italy emerged from the activist circles within the CTLN. The important, if short-lived, Partito d'Azione would leave a lasting mark on the intellectual atmosphere of the city on the Arno, symbolized perhaps most markedly by the national and international radiance of a journal like *Il ponte*.[97]

Catholicism in Florence likewise displayed an unusual vitality, no doubt facilitated by the fortunate appointment by Pius XI of Elia Dalla Costa as archbishop of Florence, a post which this close friend of Angelo Roncalli held from 1931 until his death in 1961. The protective hand of Elia Dalla Costa permitted the formation of a series of nonconformist experiments and created sufficient free space for the relatively unhindered projects of reform-minded individuals even in the dark decades of Pius XII's pontificate.[98] The internationally most renowned figurehead of Florentine progressive Catholicism was no doubt Giorgio La Pira, from 1950 to 1956 and 1960 to 1964 mayor of the city on the ticket of DC. His keen attention to the social dimension of Catholic teachings ensured his popularity amongst the popular classes of Florentine society. As mentioned already in Chapter 1, a series of high-powered East–West peace initiatives, with leading politicians from both sides of the Iron Curtain benefiting from Florentine hospitality to explore and forge personal ties with their respective counterparts—and this in the middle of the Cold

[97] See, notably, the two-volume study by Ettore Rotelli, *La ricostruzione in Toscana dal CLN ai partiti* (Bologna: Il Mulino, 1980–1), on these points, but also two superb document collections which cast vivid light on the conjuncture of 1944/5 in the Tuscan capital city: the two-volume edited collection by Roger Absalom (ed.), *Gli Alleati e la ricostruzione in Toscana (1944–1945). Documenti Anglo-Americani* (Florence: Olschki, 1988 and 2001), and another two-volume compendium edition: Pier Luigi Ballini (ed.), *La Nazione del Popolo. Organo del Comitato Toscano di Liberazione Nazionale (11 agosto 1944–3 luglio 1946)* (Florence: Regione Toscana, 1998).
[98] Bruna Bocchini Camaiani, *Ricostruzione concordataria e processi di secolarizzazione. L'azione pastorale di Elia Dalla Costa* (Bologna: Il Mulino, 1983), comes closest to a biography of this important and remarkable figure in Florentine and Italian Catholic history, though it does not cover the crucial period from 1954 until his death in 1961.

War!—firmly established the reputation of Florence as a city of peace. Predictably, it also led to criticisms of La Pira by the Catholic hierarchy including DC.[99]

Florence provided a more favourable environment—certainly as long as Elia Dalla Costa was in control—to the free development of perhaps a higher number of prescient reform-oriented progressive Catholic intellectuals and activists than any other single Italian city. One of the most famous Italian Catholic writers, David Maria Turoldo, spent a half-dozen of his crucial mid-career years in Tuscany's capital city. Ernesto Balducci spent most of his adult years in or near Florence, as did the brilliant parish priest and educator, Don Lorenzo Milani, whose 1967 *Lettere a una professoressa* became the bible of the Italian student movement and was rapidly translated into forty-odd languages. Don Bruno Borghi, an ordained parish priest, with the approval of Elia Dalla Costa, for some years in the 1950s took up full-time industrial labour and, though a lone ranger in the Italy of the 1950s, he is therefore sometimes regarded as Italy's first worker priest. Don Luigi Rosadoni, an increasingly restless and activist parish priest, played a major role in the spread of German and Dutch post-conciliar theology into Italy. Rosadoni co-founded one of the most visible of the Florentine base communities, the Comunità di Risurrezione, and became one of the animators of the *Bolletino di collegamenti*. Another one in this hall of fame of open-minded innovators was Don Enzo Mazzi, born in Borgo San Lorenzo to the north of Florence, who in 1954 at the age of 27 was appointed parish priest in a brand-new neighbourhood still mostly on the drawing board of city planners. The neighbourhood was the Isolotto, and a dozen years after Don Enzo took up his post, the Isolotto became to second wave European Left Catholicism what the Besançon watch factory LIP became for the post-1968 European New and Far Left: the internationally most famous and infamous location of visionary conflicts—in this case between Left Catholic grassroots communities and the various levels of the church hierarchy.

THE MAKING OF A BASE COMMUNITY

The Isolotto housing complex constituted one element in the remarkable series of social housing projects launched in 1949 by the Italian national government, notably promoted by the Minister of Labour, Amintore Fanfani, and then adapted to Florentine conditions by the first post-liberation mayor of the Tuscan capital, the Communist Party's Mario Fabiani. The neighbourhood,

[99] There exists an abundance of literature on this dynamic and nonconformist Catholic professor of law, antifascist, and tireless peace activist. For two highly recommended introductory biographies, see note 134 in Chapter 1.

gradually emerging between 1954 and 1961, was built on the outskirts of Florence, on the left bank of the Arno, downstream from the city centre. When Don Enzo took up his post in November 1954, there was literally no social, transport, educational, or commercial infrastructure providing services to the construction zone which gradually saw its population grow as apartment complexes were finished. One of the first projects tackled by Don Enzo was thus a makeshift social club organized in an abandoned factory, allowing space for a day-care centre, assembly halls, a library, and facilities to provide after-school coaching for the schoolchildren of socially disadvantaged families for whom the Isolotto would become a new home. In December 1957, a new church was consecrated, showcasing an innovative interior design, with the altar as the centrepiece to allow maximum interaction with the parishioners, a prescient anticipation of the liturgical innovations a few years later introduced by Vatican II. The Isolotto parish church was a joint project of the architects and Don Enzo Mazzi, with the benevolent assent of Elia Dalla Costa.

The young parish priest, outgoing and vivacious, soon forged close links with his parishioners, and the Isolotto parish rapidly developed an intensive community life, with hands-on Bible study a solid anchor, a relative rarity in the Italy of the 1950s. In July 1957, Don Sergio Gomiti joined Enzo Mazzi as vicar, with Don Paolo Caciolli replacing Don Gomiti when the latter took up a post as parish priest in a similar newly built neighbourhood adjoining the Isolotto between 1965 and 1968. The young team quickly began to involve volunteer parishioners in various tasks that were not part of strictly sacerdotal functions. More remarkably yet, Don Mazzi and his team broke with the venerable pecuniary tradition of the Catholic church which stipulates as a matter of course a system of fees for sacerdotal services rendered, such as the dispensation of the sacraments, the celebration of special masses, and the like. Most astoundingly, when individual parishioners proffered donations, the parish priests politely but consistently declined such favours. The idea was to recreate the true spirit of Christian communitarian ethics, where Christian love rather than material advantages would constitute the foundation of parish life.

Soon the Isolotto parish priests began to de-emphasize and then quietly ignore a number of non-essential, decorative elements of traditional Italian Catholic liturgy, utilizing the resulting extra time and space for an ever-greater involvement of the parishioners. The preparation of Sunday sermons was eventually no longer the exclusive preoccupation of the parish priest in his study chamber. Every Thursday evening, at first a restricted number of lay people—by the mid-1960s all parishioners—were invited to join an assembly of interested parties in order to discuss ideas and eventually to determine the content of Holy Mass for the following Sunday. The idea for such assemblies can be traced back to a particular moment in late 1958/early 1959 when a factory employing many parishioners announced a massive wave of lay-offs.

The workforce decided to stage a sit-in of the targeted Galileo factory, the struggle intensified, and the need soon arose for a general assembly of the affected workforce. On 11 January 1959 a huge crowd of Galileo workers and their families met in the spacious church placed at the disposal of the workforce by Don Mazzi and Don Gomiti. The general assembly was presided over by one of the laid-off workers. An idea had been born, though it took the intervening years—and the additional inspiration by Vatican II—for it to mature.

On 15 April 1965, while the world's bishops were still deliberating in Rome, the first general assembly of the Isolotto community took place. It was a family event with hundreds of people in attendance. Anyone who wished to speak was encouraged to do so. There were no restrictions placed on the possible topics for discussion. Weekly assemblies now became regular features of parish life for the ensuing two years. Some sessions were devoted to the discussion of specific texts. In the spring of 1967, *Populorum Progressio*, the most progressive post-conciliar encyclical, penned by Pope Paul VI in that brief honeymoon phase of progressive Catholicism when the spirit of Vatican II was not yet disturbed by the complications of global 1968, became the chosen topic. Don Enzo Mazzi decided to invite Giorgio La Pira to present the document for discussion by the enthusiastic parishioners. This is when the Florentine Catholic hierarchy decided to put a preliminary end to one of the most successful apostolates in a working-class community in all of Italy.

Elia Dalla Costa was replaced by Ermenegildo Florit in 1961 upon Dalla Costa's death. Florit had been parachuted into Florence by the conservative Pius XII in 1954 as an assistant to Dalla Costa. In reality he was to serve as a conservative watchdog to restrain the liberal instincts by Elia Dalla Costa, who had become one of the *bêtes noires* of Pius XII. The Comunità dell'Isolotto to this day is fond of recalling the words they claim were uttered in the Florence Duomo during the official welcoming ceremony of Florit presided over by Dalla Costa: 'I present to you the new bishop who has been sent to me from Rome without me having asked for him.'[100] Eleven years later, having replaced Dalla Costa as head of the Florentine Catholic church, Ermenegildo Florit forbade Enzo Mazzi to continue with his plans to have lay members of the parish discuss the papal encyclical in the open assembly inside the Isolotto church. In telephone conversations the very morning of the planned assembly, Ermenegildo Florit suggested to Don Mazzi to move the event to a cinema, if the parish really felt that it was necessary to go through with such plans. Don Enzo retorted that there was no cinema within walking distance of the Isolotto neighbourhood. Florit then proposed a compromise solution. Giorgio La Pira

---

[100] As reported by Sergio Gomiti in a conversation with the author on 21 February 2012. The words in the original Italian are: 'Vi presento il nuovo vescovo che mi hanno mandato da Roma senza che io l'abbia chiesto.'

was allowed to address the crowd, but no parishioners were permitted to speak. 'Lay people are not allowed to speak in a church.' The event took place that afternoon as mandated by the representative of the church. But the battlelines were now drawn. The general assemblies, by then regular and cherished features of parish life, were suspended until further notice. The People of God had been forbidden to speak in the House of God by a Vicar of Christ.

THE CONSEQUENCES OF A FLOOD

A few months prior to this preliminary showdown between the emerging Comunità dell'Isolotto and Archbishop Florit, on 4 November 1966, the city of Florence was devastated by a massive inundation of many low-lying parts of the city, notably including the historic city centre. A spontaneous national effort to help dig the city out from underneath the muck and rubble imme-diately got under way, with young people in particular flocking to the city to help out.[101] More importantly, with the city administration in disarray, self-help neighbourhood committees sprang up throughout the city, and in fact for a number of all-important weeks, clean-up and reconstruction work was effectively in the hands of these *comitati di quartiere*. In these committees, members of all political families worked in close daily contact, and for Catholics in particular it became a formative moment in breaking down the barriers between themselves and secular left-wing political parties. A similar learning process affected grassroots activists of the Left, who, faced with the timidity of the Centre Left municipal government in late 1966, went as far as spontaneously occupying empty houses throughout the city to provide ac-commodation for families made homeless by the flood. 'Very many progres-sive Catholic groups drew a lasting lesson from this process. They regained the sense of a commitment towards engagement with politics and an awareness of their ability to rely on themselves and to be able to take decisions on their own without delegating their powers to anyone else.'[102]

When the immediate crisis situation abated, the neighbourhood commis-sions did not disappear but, instead, refocused their activities on other

---

[101] An early scene in Marco Tullio Giordana's landmark film on the generation of the *sessantotto*, *La meglio gioventù* (Italy, 2003) emphasizes the enthusiasm and voluntary engage-ment by young Italians on this occasion, which evoked sympathy and interest far beyond the borders of the Italian state. The US folk singer Phil Ochs notably composed a song called 'The Floods of Florence'.

[102] Bruno D'Avanzo, *Tra dissenzo e rivoluzione. Gruppi cristiani a Firenze* (Bologna: Guaraldi, 1971), pp. 69–77, devotes an important chapter to the consequences of the flood; citation on p. 73.

pressing needs. The need to provide after-school coaching for schoolchildren soon emerged as a priority and the neighbourhood committees turned educators. Powerfully reinforced by the May 1967 publication of *Lettere a una professoressa*, soon a network of *doposcuole* covered the city, strongest in the socially disadvantaged neighbourhoods on the outskirts of the city.[103] The *doposcuola* in the Isolotto neighbourhood emerged as a showcase example of a particularly successful after-school project, accepted and supported by a significant cross-section of neighbourhood families, yet another proof of the successful construction of a community spirit by Enzo Mazzi, Sergio Gomiti, and Paolo Caciolli.

A COMMUNITY IN OPEN BATTLE

Then, on Sunday, 15 September 1968, Holy Mass in the church of the Isolotto was followed, as usual, by a discussion and conversation involving parishioners. This time the occupation of the cathedral in Parma of the night before, carried out by forty members of a Parma base community (see Chapter 4), dominated the discussion. Isolotto parishioners were particularly outraged by the decision of the priest officiating Holy Mass in Parma cathedral to call on the police to have the youthful activists evicted, causing a scene which filled the front pages of newspapers across Italy. No longer strangers to forthright initiatives, the Isolotto parishioners thus resolved to draw up a letter of solidarity with the Parma protesters. The next day, a committee was formed to draft such a letter. Signed by 'four priests and 102 lay Catholics of Florence', the letter was approved by the assembled parishioners and sent 'To the Christian Assembly which has occupied the Duomo di Parma', with carbon copies sent to the bishop of Parma and the pope. In subsequent days thousands more signatures were collected. The letter had the effect of a bombshell in the middle of a major windstorm![104]

Cardinal Florit sent a letter to Don Enzo Mazzi on 30 September 1968 expressing his condemnation of such an open defiance of church authorities.

[103] Again, Bruno D'Avanzo, *Tra dissenzo*, devotes a crucial chapter to this experience on pp. 79–103; but note also Benito Incatasciato, *Dalla scuola al quartiere. Gruppi di base e intervento nella scuola. Il movimento di 'scuola e quartiere' a Firenze 1968–1973* (Rome: Riuniti, 1975).

[104] Copies of this letter and most documents referred to in the subsequent paragraphs can be consulted in Alceste Santini (ed.), *Il Cardinale contestato. Da Parma al Isolotto* (Rome: Religione oggi, 1968), pp. 50–5; Marco Boato (ed.), *Contro la chiesa di classe. Documenti della contestazione ecclesiale in Italia* (Padua: Marsiglia, 1969), pp. 237–40; and Comunità dell'Isolotto (ed.), *Isolotto 1954/1969* (Bari: Laterza, 1971), pp. 152–6—in what follows I have relied on the comments and documents in this mass market paperback edition printed and first published in February 1969, which publicized the case of the Isolotto throughout Italy.

He gave Don Enzo one month to reconsider this insubordinate act. In case Don Enzo did not see fit to publicly retract his action, the Florentine arch-bishop threatened to remove Don Enzo as parish priest of the Isolotto. Mazzi, Gomiti, and Caciolli immediately realized the severity of this threat by their superior. The Comunità dell'Isolotto now decided to regroup. In a series of assemblies held in the parish church, they decided to draft an open letter to all parishioners in which the issues were restated and everyone was invited to attend a General Assembly in the parish church on Thursday, 31 October 1968, the deadline of Cardinal Florit's ultimatum, at 21:15. This 'Letter to Parishioners' further upped the ante, as could be surmised. On the morning of 23 October, the main daily newspaper of Florence, *La nazione*, appeared with the front-page headline 'Don Mazzi Disowned by the Cardinal', next to a large photo of the parish priest. Within days the case of the recalcitrant and insurgent Comunità dell'Isolotto became headline news throughout Italy, with e.g. the Rome *Il messagero*, the Milan *Corriere della sera*, and the Vatican's own *Osservatore romano* providing detailed—if rather partial—news coverage.

On the evening of 31 October an overflow of several thousand people crowded the Isolotto parish church and the neighbourhood. After an intro-ductory statement by Don Enzo, a large number of parishioners took to the floor. An eight-point summary of the proceedings expressed the community's solidarity with their parish priest and stated 'our decisive disapproval of any condemnation or other such authoritarian interruption of our experiences and our parish project', which had been constructed in fifteen years of concen-trated efforts.[105] On 6 November 1968, 108 parish priests of the Florence diocese signed a joint letter to Cardinal Florit, pointing out the democratic deficit of the Florentine diocese, which had, they argued, been kept isolated from the spirit of Vatican II, the Florentine priests enjoining the archbishop to reconsider his course of action with regard to the Isolotto and Don Mazzi. The deadline came and passed without any further action initiated by Florit. Then, on 14 November, arrived a last written warning by Cardinal Florit. On 20 November, the Comunità dell'Isolotto responded with a restatement of their unaltered firm position. Florit then engaged in one more diplomatic manoeuvre. He invited Don Mazzi for a face-to-face meeting. The Comunità dell'Isolotto decided to have a lay delegation and the other two priests accompanying Don Mazzi. After a lengthy and fruitless exchange of opinion, Florit asked all others except Don Mazzi to leave the premises. A short, hostile, verbal altercation ensued between Don Mazzi and Florit, ending by Florit pulling out a prepared letter in which the destitution of Don Mazzi as parish priest was proclaimed. Ermenegildo Florit then ostentatiously signed the

---

[105] Comunità dell'Isolotto (ed.), *Isolotto*, p. 223.

decree in front of Don Mazzi. The official act arrived in the post on 4 December 1968.

The next day, 5 December 1968, all elementary and middle schools in the Isolotto neighbourhood shut down in a protest strike promoted by the parents and teachers of these community schools. At ten o'clock in the morning the Isolotto parish church filled with an enraged crowd, and one pupil after another took the microphone to propose concrete actions. By 3 p.m. a crowd of hundreds of schoolchildren, mothers, and teachers began a protest march to the archbishop's seat in downtown Florence. At the head of the demonstrations hastily put together banners proclaimed: 'What are the people within the Church? Everything. How much do we count? For nothing. What do we want? At least something.' After a five-minute silent prayer outside the archbishop's office, whose windows had been firmly shut, the crowd then moved through the city streets to the Duomo and then Santa Maria Novella, proudly displaying as their central slogan: 'One can remove a priest but not a people!'[106] On 6 December, Sergio Gomiti stepped down as parish priest in the La Casella parish next to the Isolotto in an act of open solidarity with Don Mazzi. On 8 December 1968, a Sunday, no mass was held in the Isolotto parish church; instead a protest march of considerable proportions left the Isolotto neighbourhood for the archbishop's residence. Before returning home in light and steady rain, the demonstrators lined up their placards and banners against the main entry to the world-famous Duomo and in the staircase of the archiepiscopal palace to bear witness to the curia's attempt to crush a vibrant parish which had become an extraordinarily successful base community of huge proportions.

A flood of letters now arrived in the Comunità dell'Isolotto, expressing in often moving and heartfelt terms the solidarity of Catholics from all over Italy and Europe, often taking the form of collective letters signed by up to several dozen individuals at a time. Fifty-seven students at the Collegio Universitario Augustinianum of the Catholic University of Milan expressed their support in a letter sent on 5 December. Thirty-three seminary students from Trento sent their letter on 9 December. On 11 December a collective letter by 'The Students of the Theological Institute in Utrecht' was posted in the Netherlands. Countless individual letters poured in as well—such as a handwritten letter by 'Christoph Hahn, Amsterdam', in which the author asked Don Enzo for advice on how he could best help out: 'If you wish, we will occupy a church in solidarity with you.' A few days after Cardinal Florit's action, a petition to demand the dismissal of Florit was launched by parishioners in the Isolotto neighbourhood, spreading like wildfire throughout

---

[106] 'Cosa è il popolo nella Chiesa? TUTTO. Cosa conta? NULLA. Cosa vogliamo che conti? QUALCOSA', in Comunità dell'Isolotto (ed.), *Isolotto*, p. 264; the other slogan is on p. 265.

Florence, Tuscany, and Italy, gathering more than 20,000 signatures in one month.[107] There was little room left for compromise.

The most contentious issue now became the question of the future of Sunday church service. On Saturday, 14 December, the vicar mandated by Florit to preside over Holy Mass, Bruno Panerai, announced that mass would be offered in a nearby church, avoiding the thorny issue of what would become of the Isolotto church. On Sunday, 15 December, then, close to 2,000 faithful filled the Isolotto parish church for a reading from the Bible, as Mazzi was no longer allowed to hold Mass. On 20 December, Don Enzo Mazzi received a letter written by Pope Paul VI, the latter, in an unprecedented move, trying one last-ditch effort to conciliate the opposing camps. Then, on Sunday, 22 December, the hierarchy upped the stakes. Two emissaries sent by Florit celebrated Mass that day within the Isolotto parish church. No more than fifty persons were in attendance, half of them from outside the Isolotto parish. When the two priests left the church after the service was over, 2,000 faithful parishioners immediately filled the church for a prayer session. A game of cat and mouse began.

Christmas passed with Mass being held in the Isolotto church by emissaries representing the hierarchy. On 26 December, José María González Ruiz addressed the crowd inside the church, a courageous act of solidarity by the fearless theologian of international renown. On 29 December, the curia offered several Masses, each one attracting a paltry twenty to fifty individuals. In between Holy Mass, assemblies of the Comunità were held in the church, with the crowd of up to 1,500 parishioners either leaving the church or remaining in silent prayer when the curia's vicars arrived to hold the official ceremonies. On New Year's Day, at 10:30 a.m., more than 1,000 parishioners filled the church for a Bible reading. When the archiepiscopal emissary arrived to celebrate Mass, all but thirty persons got up and left the church. At noon, 5 p.m., and 7 p.m., the identical scenario repeated itself.

FROM COLD WAR TO OPEN CONFLICT

On Sunday, 5 January 1969, a new escalation occurred. Early church services at 7 a.m. and 9 a.m. were celebrated without incident. At 10:30 a.m., a crowd of

---

[107] Out of this substantial number, 5,408 were collected in Florence city and the province of Florence. Attentive readers of Chapter 2 will not be surprised to note that the greatest number of non-Italian signatures arrived from the Netherlands. I first learned of this remarkable initiative in a conversation with Sergio Gomiti on 22 February 2012. For the letter from the Collegio Augustinianum students, see Archivio Storico dell'Isolotto (ACI) [Florence], LT 0248; for the Trento letter, see LT 0334; the Utrecht letter is in LT 0352; and for the Christoph Hahn missive, LT 0328.

close to 2,000 parishioners arrived for a prayer session. At 11 a.m., Florit's representative, Don Alba, took the microphone announcing the beginning of Holy Mass. As had happened repeatedly before, the crowd remained silently in the church. Then, suddenly, a loud voice was heard from somewhere within the crowd: 'Under these conditions we do not wish to celebrate Mass.' Alba retorted that he did not wish to be kept from celebrating Mass by a minority of discontent. He was immediately challenged to furnish proof of his allegation, and thus Don Alba approached the microphone and exhorted the parishioners: 'Who does not wish for Mass to be celebrated, do raise your hand.'[108] It was a classic faux pas of a clueless representative of the Florentine curia. For now the unexpected did in fact occur. In complete silence, 2,000 hands went up. Alba gathered his vestments and left the building. On 6 January, the church of the Isolotto parish filled with representatives of base communities from all across Italy, who came to express their gratitude for the courageous stance of the Comunità dell'Isolotto and to demonstrate their solidarity. On 23 January 1969, the Comunità dell'Isolotto had to hand over their keys to the parish church to representatives of the Florentine curia in a highly charged and emotional act inside their church.

On 14 January 1969 the civil judiciary joined forces with the curia. Five priests from outside Florence—amongst them Vittorino Merinas of Turin's Comunità del Vandalino—and eleven Isolotto lay parishioners now stood accused of breach of the peace, instigation to commit unlawful acts, 'obscene language', and 'the disturbance of religious functions of the Catholic Church'. On 30 January 1969, the Comunità responded with an open letter, sent to the state prosecutor in Florence, signed by 702 Isolotto residents, claiming full co-responsibility for all acts supposedly committed by the sixteen accused scapegoats. The state responded by indicting a further 438 individuals, an apparently random selection of the signatories. The defence of the accused in this mass show trial now used up enormous amounts of the energy of the parishioners and solidarity activists elsewhere in Italy. In July 1970, the presiding judge granted an amnesty to eighty of the accused, i.e. to all those accused who had been either under eighteen years of age at the moment of their 'crimes' or over seventy years of age. In the end, five priests and four lay parishioners had to stand trial from 3 May to 5 July 1971, the trial ending in a full acquittal of all of the accused.[109]

In the meantime, however, the Comunità dell'Isolotto continued its fight against the curia. Space is insufficient to fully address the vicissitudes of the community's exemplary struggle which had become by then a national and,

---

[108] Comunità dell'Isolotto (ed.), *Isolotto*, p. 320.
[109] Two book-length publications cover the judicial nightmare undergone by the Comunità dell'Isolotto and their sympathizers: Comunità dell'Isolotto (ed.), *Isolotto sotto processo* (Bari: Laterza, 1971), published in April 1971 and thus before the trial itself, and the recent Comunità dell'Isolotto (ed.), *Il processo dell'Isolotto* (Roma: manifestolibri, 2011).

indeed, international cause célèbre. One further escalation of the unequal tug of war cannot be kept from the interested reader. For, although it may be difficult to imagine this, things heated up even further by the summer of 1969. No more Masses had been held inside the church since the fateful showdown of 5 January. Instead, during the first half of 1969, the Comunità dell'Isolotto regularly held prayer sessions in the open air outside the church. Slowly but surely these outdoor assemblies began to address more than merely religious issues, and the Sunday gatherings became occasions for other struggling communities in Italy, such as workers from blue-collar communities engaged in fightbacks, or spokespersons for the South African liberation movements, or Greek students reporting on their resistance against military dictatorship, to make their case. The Isolotto neighbourhood became an organizing centre of resistance to the combined powers of the curia and the state. Enzo Mazzi and Sergio Gomiti in turn formed part of the crowd of rebellious priests who attempted to lobby the 7–10 July 1969 assembly of European bishops in Chur, Switzerland (see Chapter 2). Beleaguered by the large pool of journalists, the two Florentine priests, after first refusing the honour, held a news conference on the final day of the Chur assembly, with 150 journalists from all over the world eagerly snapping up the information provided by the Florentine priests.

On 20 July 1969, then, the Comunità dell'Isolotto took a further qualitative and unprecedented step by celebrating Mass in the open air, presided over by priests from outside the Isolotto neighbourhood. Such an act of provocation could not pass without a response by the hierarchy. Cardinal Florit now threatened Don Mazzi, Don Gomiti, and Don Caciolli to revoke their ordination. Hitherto, Don Mazzi had been removed as parish priest of the Isolotto but had not lost the status of ordained priest. A period of negotiations behind the scenes ensued, and for a moment it appeared as if a total break might be avoided, with the rebel priests willing to consider compromise solutions. But the hard-line stance of Ermenegildo Florit gained the upper hand, and on 24 August the Comunità dell'Isolotto resumed its soon famous—or infamous, depending on one's point of view—*messe in piazza*. The ultimate showdown was near. On the evening of Saturday, 30 August, a spokesperson of the archbishop telephoned Don Mazzi to inform the Comunità that Cardinal Florit himself would come and celebrate Mass the following morning in the Isolotto parish church thus breaking through the impasse created by Don Alba's exit from the church on 5 January.

THE FINAL ASSAULT

Realizing that this act would constitute an irreversible breakdown in communications with far-reaching consequences, Don Enzo mobilized his resources.

A crowd began to gather at their headquarters and an automobile with loudspeakers toured the community's street from 10:40 p.m. onwards to announce the convocation of an Emergency General Assembly for 11 p.m. A dense crowd gathered, with many persons present having literally jumped out of bed to help determine a last-minute decision in the middle of the night. The—by now—seasoned activists decided to send a delegation composed of lay parishioners to the cardinal. This decision was quickly communicated to the cardinal's secretary, who was told to expect the delegation to ring the doorbell in an hour or two. The assembled members of the Comunità then drafted a statement. At 1 a.m. on Sunday morning, the letter to be presented to the cardinal finally met everyone's approval, and at 1:30 a.m. they arrived at the Villa Bifonica where the cardinal was staying that night. No one responded to their demands to be permitted entry to talk to Ermenegildo Florit. At 7 a.m. on Sunday morning, having waited outside the villa's doors all night, they were finally let in. Now ensued a most remarkable encounter in the history of the Florentine—and Italian!—church. It is not often that lay parishioners get to engage in a heated theological discussion with their archbishop.

The seven representatives—amongst them two women—handed Florit the Comunità's open letter drafted that night. In it, the Comunità provided a brief synopsis of the escalation in the preceding ten months and asked for the cardinal to make a gesture of appeasement. 'To celebrate mass together with you, our priests and our community in a symbolic gesture of reconciliation is the goal of all our efforts.' The cardinal read the letter and then addressed his interlocutors. Some excerpts of the memory protocol by the lay activists underscore what was at stake:

CARDINALE: This document is a piece of Marxist discourse. You do not constitute a Christian community, but you are a Christian spontaneous group, like there are so many others in the world today.

LAICO: We cannot accept that you deny us recognition as a Christian community.

CARDINALE: You are outside the Church because you are against me. Who is against their own bishop stands outside the Church.

LAICO: I would like you to explain to us what, then, constitutes the Church.

CARDINALE: The Church is the Pope, the bishops, the priests and the laity, the latter as constituent parts of the people of God.

LAICO: Well, then our priests do represent the Church.

CARDINALE: No, they are members of the Church, but they do not represent the Church. The only ones to represent the Church amongst you are the parish priests whom I nominated by means of the powers invested in me by God. Furthermore, your priests have been divested of their offices.

LAICO: If this is so, Eminence, give us our priests back and everything will be peaceful henceforth.

CARDINALE: This is absolutely impossible. [. . .]

[. . .]

LAICO: Eminence, your words are too harsh and unsustainable for us. We implore you to think about this and to stop by our assembly outside the church on the way to celebrate Mass and to offer us another response.

CARDINALE: A bishop cannot stop by open-air assemblies to give speeches to the crowd. I speak very little, and I speak only as a pastor, only in church.

At 10 a.m. that morning, the open space around the church was teeming with people. When the account of that morning's failed mission was read aloud, there ensued 'a dramatic moment of tension and indescribable pain, with many crying'. Yet the lowest point was reached when the cardinal arrived and entered the church, 'escorted by dozens of plainclothes police'. Apart from a handful of residents of the Isolotto, many groups of outsiders, unknown to the parishioners, had been shipped in to fill the benches of the church, some of them known local neo-fascists. When the cardinal entered, 'triumphalist songs were chanted within the church, which no one in the community had ever heard before, because such songs are never used in our parish'. The Comunità had resolved to stay outside in absolute silence, but in the face of the victory chants from inside the church, Don Enzo began to read narratives of the Passion, picked up and continued by the ten or so other priests present in the devastated crowd. When Cardinal Florit left the church after mass, his exit under police protection was accompanied by applause and chants of *Hallelujah* by the loyalist supporters of Florit. A stunned crowd of 3,000 watched in absolute silence and total despair as the cardinal stepped into the waiting car and drove off, without so much as a word addressed to or a gesture of benediction towards the assembled crowd.[110]

The Comunità dell'Isolotto, after this showdown, resumed its *messe in piazza*, with Mass often celebrated by visiting priests from elsewhere in Italy, Europe, and the world—including two Latin American archbishops—for many more years. In fact, *messe in piazza* were held outside the Isolotto church on a regular basis until the summer of 2005. Don Enzo himself, the chief target of the wrath of the Florentine curia, did not celebrate Mass until Christmas 1969 when he first did so together with Bruno Borghi and José María González Ruiz. The Comunità dell'Isolotto continued to function as a viable community, despite being forced to relinquish its church. On 14 June 1970, First Communion was celebrated in an impressive stage-managed setting in the Piazza dell'Isolotto; on 4 October 1970 the first marriage was

---

[110] The remarkable events of 30 and 31 August 1969, including the letter drawn up by the Comunità after midnight and the memory protocol—as well as the account of the Sunday morning confrontation outside the Isolotto parish church—are taken from the bulletin published by the Comunità dell'Isolotto, *Notiziario della Comunità Parrochiale dell'Isolotto*, No. 4 (September 1969).

consecrated in open air. Paolo Caciolli, who had already taken up full-time industrial labour in a Florentine manufacturing plant in 1967, eventually emigrated to Germany to make a living as a blue-collar worker and to start a family. Enzo Mazzi began working in small factories making electrical goods in 1969, then studied for a diploma and took his exams to become an elementary school teacher. Sergio Gomiti, still at the heart of the Comunità today and its competent chief archivist, from 1970 until his retirement in 1996 worked for the LAT Cooperative, charged with cleaning and reconstituting books of the Florentine branch of the National Library, devastated by the November 1966 flood.[111] The Comunità dell'Isolotto, like a number of other Italian base communities, continues to operate today. In fact, along with Spanish base communities, Italian *comunità di base* are some of the most active national networks even today, roughly fifty years after their emergence parallel to and—more forcefully—in the wake of Vatican II.

---

[111] Most of the information in this paragraph was provided by Urbano Cipriani, after consultation with Sergio Gomiti, in email communications to the author, dated 27 November and 30 November 2013.

Figure 1. General Assembly in the Isolotto parish church, 31 October 1968

Note the central place of Don Enzo Mazzi at the microphone, the parish priest purposefully placed in the middle of the church, surrounded by the parishioners. The church was expressly designed to convey the participatory atmosphere and reality of this young parish.

Figure 2. Protest demonstration from the Isolotto neighbourhood to the city centre, 8 December 1968

Figure 3. Protest demonstration from the Isolotto neighbourhood to the city centre, 8 December 1968

Rally in front of archbishop's palace at the end of the demonstration and march from the Isolotto neighbourhood to the city centre on 8 December 1968.

Figure 4. Protest demonstration from the Isolotto neighbourhood to the city centre, 8 December 1968

Demonstrators and their placards in front of archbishop's palace, 8 December 1968. Note some of the inscriptions: 'Bishop: Without Your Authoritarianism We Would All Be True Christians'—'Christ Was Born a Poor Person, Not a Cardinal'—'To Judge a People It is First Necessary to Get to Know It'.

Figure 5. Protest demonstration from the Isolotto neighbourhood to the city centre, 8 December 1968

Placard at 8 December 1968 march and rally: '[Archbishop] Florit—Serve Us as Pastor, Not Censor'.

Figure 6. Protest demonstration from the Isolotto neighbourhood to the city centre, 8 December 1968

At the end of 8 December 1968 march and rally, the protesters left their placards on the steps leading up to the archbishop's residence in central Florence, next to the Duomo.

Figure 7. Scene in the Isolotto parish church, 5 January 1969

Scene during the highly emotional and important events of 5 January 1969 in the Isolotto parish church, when it came to the final clash between the Florentine church hierarchy and the Isolotto parishioners.

Figure 8. Scene in the Isolotto parish church, 5 January 1969

A crucial moment in the contestations of 5 January 1969 in the Isolotto parish church. The photo was taken immediately after Don Alba asked the assembled parishioners: 'Who does not wish for mass to be celebrated, do raise your hand.'

Figure 9. Isolotto parish church, 23 January 1969

On 23 January 1969, the Isolotto parishioners had to hand over their keys to their church to Florentine archiepiscopal authorities. When this act of surrender occurred in the church, parishioners spontaneously took their own personal house keys out of their pockets and waved them in the air, suggesting that perhaps the church's keys had to be given away, but that the parishioners would remain the masters of their own destiny. Note the joyous, almost exuberant, expressions on parishioners' faces (as in the previous photo).

Figure 10. Outside the Isolotto parish church, 26 January 1969

From 23 January 1969 onwards, for some years, parishioners gathered in front of their closed parish church, initially in utter disbelief and shock. The photo was taken on the first Sunday after the closure of the Isolotto church: 26 January 1969.

Figure 11. General assembly outside the Isolotto parish church, 15 July 1969

One of the regular general assemblies of the parishioners outside their parish church from which they had been excluded, this one on 15 July 1969. Up to this moment, no Mass had been held in the open, 'only' the general assemblies.

Figure 12. Archbishop Florit takes possession of the Isolotto parish church, 31 August 1969

Another crucial escalation of the Isolotto conflict: Archbishop Ermenegildo Florit enters the Isolotto church to take possession at 10 a.m. on 31 August 1969, accompanied by two policemen in uniform and a representative of the Florence police headquarters (in civilian clothes, with dark glasses).

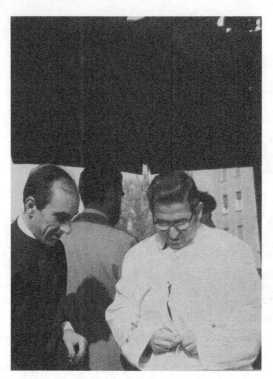

Figure 13. Outside the Isolotto parish church, 19 October 1969

Don Enzo Mazzi and José María González Ruiz at the occasion of a joint celebration of Mass on the square outside the Isolotto parish church, 19 October 1969. Of all internationally famous theologians, González Ruiz stood closest to the grassroots rebels of the Isolotto parish.

Figure 14. Outside the Isolotto parish church, 14 June 1970

The first public celebration of First Communion in the square outside the Isolotto parish church, 14 June 1970.

Figure 15. Second National Convention of 'Sette Novembre', Rome, 26 January 1974

Roberto Berton addresses the Second National Convention of 'Sette Novembre', the Italian association of radical priests, held in Rome, 26 January 1974.

Figure 16. Second National Convention of 'Cristiani per il Socialismo', Naples, 1–4 November 1974

Audience scene during the Second National Convention of the Italian section of 'Christians for Socialism', held in Naples from 1 to 4 November 1974, assembling 2,500 interested individuals.

Figure 17. Convention of Italian worker priests, Serramazzoni (Modena), 3 January 1976

Italian worker priests, gathered for their Annual Convention in an Appenine mountain village, greet the emissary representing the Italian Assembly of Bishops, Cesare Pagani, with clenched fists and singing Victor Jara's 'Venceromos', Serramazzoni (Modena), 3 January 1976.

4

From Seminarians to Radical
Student Activists

THE HIDDEN CHRISTIANITY OF LEADING
STUDENT RADICALS

'Jesus has risen; joy and thankfulness are our companions for this day; the revolution, the decisive revolution of world history has occurred, the revolution of the world by means of all-conquering love. If human beings would only fully accept this manifest love as their guiding light, the reality of the here and now, the logic of insanity, could not survive much longer.'[1] This diary entry was written on Easter Sunday, 14 April 1963, by one of the world's best-known student leaders of the generation of 1968. In all likelihood, most students mobilizing behind this charismatic figure in West Germany had no clue that Rudi Dutschke was a committed lifelong Christian. And that he was—not only on Easter morning 1963. Dutschke joined the Situationist-inspired group, *Subversive Aktion*, in early 1964. In early 1965 he joined the West Berlin chapter of the Socialist German Student League (SDS), and he subsequently turned this organization upside down. It was between early 1965 and 11 April 1968, the date of Josef Bachmann's assault on Dutschke's life, that Dutschke was propelled to the forefront of Germany's sensationalist media to become the most revered and most reviled spokesperson of Germany's student-based New Left. Though Dutschke's Christianity was usually politely overlooked by his more secular comrades, it remained a central element of the mental universe of Dutschke, the revolutionary Marxist.[2] As late as 22 November 1967, for instance, on the occasion of the Prayer and Repentance Holiday, Dutschke participated in a panel debate in an overcrowded church on 'Politics v. Christian Utopia'. A Protestant minister present at the debate told Dutschke

---

[1] Rudi Dutschke, '14. April 1963', in Rudi Dutschke, *Jeder hat sein Leben ganz zu leben. Die Tagebücher 1963–1979* (Cologne: Kiepenheuer & Witsch, 2003), p. 17.
[2] On Dutschke's strong Christian beliefs up to April 1968, see Michaela Karl, *Rudi Dutschke. Revolutionär ohne Revolution* (Frankfurt: Neue Kritik, 2003), pp. 173–81.

on the spot: 'The best Dutschke I have ever seen.' Dutschke's role models defended at the debate were, surely to no one's surprise, Dietrich Bonhoeffer, Paul Tillich, and Camillo Torres.[3]

Rudi Dutschke was a Protestant, and his case may thus stand as a useful and important reminder that the world of Protestant Christianity was just as much affected by the turbulence of the 1960s and 1970s as was the Catholic community. My second example of a leading student radical whose religiosity is often overlooked refers to the cradle of the United States American student movement, the campus of the University of California in Berkeley which, in the autumn of 1964, saw the spontaneous outbreak of what quickly became called the Free Speech Movement (FSM). The role of spokesperson for the FSM was taken up in spontaneous fashion by Mario Savio, who became to Berkeley what Dutschke later on became for West Berlin. I cannot go into any details with regard to Savio or the FSM. All I want to do is cite two passages from an autobiographical text Savio presented in November 1995:

> I grew up as a Catholic. I was an altar boy. I was going to be a priest. Now, obviously, the eldest son in an Italian Catholic family was a person who would become a priest if anyone was going to be [that]—and I was going to be that person. My two aunts are nuns. I came into it from liberation theology. I read things that probably most people in this room have not read. I read Jacques Maritain, I read Emmanuel Mounier, I read things put out by Catholic Worker people; I was very much immersed in that sort of thing.[4]
>
> I was not a careerist. I was someone who took good and evil exceptionally seriously. [. . .] And, suddenly, there's the Civil Rights Movement. And since I'm breaking away from the Church, I see the Civil Rights Movement in religious terms. In the Civil Rights Movement there were all those ministers; it was just absolutely rife with ministers, bristling with ministers. And so, to me, this was an example of God working in the world.[5]

Savio had joined civil rights campaigns in California before enrolling as a volunteer for the trail-blazing Freedom Summer 1964 campaign in Mississippi. Having literally just returned from the Deep South at the moment when the University of California administration decided to infringe University of California students' right to free speech, Savio and other veterans of Mississippi Freedom Summer then threw all their energies into a campaign which they saw as closely related and to which they gave an unsurprisingly similar name: Free Speech Movement. Mario Savio's speech to the assembled crowd

---

[3] Dutschke, '22. November 1967', *Die Tagebücher*, p. 64.

[4] Mario Savio, 'Thirty Years Later', in Robert Cohen and Reginald E. Zelnik (eds.), *The Free Speech Movement. Reflections on Berkeley in the 1960s* (Berkeley: University of California Press, 2002), p. 59.

[5] Savio, 'Thirty Years Later', p. 61.

from the top of a police car on the Berkeley campus in September 1964 made him into an icon of the student movement around the world.[6]

TON REGTIEN AND THE NETHERLANDS

This brief introductory excursion into the world of Protestantism and the microcosm of the University of California at Berkeley is meant to underscore the near-universal relevance of religious motivation for socio-political dissent in the long sixties. Very similar patterns accounted for much of the dynamic behind student dissent in Catholic Europe. The Rudi Dutschke of the Netherlands, for instance, Ton Regtien, was fundamentally influenced by his upbringing in a proletarian Catholic family in Amsterdam. Born in 1938, he entered a priest seminary in Venlo to pursue what he had chosen as his life's vocation. After two years of study, he left the seminary to enrol in a Jesuit high school, where he formed a lifelong friendship with one of his teachers, Jan van Kilsdonk,[7] the latter in 1960 one of the founders of the (in)famous Amsterdamse Studentenekklesia and, when Septuagint got off the ground in 1968, a leading activist within this flagship association of radical priests.

Obtaining his high school diploma in 1959, Ton Regtien chose the Catholic University of Nijmegen for his university study of psychology. And it was in Nijmegen, the Dutch equivalent to Leuven south of the border, where Regtien began to frequent nonconformist milieux, after initial contact with the then-hegemonic traditionalist fraternities who controlled student politics in the Low Countries. Ton Regtien quickly emerged as a prolific writer for the campus newspaper, the *Nijmeegs Universiteits Blad* (*NUB*). A report on the French Union Nationale des Étudiants de France (UNEF) by Jan Banks, member of the Roomsch Katholieke Studenten Vereniging Sanctus Thomas Aquinas in Amsterdam, pointed to the UNEF as an alternative model for student politics, inspiring Ton Regtien to pen a series of widely read articles in the *NUB* in which he extolled the virtues of a trade union for university student concerns along the lines of the UNEF.[8] The *NUB* feature propelled the idea of a student trade union—the title of the series was *Studentenvakbe-*

---

[6] See Gerd-Rainer Horn, *The Spirit of '68. Rebellion in Western Europe and North America, 1956–1976* (Oxford: Oxford University Press, 2007), pp. 60–5.

[7] Background information on the personal–political itinerary of Antonius (Ton) Aegidius Regtien is culled from the biographical entry by Niek Pas in Historici.nl: <http://www.historici.nl/Onderzoek/Projecten/BWN/lemmata/bwn5/regtien>.

[8] Antoine Verbij, *Tien rode Jaren. Links radicalisme in Nederland 1970–1980* (Amsterdam: Ambo, 2005), p. 49.

weging—into the frontline of radical student politics, and a new movement, called Studentenvakbeweging (SVB) was born.[9]

The SVB first emerged at the Catholic University of Nijmegen, and Nijmegen remained a stronghold of this challenge to the dominant role of fraternities on Dutch campuses. Yet the SVB quickly spread to other campuses. At the time of the SVB's birth in 1963, virtually 100 per cent of the Nijmegen student body was Catholic, and the SVB can thus be rightfully regarded as a product of Catholic students in search of new organizational models at a time when Dutch Catholicism was in the vanguard of a renewal of the Catholic church (see Chapter 2). Yet the SVB platform contained few if any visible traces of Catholic social theory. In fact, the SVB was a classic by-product of the simultaneous process of radicalization and secularization affecting Dutch (and European) Catholicism in the course of the 1960s and beyond. The Nijmegen historians Jacques Janssens and Paul Voestermans suggest that 'the number of students who strayed from the path of their fathers' with regard to Sunday church attendance 'began to rise at the beginning of the 1960s, and by no means solely in Nijmegen'. By 1966, however, still 47.5 per cent of Nijmegen students regularly attended mass.[10]

By the time his plea for a *studentenvakbeweging* appeared in the pages of the *NUB*, Ton Regtien had already moved to Amsterdam, where he quickly emerged as the quintessential charismatic leader of the Dutch student Left. By this time, Regtien had got caught up in the whirlwind atmosphere of student radicalism, cultural nonconformity, and provocative challenges to any number of authorities. Church affairs were no longer a matter of Regtien's real concern, and it is difficult to reconstruct whether faith and religion still played important roles for Ton Regtien. Still, when Regtien died in late 1989, two passengers in the lead car following the hearse were his lifelong friend, Father Jan van Kilsdonk, and the *spiritus rector* of Septuagint, Jan Ruijter.[11]

The academic years 1967–8 and 1968–9 witnessed an intensification of student unrest. The rapidly expanding SVB had mutated into an association with a similar action repertoire to the West German and US American quintessential student organizations of the New Left, known by their identical acronyms: SDS. By April 1968 the SVB, in alliance with a somewhat more moderate group, had managed to gain control over the umbrella organization of Dutch university student associations, the Nederlandse Studentenraad.[12]

---

[9] On the first five years of the SVB, see Hugo Kijne, *Geschiedenis van de Nederlandse Studentenbeweging 1963–1973* (Amsterdam: SUA, 1978), pp. 37–68; but also Jacques Janssens and Paul Voestermans, *Studenten in beweging. Politiek, universiteit en student* (Nijmegen: Katholiek Studiecentrum, 1984), pp. 90–121.

[10] Janssens and Voestermans, *Studenten in beweging*, p. 117 (citation) and p. 119.

[11] Conversation with Jan Ruijter, 11 December 2013.

[12] For the hot phase of Dutch student radicalism in the years 1967–9, see Kijne, *Geschiedenis*, pp. 69–126, and Janssen and Voestermans, *Studenten in beweging*, pp. 122–66.

The final spark which led to a chain reaction of radical protest across the Netherlands was struck in Tilburg, 80 km to the southwest of Nijmegen, once again strongly suggesting an intimate link between Catholic sociabilities and societal revolt. For Tilburg was the home to another Catholic post-secondary institution of higher learning, the Katholieke Hogeschool Tilburg (KHT), and it was the KHT which became the first Dutch university to explode. As late as 1963, 83 per cent of all Tilburg students at the KHT attended regular Sunday Mass.[13]

The occasion for open battle to erupt in Tilburg arose in the context of an ongoing campus-wide debate on the democratization of university administration, with students asking for co-determination on all levels. In the late evening of 28 April 1969, students organized in the Links Front took over the assembly hall where the university senate had—at 8 p.m. that evening— decided to firmly reject the students' demands. The next morning, the university's telephone exchange was likewise taken over by an angry crowd. Still, by most accounts, the storm would have passed if the university president had not then decided to shut down the university in reaction to the student protest, a drastic measure which had not been taken at any Dutch university since the Nazi occupation of the Netherlands in World War II. Now the occupation began to get support from forces far beyond the hard core of left-wing activists. From 29 April to 7 May 1969, several thousand students occupied the key building of the Katholiek Hogeschool Tilburg and lessons were held, with the assistance of sympathizing instructors, in defiance of the university administration's closure notice, in a curious role reversal for radical campus politics.[14]

A compromise agreement between the contending factions put an end to this *novum* on Dutch university campuses, but in the meantime the movement had spread to other campuses. By the time the Tilburg students celebrated a partial victory, the frontlines hardened elsewhere. The toughest battles were fought in Amsterdam where students had applied the lessons of Tilburg and occupied the Maagdenhuis, the central university administration building of the University of Amsterdam. This occupation lasted from 12 to 21 May 1969, ending in a forcible eviction, and the rapid indictment and prosecution of 570 students. It would go too far to further describe the dynamics of the Dutch student revolt. The point is that it all began at a *Catholic* university, just like the radical SVB had first taken hold on the largest *Catholic* university campus in the Netherlands in Nijmegen.

---

[13] Janssen and Voestermans, *Studenten in beweging*, p. 119.
[14] Willem Franken and Frans Godfroy, 'Vallen en opstaan van een studentenbeweging', in Werkgroep Studentenoppositie (ed.), *De verRaden Universiteit. De Tilburgse Studentenbeweging 1965-1975* (Tilburg: Katholiek Hogeschool Tilburg, 1975), pp. 4–42.

To return briefly to Tilburg. In the course of this unprecedented bout of activism on the campus of the Katholieke Hogeschool, a rapid learning process fundamentally changed the hearts and minds of an entire cohort of students. 'The free-flowing atmosphere at the college [during the period of the occupation], the intensive discussions, the mutual bonds forged in the common struggle were a unique experience which resulted in something resembling a conversion experience affecting many students, amongst them, to mention but one particular case, the then-president of the Corps Sint Olof', a leading fraternity on campus.[15] The 'conversion experience' in this case refers, of course, to a sudden radicalization of their personal and political outlook, powerfully reinforcing—if anything—the process of separation from their Catholic upbringing. It may be asked, then, what role the Catholic background of those student activists played in the course of the events in Nijmegen, Tilburg, and the Netherlands.

Ton Regtien was only one of many participant-observers who drew attention to the link between Catholicism and radical activism in the long sixties: 'Right at this time, radical currents clamouring for renewal gripped Catholic milieux. It was the time of the [Dutch] Pastoral Council, and Nijmegen and Tilburg had woken up some time ago from the hibernation induced by unquestioning obedience to Roman authorities. Not that the intonation of *The International* should be interpreted as a form of religious renewal but, at any rate, there was a mutual influence of religious and political nonconformism, by means of which the authority of the Pope as much as the authority of the Katholieke Volks Partij [the Dutch Catholic Party par excellence] came under attack.'[16] We will see similar mechanisms at work elsewhere in Catholic Europe. Perhaps a look at campus politics south of the Dutch border will help to crystallize some relevant issues.

THE ENIGMA OF LEUVEN

The Belgian Catholic '1968' in some respects ran parallel to what happened north of the border. Except that in Belgium the campus explosions happened earlier. The Belgian May 1968 in fact had already occurred in May 1966. Indeed, in the hall of fame of European university towns becoming literal battlegrounds, pride of place goes to the quaint mid-sized town of Leuven. In fact, the first Western European university to become the centre of a national controversy in the course of the 1960s was not any one of the branch campuses

[15] Franken and Godfroy, 'Vallen en opstaan', p. 28.
[16] Ton Regtien, *Springtij. Herinneringen aan de jaren zestig* (Houten: Wereldvenster, 1988), pp. 178–9.

of the University of Paris or the Free University of Berlin. The first Western European university town to witness running battles between demonstrators and police was the Flemish town of Leuven. The very Catholic University of Leuven, founded in 1425, holds the honour of having sparked a major controversy leading to militant altercations in the city's streets and the polarization of public opinion in the country-at-large. This feat, however, was initially by no means due to particularly radical action on the part of its student body, but instead was a result of some peculiarities of Western Europe's least well-known territorial state.

Space does not permit any serious incursions into the colourful details of Belgian history.[17] Suffice it to say that Belgium has been rent until the present day by various and shifting forms of internal colonization and linguistic chauvinism which, until the middle of the twentieth century, favoured the French-speaking, industrialized and increasingly secular Walloon portion over the mostly rural, heavily Catholic, and Dutch-speaking Flemish north. For various complicated reasons, by the 1960s protest movements by the Flemish population centred on the fate of the Catholic University of Leuven. Located in the Dutch-speaking half of Belgium, the traditional language of instruction in Leuven had nonetheless been French. From the 1930s onwards, Dutch was increasingly permitted to be used on campus as well, but by the 1960s the Flemish community had begun to demand the exclusive use of Dutch as the sole means of communication at this flagship university located on Flemish soil. Needless to say, the francophone community did not easily comply.

In large part as a result of this unusual set of historical circumstances, then, in Leuven 'May 1968' began two years earlier. The birth of Leuven student radicalism can be traced back all the way to May 1966, more specifically 15 May 1966, when the Belgian episcopacy made public a decision they had arrived at two days earlier. The pastoral letter took almost everyone by surprise, as it unequivocally reconfirmed the unitary and bilingual nature of the Leuven campus. Up to this moment, most Dutch-speaking Belgians had regarded the Catholic church—rock solid in the Flemish half, but weak and far more powerless in the Walloon portion of the Belgian state—as part of the Flemish community and supportive of that community's social and political concerns. To be sure, with the postwar modernization of the Flemish half of Belgium proceeding apace, a certain loosening of the umbilical cord linking many Flemish to the Catholic church could be noticed here and there already prior to the mid-1960s. With hindsight one can tell that the secularization

---

[17] Again, Horn, *Spirit of '68*, provides far greater detail not only on this quintessential Catholic student revolt but also on the socio-cultural and political context of the battle around *Leuven Vlaams*. Short passages of this and the subsequent subsection are adapted from my earlier work.

process affecting many European societies at that time was beginning to affect Belgium as well. But few contemporary observers were prepared for the sudden and unprecedented response by the hitherto rather docile Leuven student body to the pastoral letter arriving from Mechelen.[18]

In the course of Sunday, 15 May, students began to assemble in pubs and cafés in ever-increasing numbers to express their furious disagreement with this official edict, planning for an organized response the next day, Monday, 16 May, including a rally in front of city hall. Paul Goossens, the undisputed leader of the subsequent student revolt, recalls how, thus far rather disinterested in the finer points of the language issue and the modalities of a solution to the crisis of the Catholic university, he suddenly found himself at the top of the flight of outside stairs leading up to the entry of the magnificent city hall with a microphone shoved in front of his face. Later on an accomplished, charismatic speaker, but for the moment nervous and uncertain what to say, he limited his first speech to three short sentences. 'Tomorrow, out of protest, we shall go on strike.' This spontaneous, unplanned announcement fell on open ears. The second announcement was even more outrageous: 'The academic year will therefore be ending tomorrow.' Paul Goossens records 'immense joy' as his audience's response.[19]

The third and final sentence amplified in front of the growing crowd filling the Grote Markt in front of city hall warrants a brief explanatory digression onto the text of the 13 May pastoral letter. In their closing sentence, the Belgian bishops solemnly declared: 'May the Holy Ghost let us share in its light and its strength, so that the University of Leuven, in the future as in the past, may faithfully fulfil its important and indispensable mission.'[20] Here is what Paul Goossens said after calling for a student strike and the unscheduled early ending of the academic year: 'And upon special request from the Holy Ghost, the Catholic University of Leuven shall from now on become pluralist.' Goossens records in his memoirs: 'That was a direct hit.'[21] The crowd became

---

[18] The archbishop of Mechelen is the traditional *primus inter pares* of Belgian bishops. An informative and well-written recent monograph on the issues surrounding the split of the Catholic University of Leuven is Christian Laporte, *L'Affaire de Louvain: 1960–1968* (Paris: De Boeck Université, 1999). On the crucial role of language conflicts in Belgian history, note Els Witte and Harry Van Velthoven, *Language and Politics. The Situation in Belgium in an Historical Perspective* (Brussels: VUB Press, 1999).

[19] On the student reaction to the 15 May publication of the pastoral letter including the rally on Monday, 16 May 1966, see Paul Goossens, *Leuven '68 of het geloof in de hemel* (Zellik: Roularta, 1993), pp. 37–40, citations on p. 40.

[20] The document is partially reproduced in Ludo Martens and Kris Merckx, *Dat was 1968* (Berchem: EPO, 1978), p. 10. The full text can be found, entitled 'Verklaring van de Bisschoppen van België betreffende de Katholieke Universiteit van Leuven', in *Dossier Leuven. Feiten, cijfers en beschouwingen* (Leuven: De Clauwaert, 1968), pp. 114–24. I thank Patricia Quaghebeur for providing me with a copy of this rare document.

[21] Goossens, *Leuven '68*, p. 40; the demand for pluralism was a frontal attack on the uniquely Catholic orientation of this largest Catholic university outside Italy.

delirious, though quickly brought back to planet earth as the police were then beginning to clear the square with the aid of billy clubs and more.

Anger towards the church hierarchy ran so high that Goossens's impromptu strike call was effortlessly heeded the very next day. Three days later, on 20 May, the university authorities, to avoid further altercations, unexpectedly fulfilled Goossens's second point and officially declared the academic year to have prematurely ended. For, starting Monday 16 May, students and police had engaged in running battles in the city's streets. Despite the mayor's proclamation of a mini-state of siege—outlawing all gatherings of more than five people—evening after evening, as soon as nightfall provided the semblance of protective cover, students turned out in full force. Paul Goossens's three-sentence maiden speech became a declaration of independence for Leuven students from the tight embrace of their elders in various organizations and institutions, who had also agitated for the Catholic university to be transformed into a purely Flemish school, but who were generally quite unwilling to question the university's Catholic orientation, let alone to support some of the more radical slogans that could suddenly be heard.

For Paul Goossens records that, in response to his iconoclastic speech, the traditional unifying slogan, *Walen buiten* [Walloons = French speakers out!], was not to be heard that evening and instead of *Walen buiten* students shouted *Bischoppen buiten* [bishops out now!] and *Revolutie* [revolution].[22] A learning process began to get under way, which initially manifested itself in what the flagship Flemish daily, *De Standaard*, called a 'wave of anticlericalism'.[23] To cite Paul Goossens once again: 'Almost everyone present in Leuven at that time came from Catholic high schools and had experienced at least eighteen years of Catholic upbringing. There were people present who, at this particular moment, settled their accounts with that past and who shouted words which, earlier on, they had barely been permitted to think.' 'With this revolt Flanders, which had thus far lived in fear of Rome and Mechelen, lost its fear of the bishop's crozier.'[24]

It is easy to detect anticlerical sentiments within the May 1966 Leuven student revolt. And such tendencies became increasingly pronounced in succeeding years. Nonetheless, at this point in time, anticlericalism should be read as a rejection of traditional power politics by the Belgian Catholic elite and not as a rejection of Catholicism as such. One clear indication of the Catholic nature of this rebellion was the leadership role of the traditional Catholic Flemish University League (KVHV) in the Leuven student struggles of the second half of the 1960s. Indeed, Paul Goossens, who had, if rather playfully, invoked the assistance of the Holy Ghost in his speech of 16 May 1966, and who became the Leuven incarnation of Mario Savio, Rudi Dutschke,

---

[22] Goossens, *Leuven '68*, p. 40.   [23] Citation in Laporte, *Affaire de Louvain*, p. 200.
[24] Goossens, *Leuven '68*, pp. 43 and 44.

and Ton Regtien for the remainder of the decade, was elected president of the Leuven KVHV in the autumn of 1967. Crucially, like Ton Regtien, Paul Goossens had a few years earlier been enrolled in a seminary to become a priest. In Goossens's case it was more recent still. Paul Goossens began to study economics in Leuven in 1964 after leaving the seminary.[25]

THE LESSONS OF LEUVEN

This is a good moment, then, to draw some preliminary lessons from the case studies of Nijmegen, Tilburg, and Leuven. These instances of Catholic universities becoming the primary breeding grounds for radical revolt exemplify the truism that the link between Catholicism and social movements does not always have to be a straightforwardly supportive one. Catholicism can also play a negative role as a perceived authoritarian belief system against which one feels compelled to revolt. All the more so if one is Catholic oneself. Obvious manifestations of such negative mechanisms are confrontations where the concrete incarnations, so to speak, of the Catholic church are unloved—if not despised—power brokers. It should also be noted that often the particular contribution of Catholicism to the incursions of social movements consists of both elements at once, positive reinforcement and negative repulsion, even and especially within the minds of rapidly evolving single individuals. One and the same person may well be propelled by a profound sense of social justice—at least partially rooted in the lessons learned during religious instruction as a child—to question authority, notably Catholic authority figures. There is no better target for such righteous rage than a hostile university administrator at a Catholic institution of higher learning or, as was the case in Leuven, an entire episcopacy aligned against the wishes of a mobilizing community.

The linguistic orientation of the Catholic University of Leuven remained at the centre of various agitations until 1968. In early 1968 the issue once again became headline news, and it came to yet another round of mobilizations, which far exceeded the events of May 1966. When the francophone section of the university community on 15 January 1968 announced their decision, arrived at one day earlier, to keep the Leuven campus bilingual, the dyke burst once again. Far surpassing the turbulent events of May 1966, the city turned into a battlefield. The administrative offices were invaded, furniture thrown out onto the adjoining Old Market and set on fire. 'Even the most staid types continuously shouted with clenched fists: "Revolution"; and individuals

---

[25] Entry for Paul Goossens in wikipedia: <http://nl.wikipedia.org/wiki/Paul_Goossens>.

who, two weeks earlier, still personified moderation and tranquillity turned out to be frightful agitators. The entire Leuven student body seemed to have been infected by a rebellious virus and had become propagators of the most radical points of view.'[26] Or, in the words of Christian Laporte: 'An insurrectionary climate of revolutionary inspiration took over the old centre of the Brabant town: black flags were raised and one began to see wall newspapers, directly inspired by the Chinese dazibaos, while a journal with the explicit title *Revolte* explained in scientific terms how to manufacture Molotov cocktails.'[27] On 16 January, 325 students suffered arrest.

But the battle had hardly begun, with masses of students defying orders to stay clear of city streets. During the night of 20–1 January, an auditorium went up in flames; on 24 January another 675 persons were arrested by the police. Most worrisome for the authorities, the virus began to spread beyond Leuven.[28] Students at the second-largest Flemish university in Ghent expressed their solidarity with the Leuven students in no uncertain terms. And on 23 January 1968 a most extraordinary process of trickle-down activism began to affect the high school student milieu. Between 23 January and 6 February, with universities in Flanders in turmoil, tens of thousands of high school students grabbed this window of opportunity to express their solidarity with the Leuven students and to press for democratization at their own institutions, usually far more dictatorially run than any of the universities. Sometimes encouraged by emissaries from Leuven, often alumni returning to their high school alma mater to stir up the crowd, the numbers of demonstrators and the locations of such rallies speak for themselves. Small provincial towns witnessed extraordinary assemblies of angry young students. On 7 February 1968 the Belgian government stepped down. The road to Leuven Vlaams was now irreversibly cleared.

Were Leuven students the exception or did they exemplify a much larger and more general Belgian trend? Nothing demonstrates the synchronicity of Catholic and secular radicalization more persuasively than a brief summary of the corresponding evolution of two additional representative Belgian Catholic youth organizations. The Flemish Katholieke Studentenactie (KSA) organized young Flemish Catholics over the age of 6. Given the separate organizational existence of the KVHV—initially in the forefront of the Leuven student insurgency—university students were not their primary targets, though KSA members included some post-secondary students as well. What interests us here is the contingent of KSA activists aged 16 and above. In a remarkable reconstruction of this brand of KSA activists between 1965 and 1979, Iris

---

[26] Goossens, *Leuven '68*, p. 97.   [27] Laporte, *Affaire de Louvain*, p. 286.
[28] For the aforementioned (and other) facts and figures, see Mark Derez, Ingrid Depraetere, and Wivina Van der Steen, 'Kroniek van het studentenprotest', in Louis Vos et al., *De stoute jaren. Studentenprotest in de jaren zestig* (Tielt: Lannoo, 1988), pp. 124–33.

Depoorter has persuasively drawn up a picture of a previously rather trad-itionally oriented Catholic youth organization suddenly, in or about 1969, casting about for different ideological and activist guideposts. As elsewhere in the Flemish half of Belgium, the radical dynamic behind Leuven Vlaams was central to this repositioning of the 16+ age group within the KSA. 'The influence of "Red Leuven" on the KSA became apparent especially after 1971. With several years' delay, the opinions of that new generation of students began to affect the KSA. This process came about when the first generation of members, those who had lived through "May '68", left the KSA after 1971 and were replaced by a new generation which was marked even more decisively by left-wing currents.'[29] From 1972 to 1975, writes Louis Vos, within the pages of the KSA's *Werkgemeenschap +16* newspaper, the aptly renamed *Aksiekrant*, now jointly published by the similarly radicalized Jong Davidsfonds, 'criticism of the capitalist establishment based on a left-wing or Marxist social analysis provided the red thread'.[30] Vocal KSA contingents in these years were a permanent fixture of protest demonstrations on a variety of topics, marching and chanting alongside members of the Maoist AMADA and the Trotskyist RAL.[31]

The francophone Jeunesse Ouvrière Chrétienne (JOC), unsurprisingly, if anything surpassed the KSA in radical sentiments and revolutionary phrase-ology employed in publications and other interventions in the public sphere. Here, once again, the years 1969–74 were central to this experience of Catholic radicalization towards the political Left. A few examples, recorded by Paul Wynants in an important contribution to this theme, may suffice. As late as 1964, the JOC leadership habitually ended all internal correspondence with the formula, 'tous unis dans la même amitié partagée dans Notre Seigneur' [all of us united in our joint love for Our Saviour]. Ten years later four words sufficed: 'unis dans la lutte' [united in struggle]. The JOC/JOCF chose the occasion of May Day 1974 to self-proclaim itself a 'revolutionary workers' movement'. And graphic illustration of such changing trends is provided by a poster produced by the JOC at this time which reproduces portraits of

[29] Iris Depoorter, 'Van Katholieke Actie naar maatschappijkritiek. De stromversnelling in de +16-werking van KSA/KSJ (1965–1979)', unpublished licentiaatsverhandeling, Catholic Univer-sity of Leuven, Department of History, 2000, p. 74.
[30] Louis Vos, 'Traditie als bron van vernieuwing. De katholieke studentenactie in Vlaanderen, 1955–1975', *Bijdragen tot de Eigentijdse Geschiedenis* 8 (2001), p. 169. Vos, the indisputable authority on the student movement in Leuven, has now assembled his rich store of articles on this topic in Louis Vos, *Idealisme en engagement. De roeping van de katholieke studerende jeugd in Vlaanderen (1920–1990)* (Leuven: Acco, 2011).
[31] A similar situation characterized Far Left politics in French-speaking Switzerland, where a stimulating and informative report on the history of the Swiss JEC from the early 1960s to the early 1970s, written in 1971, noted that the JEC and JEC Universitaire 'today, together with the [Trotskyist] Ligue Marxiste Révolutionnaire, remain the sole student movements organized in high schools and universities'; see 'La JECU Suisse'—BDIC, JECI, F delta 1980/786.

individuals who have been 'executed because they struggled with and for the people'. Next to the predictable Jesus Christ, Mahatma Gandhi, and Martin Luther King Jr, the collection of symbolic figures included the Colombian priest and guerrilla fighter Camillo Torres; the French Maoist student Pierre Overney, drowned while fleeing French police; Rosa Luxemburg; Che Guevara; and the Catalan anarchist Salvador Puig Antich, one of the last victims of Francoist 'justice' in dictatorial Spain.[32]

FRANCE

Leuven University was by definition Catholic. Nowhere in France did a Catholic university perform a remotely similar role in terms of the centrality to national student revolts as had been the case in the Mississippi on the Dijle. And, indeed, the direct impact of explicitly Catholic (or Protestant) students on May 1968 was far less pronounced in France than in Belgium. Part of the explanation for the relative invisibility of Catholic student organizations on the barricades of the French May lies in the fact that the traditional Catholic Action grouping operating in the university milieu had already undergone a series of debilitating crises in the dozen years preceding 1968.

As early as 1957, the entire national leadership team of both the JEC and the JECF collectively resigned from their posts as a result of their superiors' opposition to the student radicals' militant campaign against the use of torture by French forces in Algeria. The national leadership structures were rebuilt soon thereafter, but the end result did not please the 'adult' monitors of JEC activism any more than the earlier cohort of JEC spokespersons. In 1965, the respective national secretaries of the JEC and the JECF were forcibly removed from their posts as a result of their engagement in openly political causes and in various struggles for progressive social change in educational matters and other issues of pressing concern for youth in the 1960s. The church authorities were once again worried that what they regarded as a small circle of radicalized Catholic student leaders had lost touch with the needs of students at the grassroots level of the JEC and were increasingly leading the ranks astray.[33]

This second crisis in less than ten years seriously damaged the JEC. Most university student members of the JEC now contributed to the setting up of a

---

[32] See Paul Wynants, 'De l'Action Catholique Spécialisé à l'utopie politique. Le Changement de cap de la JOC francophone (1969–1974)', *Cahiers d'histoire du temps présent* 11 (2003), pp. 102 ('unis dans la lutte'), 107 (1 May 1974 proclamation), and 103 (reproduction of 'Super Poster des luttes ouvrières').

[33] Denis Pelletier, *La Crise catholique. Religion, société, politique en France (1965–1978)* (Paris: Payot, 2002), provides a useful brief summary of the turbulence affecting JEC and JECF between 1956 and 1965 on pp. 78–9 of his landmark volume.

Mission Étudiante in September 1966. The JEC itself continued to operate independently, but it now mostly concentrated on the high school milieu. A small fraction of former JEC activists at the university level set up yet a third Catholic Action branch for students, the Action Catholique Universitaire (ACU), which, however, by 1970 organized a mere 1,000 members.[34] Catholic university students thus faced May 1968 divided into three separate groups, which helps to explain their limited organizational impact in the streets of Paris and the provinces. But all three umbrella groups for Catholic students experienced a similar evolution in succeeding years. If their impact on French events was relatively circumscribed on the organizational terrain, their environment affected the outlook of Catholic activists all the more.

Danièle Hervieu-Léger's history of the Mission Étudiante captures the story exceedingly well. Whereas traditional Catholic Action groups were structured along tightly centralized lines, Mission Étudiante, throughout its five-year lifespan, explicitly provided space for local initiatives, decentralized efforts, and the provision of autonomy for Catholic students, then beginning their process of radicalization towards the Left. Rather than fulfilling Catholic Action's traditional missionary role, the Mission Étudiante saw itself as a facilitator for the fruitful coexistence of an ever-growing variety of autonomous groups, be they Bible study groups, prayer groups, or Catholic grassroots organizations pursuing more overtly political causes. And, along with such strategic reorientations towards the primacy of decentralized activity, the Mission Étudiante quickly abandoned all pretence at apostolic missionary activity per se. The uppermost concern was no longer to define the optimal ways and means of influencing the university milieu; instead, the key task was seen to be the search for what it really meant to be Christian in the world of today. In a way, this stage in the evolution of the Mission Étudiante was similar to the consciousness-raising groups characteristic of the early days of second wave feminism, another social movement catalysed into reflection by the events of 1968.[35]

---

[34] On the founding of the Mission Étudiante, see above all Danièle Hervieu-Léger, *De la mission à la protestation. L'Évolution des étudiants chrétiens en France (1965–1970)* (Paris: Cerf, 1973), pp. 7–8. ACU, though operating independently from the Mission Étudiante, was also part of the loose federation of organizations nominally composing the Mission, as were the remaining structures of the JEC. On this, see the brief synopses on the organizational trajectory of ACU and JEC in Dominique Le Renn, 'Les Mouvements tels qu'ils se voient . . .', *Autrement* 8 (February 1977), pp. 200–2. (Note that, due to editing or technical errors, the entry for the ACU begins on p. 201 but continues at the top of p. 200, and the description for the JEC commences on p. 202 and continues on p. 201.)

[35] This process of reorientation and autonomous development is at the centre of Hervieu-Léger's attention in pp. 14–51 of her *De la mission*. I will have occasion to draw parallels to the early stages of second wave feminism once again when discussing the Italian case of Catholic student activism.

But, running parallel to other social and ideological milieux composing the motor forces of 1968, Catholic students did not limit themselves to contemplation, but reflection quickly led to consolidated action. And, to add insult to injury for the Catholic upper hierarchy which had beheaded the JEC in 1965 in order to avoid needless diffusion of radical ideas from the leadership level to the ranks, in the course of 1968 it became obvious to anyone who cared to see that the ideological conflicts fought most bitterly earlier on by Catholic student *leaders* now began to grip ever-growing numbers of the respective grassroots membership of Catholic student organizations as well. A phenomenon presumably isolated within small circles of intellectuals supposedly removed from the concerns of day-to-day life suddenly became a central feature of the Catholic student ranks, earlier on deemed to be inherently apolitical and passive.[36]

Activists of Mission Étudiante could be found on the streets of Paris as soon as the student movement erupted in full force in early May. Particularly visible and present in full force at the Faculty of Political Science and the Law Faculty of the University of Paris in the Latin Quarter, Catholic students played frontline roles in the occupation of these respective faculties, the installation of strike committees and the successful organization of the first of many mass meetings characteristic of the Parisian May.[37] The contribution of Catholic students to the Parisian May events was perhaps most noticeable, prominent, and notorious in the Centre Saint-Yves in the rue Gay-Lussac. Gay-Lussac had been the site of some of the earliest barricades on the night of 10–11 May. Beginning in the second half of May, the Dominican chaplains of the Centre Saint-Yves, the student social centre of Catholic law students of the Faculté de Droit, transformed the centre into a small-scale replica of the nearby Odéon National Theater, which had become the nerve centre and permanent assembly hall of the student May in France.[38]

Starting in the early afternoon and rarely ending before midnight, each day the Centre Saint-Yves became the staging ground for heated debates on any number of topics ranging from 'Individual and Collective Dimensions of Religious Belief' to 'Marxism and Christianity'.[39] The doors were open 'for everyone, students and non-students, believers and non-believers', and any

---

[36] This sea change is captured well once again by Hervieu-Léger on pp. 45–6 of *De la mission*.

[37] See note 3 on p. 95 of Hervieu-Léger's *De la mission*.

[38] The student chaplain of the Centre Saint-Yves, it should be recalled, was none other than Jean Raguénès, who later on became the messianic worker priest and inspirational prophet of the workforce at the LIP watch factory operating under workers' self-management for many months in Besançon in Eastern France; see Jean Raguénès, *De Mai 68 à LIP. Un dominicain au cœur des luttes* (Paris: Karthala, 2008).

[39] Taken from p. 158 of the chapter, 'Rue Gay-Lussac. L'Amphi chrétien permanent', in Jacques Marny, *L'Église contestée. Jeunes chrétiens révolutionnaires* (Paris: Centurion, 1968), perhaps the most evocative reconstruction of the ebullient atmosphere in the Centre Saint-Yves.

'question or position on the Church, its functioning, its ideology, the dogmatic content of beliefs, and the forms of religious expression could be formulated'.[40] As was the case literally everywhere else in Paris and France in those heady days of the second half of May, everyone was invited to speak, anyone could say anything, and everyone was eagerly listened to, even and especially if the listeners disagreed. Small wonder that Catholic participants in May 1968 later on remembered those days as an intense spiritual experience, perceived as a 'state of grace' or as a 'privileged manifestation of the Holy Spirit'.[41]

As was fashionable in other nerve centres of the Paris revolt, the general assembly of the Centre Saint-Yves created a plethora of commissions and subcommissions to elaborate positions or carry out specific tasks. One such offspring of the discussions at Saint-Yves tackled the problem of 'Revolution within the Church', soon mutating into the Comité d'Action pour la Révolution dans l'Église (CARÉ). On Pentecost Sunday, 2 June, the same day which saw seventy ecumenical iconoclasts, including the philosopher Paul Ricoeur, assemble for a joint celebration of the eucharist in a private apartment in the rue Vaugirard, members of the CARÉ streamed into the church of Saint-Séverin in Paris's Left Bank just before the celebration of Mass was to commence. Holding up placards challenging church authority, they distributed leaflets and asked for Mass to be replaced by an open forum and public debate. A community of activists having adopted the name 'Bible and Revolution' chose to interrupt Mass in Saint Honoré d'Eylau in the posh 16th *arrondissement* on 9 June 1968 at the end of the sermon, grabbing the microphone, hoisting red banners, and haranguing the scandalized audience.[42]

If the torrents of radical change made headline news above all in May and June of 1968, the subsequent period witnessed, to be sure, a reflux of activism in all social milieux. But for many student radicals now commenced a period of searching reflections. If the hectic pace of constant activism in the late spring of 1968 had captured the imagination of the entire country and a good portion of the world, it was in the subsequent months and years that the process of radicalization was consolidated, refined, and deepened.

Danièle Hervieu-Léger, a leading Catholic radical student activist at Sciences Po, five years later drew attention to a national leadership gathering of the Mission Étudiante from 30 October to 4 November 1968 in Orleans, where the spontaneous challenges arising in late spring of that year first crystallized into serious theoretical reflections on the political and religious meaning of the May revolt. Amongst the many eloquent speakers at the

---

[40] Hervieu-Léger, *De la mission*, pp. 77–8.   [41] Hervieu-Léger, *De la mission*, p. 70.

[42] Grégory Barrau, *Le Mai des catholiques* (Paris: Atelier, 1998), pp. 68–72; for more detail on the actions in Saint Séverin and Saint Honoré d'Eylau, see Marny, *L'Église contestée*, pp. 129–51 and 191–6.

Collège Saint-Euverte was Patrick Viveret, a student at Nanterre, and simultaneously a member of the Mission Étudiante and the Mouvement du 22 mars, the quintessential radical student organization of May 1968 in France, personified by its media-icon, Daniel Cohn-Bendit. Various speakers at the Orleans event began to argue that one should not limit oneself to proclaim the imminent arrival of the Kingdom of God on Earth but that one must go further to fashion a prophetic praxis to bring about the liberation of humanity in the here and now.[43] The Maritainian postulate of the separation of the temporal from the spiritual sphere, thirty years earlier the clarion call for progressive Catholics, was beginning to unravel. And the challenge in this case emerged from the Left!

The Mission Étudiante was not the only organization fundamentally transformed by the French May events. The JEC, limping along after the crisis of 1965, had hoped for a renewed lease of life by concentrating on the high school milieu. But French high school students in and after 1968 flocked to the plethora of ultraradical Comités d'Action Lycéens instead of the JEC. Nonetheless, by 1970, tension within the ranks of the JEC had reached boiling point. Adapting theses developed by the young Pierre Bourdieu, the JEC now openly chose the revolutionary road. For a number of years in the 1970s, the JEC once again openly defied authority, including Paris's Cardinal Marty. In 1977 the erstwhile JEC official, Marie Ferrier, wrote in her reminiscences published in the journal *Esprit*: 'We read the Gospel just like we read the little red book.'[44]

THE SPANISH NEW LEFT

The Spanish case is an important manifestation of the Christian spirit behind 1968, but perhaps the most important immediate and tangible contribution to the Spanish 'spirit of 1968' by Catholic students was actually made as early as the 1950s. Spanish Left Catholicism, emerging in the dire conditions of underground activism under the yoke of Francisco Franco's unbending dictatorial rule, has intellectual roots and antecedents going back at least to 1956, a cornerstone year which also happened to be the year of conception, literally and figuratively, of the transnationally operating New Left. And it was precisely in the context of the birth of the New Left that Spanish Catholic students played a singularly important role. The story of the Spanish New Left— operating in the anti-Franco underground, Franco's prisons, and in exile—is one of very many tales of great importance in this era, which is virtually unknown outside the Spanish state. In Northern European academic milieux,

---

[43] Hervieu-Léger, *De la mission*, p. 70.
[44] Cited in Pelletier, *La Crise catholique*, p. 81.

the gaze is almost entirely fixed on New Left activism in the United States,
West Germany, and, for obvious reasons, France. But the story of underground resistance to the Francoist state from the mid-1950s until the late
1960s is virtually impossible to comprehend without close attention to the
Spanish New Left, which became a key player in opposition to Franco before
largely disappearing in the course of 1969.

The Spanish New Left found its organizational expression within 'Felipe',
the Frente de Liberación Popular (FLP), and its affiliated but autonomous
sections in Catalonia and the Basque Country. In both Madrid and Barcelona,
the two hot spots of New Left activism early on, the original nucleus was called
University New Left (Nueva Izquierda Universitaria in Madrid and Nova
Esquerra Universitaria in Barcelona), and both groups were almost exclusively
composed of devout and practising Catholic students, searching for an alternative to both Francoist repression and the strictures of the traditional Old
Left. 'Catholicism was so very much present that very often the same meeting
places [used by New Left circles] were also utilized to hold theology seminars',[45] and the name quickly chosen by the Spanish New Left, FLP, was a
conscious combination of the acronym of two organizations that served as
inspiration for the Spanish New Left in the 1950s: the Algerian FLN, the Front
de Libération National, and the French MLP, the Mouvement de Libération
Populaire. Almost everyone will be familiar with the Algerian FLN, which,
after a decade of bloody struggles against French colonial power, managed to
force out their Gallic superiors in the early 1960s. But who was the French
MLP? The Mouvement de Libération Populaire by the mid-1950s had become
a rather marginal force on the fringes of the French Left. In the mid-to-late-
1940s, under a different label, the Mouvement Populaire des Familles (MPF),
it had been the quintessential social action organization of the activist French
Catholic Left. With a membership which at times exceeded 100,000 adherents,
the MPF (later on changing its name to MLP) led direct action campaigns,
including housing squats, protest rallies, and other militant pressure tactics to
draw attention to the miserable housing, working, and general living conditions of urban working-class residents in the industrial strongholds of post-
liberation France, such as the Nord, Lyon, Saint-Étienne, Marseilles, and, of
course, Paris.[46] For the Spanish New Left to have adopted a composite
acronym locating its intellectual and activist traditions within Third World

---

[45] Julio Antonio García Alcalá, *Historia del Felipe (FLP, FOC y ESBA). De Julio Cerón a la Liga
Comunista Revolucionaria* (Madrid: Centro de Estudios Políticos y Constitucionales, 2001),
p. 42.

[46] For an English-language summary of the contributions of the MPF/MLP to French social
movement culture between 1945 and 1968, see Bruno Duriez, 'Left Wing Catholicism in France.
From Catholic Action to the Political Left: The Mouvement Populaire des Familles', in Gerd-
Rainer Horn and Emmanuel Gerard (eds), *Left Catholicism, 1943–1955. Catholics and Society in
Western Europe at the Point of Liberation* (Leuven: Leuven University Press, 2001), pp. 64–90.

liberation movements and European Left Catholicism needs few additional comments.

Nonetheless, to underscore my point, I would like to draw attention to two more texts that showcase the exceptional centrality of the Catholic Left in underground Spain. The first is a citation from the first serious attempt to trace the organizational and spiritual heritage of the Spanish Felipe, a monograph by Julio Antonio García Alcalá. The brief citation highlights the unorthodox nature of the international current of the New Left in general, and the heavily Catholic influence of the Spanish New Left in particular: 'In contradistinction to the monolithic nature of other [underground] parties, it [the FLP] preferred the free association and interpretation of the most varied authors, usually explicitly of a heterodox nature. The [FLP] activists would thus simultaneously read Rosa Luxemburg, Lenin, Mao, Trotsky, Marx, André Gorz, Teilhard de Chardin or [Emmanuel] Mounier, exemplifying a pluralism that connected the various traditions which served as source and inspiration for the *felipes*, such as Marxism, Christian humanism and libertarian thought.'[47]

The second quotation is from a text by Alfonso Carlos Comín, a well-known journalist and social scientist, who had this to say about the early New Left milieu which developed into a central powerhouse of anti-Francoist determination and resolve: '[T]he young Spanish university students, preoccupied and unsettled, studied the official syllabi in order to obtain the necessary qualifications and their academic titles, but they regarded those books as ever-so-many lifeless pages. Simultaneously, they avidly devoured books at the margins of the official reading lists, which they discussed in their get-togethers and their seminars, such as the works by Mounier, Teilhard, Congar, Rahner, Lukács, Sartre, Camus.'[48] Once again, the ideological heterodoxy and pluralism of New Left beliefs emerge crystal clear, but here the centrality of Left Catholicism emerges if anything even more centrally than in the above citation by García Alcalá.

The Spanish New Left, as elsewhere in Europe and the First World, is a product of the complications of the international conjuncture of 1956. Whereas elsewhere in Europe the combined impact of Algeria and Suez, coupled with Stalinist interventions in Hungary and Poland, led to the birth and development of a 'New Left' to the left of social democracy and Communism,

---

I devote a central chapter to the MPF in my *Western European Liberation Theology. The First Wave, 1924–1959* (Oxford: Oxford University Press, 2008), pp. 175–224.

[47] García Alcalá, *Historia del Felipe*, pp. 21–2.

[48] Alfonso Carlos Comín, cited in Daniel Francisco Álvarez Espinosa, *Cristianos y marxistas contra Franco* (Cadiz: Servicio de Publicaciones de la Universidad de Cádiz, 2003), p. 187. On Comín, there now exist two stimulating monographs: Francisco Martínez Hoyos, *La cruz y el martillo. Alfonso Carlos Comín y los cristianos comunistas* (Barcelona: Rubeo 2009), and José Antonio González Casanova, *Comín, mi amigo* (Barcelona: Lector, 2010).

Spain experienced its own Golgotha. In February 1956, heated confrontations erupted in the Law Faculty of the University of Madrid, leading to the detention of activists and the temporary closure of the university. It was the first serious challenge to unmitigated Francoist rule since the end of the Spanish Civil War in 1939. Spanish opposition politics dates its revitalization precisely to these events in early 1956.

The historian of this student uprising, which opened a new era in Spanish politics, Pablo Lizcano, points out the decisive contributions of Catholic circles to the events which gave rise to what has since become regarded as 'the Generation of 56'. Already in the course of 1955, the Madrid University branch of Catholic Action had organized a cycle of presentations and colloquia on various topics, including the relevance of Marxism and the overall contributions of the labour movement, sometimes chaired by students belonging to the secular underground Left, occasionally by activists in the Spanish detachments of Catholic Action oriented towards working-class milieux, the JOC and the HOAC (more on both in Chapter 5). The seminar series in the Economics Faculty of San Bernardo provided a first free space for dissident tendencies within Catholicism and other free thinkers under the Francoist yoke.[49] Pablo Lizcano also furnishes detailed information on the subsequent contributions of Spanish dissident Catholics to the genesis of the Spanish New Left.

STUDENT RADICALISM IN THE SPANISH SIXTIES

Yet Spanish Catholic dissidence within the student milieux did not solely find its outlet in the ranks of the rapidly swelling Frente de Liberación Popular. They also joined forces with secular anti-Franco activists to found an underground university student federation, the Unión Democrática de Estudiantes (UDE), in 1957, which eventually merged into a larger umbrella of underground student organizations, the Federación Universitaria Democrática Española (FUDE), founded in late 1961.[50] The sole officially approved university student organization was then the regime-friendly Sindicato Español Universitario (SEU). Spanish student politics, however, soon got so heated that the dictatorship decided in 1965 to dispense with the SEU, as it no longer served as a smooth transmission belt of regime policy on the university level. Along with the FUDE, yet another product of Catholic dissidence, the Unión

---

[49] Pablo Lizcano, *La generación del 56. La Universidad contra Franco* (Madrid: Saber y Comunicación, 2006), pp. 177–9 (seminar series in San Bernardo) and pp. 215–25 (Catholic origins of Felipe).

[50] Gregorio Valdelvira, *La oposición estudiantil al franquismo* (Madrid: Síntesis, 2006), p. 34.

de Estudiantes Demócratas (UED), had contributed to the marginalization and eventual disappearance of the Francoist SEU. In fact, the historian of the Spanish student opposition to the dictatorship, Gregorio Valdelvira, writes: 'The collaboration between FUDE and UED was one of the key forces in the ultimate struggle against the SEU and in favour of autonomous student organizations.'[51] The massive and almost continuous student mobilizations against Franco in the succeeding years between 1965 and 1968 saw the FUDE and UED battling side-by-side, together with the underground Spanish Communist Party (PCE) and the New Left FLP.

One of the most important component parts of the largely Catholic UED was the Spanish section of the Jeunesse Étudiante Catholique Internationale (JECI), the Juventud Estudiante Católica (JEC).[52] Already in the late fifties, this classic organization belonging to the core groupings of specialized Catholic Action had begun to embark on an autonomous and regime-critical path. The adoption of the organizational principles of specialized Catholic Action almost inevitably—given the contours of Spanish underground politics in the university milieu—led to a cycle of ever-increasing radicalization. By the mid-1960s, the JEC formed part and parcel of radical university student politics and at first concentrated on work within the UED. After the removal of the SEU from campuses by 1965, the JEC threw all its forces into the emerging wave of ever-multiplying, seemingly unstoppable student activism *tout court*. A former member of the JEC national leadership team recalls that now 'JEC activists mutated from engagement with underground student unions of Christian Democratic orientation (UED) towards activism within groups of the [largely secular] Left, such as the FUDE or within political parties, such as the PCE or the FLP.'[53]

A former national student chaplain of the JEC reports that 'in those years, until 1967, the JEC as such—obviously more directly on some campuses than in others—played a strong and dynamic leadership role within the overall student movement'.[54] By the mid-1960s, the Spanish JEC witnessed a multiplication of its membership to roughly 5,500 active members.[55] In 1959, the predecessor organization of the JEC had reported a core membership of a

[51] Valdelvira, *Oposición estudiantil*, p. 61.

[52] On the relevance of the JEC for the dissident Catholic UED, see for instance José Álvarez Cobelas, *Envenenados de cuerpo y alma. La oposición universitaria al franquismo en Madrid (1939–1970)* (Madrid: Siglo XXI, 2004), p. 127.

[53] Francisco Tauste Alcocer, 'La crisis de la JEC en la época de la contestación universitaria (1967–1970)', in Feliciano Montero (ed.), *Juventud Estudiante Católica 1947–1997* (Madrid: JEC, 1998), p. 95.

[54] Jesús Lasagabáster Medinabeitia, 'La JEC de los años sesenta. Testimonio del consiliario nacional', in Montero (ed.), *Juventud*, p. 91.

[55] Inmaculada Franco Candel, 'El final de la crisis. Primeros pasos de un movimiento renovado (1974–1978)', in Montero (ed.), *Juventud*, p. 120.

mere 521 activists.[56] Much of the growth in membership in the first half of the 1960s had been due to a phenomenal increase in high school student interest.[57] But even within the university milieu, the relatively low membership figures should not be misinterpreted as a sign of minimal presence. The Spanish university system under Franco had then not yet embarked upon the huge expansion of student numbers characteristic of much of the rest of Western Europe.[58] Moreover, as most Spanish university students were then still practising members of the Catholic church, the ideological influence of the JEC 'was far superior to its actual physical presence';[59] and, last but not least, JEC members, as already mentioned, often expended most of their energies in activism within larger umbrella groups where their efforts could have a multiple, if somewhat indirect, effect.

The cycle of radicalization by Spanish JEC members was merely one element—though a crucial one—in a more general radicalization of specialized Spanish Catholic Action. In response, from 1966 to 1968, the Spanish Catholic hierarchy unleashed a no-holds-barred campaign of intimidation and repression against the rebellious divisions of both the youth and the adult wings of specialized Catholic Action. For the JEC, as for other battalions of the fledgling Spanish Catholic Left, this had disastrous consequences. The entire logistical infrastructure was dismantled, leading to massive membership loss. A former member of the JEC national leadership in the years 1969–73 suggests that, in 1969, JEC membership in Spain as a whole had melted down to a grand total of 141 activists.[60] By 1972, numbers had increased to 680 members, of whom 400 were high school students, still a pale shadow of its former glory days.[61] It was a setback from which the JEC never really recovered.[62]

The years after 1966 were crucial years for Spanish underground politics. Until 1968, student—and worker! (see Chapter 5)—radicalization proceeded apace. From 1968 onwards, new waves of repression hit university campuses,

---

[56] Feliciano Montero García, 'De la JUMAC a la JEC. Aproximación a la historia de la A.C. Estudiantil', in Montero (ed.), *Juventud*, p. 48.

[57] Franco Candel, 'El final de la crisis', p. 120, reports that of the 5,500 JEC members in the mid-1960s, 4,000 were high school students. Further information on the importance of the high school student milieu within JEC circles is provided in an email communication by Feliciano Montero to this author, 9 December 2013.

[58] Concrete data to this effect are provided in Montero to author, 9 December 2013.

[59] Álvarez Cobelas, *Envenenados*, p. 127.

[60] Manuel Álvarez Fernández, 'El paso del desierto. Desde la ruptura hasta el inicio del despegue (1968–1973)', in Montero (ed.), *Juventud*, p. 101.

[61] Franco Candel, 'El final de la crisis', p. 120.

[62] On the crisis of Spanish specialized Catholic Action, see above all Feliciano Montero García, *La Acción Católica y el franquismo. Auge y crisis de la Acción Católica Especializada en los años sesenta* (Madrid: Universidad Nacional de Educación a Distancia, 2000). More generally on the radicalization of significant sections of Spanish Catholicism after 1956, see Feliciano Montero, *La Iglesia. De la colaboración a la disidencia (1956–1975)* (Madrid: Encuentro, 2009), especially his third chapter, 'De la Democracia Cristiana al Cristiano-Marxismo', pp. 171–219.

but in the end this merely served to further heat up campus politics. With Catholic dissidence under frontal attack by the Catholic hierarchy, the path was thus artificially widened for the almost uninterrupted growth and development of the secular Left which, in turn, underwent a further important evolution in the wake of 1968. The pluralist and anti-authoritarian New Left (FLP) dissolved in 1969 and gave rise to a plethora of mostly Trotskyist and Maoist organizations of the Far Left, further hardening the battle lines.

The UED, the predominantly Catholic underground student federation, got caught up in the rapidly changing atmosphere and dissolved itself in 1967, many of its members joining the revolutionary Left, as did one of the UED's founders and principal actors, Julio Rodríguez Aramberri, who switched his allegiance to the Trotskyist Liga Comunista Revolucionaria.[63] What had remained of the JEC succumbed to identical temptations. JEC members' activism within political parties of the secular Left became the norm in the period of its greatest radicalization from 1968 to 1973. Such double membership, however, only further complicated the situation 'as not all JEC members carried out political work within the same party. By this is meant that some placed their bets on the Communist Party, others on the [Trotskyist] Liga Comunista. Some cast their lot with Moscow, others for Beijing'; each choice entailed distinct and often conflicting strategies.[64]

The upshot of the cycle of radicalization of Spanish (in this case: student) politics, coupled with repression by the Spanish curia, was thus a curious contradiction and a missed encounter. The uncompromising engagement by grassroots Catholic (here: student) activists against the vicious dictatorship by the late sixties had resulted in a growing acceptance of Catholic militants as equal partners by activists in the Spanish secular underground Left, who had earlier on, certainly up to and including the mid-1960s, on occasion expressed grave reservations against the presence of Catholics amongst their ranks. But by the end of the decade, the church hierarchy's determined crushing of specialized Catholic Action reinforced the incipient trend of Catholics to agitate within the ranks of the secular Left. Growing distance from the official church furnished powerful energies for the deepening of the trend towards secularization. 'Some of the leading activists within Marxist organizations in the second half of the sixties and the first half of the seventies emerged out of this particular conjuncture.'[65]

---

[63] Lizcano, *La generación del 56*, p. 289. Álvarez Cobelas, *Envenenados*, p. 191, reports 1967 as the endgame for the UED. Valdelvira, *Oposición estudiantil*, p. 235, laconically notes on the fate of the UED: 'It was likewise swept away by the tempest of radical leftism.'

[64] Rafael Rubio Gómez-Caminero, 'De Hellín a Valladolid. El debate politico en la JEC (1972–1975)', in Montero (ed.), *Juventud*, p. 112.

[65] This paragraph is based on Francisco Fernandez Buey, 'La influencia del pensamiento marxista en los militantes cristianos durante la dictadura franquista', in José María Castells, José Hurtado, and Josep Maria Margenat (eds), *De la dictadura a la democracia. La acción de los*

ITALY

'1968' was a transnational phenomenon. That much is beyond doubt. But it is also unmistakably obvious that the social movements of 1968 affected different countries to different degrees. Scholars and the interested public in the Anglo-Saxon world usually place emphasis on the French events. And there is no doubt that the overarching social crisis of May/June 1968, which witnessed not only student protests but a three-week-long general strike, was without parallel in the years of open conflict from the mid-1960s to the mid-1970s. But there was one other country where the political, cultural, and social crises of this red decade were yet more pronounced, more long-lasting, and more deep-going than in France. This country is, of course, Italy.

Long before Parisian students could even dare to dream about occupying the Sorbonne, the Italian university system had ground to a halt. The autumn term of 1967 and the winter term of early 1968 saw a constantly ascending cycle of student protests, leading to increasing numbers of campuses being rent by division. After the infamous police riot of 1 March 1968 in the Parc of the Villa Borghese in central Rome—the Battle of Valle Giulia—the month of March 1968 saw virtually all campuses throughout Italy, large or small and north or south, effectively shut down. Classes were boycotted, blockades kept lecture halls empty, and university administrators pre-emptively suspended all teaching operations in those locations where students had not yet succeeded on their own. Only large-scale ignorance of Italian affairs—and the Italian language, I should add—has kept the Italian Movimento Studentesco from taking up its rightful central place in the annals of social movement history of what I have called the 'red decade': the period of 1966–76.

Small wonder that, for Catholics too, the radicalization exceeded the already not inconsiderable efforts of their French comrades-in-arms. The degree to which ferment in the Italian church exceeded similar processes in France can be gauged, for instance, by a comparative glance at the phenomenon of base communities, discussed for the early stages of their Italian manifestation in the preceding chapter. Some French base communities preceded the May '68 explosion as well, but these early precursors of what became a popular movement after May 1968 were few and far between, and members often felt an acute sense of painful isolation prior to the sudden flowering of such experiments ushered in by the springtime struggles of 1968. In Italy, too, many base communities first emerged in the student milieu, and here too some could be traced back to the mid- or even early 1960s. But in Italy the moment when this 'fashion' began to take on a certain dynamic of its own was the biennium of 1966–7. At the end of 1967, when French Left Catholics still considered themselves in internal exile cut off from the mainspring of French Catholicism, there existed already more than 1,000 autonomous groupings up and down the Italian boot[66]—more than the maximum number of French equivalents in the heyday of second wave French Left Catholicism in the first half of the 1970s.

Corresponding to their greater numerical strength and social implantation compared to their comrades in France, Italian base communities survived far longer. Whereas French analogues entered a period of notable decline by the mid-1970s at the latest, Italian communities were strong throughout the decade of the 1970s. The national assembly which can be regarded with some degree of justification as the last gasp of the French communities was the June 1974 gathering in Dijon. National conventions in Italy take place on a regular basis right up to today, if on a lesser scale since the 1980s. Also, whereas such national conferences in France never left very many written traces, once the Italian base community conventions became 'institutional-ized', their proceedings were regularly published and thus easily entered into the much vaster national dialogue with the burgeoning Left Catholic audience in the country as such.

Italian Left Catholicism, naturally, by no means solely focused on the build-up and expansion of a dense network of *communità di base*. Student radicals likewise did their level best to transform pre-existing organizations within the vast lifeworld of Italian Catholicism, most often concentrating their activities within the broad umbrella of Catholic Action. The Catholic University Student Federation (FUCI), meeting in Verona in August 1969, passed reso-lutions calling for the abolition of the Concordat, the separation of church and state, an end to the obligatory support for Democrazia Cristiana, and a complete overhaul of the social doctrine of the Catholic church. Virtually identical sentiments began to dominate the Movimento dei Laureati Catto-lici.[67] There is no better graphic illustration of the radicalization of Italian Left Catholicism than the inside story of the final years of the Intesa Cattólica, the umbrella organization coordinating Catholic student organizations at the university level, penned by the participant-observer Raoul Mordenti. Largely paralleling the fast-paced (r)evolution of *gruppi spontanei* at precisely the same time, between November 1967 and December 1968 the Intesa rapidly adopted the ideology and organizational principles of the Italian New Left, and almost seamlessly merged into the Movimento Studentesco, the new star on the horizon of Italian radical politics.[68]

[66] Mario Cuminetti, *Il dissenso cattolico in Italia. 1965–1980* (Milan: Rizzoli, 1983), p. 118.

[67] Giorgio Vecchio, Daniela Saresella, and Paolo Trionfini, *Storia dell'Italia contemporanea. Dalla crisi del fascismo alla crisi della Repubblica (1939–1998)* (Bologna: Monduzzi, 1999), p. 442.

[68] Raoul Mordenti, 'Appunti per una storia dell'Intesa universitaria e una interpretazione del suo scioglimento', in Lorenzo Bedeschi et al., *I cristiani nella sinistra. Dalla Resistenza a oggi* (Rome: Coines, 1976), pp. 147–83, especially pp. 176–83.

Symbolically, it was precisely at the influential Catholic University of Milan, La Cattolica, that events propelled Italian Left Catholic student activism to central place in Italian national political culture of the late 1960s. As was the case with the University of Leuven, La Cattolica appeared to many as an unlikely venue for student activism. Traditional university authorities' paternalism was magnified by conservative Catholic values which cast a shadow over the most minute details of students' everyday life. All entrants to La Cattolica had to be members of the Catholic church. Students or faculty found to be 'living in sin' were automatically expelled. To ensure that such temptations were minimized, female students were regularly placed with families. Small wonder that an absence of left-wing political traditions—a very *un*-Italian feature of universities in the 1960s—characterized La Cattolica. Still in 1968, 65 per cent of La Cattolica's students attended church services regularly.[69]

It is therefore of considerable interest that the cycle of university student protest which brought Italian higher education to a screeching halt by the late winter and early spring of 1968 commenced precisely on the campus of this ideologically most sheltered university in all of Italy. A general assembly of more than 1,000 students on 17 November 1967, after many hours of heated debate, decided at midnight to occupy the campus for an indeterminate period of time to protest against an impending 50 per cent increase in student fees. Occupation of key buildings, of course, was a traditional tactic in times of crisis by Italian students and had occurred already earlier in the 1960s, though never at La Cattolica. Yet what escalated this action beyond all expectations of everyone involved was the response by the administrators of La Cattolica. Three hours after the call for a campus occupation emerged from the night-long mass meeting of irate students, the police invaded the campus at 3 a.m., forcibly removing hundreds of students from university grounds. 'Had the police not been called, it seems likely that the mobilisation would have fizzled out, especially in the absence in mid-November of a wider national movement.'[70]

In the *ventennio*, the dark twenty years of Italian fascism, La Cattolica had managed to remain one of the few islands in the Italian state where the brutal tentacles of the fascist police had never dared to interfere. Despite the presence of oppositional thinkers amongst La Cattolica's students and lecturers, not once had the forces of fascist law and order stepped onto La Cattolica's grounds. Now, in the wee hours of the morning of 18 November 1967, this proud tradition was broken—by open invitation of the Vice Chancellor.

---

[69] Robert Lumley, *States of Emergency. Cultures of Revolt in Italy from 1968 to 1978* (London: Verso, 1990), pp. 77–86, provides an insightful and stimulating overview of the parameters of student life at La Cattolica in 1967–8.

[70] Lumley, *States of Emergency*, p. 80.

This move engendered the reconsideration of other Catholic traditions, not the least of which the habitual submission to Catholic authorities by Catholic believers. For a half-dozen years, La Cattolica became a hotbed of student radicalism in the Italian state and a central point of reference by activists elsewhere.

La Cattolica had been for many decades the training ground of the Italian Catholic elite, and Amintore Fanfani was only one amongst many prominent Italian Catholics to graduate from this venerable institution. Within Milan, La Cattolica was the largest of the four universities existing at that time. By contrast to its rival institutions, students at La Cattolica hailed from all corners of the Italian state,[71] an important feature soon serving as a reverse transmission mechanism for radical ideas throughout the country, as students from Milan spread the news of struggles at La Cattolica throughout the country. What was the specifically *Catholic* contribution to the explosion at La Cattolica?

Agostino Giovagnoli claims that the events at La Cattolica may not be the best barometer for social ferment amongst Italian Catholics in the late 1960s, as students were then unquestionably already beginning to be influenced by other processes and ideologies across the land.[72] Perhaps so, but in 1967 and 1968 it seemed that the universe of Catholic beliefs still dominated most students' personal behaviours more than any rival ideology. Some snapshots made by (dis)interested observers may underscore this view.

The undisputed charismatic student leader at La Cattolica in 1967–8 was Mario Capanna. In his memoirs Capanna recalls the stressful programme of study, including the constant pressure to excel at exams. Failure to obtain the highest marks resulted in loss of stipends, leading to quasi-automatic termination of university studies in the case of those not fortunate enough to be born into the higher echelons of Italian class society. 'We studied, therefore, day and night. But not solely to prepare for exams.' Capanna and his immediate circle of friends may have been unusual at La Cattolica for their early interest in 'Marx and other Marxist authors', but such forbidden fruits constituted by no means the sole object of extracurricular exploration: 'And we read theologians who were then regarded as innovative and cutting-edge, such as Karl Rahner, Edward Schillebeeckx, Hans Urs von Balthasar. On any number of them we had frequent discussions which lasted into the morning hours.'[73]

The centrality of Catholic thinkers (and the relative irrelevance of Karl Marx) emerges from countless reports of ferment at La Cattolica in 1967

[71] On this, see yet another contribution by Robert Lumley, 'Il Movimento Studentesco di Milano', in Aldo Agosti, Luisa Passerini, and Nicola Tranfaglia (eds), *La cultura e i luoghi del '68* (Milan: Franco Angeli, 1991), pp. 267–74.
[72] Agostino Giovagnoli, 'Cattolici nel Sessantotto', in Agostino Giovagnoli (ed.), *1968: fra utopia e Vangelo. Contestazione e mondo cattolico* (Rome: Ave, 2000), p. 39.
[73] Mario Capanna, *Formidabili quegli anni* (Milan: Rizzoli, 1998), p. 18.

and 1968. An account published in Italy's Communist daily, *L'unità*, on 22 November 1967, five days after the ill-fated occupation, makes clear that amongst the most frequently cited authorities in the early moments of student activism at La Cattolica were not any Marxists but 'Saint Paul and Saint Augustine, John XXIII and Vatican II; and the most popular tune sung by the movement was *Glory, Glory Hallelujah*'. When students and lecturers arrived from the State University of Milan and began to sing 'Bandiera rossa', La Cattolica's students shut them up by loud and unfriendly hissing.[74] Eight months later, during one of many site occupations by La Cattolica's restless students, a two-week stretch of protests in late May and early June 1968, Mass was celebrated daily in the university chapel with great throngs present. 'Apart from Biblical texts, parts of speeches by John F. Kennedy were read out loud, and Negro Spirituals resounded together with traditional songs. Frequently, at the very end, the celebrants intoned *We Shall Overcome*, whose melody and words well-expressed the hope of the young activists for the success of the ideals which animated them.'[75]

THE RADIANCE OF GIOVENTÙ STUDENTESCA

One of the organizations which aided La Cattolica to enter the activists' hall of fame was Gioventù Studentesca (GS), an organization whose origins lay within the network of secondary schools in Milan. Quickly making its presence felt at La Cattolica as well, GS achieved a degree of notoriety second to none, and the classic English-language account of Italy's red decade (1968–78) notes that, at the University of the Sacred Heart, GS 'became a cauldron of open debate and discussion', where '[h]umanist and populist ideas linked up with Marxist theories, and evangelism took on the form of overtly political activism'.[76] Given the conjunctural importance of GS, whose radiance far exceeded the city limits of the Lombard capital, and the ongoing fame of its successor organization of sorts, Comunione e Liberazione (CL), it is instructive to take a closer look at GS whose history remains largely unknown. In fact, given the central role within GS and CL by Don Luigi Giussani, a short glance at his intellectual biography will point out the solid roots of Giussani within the discourse of the Italian—and indeed European—Catholic Left.

---

[74] Reported in Roberto Beretta, *Il lungo autumno. Controstoria del Sessantotto cattolico* (Milan: Rizzoli, 1998), p. 28.

[75] Interview of Father Nello Casalini in 1997, taken from Beretta, *Il lungo autumno*, pp. 62–3. Along with Mario Capanna, Nello Casalini was a key student leader at La Cattolica, the chairperson of practically all student general assemblies held for the duration of the long '1968' on Milan's campus. Casalini joined the Franciscan order in 1973.

[76] Lumley, *States of Emergency*, p. 79.

At the Catholic elite school where Luigi Giussani received his secondary and seminary education from 1937 onwards, the Seminario di Venegono, Giussani crucially came under the influence of prominent representatives of Italian progressive Catholicism. An authority on GS and Luigi Giussani, Massimo Camisasca, repeatedly highlights the particularly formative influence of Gaetano Corti amongst the faculty at Venegono.[77] Symptomatically, it was precisely Gaetano Corti who incorporated the teachings of three of the most important schools of innovative Catholic theology in the 1930s: progressive Dominican strands at Le Saulchoir, progressive Jesuits at Fourvière, and the Innsbruck school of kerygmatic theology.[78] Luigi Giussani's ideas did not exactly fall from the sky.[79]

Taking over a small Milan grouping in existence since 1945, Gioventù Studentesca, from 1954 onwards Giussani devoted much of his intellectual and organizational energies and skills to turn the hitherto unremarkable circle into the most dynamic organization within the plethora of Italian Catholic organizations in the run-up to 1968. Considering Catholic Action, as it then existed in Italy, as animated by 'a well-groomed, hortatory enthusiasm, challenged into action [solely] by ceremonial aspects',[80] Luigi Giussani struck out in—for Italy—entirely new directions. Realizing that, even in Italy, Catholicism was losing its hold over ever-larger segments of the population, Giussani developed in the course of the 1950s a novel approach to regain and retain influence over young Italians in the largest population centre of northern Italy, Milan, which Archbishop Montini in 1957 had declared *terre de mission.*

GS was initially exclusively implanted in several Milanese high schools, and it was in this seemingly inhospitable environment in the classic period of the post-1945 economic miracle where Giussani netted his first successes. Unlike traditional Italian Catholic Action, which focused above all on the religious dimension, sometimes—as was also the case with the FUCI—likewise on the elite and electoral dimension of Italian Catholic politics, Giussani encouraged GS to concentrate on the social and cultural dimension of missionary activism. In fact, Giussani inspired his followers to devise a 'holistic' technique of creating an environment and atmosphere which shaped GS into a lively organization serving simultaneously as vehicle for expansion and as a social centre where free expression of ideas would encourage personal growth of GS

[77] Massimo Camisasca, *Comunione e Liberazione. Le origini (1965–1968)* (Cinisello Balsamo: San Paolo, 2001), pp. 76 and 81.

[78] Salvator Abbruzzese, *Comunione e Liberazione* (Bologna: Il Mulino, 2001), pp. 31–2.

[79] The influence of one of the key activists in the first wave of nonconformist Italian Left Catholics, Don Primo Mazzolari, on Luigi Giussani is noted in Maria Bocci, '"La Chiesa in quanto tale". Il Concilio indiviso, da Gioventù Studentesca a Comunione e Liberazione', *Bollettino dell'Archivio per la storia del movimento sociale cattólico in Italia* 45/2–3 (May–December 2010), p. 204.

[80] Luigi Giussani's words, cited in Abbruzzese, *Comunione e Liberazione*, p. 17.

members. From the beginning, weekly assemblies at its headquarters in Via Statuto were occasions when members could freely air issues, ideas, and problems which preoccupied their minds, having arisen in the context of their daily lives. For young Catholic high school students on the receiving end of paternalism in their families, at their schools, and in the church, GS thus quickly became a cherished home away from home. For an idealistic generation of young people, GS thus literally and figuratively appeared to prefigure the most desirable features of utopian Christian communities based on honesty and authenticity.[81]

In effect, the weekly assemblies served a function very similar to consciousness-raising techniques applied by early second wave feminist circles a few years later, helping to forge close, intimate, affective bonds between GS members. What further strengthened the community spirit of GS were a series of charitable projects constituting a central aspect of GS activities. Students from the mostly middle-class secondary schools, where GS had grown strong roots, went on regular visits to the proletarian and sub-proletarian districts on the outskirts of industrial northern Italy's largest town in order to assist the socially disadvantaged in various ways, not dissimilar to what the Comunità di Sant'Egidio would be doing in the wake of 1968 in Rome. From 1963 onwards, GS also organized summer camps in rural Calabria in Italy's underdeveloped South for similar charitable purposes. Already in 1960, a missionary programme in Brazil had been launched under the auspices of GS.[82]

With many GS high school students soon graduating and many of them becoming university students, GS soon branched out into the world of post-secondary higher education, quickly making inroads in these milieux as well. Geographically, GS soon spread outside Milan proper, with new branches being founded throughout Lombardy but also elsewhere throughout Italy. Two mechanisms played a particularly favourable role in this growth of the organization into a nationally organized group. The preferred summer holiday destinations of Milanese middle-class families were then the coastal towns of Liguria and the Romagna. Young *giessini*—as GS members were referred to by the initials of their organization—finding themselves in significant numbers in such resort communities, quickly began to reconstitute GS circles on location, often inspiring young students permanently living at the Ligurian and Adriatic

---

[81] A marvellous and evocative description of these mechanisms, which contributed significantly to forge a powerful communitarian spirit within GS, is Luca Perrone, 'Rinnovamento religioso e civile nell'esperienza di "Gioventù Studentesca"', *Il mulino* 16/7 (no. 177), July 1967, pp. 493–522. Perrone was then the editor of the GS newspaper, *Milano studenti*, and it was under his editorial guidance that GS evolved into a component part of the Italian New Left. At the time Perrone wrote this piece, however, much of this evolution was yet to materialize, and the article is therefore a rare snapshot of a social movement in rapid motion.

[82] Detailed narrative descriptions of these charitable works in the Bassa Milanese, Calabria, and Brazil can be found in Camisasca, *Comunione e Liberazione*, pp. 179–204.

coasts, who had come into contact with visiting Milanese *giessini*, to found local chapters. When GS had begun to infiltrate the university milieu, another diffusion mechanism began to click in. After finishing university studies, many graduates returned to their respective home towns, bringing the gospel of GS organizational techniques to previously untouched locations.[83]

Yet perhaps the most revolutionary feature of GS was Giussani's insistence on co-education within GS, at a time when for several decades to come Italian Catholic Action groupings were always and everywhere expending much energy on the continued existence of separate organizations for the two sexes. For Giussani, the overarching principle of GS was its mirroring of real life situations and contemporary sociabilities. Day trips and vacation colonies—not just activities at their home base—thus saw members of both sexes spending quality time together away from home and school, clearly one additional source of the growing popularity of GS amongst the high school crowd. Small wonder that the Catholic hierarchy soon began to air some concerns about the existence and the comportment of GS, which stood apart from all similar organizations within the galaxy of Italian Catholic Action. In addition, the charitable work in the Bassa Milanese and later on Calabria slowly undermined another principle of Italian Catholic Action, its firm support to traditional parishes as the fundamental building block of associational life, as *giessini* from a large mix of Milanese parishes joined forces in these encounters with the darker side of the Italian economic miracle in the 1950s and 1960s. By the late 1960s, Don Giussani even began to go beyond diocesan—and not just parish—boundaries when helping to set up cultural centres for his movement, which served as powerful magnets attracting new crowds.[84]

THE SPIRIT OF '68

Until the mid-1960s, however, this challenge to church traditions was not part of any larger plan to question authority as such. In fact, though GS was open to the spirit of Vatican II, it did not engage in challenging political campaigns. Indeed, when other Catholic organizations, such as the FUCI, began to champ at the bit, such as in October 1962 when the FUCI supported a student strike

---

[83] Perrone, 'Rinnovamento', pp. 510–12, devotes some stimulating passages to the spread of GS throughout Italy. Further narrative detail on this expansion is in Camisasca, *Comunione e Liberazione*, pp. 212–34. One local high school student in Rimini on the Adriatic, who first got into contact with GS in such a coastal resort, was Andrea Riccardi, the *spiritus rector* of the Comunità di Sant'Egidio some years later. Conversation with Roberto Morozzo, 16 April 2012.

[84] The significance of the establishment of such *centri culturali* as implicit challenges to diocesan control is underlined by Abbruzzese, *Comunione e Liberazione*, pp. 24–5.

in solidarity with the Spanish anti-Franco underground, GS kept its distance from this campaign, though characteristically taking care not to align itself with the position of the curia either. If there was a strong authoritarian influence within GS, it lay in the unquestioned veneration of Luigi Giussani who, a charismatic figure by all accounts, for all practical purposes directed GS. Even the weekly consciousness-raising sessions run by GS had a distinct component which made the atmosphere within GS different from similar free expressions of ideas within specialized Catholic Action on the other side of the Alps, which had already propelled the latter to international fame in the interwar period. The weekly assemblies in Milan always 'ended with the most mature person present (often a priest) furnishing a synthesis [of what the young *giessini* had aired]', attempting to channel youthful energies in acceptable directions.[85]

Still, in the course of the second half of the 1960s, GS—not unlike other sections of Italian Catholicism—was irreversibly shifting to the left. Whether the removal of Giussani as leader of GS by the Milanese hierarchy in 1965 can be blamed for this evolution may be subject to doubt. At any rate, missionary activity in Brazil had brought GS in close contact with radical currents hitherto unknown to them. It was subsequently only a small step for Third World solidarity activists to apply their perceived lessons from the extra-European context to the socio-political situation on their own doorstep in First World countries. And so it came to be in industrial northern Italy. Oriented towards the student milieu, *giessini* quickly mutated into student radicals, responding enthusiastically to the signs of the times. With Luca Perrone as editor, the GS house organ, *Milano studenti*, reaching a distribution of 15,000 copies per issue in the run-up to 1968, turned its attention 'towards the problem of the Third World, revolution in Latin America, situations of deprivation and poverty, thus drawing attention to themes and issues which were now coming to the surface within the movement [i.e. GS] and which would lead to the crisis of 1968'.[86]

The critical spirit and the open-minded attitudes towards all sorts of innovations, characteristic of GS from its very beginning, now began to take their toll. As happened with the Intesa Cattólica, GS membership began to melt away, swelling the ranks of the rapidly expanding ecumenical and secular Movimento Studentesco in inverse proportion. Salvatore Abbruzzese reports that 'virtually the entire leadership of GS, half of its rank-and-file, the entire Rimini section of GS, all *giessini* working in Brazil except for the founder of the Brazil outpost, Don Pigi Bernareggi, abandoned GS to enter into the fledgling

---

[85] Abbruzzese, *Comunione e Liberazione*, p. 20.

[86] Camisasca, *Comunione e Liberazione*, p. 204. Maria Bocci, 'La Chiesa in quanto tale', p. 250, writes: '"Milano Studenti" now concentrated on socio-political themes which had up to then been of secondary concern compared to articles on cultural or ecclesial topics.'

Movimento Studentesco, a process revealing an inner sensibility within GS, which had somehow been fashioned in the preceding years and which its working methods, constantly open towards new experiences, and its communitarian lifestyle, encouraging discussion and activist engagement, had nourished all along'.[87] Even and especially at the epicentre of GS activism, Milan, the defections were devastating. Almost all university students with GS affiliation at La Cattolica shifted their allegiance to the Movimento Studentesco; in total half of all *giessini* in Milan jumped ship.[88] The remainder of GS, under the leadership once again of Luigi Guissani, now profoundly changed direction and rapidly evolved towards what soon became best known under the label of Communione e Liberazione.

TRENTO AND PARMA

Continuous frictions and bouts of campus occupations after November 1967 made La Cattolica a national symbol of Catholic dissent. But there were other locations which exemplified the spirit of 1968, several of them associated in particular with student activism. One such *lieu de mémoire* became the University of Trento, a brand-new campus founded in 1962, de facto a Catholic institute of higher education. Trento University students preceded La Cattolica's students in taking to the streets, starting with a first campus occupation in January 1966. By the time La Cattolica in Milan joined the fray, Trento already possessed seasoned student leaders. I have addressed events in Trento in detail elsewhere.[89] In the context of this chapter I merely wish to draw attention to an event on 26 March 1968. On that Tuesday at a quarter past seven in the evening, between fifty and sixty students literally invaded the Trento cathedral where a church service was being held, challenging the priest who was known for his conservative views and then shouting: 'This is not true! Everything is a lie!' Irate parishioners quickly removed the sociology students. Headed by the devout Paolo Sorbi, several days later another group of thirty to forty students sat down in the front rows of the Trento Cathedral, quietly rising from their seats as soon as Mass began to be celebrated. The students silently marched out of the building and then commenced a

---

[87] Abbruzzese, *Comunione e Liberazione*, p. 58.
[88] Camisasca, *Comunione e Liberazione*, p. 286.
[89] See the relevant pages in my chapter on student activism in my *Spirit of 1968*, pp. 74–83. The most comprehensive treatment of radical Catholic activism at Trento is now Alessandro Chini, *Il dissenso cattolico. Dal postconcilio al referendum sul divorzio in Italia e a Trento* (Trento: Edizioni U.C.T., 2009), which, on pp. 49–200, draws a rich portrait of events at this cradle of the Italian student movement.

counter-celebration in front of the cathedral, reading from texts by dissident Catholics, such as Don Lorenzo Milani or Don Ernesto Balducci.[90]

Yet the most shocking and prominent challenge to church traditions, coupled with an invasion of sacred ground, was the church occupation in Parma on 14 September 1968. The following account is largely based on a reconstruction of this action by Brunella Manotti. Her evocative description commences several years before this headline news event. The story of the base community of Santa Maria della Pace may stand for other personal and political itineraries of dissident Catholics up to 1968. The sole difference consists in the unusual climax of their organizing efforts which can be traced back to 1963.[91]

A branch of the Gioventù Studentesca had been founded in the parish of Santa Maria della Pace in Parma to enable a group of mostly high school students to provide an alternative to the regular fare of church-sponsored activities. In November 1964, this small circle of friends obtained an important ally with the appointment of the 24-year-old Don Pino Setti as parish priest. He energized the informal group, and soon they published a small magazine, *Il ponte*, initially subtitled 'Internal Bulletin of Gioventù Studentesca'. By 1966 they gave themselves a proper name: I Protagonisti. Don Pino Setti offered a range of options for his parish youth, including frequent outings into the open air, where Mass was held and ideas were freely debated. The balance of activities and ideas was clearly tilting towards the left. Young people, who had few other outlets for creativity and the exchange of limitless ideas, were encouraged to speak out. For women members of this group in particular, I Protagonisti is remembered still decades later as a source of great empowerment. New non-alienated and non-hierarchical interactions between priestly authority and laity were central to the success of this particular group.

Links were established to other base communities. Dissident Catholic thinkers were invited as guest speakers, including the Florentine iconoclast Ernesto Balducci. I Protagonisti established study groups where the works of nonconformist intellectuals and activists were discussed, including such figures as Pier Paolo Pasolini, Ignazio Silone, and the famous songwriter and musician from Genova, Fabrizio De André. When I Protagonisti began to explore the meaning and the message of Luigi Tenco, an icon of Italian youthful rebels in the 1960s who had committed suicide in January 1967, I Protagonisti began to make inroads into a previously untapped group of cultural rebels, the countercultural milieu, exemplified by provocatively

[90] A detailed account of this challenge to Catholic authority is the chapter, 'Trento. La protesta entra in chiesa', in Beretta, *Il lungo autumno*, pp. 74–81.

[91] Brunella Manotti, '"La mia religione era un profumo": Parma e il dissenso cattolico. Il caso de I Protagonisti', in Margherita Becchetti et al., *Parma dentro la rivolta. Tradizione e radicalità nelle lotte sociali e politiche di una città dell'Emilia rossa 1968–1969* (Milan: Punto Rosso, 2000), pp. 33–84.

dressed young women and young men with ostentatiously long hair, *i capel-loni.* One such recruit to I Protagonisti via the focus group on Luigi Tenco was the Parma-based Francesco Schianchi, a student at Milan's La Cattolica, about whom more below.

In March 1967, Don Pino Setti decided to organize an event which put Parma on the map of dissident Catholicism in the Italian state. Profiting from new links to countercultural iconoclasts, he arranged for one of Italy's most infamous rock bands, I Corvi, to join Don Setti for what became Italy's first Beat Mass. The event drew a substantial crowd. Not only was the church filled with unusual musical sounds, but appeals for peace in Vietnam were launched from the pulpit, and loudspeakers carried the message to the overflow crowd assembled outside. The conservative local paper, the *Gazzetta di Parma*, described the scene in rather unflattering terms, concentrating on what local notables regarded as scenes more appropriate to an inferno than to a holy site: 'Ragazze in minigonna, capelloni e barboni.' [Girls in miniskirts, young men with long hair and shaggy beards.] Don Pino Setti now drew the attention of his superiors as well.

In November 1967 I Protagonisti decided to link up with a Walk for Peace in Vietnam, heading across Italy from Milan to Rome and making a stopover in Parma. Don Pino Setti wanted to join up as well, but church authorities explicitly forbade him from joining the youthful crowd. Don Pino ignored his superiors and along with secular and other religious figures, including Danilo Dolci, he addressed an immense crowd from a balcony overseeing the Piazza Garibaldi in Parma's city centre. The authorities now directly intervened, and Don Pino was removed from his post and sent into internal exile to serve as a village priest in a remote mountain hamlet in the Appenines. I Protagonisti were besides themselves with rage and plotted further actions, now no longer relying on Don Pino's advice. At first they believed that they could persuade church authorities in Parma to lift the ban on Don Pino. They met with the bishop, but the conversation led nowhere. Only when I Protagonisti felt that all other avenues had been tried and tested did they decide on the action which made I Protagonisti, still mostly composed of local high school students, into a household term for the Italian Catholic Left.

At this point it is worth stressing the arrival of Francesco Schianchi on the scene in the wake of the study group's intense discussion of the meaning of Luigi Tenco's life. A student at La Cattolica, Francesco Schianchi had partici-pated in the student unrest in Milan, including the never-ending succession of site occupations. The idea to occupy the Parma cathedral was launched by none other than Francesco Schianchi;[92] as soon as it was aired, I Protagonisti set about to implement this plan. A member of I Protagonisti recalls: 'There

---

[92] On the catalytic role of Francesco Schianchi, see, once again, Beretta, *Il lungo autumno*, pp. 72 and 147.

had been the occupations of the universities. The student movement occupied the university; we are Catholics, so we occupied our home. For us the church was our home; we did not regard it as the home of priests only. We are the people of God ... We were in line with Vatican II.'

On 14 September at 4:30 p.m. about a dozen activists walked into the Dome and sat in a circle around the altar. Emulating the practice of university students who frequently used campus occupations to hold alternative seminars and discussion groups on topics frowned upon by traditional authorities, I Protagonisti began to host a teach-in on the theme of poverty. A much larger crowd of supporters soon gathered; outside the Dome in central Parma a banner soon proclaimed: 'La Cattedrale è occupata.' Church authorities in Parma were bewildered and responded by the sole means they felt would restore their authority. They called on the police to evict the students from the temple of God.

Three hours after the initial nucleus of protagonists had walked into the church, a much larger number of dissidents were literally carried out of the church. With protesters employing passive resistance techniques, police began to manhandle the demonstrators with impunity. Photographers from the local press were clicking away, taking great pleasure in producing shots that would shock and please their conservative and voyeuristic readers. Aiming to cast aspersions on the morality and ethics behind the students' actions, the cameras recorded in particular images of young women dragged away by policemen, unable to straighten their skirts while in the hands of the law enforcement officers. The Dome in Parma was returned to its previous state of austere silence, but the effect of this event sent shockwaves across Italy.

Solidarity statements were sent from base communities across the land, principled statements which in turn engendered serious consequences for some of their authors, who explicitly declared their agreement with the act of disobedience by Parma students—such as Don Enzo Mazzi and the Comunità dell'Isolotto. It would lead too far astray to detail further steps along this road which led to the flowering of dissident Catholicism in Italy throughout the decade of the 1970s. But the point has hopefully been made. Not only did Italian Catholicism begin to experience serious challenges from within, but Catholic students took up front-line positions in this fight.

THE JEUNESSE ÉTUDIANTE CATHOLIQUE INTERNATIONALE

The umbrella organization of this amazing welter of Catholic student organizations rapidly evolving towards the left reflected the multiplicity of approaches and the rapid succession of answers given to the issues at the centre of European student concerns. The history of the Jeunesse Étudiante Catholique Internationale (JECI) remains to be written.[93] Like literally all other international federations of specialized Catholic Action branches, whose archives are readily accessible but which await their historian,[94] the trajectory of the JECI at the highpoint of student struggles in Europe and the world reflects the ups and downs of student movements and their ideological debates in almost perfect laboratory conditions.

During the first half of the 1960s, the JECI was in tune with progressive currents in the Catholic church, and the experts invited to their conferences and study sessions hailed from the milieu of theologians representing the currents which helped shape Vatican II. Thus, the summer camp of the university branch of the JECI in Anseremme along the River Meuse in the Walloon Ardennes saw the Belgian-born Dutch reform theologian Edward Schillebeeckx as the central referee.[95] What is worth highlighting, however, is that, already in the early-to-mid-1960s, Spanish theologians were unusually prominent amongst the invited experts, no doubt reflecting the ferment then erupting in the Spanish underground, which cast a bright light over JECI sections in other European states. In 1962, for instance, on the occasion of the 1962 summer camp of the university branches of the JECI in Switzerland, Luis Maldonado, theology professor at a branch campus of the University of Salamanca in Madrid and, in 1962, the chaplain of JEC students at the University of Madrid, introduced the vacationing students to the theology of Karl Rahner.[96] At the European Study Session of the JECI in Folkestone, England, in September 1965, it was the chaplain of the Spanish JEC from 1962 to 1967 and, in 1965, simultaneously the chaplain of the JECI, Jesús Maria Lasagabáster Medinabeitia, who presented his thoughts on 'The Role of the Christian in the World and the School of Today' to his audience, basing his reflections on the works of Rahner, Schillebeeckx, and other reform theologians, but also devoting significant space to the theology of José María González Ruiz.[97]

---

[93] I intend to address the vagaries of JECI politics in the 1960s and 1970s in a future article. This subchapter of Chapter 4 is merely designed to trace the vague outlines of the turbulences affecting the life and times of the JECI in *les années 68*.

[94] To mention but one goldmine: the archive of the Jeunesse Ouvrière Catholique Internationale (JOCI) in Brussels is extremely well organized and enormously rich—though, thus far, painfully ignored by scholars.

[95] Report on the 'Universitätslager der IKSY', 'Anseremme, 30. VIII–12. IX [19]60'—Bibliothèque de documentation internationale contemporaine (BDIC), Fonds Jeunesse Étudiante Catholique Internationale (JECI), F delta 1980/106.

[96] The French text of his allocution, 'El sentido del trabajo estudiantil en el plan de Dios', can be consulted in BDIC, JECI, F delta 1980/110.

[97] 'Le Rôle du chrétien dans le monde et l'école d'aujourd'hui', 'Session d'études européennes de la JEC Internationale, Folkestone (Angleterre), 6–11 septembre 1965'—BDIC, JECI, F delta 1980/810.

If the Iberian dictatorships served to alert European JECI activists to the fragility of democracy, the political and social realities of Latin America contributed to the politicization of the JECI even further. For the JECI was, by definition, not a European but a world association of Catholic students. Latin American students played prominent roles in the JECI from the 1950s onwards. Thus the Brazilian Luis Alberto Gómez do Souza was elected Secretary General of the JECI at the 1958 World Council session in Dakar, Senegal. More importantly, for many crucial years during the wave of radicalization of student politics, the chaplain of the JECI, headquartered in Paris, was Father Luis de Gonzaga di Sena, formerly an instructor at the priest seminary of Olinda and the University of Recife, forced to leave Brazil as a political exile.[98] Radical ferment had gripped Latin American campuses long before it began to affect most European campuses north of the Pyrenees, and their ideas rapidly gained followers within European sections of the JECI by the late 1960s.[99] The Portuguese delegation to the 1970 London Conference of the JECI, themselves no strangers to bold initiatives, in their internal conference report prominently noted:

> Of all groups present in London, those who impressed us by far the most were the Latin Americans—and this for various reasons. Apart from being extraordinarily communicative, everyone there felt that their contributions to our gathering were the most precious. They are individuals used to thinking for themselves, full of ideas and questions, capable of always expressing what is on their minds when they have something to say, truly committed to the tasks at hand. One virtually senses how their brains are continuously active, always tackling issues straightforwardly, focusing on the reality of their home countries and the entire world. Their thought processes were continuously stimulated by their confrontation with these realities, always ready to take up the challenge to think for themselves. One could tell that they have a deep-going understanding not only of their own situation but, more generally, of the world situation as such.[100]

[98] Father Sena arrived in France in 1964. Later on assuming the position of chaplain of the JECI, he served in this capacity until 1974; see 'Merci Sena', in *Lettre au Conseil* 12 (70–4), March 1974—BDIC, JECI, F delta 1980/213. None other than Dom Hélder Câmara in 1964 became archbishop of Olinda and Recife, the home base of Father Sena.

[99] A classification of organizations belonging to the JECI, based on an internal questionnaire sent to JECI sections in 1970, which asked for clarification on their preferred strategies for social change, clearly shows Latin American sections in the vanguard of radical sentiments, with sections from all other continents clearly trailing behind their Latin American cohort in the degree of commitment to radical solutions; see 'Rapports de la Session Mondiale de la JECI', 'Londres 1970': Peter Praetz, 'Introduction générale', p. 14—BDIC, JECI, F delta 1980/46.

[100] 'Informaçao sobre a sessão mundial e o conselho mundial da JEC Internacional (Londra, 23 jul. – 18 ago. 1970)', pp. 10–11—BDIC, JECI, F delta 1980/1062. I thank Roberto Zaugg for valuable assistance in translating this passage.

FROM APOSTOLIC MISSIONARIES
TO THE RADICAL LEFT

But, of course, it was not solely the influence of Latin American sections, magnified no doubt by the presence of Luis Sena in the JECI headquarters in Paris,[101] which opened the eyes of *jecistes* to global inequalities and the lack of justice in the world. The 1960s was a time when, triggered into action by the Algerian and Cuban revolutions and then further scandalized by the Vietnam War, First World activists began to 'discover' the Third World. The 1964 World Council of the JECI, held in Montreal, devoted its study session—a regular feature of such world councils—to 'The Mission of Students in the Face of Underdevelopment'. The official report on the Council deliberations, written by the Argentinian General Secretary of the JECI, Paco del Campio, prominently underscored: 'The deliberations of the Council during those twelve days focused on two fundamental aspects of the problem of domination in the world of today: the problematic of the struggle against underdevelopment which concerns all of humanity because of its global implications, and the quest for—and respect and development of—the original character particular to each region and each culture', an agenda with unlimited implications, to say the least.[102]

The events of the calendar year of 1968—not only but above all in France—then added further fuel to the flames. A call for a meeting of Regional Secretaries of the JECI in early 1969 vividly paints a picture of a scenario bound to create further uncertainties. The document underscores 'the acceleration of the transformations which today's world is undergoing, the speed with which the student milieux are undergoing a learning process, mobilizing themselves and agitating within society, all the while undergoing a profound inner transformation, both with regard to ideas and actions'. At the same time the circular noted 'the crisis which the Church is experiencing and which the Holy Father did not hesitate to call "a crisis of self-destruction"', and the document goes on to suggest that 'the fight against the societal status quo is the sole means which students have developed in order to demonstrate their desire to participate in the building of this world. Contestation—we utilize this expression for the moment without deeper reflection on its utility—is the language peculiar to the student movement in the underdeveloped and the developed world today.'[103]

---

[101] The central role of Luis Sena in the rapid evolution of the JECI to the left precisely in the conjuncture at the end of the 1960s and the very beginning of the 1970s was underscored in a recent email communication by Peter Praetz, who was then a member of the JECI leadership team in Paris; email by Peter Praetz to Gerd-Rainer Horn on 24 October 2011.

[102] Paco del Campio, 'Rapport du Conseil Mondial', 'Montreal 1967'—BDIC, JECI, F delta 1980/37.

[103] 'Circulaire aux Secrétaires Régionaux', 26 mars 1969, p. 1—BDIC, JECI, F delta 1980/103.

After a period of what could in retrospect be regarded as Third World solidarity work, the focus of European sections now shifted back towards their own societies at home. Virtually all European sections underwent a period of intense radicalization, but a radicalization at two different speeds resulting in two potentially—but not necessarily—conflicting strategies. One sought to forge close links with other sections of society 'and concentrated on an exploration of the reasons for the distrust of the student protests by the proletariat and the need for a strategy which aimed at solidarity between militant students and workers. The second assumed that the political neutralization of the masses of workers would not be overcome in the foreseeable future, and therefore called for a strategy aimed at undermining the support of the new capitalism by the intelligentsia and the absorption of socialist ideas into the educational system.'[104] Both views on how to change the world were a far cry from what the JECI had been all about a mere half-dozen years earlier.

New strategies called for new spiritual guides, and Edward Schillebeeckx and Karl Rahner were replaced by representatives of what can be regarded as the Far Left within progressive Catholic milieux. The star of the 1970 World Council in London was now Paul Blanquart, the Dominican radical priest who excited his audience by his invocation of the centrality of 'utopia' as inspiration for concrete action in the here-and-now. Religious belief can powerfully assist socialist action, he persuasively argued, precisely if it utilizes utopia as the intermediary—the point of contact—between faith and political action.[105] And the archives abound with statements with regard to the great impact made by Blanquart at the London gathering.[106] Paul Blanquart became a much-sought-after tribune at conferences all over Europe in subsequent years.

Four years later, at the next World Council of the JECI in the Dutch village of Cadier en Keer near Maastricht in 1974, it was Gustavo Gutiérrez who spellbound his audience with a magisterial survey of the ways in which faith had made an impact on the contemporary world, 'Experiencia de Fe'. Explicating the various contributions of earlier or contemporaneous radical theologians, notably theologies of development, theologies of revolution, and theologies of violence, Gutiérrez underscored the particular vitality of the radical new theology with which his name has since become associated: the

---

[104] 'The European Student Conference, 1969', 'Gwatt, Switzerland, March 23–27', p. 1—BDIC, JECI, F delta 1980/785.

[105] Material on the crucial 1970 London World Council can be found in F delta 1980/43–6, including the text of Blanquart's intervention, 'Éléments pour l'interprétation et la critique de la société', a presentation of high intellectual niveau, using the language of unorthodox non-structuralist, indeed revolutionary, Marxism, followed by a lengthy discussion by various participants and a final response by Blanquart in F delta 1980/46.

[106] Note, for instance, the reminiscence of the then-chaplain of the Spanish JEC, José Pachón Zúñigo, in 1978: 'In 1970 the JEC was profoundly marked by the ideas of Father Blanquart put forth at the World Council in London'; see Zúñigo's 'Memoria Cristiana de la JEC. 1969–1977', p. 3—BDIC, JECI, F delta 1980/820.

theology of liberation. Gutiérrez offered the theology of liberation as the most radical solution of all such professions of faith, exceeding in explosive power all rival radical theologies then much in vogue throughout the world. The Spanish language version of his intervention notably includes a fascinating sixty-page transcript of the ensuing discussion with Catholic student revolutionaries at Cadier en Keer.[107]

It would go too far to further describe and analyse the remarkable radicalization undergone by the JECI in the late sixties and the first half of the 1970s in particular; but this brief invocation of the overall contours of this development will hopefully have further underscored—if there was any remaining doubt—that Catholic student politics in the red decade between 1966 and 1976 was a constituent part of—and key force behind—radical student politics in Europe as such. Where Catholic students did not outright join the fledgling groupings of the New and the Far Left, many of their organizations became close allies and forged intimate ties with their radical secular cohort to the left of the Old Left.

[107] Material on the 1974 Cadier en Keer World Council is in BDIC, JECI, F delta 1980/47–54; the text of Gutiérrez's fiery speech, complete with the minutes of the subsequent debate it engendered, is in F delta 1980/54.

5

The Working Class Goes to Paradise

THE CONFEDERAZIONE ITALIANA SINDACATI DEI LAVORATORI (CISL)

It is by no means easy to pinpoint the specifically Catholic roots of activism amongst students belonging to the generation of '1968'. This forensic task constitutes an even greater challenge when attempting to assess the Catholic motivations behind working-class militancy, which is equally characteristic of the conjuncture of '1968', certainly in Mediterranean Europe.[1] For student leaders, benefiting from their familiarity with texts and written expression of ideas, frequently penned autobiographies, if they did not become the outright objects of biographical studies themselves. Working-class leaders had far fewer occasions to devote precious free time to the production of reflections on their own personal and political itineraries. Given the particular volatility of the Italian cauldron of multiform social movement activity for several years after 1968, sufficient material has been published on the veritable laboratory of radical working-class action south of the Alps to permit at least an approximate picture of the issues at hand. Characteristically, much of the material allowing much-needed and hitherto much-occluded insight into the Catholic motivation for radical working-class insurgency stems from sources closely identified with 'Catholic' workers' associations, above all the quintessentially Catholic trade union federation, the Confederazione Italiana Sindacati dei Lavoratori (CISL).

From 1968 till 1976, no country in Europe experienced such a seemingly permanent wave of working-class struggles and working-class gains quite like that in Italy. Especially in the upswing phase of 1968–72, the CISL occupied pride of place within the range of contestations which made Italian factories

---

[1] For a survey of the working-class dimension of the upsurge in activism in the late 1960s and early 1970s, see my chapter, '"Vogliamo Tutto". The Working-Class Dimension of "1968"', in *The Spirit of '68. Rebellion in Western Europe and North America, 1956–1976* (Oxford: Oxford University Press, 2007), pp. 93–130.

and offices almost 'liberated zones' compared to anywhere else in Europe.[2] For anyone familiar with the history of Italian trade union federations—and especially that of the CISL—this was a wholly surprising and unpredicted turn of events. For the CISL had been created to provide a moderate counterweight to the hegemonic Communist current dominating trade union politics in the wake of liberation in 1945. For a few years after liberation, virtually all Italian trade union currents operated within the unified Confederazione Generale Italiana del Lavoro (CGIL). But in 1948, the Catholic current split from the CGIL in the context of emerging Cold War politics, first setting up what became known as the Libera CGIL (Free CGIL), then renaming itself in 1950 as the CISL. For two decades the CISL performed the role of a moderate, pro-Western alternative to the Communist-dominated CGIL. With good reason, the CISL was thus identified as the Catholic answer to 'Communist' intransigence. How could a trade union federation wholly devoted to business unionism turn into a vehicle of societal revolt?

In fact, unlike virtually all other European national Catholic (or Christian) trade union federations set up or revitalized at the onset of the Cold War, the CISL adopted the orientation towards 'secularism' [*laicità*] as an operating principle and ideological identity from the start. From the outset, no formal ties bound the CISL to the Catholic church. Especially in Italy, where the Catholic church could boast of a huge array of capillary organizations within and beyond Catholic Action, this choice of a secular orientation was wholly atypical and was recognized as such by friend and foe. Nonetheless, for all their open advocacy of a pluralist orientation, the CISL was part and parcel of the Italian Catholic universe. In fact, as one of the most astute members of the CISL leadership team, Bruno Manghi, once stated perspicaciously, it was solely because of the deeply Catholic convictions of the founding generation of CISL leaders that the CISL could afford to adopt a lay orientation. In the late 1940s, the Catholic roots of the *cislini* were universally recognized as an outstanding feature of their organization, and thus their embrace of nominal secularism was questioned by few observers at the time.[3]

If the choice of *laicità* was based on the indisputable strength of Catholic convictions within the CISL's leadership and ranks, it nonetheless opened the doors towards a genuinely pluralist orientation. And one way in which this autonomy from the Catholic church was able to manifest itself was in the choice of ideological role models. The traditional social doctrine of the church remained the unquestioned key ideological reference point for quite some

[2] The classic cinematographic expression of this era remains Elio Petri, *La classe operaia va in paradiso* (Italy, 1971).
[3] Note the relevant passage in an interview with Bruno Manghi, 'Una pigra unanimità affievolisce la democrazia', in Fondazione Vera Nocentini (ed.), *Sindacalismo e laicità. Il paradosso della Cisl* (Milan: FrancoAngeli, 2000), p. 46.

time. Catholic social theory viewed society as an interlocking series of relationships based on natural law, where each link performed an assigned role in a quasi-organic harmonious mechanism assuming social peace as a permanent primordial value. But other traditions could also find a toehold in the official culture of the CISL. Given the fascination with American culture as the pinnacle of Western civilization in the era of the Cold War, American trade union practices were widely admired by CISL leaders, and the United States AFL-CIO performed the function of role model in the heyday of Cold War politics in the 1950s and early 1960s.[4]

Yet, for all its Cold War blinkers, even within the AFL-CIO there operated a variety of sometimes conflicting traditions. For the metal workers' federation (FIM) operating within the CISL in the period of incipient reorientation within the CISL (1958–63), Walter Reuther and the early postwar United Automobile Workers (UAW) were a key source of inspiration. And, of course, within the spectrum of American trade union politics, the Reuther period of UAW activism stood at the left margins of the kaleidoscope of US working-class politics.[5]

Yet, more generally, the infatuation with the American role model, in the context of stultifying Italian Cold War politics, frequently introduced into the CISL not just a breath but entire breezes of fresh air. In the face of the hegemony of traditional Catholic social theory, American pragmatism opened up new vistas for *cislini*.[6] What fascinated the CISL the most about their American godfather were the democratic impulses, still visible in AFL-CIO practices in the course of the 1950s, but also the advocacy and practice of unity amongst formerly competing federations[7]—the erstwhile 'enemy brothers', the American Federation of Labor and the Congress of Industrial Organizations, merged into a unitary federation in 1955! Another feature of American culture, the rising star of academic sociology in the 1950s and 1960s, also left a lasting impact on CISL theory and practice.[8] Certainly the important training

---

[4] Note, for instance, Silvana Sciarra, 'L'influenza del sindacalismo "Americano" sulla Cisl', in Guido Baglioni (ed.), *Analisi della Cisl. Fatti e giudizi di un'esperienza sindacale* (Rome: Lavoro, 1980), pp. 283–307.

[5] Bruno Manghi, 'La Fim. Una federazione in un sindacato di categorie', in Baglioni (ed.), *Analisi della Cisl*, p. 663. For the role of the UAW and, in particular, Walter Reuther in the postwar conjuncture of US politics, see Nelson Lichtenstein, *Walter Reuther. The Most Dangerous Man in Detroit* (Urbana, Ill.: University of Illinois Press, 1997).

[6] Again, Bruno Manghi is excellent at teasing out the various strands and consequences of the fascination with United States' practices within the CISL; note his 'La Fim-Cisl. Apologia di un processo di liberazione', in Lorenzo Bedeschi et al., *I cristiani nella sinistra. Dalla Resistenza a oggi* (Rome: Coines, 1976), p. 216.

[7] Interview with Franco Bentivolgi, 'La laicità nell'esperienza formativa dei dirigenti Cisl', in Fondazione Vera Nocentini (ed.), *Sindacalismo e laicità*, p. 56.

[8] For the unusually prominent role of trained sociologists in CISL leadership bodies, note the relevant comments to this effect in Emilio Reyneri, 'Il ruolo della Cisl nel ciclo di lotte 1968–1972', in Baglioni (ed.), *Analisi della Cisl*, p. 749. For a discussion of a similarly

school for CISL cadres, founded in Florence in 1951, for the most part kept Catholic social theory at arm's length in its syllabi and associated practices, preferring to draw on the traditions of the more open-minded American theories and experiences.[9]

Nevertheless, for all practical purposes, up to 1958 and in some respects all the way up to 1968, the CISL was a moderate and 'acceptable' alternative to CGIL radicalism. Even when Giulio Pastore, co-founder and first president of the CISL from 1950 to 1958, stepped down from a cabinet post in the Italian national government in 1960 in protest against the collusion of the Christian Democratic Prime Minister, Fernando Tambroni, with the neofascist Movimento Sociale Italiano, whose votes had been crucial to allow Tambroni to narrowly survive a vote of confidence, the CISL remained wholly absent from the subsequent social and political convulsions affecting Italian civil society.[10] The CISL by and large performed the role assigned to it for close to two decades. If there were no official ties to the Catholic church, the close relationship with conservative Christian Democracy more than made up for this.

THE BREACH OF BRESCIA

Yet, from the late 1950s onwards, concentrated within its metalworking federation (FIM), changes began to be noticed here and there. As is often the case in large organizations, such efforts at tentative reorientations could first be noted at the periphery rather than the centre of CISL operations based, as was the case with the CGIL, in Rome. 'This switch began to be prepared from 1955 onwards, but was first translated into actual practices between 1958 and 1972, first in Brescia, then in Turin, in Milan, in Genoa, in Bergamo.'[11] 'Historically, Brescia was the starting point: a Catholic working-class milieu with distinct characteristics had given rise to an autonomous leadership group'[12] based on the strong presence of skilled workers in the industrial zones of the Val Trompia in the foothills of the Alps to the north of Brescia.

contradictory role of American sociology in the cradle of the Italian student movement, the Higher Institute of Social Studies in what became the University of Trento, note the discussion of 'Sociology in Trento' in Horn, *The Spirit of '68*, pp. 74–7.

[9] On the conspicuous absence of the social doctrine of the church from the learning outcomes of the Florentine study centre, see Bentivogli, 'La laicità', pp. 54–5. For the parameters guiding the training of *cislini* cadres and other elements of continuing education within the CISL's ranks, see Silvio Costantini, 'La formazione del gruppo dirigente della Cisl (1950–1968)', in Baglioni (ed.), *Analisi della Cisl*, pp. 121–57.

[10] Pasquale Colella, 'Cisl e mondo cattolico', in Elisabetta Benenati Marconi et al., *CISL 1948–1968* (Messina: Hobelix, 1981), p. 260.

[11] Manghi, 'La Fim-Cisl', p. 217.   [12] Manghi, 'La Fim', p. 664.

Based on a tradition of deep-rooted Catholic antifascism in the province of Brescia, this courageous and radical nucleus of activists soon made inroads into Brescia proper. Catholic radical populism in Brescia deserves a much closer inspection.

Until 1960, the local CISL leadership team, together with representatives of all other local Catholic associations, each Christmas paid the local church authorities a visit 'as a sign of devotion' and to express their best wishes for the upcoming year. Normally, the CISL had little direct contact with the local church authorities, leaving all direct negotiations in the hands of the Catholic Action organization designated to assist blue-collar workers, the Associazioni Cristiane dei Lavoratori Italiani (ACLI). Yet by 1963 the ACLI and the CISL representing *bresciani* Catholic workers went separate ways, the ACLI then still closely allied to the hierarchy, with *cislini* evolving towards greater independence.[13] What had happened to cause the break-up of this apparently seemless alliance?

The decisive first step by Brescia Catholic workers towards emancipation had been a series of conflicts at the important FIAT subsidiary OM in Brescia around the issue of bonuses paid to workers in return for a no-strike pledge. Radicalized by the Left Catholic sentiment spreading southwards into Brescia proper from the Val Trompia, local CISL leaders began to reconsider the entire tradition of social Catholicism which militated in favour of peaceful labour relations. They were assisted in this reconfiguration of attitudes towards class relationships and class struggle by several local figures within Brescia Catholicism. The premier diocesan theologian, Tullio Goffi, invited to do so by the Brescia CISL, published a widely noted article in the province-wide CISL publication in which he encouraged local *cislini* to strike out in the direction of emancipation and greater autonomy for lay activists. Father Giulio Bevilacqua, a lifelong friend and confidant of Giuseppe Battista Montini, the latter soon to become Pope Paul VI, likewise exhorted *cislini* to rely on their own resources. Asked to intervene in the flagship conflict at OM, Giulio Bevilacqua declined the honour, exhorting lay unionists to assume and rely on their own responsibility and authority if they wished to achieve their goals.

Pope John XXIII's May 1961 encyclical, *Mater et Magistra*, then provided powerful papal support. For *Mater et Magistra* explicitly called for a greater say for workers in the running of their own affairs and in the running of their enterprises, a radical inversion of Catholic social theory. John XXIII also advocated—another first in the history of official papal documents—a more

---

[13] The key study of Catholic working-class politics in postwar Brescia is Franco Gheza, *Cattolici e sindacato. Un esperienza di base. La Fim-Cisl di Brescia* (Rome: Coines, 1975). The move from harmony towards a rift in the relationship between the Brescia CISL and ACLI in the early 1960s is sketched on pp. 189–91 of this important book, citation on p. 189. The remainder of this subsection relies on this indispensable source.

nuanced, historical approach to the Marxist tradition, effectively abandoning
the hitherto unbending wholesale condemnation of Marxism in all its variants.
Mater et Magistra thus not only validated a more conflictual trade union
strategy vis-à-vis employers, but it also gave an implicit green light to efforts to
bridge the divide between the two 'enemy brothers', CISL and CGIL. But by
the time the *cislini* in Brescia felt further empowered by *Mater et Magistra*, the
initial example of Brescia had been emulated elsewhere already. And, of
course, it was not solely *Mater et Magistra* which blew wind in the sails of
the *cislini*, with Turin *cislini* following in the footsteps of their *bresciani*
colleagues almost immediately. The Decree on the Lay Apostolate proclaimed
by Vatican II, approved in the closing moments of the World Council on 18
November 1965 by an astounding 2,340:2 majority, not only created free space
for the deployment of lay energies and initiatives. *Apostolicam actuositatem*
went even one step further and explicitly prodded the laity to take an active
role in the development of Catholic social theory![14]

Nevertheless, the radicalization of the CISL proceeded along hesitant and
contradictory lines. 'It all happened in a process which was by no means linear
but evolved via internal tensions which only got worse as the decade proceeded, with new insights guiding this evolution, some of them fundamentally
changing over time from the initial and original intuitions.'[15] And, for all the
importance of the impulse emanating from Vatican II, these clarion calls for
qualitatively enhanced freedoms for lay activists in the last analysis merely
further stimulated processes that were already under way. If there was one
starting point, it was the aforementioned 1958 conflict at Officine Mecchaniche
(OM) in Brescia, a car factory, which happened at a moment when Pius XII
was still ruling the roost. But, in turn, Brescia stood in the front ranks of
progressive change within the Italian Catholic universe in part because of the
tenacity of the radical popular Catholicism in the province of Brescia and, most
pointedly, in the Val Trompia. Giulio Bevilacqua was only the most prominent
local representative of this local tradition. In short, theological influences, local
heritage, and pragmatic engagement in fearless battles on the factory floor all
played a role in the crystallization of a radical Catholic working-class current. It
was a virtuous circle of interlocking influences which shaped Brescia—and
then Turin, Milan, Bergamo, Genoa—into a beacon of change.[16]

---

[14] The most convincing depiction of the impact and relevance of the innovations of Vatican II
as well as John XXIII and Paul VI for the daily practice of the CISL is Mario Reina, 'L'orienta-
mento dell'insegnamento sociale della chiesa e le linee dell'azione sindacale', in Guido Baglioni
et al., *Lavoratori cattolici e sindacato* (Rome: Lavoro, 1979), pp. 13–33.

[15] Tiziano Treu, 'Cultura e valori dei lavoratori cattolici e concezione sindacale della Cisl', in
Baglioni et al., *Lavoratori cattolici*, p. 43.

[16] It is perhaps accidental but certainly symbolic that Guido Baglioni, the foremost social
scientist to cast light on the multiform conjunctures of *cislini* traditions and the long-time head
of the CISL's Florence Study Centre, was born and raised in the Val Trompia.

THE ROOTS OF *CISLINI* AUTONOMY: CATHOLIC EVERYDAY PRACTICES

More generally, everyday Catholic working-class culture, by no means limited to the early strongholds of *cislini* changes in orientation from the late 1950s onwards, played an additional powerful role in eventually transforming the CISL from moderate proponent of business unionism to a key force in making Italy's factory floors in the early 1970s literally ungovernable by traditional management methods. No one has contributed greater insights into these invisible mechanisms than the sociologist and CISL activist Bruno Manghi. It is instructive to cite a few methodological comments penned by Manghi in the heat of the struggle, referring back to the decade of the 1950s when the CISL was anything but the protagonist of valiant anti-hierarchical battles.

'In the Italian case', Manghi asserts, 'one must emphasize the communications, exchanges and socialization patterns which began to change the points of production from—at the very least—the early 1950s onwards. The factory floor became a crossroads of ideas, languages and dialects, reflecting the variety of regional origins as much as the presence of a number of different political and religious families.'[17] And in each section of each factory, 'the microcosm of individual points of production, the movements to be effected, the objects which each worker has to appropriate for himself, often to defend his individual identity', helped shape his self-understanding and mental universe. The same held true for each worker's interactions with other workers, including relationships of 'friendship, competition and sometimes love, hate, desire, sympathy, mutual protections and frustrations'. And out of these individual situations emerged 'worlds of ideas and conversations. Furthermore, each worker lives the experience of the wage received, his career, his qualifications, his reassignments to other posts. But', and here Manghi becomes even more suggestive, 'the work environment is not just a reflection of itself. It mirrors the world at large. It reflects the influence of each worker's family, illnesses, births, sex, his pleasures, his tastes, the food he eats, the clothes he wears.'[18]

And in this context the Catholic upbringing and lifeworld of many *cislini* begins to play a clear and present role. Manghi describes a number of different Catholic subcultures of the 1950s which eventually fed into *cislini* activism, with many later union leaders of the 1960s and 1970s emerging precisely from these milieux. One such important source of energy was 'young people who grew up within the multiform associations provided for Catholic youth, from Catholic leisure associations, from the innermost recesses of parish life'.

[17] Bruno Manghi, 'La presenza quotidiana dei cattolici nei luoghi di lavoro', in Baglioni et al., *Lavoratori cattolici*, p. 60.
[18] Manghi, 'Presenza quotidiana', p. 59.

For, while certain parishes were clearly dominated by conservative if not openly right-wing ideologies and practices, this was by no means everywhere the case. 'There existed also another tradition, parishes where the young themselves were in control, or which were run by friendly assistant parish priests, leisure time associations which reflected young people's concerns, parishes where the president of the Catholic youth association was a black sheep in the eyes of the parish notables. And within such parishes arose instances of generational conflict which increasingly took on the overtones of social and pre-political dissent.'[19]

Even the cults of courage and physical engagement promoted in the daily practice of popular sports within these Catholic youth associations 'are experiences which acculturate young apprentices, the graduates of trade schools, the adolescent pupils of technical and professional schools, just as much as the sons of sharecroppers, towards a growing insubordination vis-à-vis the existing order of things'. And Manghi then makes an important observation. 'Few of these pupils read Mounier and Maritain. No one has ever encountered such marginalized Catholics within the ranks of the openly politicized Left. Few of them know *Adesso* by Mazzolari, even fewer will ever read *Esperienze pastorali*. Nonetheless, a new generation arose on factory floors and office suites which is less malleable, ready to transfer' their newly acquired skills and their fearless courage onto the plane of social and political action.[20]

'By no means do I wish to say', adds Manghi, 'that, out of those football camps or out of the halls where Don Bosco-type films were projected, a throng of activists arrived onto the factory floor. But the cult of youth, the intense activism and the experience of collective action within their Catholic universe had broken open the crust of resignation in thousands of young people, providing a powerful push towards self-realisation which for many could no longer be carried out within the tight restraints of industrial and peasant labour.' 'Sometimes the trade union became the form of associational life which substituted for the parish, the latter often deemed too restrictive, with little relationship to real life, under excessive control from above. Sometimes both experiences existed side-by-side and mutually influenced each other.' 'Out of such microcosms of Catholic associational life in the years up to 1964–5 emerged countless trade union leaders.'[21]

Even less combative Catholic subcultures contributed their own fair share to the transformation of Catholic workers' associations in subsequent years. There were, for instance, plenty of *cislini* who abstained from any sort of

[19] Manghi, 'Presenza quotidiana', p. 63.

[20] Manghi, 'Presenza quotidiana', p. 64. *Adesso*, until his death in 1959 published by Don Primo Mazzolari, was then the flagship journal of the Italian Catholic Left. The 1958 *Esperienze pastorali* was the first (and only) book-length study published by the iconoclastic darling of the Italian student Left in the late 1960s, Don Lorenzo Milani.

[21] Manghi, 'Presenza quotidiana', p. 64.

oppositional politics, who felt more at home in the stable social world extolled by traditional Catholic social theory. But, for all their apparent lack of interest in the practices of contestation, 'they never became defenders of authoritarian solutions or apologists for their employers. They never identified themselves with their bosses or the latter's cultural and political organizations, nor did they embrace the ideology of competition and economic success, whatever the cost. In fact, once the trade union became a regular and legitimate presence at their workplace, a number of these workers agreed to join the CISL, participating in assemblies and the election of delegates, even if they retained a reserved attitude in the face of militant activism.'[22] Indeed, even in the heyday of Cold War politics, the CISL never became an organization prone to accede to employers' demands.

A similar uneasy relationship of forces between local notables and grass-roots sullenness and growing discontent characterized associational life in parishes and Catholic Action. 'It is certainly correct to say that employers frequently succeeded for many years in utilizing and controlling the universe of Catholic associationism. But almost never did they succeed in simply attaching this plethora of groupings in an organic fashion to their zone of cultural and social domination.' There always remained a residual antipathy and resistance towards their social superiors, often based on traditional Catholic values. Solidarity and collective action remained high on the list of principles which shaped the mental universe of Catholic workers even in the darkest days of the Cold War. Moreover, Catholics retained a healthy disregard for the myths of productivism, preferring a solidaristic environment. Catholics likewise held in very high esteem what is sometimes regarded as 'non-labour time'. 'The high regard with which feast days, rituals and the family—all concentrated in moments of the life cycle outside of working hours proper—were held underline the superior quality of non-labour time. And the first timid polemics targeting the employing classes emerged in certain dioceses in the 1950s precisely over the issue of Sunday work.'[23]

Respect for authority but also a high regard for equality were likewise common Catholic values which could, on occasion, clash and produce unexpected outcomes. Even the mere appreciation of authority, a product of Catholic socialization since time immemorial, could turn out to favour subversion. If authority figures in a factory were exposed as incompetent and/or immoral, support for traditional leadership figures could be quickly withdrawn. When the cycle of working-class activism entered the 'hot phase' after 1968, other ideological idiosyncrasies of Catholic workers could quickly transform the CISL from a moderate brake on union militancy compared to the CGIL into the key promoter of radical changes. Nostalgia for a mythical

---

[22] Manghi, 'Presenza quotidiana', pp. 65–6.   [23] Manghi, 'Presenza quotidiana', p. 68.

and mystical past, a standard feature of Catholic social theory prior to Vatican II, could rapidly become a tool for the anticipation of a non-alienated future. It is high time to take a close glance at some mechanisms which helped propel the CISL—in the conjuncture of the *sessantotto*—to pride of place as a beacon and leading promoter of unfettered radicalism.

A VIRTUOUS CIRCLE

The CISL had traditionally attracted young unskilled and white-collar workers precisely because of its image of greater moderation vis-à-vis the CGIL, the latter having often relied on skilled workers' radical instincts to sustain its confrontational image in the 1950s and early 1960s. One of the characteristics of the post-1968 period in Italy, of course, was the prominent role of unskilled young workers and white-collar employees as shapers of their radical destiny. As these hitherto rather passive strata abandoned their deferential attitudes from 1968 onwards, the CISL became their natural organizational vehicle. Unskilled workers were the key forces pushing to reject Taylorism, piecework regimes, and other unwanted features of late-capitalist productivism. Building on the pre-existing substructures of traditional Catholic esteem for egalitarianism, the CISL after 1968 became the key organization for the promotion of anti-hierarchical, anti-capitalist demands, which were now all the rage on the factory and office floors. The CISL, hitherto not particularly well implanted in classic blue-collar industries, suddenly benefited from the influx of new and radicalized members. Unlike the CGIL, which had engaged in many confrontations during the Cold War decades, the CISL had few memories of battles lost in earlier years. Coupled with the rush of new members, the CISL was thus ideally poised to give organizational expression to these newly popular spontaneist and anti-hierarchical milieux. As the weaker union in blue-collar industries up to 1968, the *cislini* felt that they had little to lose and could embark upon new engagements and experiences. In turn, this newly emerging image of the CISL fuelled by anti-hierarchical, spontaneist, and libertarian energies fed a constant stream of new recruits from within the burgeoning Italian New Left, the PSIUP, and notably the legion of activists radicalized in the ranks of post-Vatican II Catholic dissent.[24]

---

[24] By far the most convincing portrayal of the process of fundamental reorientation in outlook and strategies by the CISL after 1968 is Emilio Reyneri, 'Il ruolo della Cisl', already cited in note 8, from which this subsection heavily draws. The Partito Socialista Italiano di Unità Proletaria (PSIUP) was the key political party which gave organizational expression to New Left sympathies at that time.

A major source of energies stimulating *cislini* activists to seemingly reach for the sky was the absence of a strong and authoritative political filter. Having increasingly abandoned Christian Democrat tutelage in the years between 1958 and 1968, there was no political organization to which *cislini* could turn for experience and advice. The CGIL, by contrast, was still led on a relatively short leash by the PCI, even though the PCI was far less authoritarian in this regard by comparison with the attitudes of the PCF vis-à-vis the CGT in France. But the newly dominant CISL radicalism operated in truly autonomous fashion. And, in a period when production relations were turned upside down, the implications of such a turn were literally and figuratively unlimited.

In the years of moderation, the *cislini* had enthusiastically engaged in contract negotiations over production goals and the technical division of labour on the factory floor, including piecework regulations. The CGIL, by contrast, systematically rejecting such attempts to shape the contours of production within the limits of capitalist rationality, traditionally had refused to engage in such negotiations. Now, after 1968, when the *cislini* reoriented towards stridently anti-capitalist goals and methods, there was no organization better placed to contest and reject piecework, line speeds, and similar trappings of technical management of the factory floor than the CISL, which knew better than any other organization what such a Taylorist approach concretely implied. Up to 1968, individual contracts negotiated at factory-level had tended to adopt gains obtained in, often difficult, national negotiations. From 1968 to 1972, this relationship was essentially reversed. National contract terms now, instead, adopted gains which particularly combative and successful local workforces in flagship factories had managed to achieve. Individual factories—rather than national negotiation teams—were driving the system in this period of rapid change. The CISL, hitherto playing second fiddle on the national scale, was once again well poised to benefit from this role reversal. With individual factory battles setting the tone, the political centrality of the factory became the watchword of the day. Once again, the *cislini*, with no political party as their brains trust behind the scenes, felt perfectly at ease in this new and highly politicized spontaneist environment. In turn, their elevation of the factory to the primary locus of contestation attracted yet another non-traditional left-wing milieu which had quietly grown in influence from the late 1950s onwards: the *operaisti*.[25]

---

[25] *Operaisti* placed emphasis on autonomous working-class action to achieve radical goals, unencumbered by the constraining role of traditional left-wing political parties or trade union federations. First making waves in the late 1950s, this current obtained a particular popularity in Italy, often having prepared the ideological and activist terrain in grassroots efforts in the run-up to 1968. The most accessible English-language study of *operaismo* is now Steve Wright, *Storming Heaven. Class Composition and Struggle in Italian Autonomist Marxism* (London: Pluto, 2002).

In hindsight, the high value placed traditionally by *cislini* on contract negotiations, originally fed by pre-Vatican II organicist Catholic social theory promoting social peace, had unwittingly prepared the CISL to become the quintessential union federation of this hot phase of radical working-class struggles after 1968. Their traditional promotion of a decentralized approach to interactions with employers, an attitude emerging as much from their position as the underdog vis-à-vis the CGIL as from the traditional Catholic veneration of 'substitutionism', favouring decentralization of decision-making whenever possible, further aided the radiance of CISL factory-centred activism after 1968. The CISL—and the FIM always performing a vanguard role in this stage of *sessantotto* activism—kept its eye on the prize of the individual factory floor, and the CISL was therefore also much better prepared than the CGIL to promote and foster internal union democracy and the rotation of tasks amongst its members. *Cislini*—again with the FIM in pole position—regarded its grassroots base as the source of and the locus of debates on policies and objectives. The CISL was constitutionally far less inclined to view the rank-and-file as a constituency which could be mobilized instrumentally to support ideas generated at the top. It is easy to see how such egalitarian, anti-hierarchical attitudes could promote the virtuous circle of attracting anti-authoritarian activists emerging from the milieux of *gruppi spontanei* and the Movimento Studentesco to further feed the flames of CISL radicalization.

If, then, the CISL's rise to prominence owed much to circumstantial accident—in the terms of Vatican II: the happy conjuncture of the 'signs of the times'—certain Catholic dispositions contributed their own fair share to this process. Thus, to furnish one additional example of the capacity of Catholic traditions to facilitate radicalization, the study of CISL attitudes towards participation in the running of their enterprises is curiously instructive. In the 1950s and early 1960s, still under the sway of organicist conceptions of factories as harmonious production units, this willingness meant above all the negotiations of piecework rates, line speed, and other features of technical factory regimes. There was no sense, then, of such contract negotiations challenging the underlying rationale of enterprises running along capitalist lines. After 1968, the meaning of 'participation' changed rapidly and profoundly. It now no longer meant the stipulation of the rate of exploitation, but instead it was reinterpreted to mean workers' control and workers' self-management. The principle of engagement with the running of an enterprise was still the same, only the concrete contours and ultimate goals had changed in radically new directions.[26]

Pierre Carniti, the long-time CISL leadership figure, once asked himself 'why Catholics within unions appear to engage in experiences which are richer

---

[26] Treu, 'Cultura e valori', pp. 51–4, is particularly insightful on the changing meaning of 'participation' within the culture of the CISL.

and more advanced than others'.[27] Leaving aside a host of factors already addressed earlier in this chapter, Carniti highlighted in his answer one additional mechanism or, rather, a complex of issues that can be traced back to traditional Catholic belief systems. Carniti pointed to elements of Catholic faith which, 'though firmly anchored in concrete time and concrete history, do not fully exhaust themselves with actions, projects, politics or ideology. There is also the presence of hope, hope in total liberation, constantly invoked by tensions encountered in everyday struggle, in view of the final destiny of humanity.'[28] The striving for equality, an authentically egalitarian future, cannot be subsumed solely by reference to improvements in work schedules, working conditions, or a more rational reshuffling of necessary labour time, 'but it also means the realization of another quality of life, a transformation of values able to oppose individualism and to promote solidarity and equality in the face of competition'.[29] Or, as Pierre Carniti was fond of saying, 'Jesus Christ was certainly not a Menshevik'.[30]

ACLI, BELGIUM, AND THE CFDT

The CISL was of course by no means the only Catholic workers' association which was profoundly affected by the spirit of Vatican II and the associated wave of social movements inspired by Rome's unexpected course correction. In Italy alone there existed an amazing—and sometimes confusing—welter of organizations within Catholic Action which had as their major goal to carry out work within the working-class milieux. For instance, the flagship Catholic Action organization for working-class youth, the Movimento Lavoratori di Azione Cattolica (MLAC), underwent some very important changes in this time period.[31] But the most astounding experiments occurred within one of the very largest mass organizations of Catholic workers in Italy as a whole, the aforementioned ACLI.

The ACLI had been founded in newly liberated Rome in the summer of 1944, and one of its original missions had been to organize the nucleus of what might eventually become a Catholic trade union federation when all of Italy would be liberated, which did not happen until late April 1945. Eventually the CISL emerged to take on this particular task. The ACLI, thus, primarily took on the function of Catholic Action organization for Catholic workers,

---

[27] Pierre Carniti, 'Lavoratori cattolici, conflitto, classe', in Baglioni et al., *Lavoratori cattolici*, p. 107.

[28] Carniti, 'Lavoratori', p. 108.   [29] Carniti, 'Lavoratori', p. 109.

[30] Carniti, 'Lavoratori', p. 107.

[31] The standard reference work on the MLAC is now Valentino Marcon and Tino Mariani, *Storia del Movimento Lavoratori di Azione Cattolica* (Rome: Ave, 2005).

although it developed additional roles. For much of the 1950s and into the 1960s, the ACLI remained loyal to the hierarchy's vision for Catholic Action groupings, and there was no question about the ACLI's role as a transmission belt for DC policies. When the CISL began to develop an appetite for an autonomous course in the late fifties and early sixties, it was the ACLI which served as a moderating influence in this milieu. But by the mid-1960s the ACLI, too, began to flex its muscles.

By 1966, voices openly critical of the guiding role of conservative DC could be heard with increasing frequency and resonance within the ACLI leadership and within its ranks. A first intellectual and organizational crystallization of such a new course occurred at the June 1969 national ACLI congress in Turin. The ensuing Hot Autumn of 1969 ensured that this radical turn towards autonomy and independence would emerge victorious. The 1970 Summer School in the Vallombrosa, the traditional summer retreat of ACLI activists, signed and sealed the ACLI's determination to break with DC and to openly proclaim the need for a socialist solution to the problems and issues confronting Italian politics and society. A mass organization of Catholic Action, which in 1969 counted at least 600,000 members in 7,205 local sections throughout Italy, had broken with the traditionally conservative Catholic mainstream tradition and struck out on a path of its own.[32]

And, of course, it was by no means 'just' Italy which reflected the new winds blowing in the wake of Vatican II, powerfully reinforced by global '1968'. The Belgian Catholic workers' movement, for instance, from 1970 onwards proved to be even more enthusiastic than its Socialist counterparts to adopt 'self-management' as its own banner. Wildcat strikes and factory occupations found more practical assistance and support within the ranks of the Catholic trade union federation, dominant in the Flemish half of Belgium, than in the Socialist federation. The Catholic Confédération des Syndicats Chrétiens in 1971 published a programmatic brochure, *The Democratization of the*

---

[32] On the history of the ACLI, consult Carlo Felice Casula, *Le ACLI. Una bella storia italiana* (Rome: Anicia, 2008), notably the interview with Emilio Gabaglio, who was ACLI President in the hottest phase of radical action, 1969–72, on pp. 29–52. The most detailed account of the period of rapid and far-reaching changes within ACLI remains Maria Cristina Sermanni, *Le ACLI. Alla prova della politica 1961–1972* (Naples: Dehoniane, 1986). An astute and concise insider's perspective is also accessible in Fausto Tortora, 'Le ACLI e la scelta socialista', in Lorenzo Bedeschi et al., *I cristiani nella sinistra. Dalla Resistenza a oggi* (Rome: Coines, 1976), pp. 199–213. An informative collection of Italian newspaper articles on key moments in ACLI history is presented by Mariangela Maraviglia (ed.), *ACLI. 50 anni a servicio della Chiesa e della società italiana* (Cinisello Balsamo: San Paolo, 1996). The concrete membership data for 1969 are taken from Ivan Moscati, 'Le ACLI e lo spontaneismo', *Tempi moderni* 7 (1971), pp. 125–8. I thank Giovanni Scirocco for sending me this reference. Internal ACLI documents for that period claim up to one million members!

Workplace, in which it explicitly advocated self-management not just for factories and offices but for society as a whole.[33]

Perhaps the most internationally famous manifestation of such trends could be observed within the quintessential French Catholic trade union federation, the Confédération Française Démocratique du Travail (CFDT), which, nominally, had separated from the Catholic church in 1964 but whose membership and leadership remained fundamentally influenced by Christian social theory for quite some time. It was the CFDT, rather than the Communist Confédération Générale du Travail, which proved itself to be open to the spirit of '68. And it was the CFDT, marching in step with radical students, which proudly proclaimed on 16 May 1968, at the very onset of the three-week-long general strike which shook the foundations of the French state: 'To civil liberties and rights within universities must correspond the same liberties and rights within enterprises; in this demand the struggle of university students joins up with those which workers have fought for since the origin of the labour movement. We must replace industrial and administrative monarchy with democratic structures based on workers' self-management.'[34]

The CFDT would remain in the thick of social movement unionism until the early 1980s. Thus, it played a singularly important role in the flagship factory occupation and subsequent attempt at production under workers' self-management by the workforce at the watchmaking plant of LIP near Besançon. From June 1973 to January 1974, the LIP watch factory became the internationally most famous cause célèbre of the radical Left, including notably the increasingly radicalized battalions of the Catholic Left. In Besançon itself, virtually the entire Catholic community in this strongly Catholic town stood behind the LIP workers, notably the archbishop of Besançon, Marc Lallier.[35] But, if the cauldron of France in the aftermath of 1968 and the Italian

---

[33] Patrick Pasture, 'Histoire et représentation d'une utopie. L'idée autogestionnaire en Belgique', in Frank Georgi (ed.), *Autogestion. La Dernière Utopie?* (Paris: Publications de la Sorbonne, 2003), pp. 143–56. On parallel sentiments percolating within the ranks of the influential Flemish functional equivalent of the ACLI, see Walter Nauwelaerts, 'Le Kristelijke Werknemersbeweging', in Emmanuel Gerard and Paul Wynants (eds), *Histoire du Mouvement Ouvrier Chrétien en Belgique*, Vol. II (Leuven: Leuven University Press, 1994), pp. 501–43.

[34] The key study of the transformation of the erstwhile Catholic trade union federation into the motor force of radical societal, self-management-oriented change is Frank Georgi, *L'Invention de la CFDT 1957–1970* (Paris: Atelier, 1995). The same author furnishes a superb analysis of the specifically Christian impulses behind this revolution; see Frank Georgi, 'De la CFTC à la CFDT. Un choix chrétien?', in Bruno Duriez et al. (eds), *Chrétiens et ouvriers en France, 1937–1970* (Paris: Atelier, 2001), pp. 183–93. Perhaps the most inspiring overall survey of the history of the CFDT from the 1940s to the 1980s remains Pierre Cours-Saliès, *La CFDT. Un passé porteur d'avenir. Pratiques syndicales et débats stratégiques depuis 1946* (Montreuil: La Brèche, 1988). The 13 May 1968 citation is taken from Albert Detraz, 'Le Mouvement ouvrier, la CFDT et l'idée d'autogestion', in Edmond Maire, Alfred Krumnow, and Albert Detraz, *La CFDT et l'autogestion* (Paris: Cerf, 1975), p. 77.

[35] Jean Divo, *L'Affaire LIP et les catholiques de Franche-Comté* (Yens-sur-Morges: Cabédita, 2003).

Hot Autumn seem highly unusual venues for working-class missionary work in the fulfilment of a newly reinvented social doctrine of the Catholic church, an even more astounding case is provided by Francoist Spain, often left completely outside the orbit of scholars concerned with the vagaries of social Catholicism in post-World War II Europe.

THE BIRTH OF THE HOAC

The most important organization representing Catholic working-class milieux in Spain was the Hermandad Obrera de Acción Católica (HOAC), founded in 1946 on the initiative of the ultra-conservative Catholic curia. In fact, the initial stimulus for the creation of the HOAC was a communication by Pope Pius XII, himself not exactly a friend of innovative experiences within and beyond Catholic Action, on the occasion of a visit to the Vatican by the Spanish hierarchy. Pius XII had become rather concerned at the seemingly unbridgeable gulf between much of the Spanish working class and the Spanish Catholic church in the wake of the victory of Francoist forces, enthusiastically supported by the church, in the exceedingly brutal conflict of the Spanish Civil War. Taking as its model the Italian ACLI, the Spanish hierarchy, prodded by the pope, then set in motion plans to fashion a Spanish Catholic Action organization designed to evangelize the adult working-class milieu. Again following the example set by the ACLI, the second function of the HOAC was to serve as the working-class wing of the (in the case of Spain, eventual) development of a Spanish Christian Democracy.[36]

Yet the desperate circumstances of Spanish working-class existence under the Francoist yoke soon influenced the HOAC to become an advocate for working-class causes, a choice which, of course, was also a result of the absence of any other legal outlet for working-class demands. Founded on 16 September 1946, its flagship newspaper, *Tu!*, appeared from November 1946 onwards. By February 1947, the first voices could already be heard criticizing *Tu!*'s increasingly political orientation.[37] The increasingly strident anti-capitalist orientation of *Tu!* led to a first suspension of the newspaper by the Spanish government in the second half of 1947.[38] By 1949 HOAC membership

---

[36] The outstanding historian of the HOAC is Basilisa López García. The circumstances behind the creation of the HOAC in 1946 are amply developed in her *Aproximación a la historia de la HOAC, 1946–1981* (Madrid: HOAC, 1995), pp. 27–35. López García also published, amongst many other items, a useful brief survey of HOAC's history, 'Dilemas constantes en el desarollo histórico de la HOAC', in a special issue of the journal *XX Siglos* 4, no. 16 (1993), pp. 15–25, which furnishes some additional detail.

[37] López García, *Aproximación*, p. 41.

[38] Comisión Permanente de la HOAC, *Guillermo Rovirosa, ¡ahora más que nunca!* (Madrid: HOAC, 2006), p. 35.

surpassed the 5,000 mark.[39] *Tu!* filled a vacuum of information for working-class communities across Spain. In 1951, *Tu!* in fact sent a special reporter to cover one of the first major strikes in post-Civil War Spain, the strike of urban transportation workers in Barcelona.[40] The regime daily, *Arriba*, promptly accused the HOAC of fomenting strikes. Having reached a circulation of 45,000 copies per issue in April 1951, *Tu!* was given the choice of submitting to strict censorship or of closing down. HOAC leaders opted for the latter course.[41]

Yet it was not solely as a result of the peculiar Spanish condition of brutal dictatorship, assisted by the Spanish Catholic hierarchy, that an unusual free space developed for Catholic Action organizations set up by the hierarchy, such as the HOAC. The HOAC's leadership in addition benefited from the presence of some extraordinary individuals in its ranks who, in turn, were the product of the bitterly divisive and conflict-ridden history of Spain in the years leading up to and including the ferocious Spanish Civil War. The indisputable intellectual figurehead of the early HOAC was Guillermo Rovirosa. Born in 1897, Rovirosa, during the crucial years of the Civil War, worked as an engineer in a Madrid factory. After the outbreak of the Civil War, he was unanimously elected to preside over the workers' committee which henceforth administered the plant in Republican Madrid. He carried out this function until the fall of Madrid towards the end of the civil war, and was subsequently sentenced by the victorious Francoists to twelve years in prison for his role as head of this institution of workers' control. Released after only one year in jail, he returned to his profession, but he now also deepened his religious orientation, which he had commenced in the early 1930s when living in Paris.[42]

GUILLERMO ROVIROSA

As was the case with many other leading figures in the HOAC, Guillermo Rovirosa was profoundly affected by the Civil War, in his case by the experience as head of a workers' committee administering the factory in which he had worked for some time in Madrid. Madrid, though run by a Defence Committee dominated by orthodox Communists, experienced several years

[39] López García, *Aproximación*, p. 49.
[40] López García, *Aproximación*, p. 55. A first-hand account of this heroic strike is Angel Alcázar, 'La huelga de tranvías de Barcelona del año 51', *XX Siglos* 5, no. 22 (1994), pp. 87–91.
[41] López García, *Aproximación*, pp. 56–7.
[42] The sole book-length, single-author biography of Rovirosa remains Xavier García, *Rovirosa. Comunitarisme integral. La revolució Cristiana dintre el poble* (Barcelona: Pòrtic, 1977), which covers the civil war years on pp. 127–35. Some additional information used in this paragraph is provided by López García, *Aproximación*, p. 36.

of revolutionary experiments which, elsewhere in Spain, Communists were desperately and brutally trying to crush. 'In the defence of Madrid, the Junta [the Defence Committee] employed methods that the men of the [anarcho-syndicalist] CNT and [Left Socialist/Trotskyist] POUM had advocated else-where, in Irún and San Sebastián: arming the people, omnipotence of the Committees, action by the masses, and summary revolutionary justice.'[43] Collectivizations, grassroots democracy in emergency conditions, and the experience of solidarity under extraordinarily tense circumstances thus formed part of Rovirosa's intellectual baggage, just as much as the intensive study of the social doctrine of the church. Given the task of organizing and developing the newly founded HOAC after 1946, Guillermo Rovirosa set out to accomplish this mission with a peculiar combination of ideological influ-ences guiding his actions. A tireless organizer, Rovirosa then criss-crossed Spain to construct the HOAC, penning countless articles in *Tu!* and the HOAC's internal discussion journal, the *Boletín de dirigentes*, but also some-how finding time to compose programmatic statements.[44]

On the occasion of the hundredth anniversary of *The Communist Mani-festo*, for instance, Rovirosa wrote what he regarded as the Christian answer to Karl Marx, *The Communitarian Manifesto*, published one year later in 1949. Equally opposing unbridled capitalism and the horrors of totalitarian collect-ivizations in the Communist world, Rovirosa developed an alternative vision. He criticized Marx for his belief that private property undergirded capitalist inequalities. In fact, Rovirosa contended, it is precisely capitalism which is the fiercest enemy of private property. Under capitalism most individuals are left penniless and property lies in the hands of a tiny handful of individuals. Rather than attacking capitalism for its supposed reliance on private property, Rovirosa contended, Marxists and anarchists should have pointed out that capitalism is by nature hostile to the right of everyone to their fair share of property. By falsely accusing capitalism of the one thing which capitalism did not do, Marxism inadvertently strengthened the ideological defences of cap-italism, thus helping to consolidate a socio-economic system both Marxists and Rovirosa passionately hated.

For Rovirosa, the right to private property is a mainstay of human rights and a pillar of social justice. But Rovirosa, of course, proposed a somewhat non-traditional definition of private property and a correspondingly noncon-formist view of the ideal society based on the inalienable right to property. In fact, for Rovirosa, his utopian ideals were very close to what others would call self-governing autonomous communities and for which nineteenth-century

---

[43] Pierre Broué and Emile Témime, *The Revolution and the Civil War in Spain* (Cambridge, Mass.: MIT Press, 1972), p. 247.

[44] The key source for this aspect of Rovirosa's life is Comisión Permanente de la HOAC, *Guillermo Rovirosa*; the following paragraphs likewise draw from this source.

utopian socialist communes or, indeed more likely, the anarchist collectives in Catalonia and Aragón after the outbreak of the Spanish Civil War probably served as distant role models. For Rovirosa, such authentic communities were to be governed by the principles of fraternity, equality, and solidarity. But he insisted that each person and each family would remain owners of their home and of the tools and means of production. All enterprises, services, or land would fully remain in the hands of those who worked in these sectors of the communitarian economy. Inequalities were to be nipped in the bud by insisting that each person would solely receive the fruits of the labour that they had personally contributed.[45]

To most unbiased observers, it was clear that Rovirosa's communitarian idea stood much closer to Karl Marx than to Adam Smith. And this anti-capitalist spirit provided a red thread for Rovirosa's copious writings. In fact, it was a biting critique of capitalist enterprises, ending with the invocation of the need for a principled defence of the dignity of workers in the face of the 'false dignity' of money, which led to the temporary suspension of *Tu!* in 1949. But Rovirosa's polemical pen did not relent: 'Capital and capitalism constitute a festering open wound'; 'in the age of Saint Paul, those who did not work did not eat; today, seeing that we have progressed, those who work do not eat'.[46] It is evident that the HOAC had embarked upon a free flight into uncharted terrain, and this under enormously difficult objective circumstances. Needless to say, neither secular nor ecclesiastical authorities in Spain appreciated this turn of events.

WORKING-CLASS APOSTLES

The second crucial personality in the early years of the HOAC was Tomás Malagón, born in 1917 and ordained as a priest in 1943. As had been the case with Guillermo Rovirosa, Malagón had spent the Civil War years on the Republican side. A seminary student at the Pontifical University of Comillas in Santander when war broke out, he abandoned his studies and joined the Republican military where he rubbed shoulders with socialists, communists, and anarchists, an experience which, Malagón later on insisted, affected his

[45] The text of the 'Manifiesto comunitarista' is perhaps most easily accessible in Guillermo Rovirosa, *Obras Completas*, Vol. I, *Cooperación y comunidad* (Madrid: HOAC, 1995), pp. 49–90. In interpreting the meaning of this text, I have found the relevant pages in Xavier García, 'El pensamiento social de Rovirosa', in Xavier García, Jacinto Martín, and Tomás Malagón, *Rovirosa, apóstol de la clase obrera* (Madrid: HOAC, 1985), pp. 146–61, particularly helpful.

[46] These two paradigmatic citations are taken from Comisión Permanente de la HOAC, *Guillermo Rovirosa*, p. 44.

intellectual and moral outlook profoundly. He joined the Spanish Communist Party during the Civil War.[47] Tomás Malagón, in the words of one of the outstanding historians of Spanish Left Catholicism, Rafael Díaz-Salazar, 'was a precursor of political theology and the theology of liberation when they did not yet exist as such. He performed the role of liberation theologian in Spain already in the course of the 1950s.'[48] Malagón employed such categories of analysis as 'the mystical body of Christ' and 'class struggle' at a time when such a terminology—certainly in combination!—was still frowned upon in Catholic circles even in neighbouring France.[49]

In July 1953 Guillermo Rovirosa and Tomás Malagón met for the very first time, and within two months Rovirosa offered Malagón the post of spiritual adviser to HOAC. Now began an extraordinarily fruitful period of intellectual refinement and renewal for the HOAC leadership team and for the organization as a whole. The radical imagination of the lay activist Rovirosa joined forces with the fearless theological innovations of Malagón. The intuitions of Rovirosa could now benefit from the doctrinal training of Malagón, who gave systematic shape to the instincts of the former. The duo was soon referred to by admirers as possessing 'one soul in two separate bodies'.[50] This fertile combination of talents more than made up for the loss of the HOAC's key journalistic product, *Tu!*, a few years earlier.

In fact, the need to find a new way to interact with their targeted audience, the Spanish working class, after the closure of *Tu!* soon turned out to be an opportunity in disguise. The Francoist government had hoped that the forcible removal of *Tu!* as a weapon for the nascent HOAC would have as an intended consequence the rapid demise of the HOAC. But Guillermo Rovirosa soon developed a new and far more dangerous weapon in the overall project to give a voice and potential power to the atomized Spanish working class. At the height of influence of *Tu!*, there had been consistent voices who had criticized the HOAC's almost single-minded orientation towards journalistic campaigns in the struggle against the enforced disenfranchisement of the Spanish working-class poor. Rather than educating working-class activists to become the agents of their own liberation, the HOAC was seen by some as expending much energy in order to perfect a journalistic tool. With *Tu!* removed from the scene, now the path was wide open to begin a consistent programme of training workers to become apostles of a better future amongst their cohort of working-class poor. Rovirosa began to develop a systematic plan to train

---

[47] The two key biographical sketches of Tomás Malagón are Alfonso Fernández Casamayor, *Teología, fe y creencias en Tomás Malagón* (Madrid: HOAC, 1988), and Basilisa López García, *Tomás Malagón Almodóvar, 1917–1984* (Toledo: Almud, 2014).

[48] Cited in Casamayor, *Teología*, pp. 61–2.

[49] These are the telling examples of some of Malagón's preferred intellectual tools cited in López García, *Tomás Malagón*, p. 56.

[50] Casamayor, *Teología*, pp. 61–2.

HOAC rank-and-file activists to become spokespeople for their own class. A three-year-long training programme consisting of a series of carefully selected courses was set up which would create a continuous fresh supply of working-class cadres who, it was hoped, would then become leading activists in the hoped-for self-emancipation of the Spanish working class.[51]

And working-class apostles they became. It so happened that from 1958 onwards—and then much more forcefully after 1962—industrial unrest in Spain experienced a serious revival which began to undermine the foundations of the Francoist order. Even the regime-sponsored official working-class associations were sometimes playing crucial roles in this subversion of the status quo. More frequently, however, embryonic underground trade union formations saw the light of day, often relying to a significant extent on Catholic milieux for support and encouragement. The dates when such proto-union structures were first set up reflect the revival of industrial action in Spain. Out of the 1958 mineworker strikes in Asturias emerged the Federación Sindical de Trabajadores (FST), with activists from the youth wing of Spanish specialized Catholic Action for the working-class milieu, the Juventud Obrera Católica (JOC), playing the central role. Likewise in 1958 arose the Catalan equivalent of the FST, the Solidaridad de Obreros Cristianos Catalanes (SOCC), animated by Catholic Action forces from the JOC, HOAC, and other groups. The year 1960 saw the creation of the Unión Sindical Obrera (USO), initially in the Basque Country, once again largely propelled by members of the JOC. By 1962, the Acción Sindical de Trabajadores (AST) joined the fray, frequently set up by HOAC activists, but with a Jesuit workers' network, the Vanguardias Obreras, playing an even more important role.[52] The year 1958, of course, also witnessed the first tentative steps towards the setting up of underground Workers' Commissions (Comisiones Obreras—CC.OO.), which eventually became the leading force of anti-Franco industrial unrest, rapidly becoming an umbrella organization, often benefiting from the practical cooperation of some of the aforementioned, originally largely Catholic-inspired, underground union federations.

The CC.OO are today frequently regarded as an organization closely linked to the PCE, certainly when they first operated in the anti-Franco underground. Doubtless, Communist workers often played leading roles in the CC.OO from the very beginning; and, in the second half of the 1960s, they consolidated their hold over these CC.OO. Yet, in the early stages of the CC.OO, the Catholic contribution towards the conception, birth, initial growth, and development of CC.OO had been crucial. A brief glance at the founding moments of these radical rank-and-file committees, which, for quite some time,

---

[51] López García, *Aproximación*, pp. 61–4.
[52] López García, *Aproximación*, pp. 130–3, provides a short and informative survey of this effervescence in Spanish working-class milieux.

due to the constraints of Francoist dictatorial control, were forced to remain relatively isolated and autonomously operating local or, at best, regional organizations, speaks volumes with regard to the indispensable role of Catholic workers.

THE CATHOLIC CONTRIBUTION TO
THE BIRTH OF THE CC.OO

For much of the first half of the twentieth century, Asturias had performed a central role within the labour movement in Spain, and it thus only stood to reason that some of the very earliest tender shoots of CC.OO activism under the Francoist yoke could be traced back to this combative province. Tentative moves towards the construction of workers' commissions took place from 1956 onwards, and the two political subcultures which stood in the vanguard of such moves were the PCE and the HOAC. HOAC activist Manuel Hevia Carriles had been arrested for a militant speech on the occasion of an apostolic campaign in Gijón as early as 1952, as had HOAC activist José Borbolla in 1954 in Avilés. HOAC's crucial contribution to the growth of CC.OO in its heartland territory of Asturias was thus a natural consequence of its outlook and orientation in previous years.[53]

The first workers' commissions destined to survive for some time and to inspire similar formations elsewhere—and now generally regarded as the classic example of a CC.OO operating successfully in adverse conditions—was the Comisión Obrera at the mining complex of La Camocha. Paradigmatically and symbolically, here—as in neighbouring Asturian mining communities—HOAC activists played indispensable roles. In fact, at La Camocha, the local parish priest was a member of its coordinating commission from the very outset.[54] The 1962 strike wave was centred on Asturias and the neighbouring Basque provinces of Vizcaya and Guipúzcoa, where the Madrid government clamped down by proclaiming a state of emergency. The mining valleys southeast of the capital city of Asturias, Oviedo, were at the very centre of the conflict. On 24 April 1962 all mines in the area shut down in a coordinated action. That very same day delegates from all affected pits gathered for a meeting which elected another novelty for underground Spain: a strike committee. The meeting was moderated by a leading HOAC activist,

[53] Rubén Vega García, 'Cristianos en el movimiento obrero asturiano durante el franquisme. Un apunte', *XX Siglos* 5, no. 22 (1994), pp. 4–5.
[54] Javier Domínguez, 'Las Vanguardias Obreras en la lucha por la democracia', *XX Siglos* 4, no. 16 (1993), p. 70.

Manuel Morillo, with the central organizer of national HOAC trade union work, Jacinto Martín, advising the proceedings from behind the scenes.[55]

Catholic workers agitated side-by-side with PCE members in the mining and industrial conflicts in the Basque country. In Vizcaya, the strike wave rapidly resulted in the arrest of fifty-two activists. Local workers' commissions elected five spokespersons to engage in negotiations with the authorities to obtain their release. The majority of this leadership body consisted of HOAC members. This emergency coordinating committee eventually mutated into the Vizcaya provincial leadership of area CC.OO, the very first such province-wide CC.OO in all of Spain! And here again HOAC (and JOC) activists continued to exercise important functions.[56] Other locations where Catholic—and, in particular, HOAC—activists played crucial roles in the launching of CC.OO include Burgos;[57] the Basque province of Álava, where the CC.OO for all practical purposes arose within radicalized Catholic associations including HOAC members, to be sure, but also activists of the radical Jesuit network, Vanguardias Obreras;[58] Andalusia;[59] and many other important industrial and mining areas throughout Spain. An autobiographical account by the secretary of the very first workers' commission in Barcelona, Angel Alcázar, might stand for the experiences of many other *hoacistas*.

A bank employee in the Central Contable de Banesto in Barcelona, Alcázar was centrally involved in drawing up a list of company-specific grievances over working hours, working conditions, and remuneration which, to everyone's great surprise, management accepted in full. The year was 1957. The action committee consisted of a group of Christian white-collar workers, animated by a Jesuit. News of their victory travelled fast to other Barcelona banking institutions, where employees began to draw up similar lists. A qualitative

---

[55] López García, *Aproximacíon*, p. 144. Jacinto Martín, like so many other key HOAC leaders, had been profoundly influenced by anarcho-syndicalist theory and practice in his youth, introducing many of its principles into Catholic social theory and practice within the HOAC in 1950s and 1960s Francoist Spain. Manuel Morillo had once been a member of the PCE.

[56] Pedro Ibarra Güell and Chelo García Marroquín, 'De la primavera de 1956 a lejona 1978. Comisiones Obreras de Euskadi', in David Ruiz (ed.), *Historia de Comisiones Obreras (1958–1988)* (Madrid: Siglo XXI, 1993), p. 116.

[57] Enrique Berzal de la Rosa, *Sotanas rebeldes. Contribución cristiana a la transición democrática* (Valladolid: Diputación de Valladolid, 2007), pp. 82–3.

[58] Güell and Marroquín, 'De la primavera', p. 118.

[59] For much important detail on the Andalusian context, see José Hurtado Sánchez, 'Sevilla: Obreros cristianos en la lucha por la democracia', in José María Castells, José Hurtado, and Josep Maria Margenat (eds), *De la dictadura a la democracia. La Acción de los cristianos en España (1939–1975)* (Bilbao: Desclée de Brower, 2005), pp. 366–7; and Carmen R. García Ruiz and Alberto Carrillo Linares, 'Cobertura de la Iglesia a la oposición. La colaboración con CC.OO. Los casos de Málaga y Sevilla', in Castells, Hurtado, and Margenat (eds), *De la dictadura a la democracia*, pp. 411–21.

breakthrough then occurred, as elsewhere in Spain, during the strike wave of 1962 which also spread throughout Catalonia. Bank workers, already familiar with each other due to their earlier cycle of mobilization, now joined forces, produced and distributed leaflets and information sheets, deciding to adopt the label 'workers' commission' for their group, which became La Comisión Obrera de Banca. According to Alcázar 'it was in the apostolic workers' movement where we developed those ideas through person-to-person inter-action and where we consequently lost our fear of joining forces with Communist activists'.[60]

In September 1964, then, at the instigation of the workers' commission at the Montesa works, where JOC and HOAC activists played crucial roles, forty activists from a range of enterprises and industries met in the building of the Parish of San Miguel de Cornella. The gathering constituted itself as the Central Workers' Commission of Barcelona. With characteristic self-deprecation, Angel Alcázar notes: 'I was chosen to become its Secretary, probably because of my professional experience with administrative tasks. This Central Commission met every week, always in buildings belonging to the Catholic Church.' In November 1964, the Central Commission organized a general assembly in the Parish of Sant Medir, to which 300 workers came, approving a list of far-reaching demands, including a 'minimum wage, a sliding scale of wages, the right to form trade unions, and the right to strike'.[61] A second general assembly—also in the Parroquía de Sant Medir—in 1965 elaborated a concrete action plan, then decided to present their grievances to the regime-friendly official trade union federation in central Barcelona in a show of force during the early evening of 23 February. Three days before the target date, the entire Central Commission were arrested, along with others. If anything, however, this repressive act had the opposite effect from the intend-ed intimidation. At the appointed date and location, 15,000 workers gathered for a lively demonstration. The CC.OO de Barcelona were there to stay.[62]

---

[60] Angel Alcázar, 'Los cristianos en la creación de Comisiones Obreras', *XX Siglos* 5, no. 22 (1994), p. 120.

[61] Alcázar, 'Comisiones Obreras', p. 120.

[62] Alcázar presents an informative insider's view of the overall stages of the development of the Barcelona CC.OO until the early 1970s in his 'Comisiones Obreras', pp. 118–26. For more detail on the important Barcelona CC.OO from an insider activist perspective, note José Antonio Díaz, *Luchas internas en Comisiones Obreras. Barcelona 1964–1970* (Barcelona: Bruguera, 1977), and Julio Sanz Oller, *L'Espoir demeure. Les Commissions Ouvrières de Barcelone* (Lyon: Federop, 1975). For a stimulating academic study on the development of the Barcelona CC.OO in an important industrial zone, see Emili Ferrando Puig and Juan Rico Márquez, *Les Comissions Obreres en el franquisme. Barcelonès Nord (1964–1977)* (Barcelona: Abadia de Montserrat, 2005). On the HOAC in Catalonia, the standard reference work for years to come will remain Emili Ferrando Puig, *Cristians i rebels. Història de l'HOAC a Catalunya durant el franquisme (1946–1975)* (Barcelona: Mediterrània, 2000).

SAINT JOSEPH THE WORKER

If the CC.OO became the quintessential organizational vehicle for anti-Franco working-class dissent, the most symbolic action to occur in the decades-long struggle to obtain elementary democratic rights for working-class constituencies was the May Day celebrations. A mainstay of Marxist- and anarchist-inspired celebrations of labour and of labour movements ever since the Chicago Haymarket massacres in 1886, by 1955 Pope Pius XII had decided to counteract this popular, secular, left-wing tradition by proclaiming the first of May the feast day of Saint Joseph the Worker, honouring the husband of Mary, mother of Jesus: the carpenter Joseph. In most countries around the world, this ideological counteroffensive did not exactly turn out to become a full-blown success, but in Spain this new holiday took on a life of its own.

Celebrations organized to venerate Saint Joseph the Worker quickly mutated into anti-regime expressions of increasingly radical intent. Thus, for instance, as early as 1961, in the Asturian industrial port city of Gijón, the festivities to honour Saint Joseph, organized by the JOC and HOAC, went somewhat astray. The auxiliary bishop in the course of the morning celebrated the eucharist in the Parish of San José (Joseph), then presided over a public gathering which attracted 2,000 participants. On this occasion, several Christian activists took to the floor and developed stridently critical assessments of the economic and socio-political situation in Gijón, Asturias, and Spain as a whole. Enraged, the auxiliary bishop then delivered a closing address in which he sharply criticized the earlier speeches and expressed his fundamental disagreement with what had been said by the Catholic Action representatives. In the afternoon of 1 May 1961, the diocesan chaplains of the HOAC and the JOC were promptly removed from their positions, and other dissident parish priests were subsequently forced to relinquish their posts as well.[63] But a pattern had become established.

An information bulletin on the events surrounding the first of May celebrations in Bilbao in 1965 further exemplifies which way the wind was now beginning to blow. From early April onwards the workers' organizations of Catholic Action (HOAC and JOC) had begun to plan for their—by then—traditional public celebration, 'whose purpose is the evangelization of the world of labour, familiarizing this milieu with the social doctrine of the Church within which there exist solid bases for the just aspirations of the working class'. In the course of April 80,000 leaflets and 3,000 posters

---

[63] Oscar Iturrioz Fanjul, 'La Iglesia asturiana en la transición política española', *XX Siglos* 4, no. 16 (1993), p. 129.

were distributed throughout the diocese, 'causing a massive buzz of activity within working-class communities'.[64]

The organizers of the event had chosen a neighbourhood high school as their venue. Then, on 29 April, the Bilbao Police Chief suddenly called in the high school principal, alerting him to the fact that the school was located in a neighbourhood in which the clandestine labour movement had selected to stage a demonstration on 1 May. The Police Chief informed the principal that the authorities could not be held responsible for any damages to the school facilities that would be likely to occur. And he suggested that the principal should refuse to rent out his building to the Catholic Action groups in order to avoid complications. Incredibly, the high school principal refused to break the agreement he had entered into with the apostolic movements. Secular and ecclesial authorities now intensified their attacks against the organizers of the Catholic Action celebration of Saint Joseph the Worker, which may perhaps have been scheduled for that particular high school because of the simultaneous illegal action planned by the CC.OO and other labour movements operating in the underground.

At 8:15 p.m. that very same evening, Thursday, 29 April 1965, the official representative of the Spanish curia in the Bilbao diocese, Don Teodoro Jiménez Urresti, paid a visit to the offices of the diocesan branches of the HOAC and JOC. He informed the stunned activists present of a flurry of activity earlier on that evening. The Bilbao Police Chief had apparently telephoned the bishop of Bilbao in the late afternoon, warning the bishop of the possible consequences of the celebration of Saint Joseph the Worker planned for the Colegio Santiago Apostól. At 6 p.m., the bishop then had a conversation with Don Jiménez, in which Don Jiménez informed the bishop that he, the episcopal emissary in Bilbao, had decided on his own to suspend the public celebration in the Colegio Santiago Apostól. And now, Don Jiménez announced to the assembled working-class 'apostles' that he was paying a visit to the offices of the HOAC and JOC to inform them of this decision. The activists listening to Don Jiménez immediately lodged vocal protests with him, but the latter simply responded 'that I did not come here to engage in dialogue, but to impose this decision which is irrevocable. And to inform you that I have already sent a note to the local newspapers', the text of which Don Jiménez then read aloud, in which the suspension of the public celebration in the Colegio Santiago Apostól was proclaimed.[65]

On Friday, 30 April, the local newspapers published Don Jiménez's note, and the local radio stations likewise publicized Don Jiménez's authoritarian

---

[64] 'Informe de los acontecimientos ocurridos en Bilbao ante la suspensión del Acto que los Movimientos Obreros de la A.C. tenían previsto celebrar el Primero de Mayo', p. 1—Archivo de la HOAC (AHOAC) [Madrid], 31.5.

[65] 'Informe de los acontecimientos', p. 1.

decision. The subtext clearly suggested that the HOAC and JOC should regroup for a celebration of Saint Joseph the Worker at some other time and place. The working-class Catholic Action groupings of the Bilbao diocese responded in kind. They drew up and printed their official response to Don Jiménez's missive. They distanced themselves from Don Jiménez's decision, and then concluded: 'We do not intend to celebrate this act at some other date, which would not make any sense.'[66] To celebrate Saint Joseph the Worker on a date other than 1 May was no option for the HOAC and the JOC. The 1965 Bilbao feast in honour of Saint Joseph thus never did occur, but the consequences of such arbitrary actions by church and secular authorities were no doubt manifold.

MAY DAY 1968 IN SANTANDER

The Spanish underground labour movement grew yet more visible and strong in the following two years. In June 1967, CC.OO delegates gathered for the first-ever national assembly. Then, in October 1967, a national Day of Action brought the atmosphere to boiling point. Huge demonstrations of up to 100,000 workers took to the streets in the activist hotspots of the Spanish peninsula. Police repression was correspondingly ferocious. The calendar year of 1968 thus saw an understandable decline in working-class mobilization across Spain. Catholic workers remained in the thick of the movements. But the consequences of their recalcitrance were correspondingly tragic. A brief snapshot of the 1968 feast day of Saint Joseph the Worker in Santander provides insight into the dynamics under way.

At 10:15 in the morning of 1 May 1968, a crowd of about 250 workers, hailing from various locations throughout the province, gathered at a pre-determined location where they remained assembled until just before 11 a.m. The police then arrived and dispersed the crowd without major incident. At noon, about 200 people gathered in the centre of Santander, rapidly targeted by armed police. With police reinforcements arriving, 'a hailstorm of beatings by fists and truncheons was launched against the workers who stood with arms tightly linked, without even once attempting to defend themselves against the brutal police aggression. Witnessing this shameful spectacle of workers and a group of students being beaten to a pulp with indescribable fury and blind rage, falling to the ground, tossed in all directions and continuously punched, countless people, young and old, began to shout: "Assassins!",

---

[66] 'Informe de los acontecimientos', p. 2.

"Riffraff!", "You have no right to do that!", "Bloodhounds!" and similar epithets.'[67]

One particular group was isolated from the rest of the victims and suffered further 'brutal aggression of unimaginable extremes', before being summarily arrested. Between 20 and 25 demonstrators were jailed, some of them quickly released, leaving nine protesters in prison, three of them women. All but one of these victims were members of the Santander HOAC. At 5:30 p.m., the HOAC attempted to hold the traditional Mass associated with this feast day, 'as they had done in all previous years, a mass exclusively dedicated to the honour of our patron saint, Saint Joseph the Worker', only this time things turned ugly in the church. The regular parish priest of the chosen church, San José (Saint Joseph) in the neighbourhood of Tetuán, had been placed under house arrest by the police, forcing the organizers to quickly find a replacement. But Mass was never held in Santander on 1 May 1968. About 100 people entered the chosen church but, mere minutes before Mass was scheduled to begin, a large number of police arrived, 'blocking off in a spectacular coordinated manoeuvre the adjacent streets and the entry to the church, demanding identification cards from all present and barring access to the interior of the church to others. Several police officers entered the church with the intention of carrying out arrests, ignoring the protests of the priest.'[68]

The streets of Santander did not become quiet until after midnight. The human toll was significant. Apart from numerous individuals suffering severe bruises and related injuries necessitating medical interventions, a 23-year-old was hospitalized with multiple face wounds and the loss of vision in one eye. Another 20-year-old with similar injuries, 'but in an even worse state', was likewise battling to retain vision in one eye. Was Saint Joseph the Worker looking the other way?

THE *GLEICHSCHALTUNG* OF SPANISH CATHOLIC ACTION

The HOAC—but, it should be clear by now, not only the HOAC—was in the midst of one of the most dynamic and tragic struggles by working-class forces to obtain justice in post-World War II European history. And the upper ranks of the Spanish Catholic hierarchy closed ranks with the oppressor. There was probably no country in Western Europe where the Catholic community was as deeply divided as Spain. An unabashedly traditionalist

---

[67] 'Informe de los hechos ocurridos en Santander, con mótivo de la celebración del Primero de Mayo'—AHOAC, 32.4.

[68] The citations in this and the following paragraph are from 'Informe de los hechos', p. 2.

curia faced off against an increasingly restless and recalcitrant grassroots flock. Of course, by no means all Catholics in Spain took sides against secular and ecclesiastical authorities. Far from it! But when people began to actively engage in the quest for individual and collective liberation, a stark line was being drawn. It was for good reasons that the Council of Ministers, the highest body of policy makers in Franco's Spain, discussed papal encyclicals and the documents emanating from Vatican II in its regular sessions.[69]

In earlier years, ecclesiastical authorities had mostly targeted individual figureheads when the need was felt to emphasize the consequences disobedience might entail. Guillermo Rovirosa, the tireless agitator for working-class emancipation and a communitarian future, in late 1955 was removed as editor of the most important publication geared towards HOAC members, the *Boletín de militantes,* earlier called the *Boletín de dirigentes,* the name change itself already symbolizing the switch towards grassroots activism under way within Spanish Catholic Action. In 1957, he was then removed from all positions he held within his brainchild, the HOAC.[70] In 1964, the theologian and soulmate of Rovirosa, Tomás Malagón, was forced to relinquish his position as national chaplain of the HOAC.[71] Yet, contrary to the expectations of ecclesiastical and secular authorities in Francoist Spain, opposition sentiments kept growing. And Catholic workers stood in the vanguard of this liberation movement from below.

As to the HOAC, in 1963 it further increased the stakes by creating a publishing house, ZYX, which, along with similar HOAC ventures, 'became the very first initiative to introduce radical working-class writings into Spain in the early 1960s'. The classics of the Spanish socialist and anarchist tradition, including works by the veteran socialist Julián Zugazagoitia and the anarchist Ángel Pestaña, were republished and thus made available to a popular audience for the first time in a quarter of a century. Studies of Yugoslav self-management or of topics such as the agrarian revolution in Castroist Cuba were published by Editorial ZYX. ZYX—and the HOAC in general—soon became a trusted ally of the secular Left. The widow of one of the foremost leaders of Spanish social democracy, Julián Besteiro, transferred the copyright of her late husband's writings to Editorial ZYX, 'and Cipriano Mera, the [legendary veteran] anarcho-syndicalist leader, offered his archive to the management team of this publishing house'.[72] But, of course, it was not only

---

[69] López García, *Aproximación,* pp. 160–1.
[70] Comisión Permanente de la HOAC, *Guillermo Rovirosa,* pp. 69–74.
[71] Casamayor, *Teología,* p. 107.
[72] Citations taken from Rafael Díaz-Salazar, *Nuevo socialismo y Cristianos de izquierda* (Madrid: HOAC, 2001), p. 56. The remarkable story of the Editorial ZYX is described in somewhat greater detail in Carlos Díaz, 'De ZYX, aquel cristianismo sociopolítico, al Instituto Emmanuel Mounier', *XX Siglos* 5, no. 22 (1994), pp. 96–106; and, perhaps most readily accessible, in López García, *Aproximación,* pp. 191–5. The HOAC archival holdings include

HOAC which shifted considerably to the left in Spanish Catholic milieux in the course of the troubled Spanish sixties.

By 1966, the Spanish curia had seen enough. It went onto its final offensive against the most forceful and imaginative defenders of progressive Catholicism in Europe at that time. Less than nine months after the closing ceremony of Vatican II, the Spanish hierarchy began its concerted and coordinated campaign to break the back of recalcitrant specialized Catholic Action. Precisely at the moment when progressive Catholics in Spain had managed to successfully overcome the traditional hostility of the Spanish secular Left against all things Catholic, precisely when specialized Catholic Action groups were forging close alliances with other opposition forces, the curia began to shut down the infrastructure of offices and other support systems for the HOAC, the JOC, and similar organizations belonging to both the youth and the adult wings of specialized Catholic Action.[73]

The Spanish curia in many ways achieved its goals. The dynamism of specialized Catholic Action was halted in full flight. Under attack from both secular and ecclesiastical authorities, Catholic Action members now were forced to focus on defending their home turf within the structures of the church. The social impact of progressive Catholicism was, thus, dramatically—and, one should add, artificially—cut short and reduced precisely at a moment when opposition movements within and outside the Catholic church had become seemingly unstoppable. Membership in specialized Catholic Action drastically declined. In one sense, Spanish progressive Catholics never recovered from this dramatic loss of power and influence within the anti-Francoist parallelogram of forces. When the curia-driven campaign came to an end, the former flagship organizations of Catholic Action were a pale shadow of their former selves.

By the 1970s, it was the secular Left which clearly began to pull nearly all the strings in opposition movements to Francoist rule. Moreover, secular Marxist

countless informative documents on ZYX in AHOAC 140, including such items as, for example, the detailed and stimulating text of a speech by Teófilo Pérez Rey, 'La Editorial. Nacimiento y evolución'—AHOAC 140.20.

[73] The historian of this counterattack by the hierarchy is Feliciano Montero García, whose *La Acción Católica Especializada en los años sesenta* (Madrid: Universidad Nacional de Educación a Distancia, 2000) will remain the indispensable reference work on this massive wave of unabashedly reactionary repression by church authorities at the beginning of the final ten years of Francoist dictatorial rule. Montero, it should be pointed out, is the most outstanding historian of Spanish Catholicism, including dissident Catholicism, in the crucial third quarter of the twentieth century. Another modern classic is his *La Iglesia. De la colaboración a la disidencia (1956–1975)* (Madrid: Encuentro, 2009). A major resource and theological compendium focusing precisely on the conflict between the curia and Spanish Catholic Action is Antonio Murcia, *Obreros y obispos en el Franquismo. Estudios sobre el significado eclesiológico de la crisis de la Acción Católica Española* (Madrid: HOAC, 1995), with a foreword by none other than Johann Baptist Metz.

underground groupings were now frequently benefiting from an influx of disenchanted radical Catholic activists, who now joined the secular Left in significant numbers, some of them now discarding their religious faith along with the Catholic Action membership cards. Tragically, it was only at this nadir of progressive Catholicism in Spain that a major sea change began to affect the ranks of the Spanish curia. From one of the, quite literally, oldest— and one of the most conservative—Catholic national hierarchies in all of Europe, the Spanish curia underwent an inevitable generational change in the space of a few years. By the early 1970s, the Spanish curia suddenly became a force for change, not only ecclesiastical but also political change. Spanish progressive Catholicism obtained a second wind, but it was perhaps too little and, definitely, too late. Spanish progressive Catholics would never again play such a central role as they had in the heyday of specialized Catholic Action up to the late 1960s, when in particular its working-class organizations appeared to lead the way.

THE MOUVEMENT MONDIAL
DES TRAVAILLEURS CHRÉTIENS

Both the HOAC and the ACLI belonged to an international association of Catholic workers' organizations which served as an umbrella for Catholic Action groupings oriented towards the adult working-class milieu. Catholic trade unions were usually operating within the orbit of the International Federation of Christian Trade Unions, perhaps best known under the French initials CISC (Confédération Internationale des Syndicats Chrétiens). Specialized Catholic Action organizations targeting young Catholic workers had already begun to establish an international umbrella for such youth groups in the inter-wartime period, given that the Jeunesse Ouvrière Chrétienne had been launched—first in Belgium, then in France, then elsewhere—earlier than their equivalent adult groupings.

It was not until 1951 that an International Federation of the Christian Workers Movement was created for the purpose of grouping Catholic Action organizations active within the adult working-class milieu, thus setting up a third pillar of international Catholic organizations targeting workers alongside the CISC and the International of Young Christian Workers.[74] Its first dozen years or so were, to some extent, hampered by internal divisions which centred on the decision by some groupings to create a Catholic pillar in their respective

---

[74] 'International Christian Workers' Movement—Some Historical Facts', p. 2—Archief Mouvement Mondial des Travailleurs Chrétiens (MMTC), Documentation and Research Centre for Religion, Culture and Society (KADOC) [Leuven, Belgium], 1.1/3.

societies from cradle to grave, complete with the provision of Catholic trade unions and political organizations, whereas other branches concentrated on evangelical tasks, leaving it up to individual members to choose their terrain for trade union and political work within pre-existing secular organizations. By the late 1950s, a decision was taken to restructure the international federation to enable the two potentially conflicting tendencies to overcome those obstacles and to create what became the World Movement of Christian Workers, again probably best known internationally by its French initials: MMTC.

After several hiccups, the MMTC finally got off the ground in May 1966 at the seventy-fifth anniversary celebrations of the first important papal social encyclical, *Rerum Novarum*. The official call for this 'Constituent Assembly of the World Movement of Christian Workers' proudly proclaimed in its English-language version: 'More than 20,000 workers from European countries, together with a great number of delegates from other continents, will attend a mass, presided by Pope Paul VI, in the Basilica of St. Peter in Rome. Mass will be followed by a solemn audience during which the Pope will address to the workers a message which will resound as a powerful echo of the Vatican Council. The Assembly itself will open on Monday, 23 May. It is neither a General Convention nor a public meeting. It will be kind of a working party, lasting the whole week', with select representatives from various national constituent organizations taking active part in it.[75]

Total membership of the MMTC approached the two million mark for its European sections alone. The single largest battalion within the MMTC was none other than the Italian ACLI, followed by the four Belgian groupings belonging to the MMTC, together accounting for more than half a million members, with Germany ranking third with more than 400,000 members.[76] The MMTC was thus a giant workers' organization representing significant parts of the Catholic working-class communities in various countries; and it is thus astounding to realize that, to date, there exists no published study of this influential federation.[77] As was the case in my subchapter on the Jeunesse Étudiante Chrétienne Internationale at the end of Chapter 4, I cannot do full justice to the wealth of discussion, activism, and exchanges within the MMTC

[75] 'The Constituent Assembly of the World Movement of the Christian Workers. Rome, 23–29 May 1966', p. 1—MMTC, 1.1/3.

[76] Robert de Gendt, 'Continental Report Europe', written on the occasion of the founding conference. To appreciate the Belgian figures, one should note that the entire country only counted ten million citizens!—MMTC 1.1/11.

[77] The most informative unpublished attempt to portray the outlines and contours of the MMTC remains the June 1995 licentiaatsverhandeling by Ann Daenens, 'De Wereldbeweging van Christelijke Arbeiders (1961–1983). De mundialisering van de christelijke arbeidersbeweging', Katholieke Universiteit Leuven, Faculteit Letteren, Departement Geschiedenis. Daenens, however, pays relatively little attention to the issues at the centre of my own concern in this chapter.

in this subchapter. All I wish to do, for the moment, is to draw attention to the indisputable fact that the MMTC got caught up in the whirlwind of post-Vatican II sentiments reinforced by the spirit of '68, just as much as virtually all other Catholic international associations within and outside Catholic Action.

The remarkable story of the HOAC's precocious radicalization as early as the 1950s stands, of course, without parallel in the history of the MMTC, and this Spanish *Sonderweg* is entirely due to the Iberian peculiarities described earlier in this chapter. In virtually all other cases, the MMTC's sections remained loyal subjects of the Catholic hierarchy far into the 1960s. But when the impulses delivered by Vatican II were quickly followed by the explosions of social movements starting in and around 1968, the dyke burst within the MMTC as much as in most of its individual sections.

THE RADICAL TURN AT OSTEND

Certainly by the closing years of the 'sixties', a careful perusal of documentation extant within the copious archives of the MMTC betrays a quickening sense of questioning and challenging of the status quo within society—and within the church. Space does not permit a more detailed exploration of such trends; instead a brief glance at the first world conference after the 1966 founding session in Rome will outline a number of distinct evolutions in the outlook and the action repertoire of the MMTC. When in early October 1970 150 delegates from fifty countries and all five continents assembled for the Second General Assembly, a new era was already under way. The vacation colony of the Belgium Christian Trade Union of Woodworkers and Construction Workers in Mariakerke near Ostend on the Belgian coast was a beehive of activity from 4 to 11 October.[78]

A series of workshops assembled the international delegates, producing documents which showcase the quasi-volcanic activities at grassroots levels, mediated by the elected representatives deliberating in Ostend. Perhaps the most clear-cut manifestations of the new winds blowing within international Catholicism were, however, two central speeches. One was delivered by the MMTC chaplain, the Portuguese Father Agostinho Jardim Gonçalves. Father Jardim publicly launched an 'Appeal for Liberation', a call to action definitely not meant to be adulterated by 'a bourgeois interpretation or a sentimental

---

[78] Astute and informative commentaries on the Ostend proceedings were published, amongst others, in the mainstream French Catholic daily newspaper, *La Croix*, with statistical information presented in Félix Lacambre, '150 délégués de 50 pays examinant le développement integral des travailleurs', *La Croix*, 7 October 1970—MMTC, 1.2/12.

pietism'—Jardim's words—designed to defer concrete measures to a distant future age. For Jardim, liberation was meant to become liberation in the here and now, and the opening lines of his Appeal for Liberation suggested some ideas for the specific tasks lying ahead:

> It corresponds to the profound aspiration of all workers: to liberate themselves from the conditions which have rendered them slaves; to rise from lethargy and the suffocating slumber which are the consequences of misery, in order to go forward with resolve and dignity; to banish all that which may stand as an obstacle to self-affirmation and pride in one's class, paternalistic attitudes included. [...] When workers refuse to resign themselves to unjust situations to which society condemns them; when they ask for higher wages, more dignified housing, concrete access to education, an effective participation in the building of society—then they call for a liberty which allows them to develop their talents and their capacities, their physical energies and the free development of their spirits.[79]

The other keynote speaker was François Houtart, then teaching at the University of Leuven, a Belgian priest and sociologist who had served as peritus at Vatican II. In the words of the *La Croix* journalist Félix Lacambre, at Ostend Houtart 'carefully analysed the internal and external mechanisms responsible for global underdevelopment, the consequences of political, economic, cultural, military and social domination in the framework of the capitalist world system. Yet, for all his criticism of the western way of life, he also disapproved of the Communist regimes in Russia and China.' In fact, the headlines and the three bullet points introducing Lacambre's article nicely capture Houtart's keynote presentation at the MMTC's world congress: 'The exploitation of workers gives birth to violence.' 'The voice of the people who suffer and that of Christ who liberates.' 'To change the structures generating hunger.' 'Do not judge those who resort to arms.'[80] It is perhaps useful to supplement Lacambre's comments with a direct citation from Houtart's incendiary speech:

> We can detect a sense of growing solidarity within the struggles occurring throughout the world today, amongst the revolutionary movements of Latin America, the liberation movements in the Portuguese colonies, the South Vietnamese National Liberation Front, and even within pockets of the "Third World" existing within the interstices of the rich portions of the world, such as the Black Panthers. [...] In fact, the third world war has already begun: that of the rich people against poor people. And it is a war of truly global proportions: the war in Vietnam toppled an American president; the guerrilla fighters in Guatemala cause headaches for the West German government; national liberation fighters in Angola and Guinea–Bissau are mowed down by the bullets coming out of

---

[79] 'Réflexion doctrinale du Père Jardim', in 'Compte-rendu de la Deuxième Assemblée Générale', in *Infor MMTC* no. 13 (November 1970), p. 29—MMTC 1.2/16.

[80] Félix Lacambre, 'L'Exploitation des travailleurs fait naître la violence', *La Croix*, 10 October 1970.

Belgian-made rifles and American napalm. It is precisely this imperialism of moneyed interests—which *Populorum Progressio* addresses—which lies at the root of injustice and which is why the new name for peace is development.[81]

As a later summary of the MMTC's history astutely remarked, the Ostend assembly ushered in a massive reorientation of its global outlook and its daily work. 'Liberation' subsequently became a household term in MMTC's deliberations and publications, and it was explicitly defined to denote a complete redistribution of resources and change of values throughout the world, rather than an incremental increase in income for workers. And if Houtart's call for development as the new tonic to combat global underdevelopment could perhaps be misunderstood to mean a mere reshuffling of resources without the need for new overall parameters, the MMTC's balance sheet drawn up in 1974 dotted all the i's in this respect as well: 'The discussions held in 1970 in Ostend very quickly led the MMTC to realize that the idea of thorough and long-lasting development must give rise to another set of more outwardly oriented and global ideas, which will more effectively sweep away the reformist sense still attached to development projects today.'[82]

   The following observations were made in a document internal to the French section of the MMTC, the Action Catholique Ouvrière (ACO), but the spirit holds true for large sections of the MMTC as a whole: 'By means of this active presence within workers' struggles and our constant efforts to discuss and update our practices, many leaders of the ACO have become convinced that it is no longer they who introduce workers to the message of Christ, but that in effect Christ has preceded them and reveals himself in the signs of the times' manifested in everyday battles.[83] The apostolic missionaries of Catholic Action underwent a learning process identical to that reported by second-wave worker priests described in Chapter 2.

THE 1974 GENERAL ASSEMBLY IN ROME

The December 1974 General Assembly of the MMTC met once again in Rome. But the proximity of the Vatican did not temper spirits in the least. The Four-Year-Plan agreed upon in Rome included the following telling passage under the heading 'Overall Objectives':

[81] 'Conférence prononcée par le chanoine F. Houtart', in 'Compte-rendu', p. 18.
[82] 'Rapport: Révision et Orientation', '2ème partie: Action du MMTC et de ses mouvements membres', in 'Documents de Travail. Assemblée Générale MMTC 1974', p. 7—MMTC, 1.3/11.
[83] 'Rencontre de l'ACO française et du Bureau (Paris, 1–6 Octobre 1973)', p. 2—MMTC, 2/2.

A) Together with all other workers, to pursue the construction of a new society. The latter emerges out of the daily lives of workers, from the fundamental values and aspirations of workers which we share. We would like to stress that it is by means of concrete action at the point of production that this new society will advance. We wish to place particular stress on the importance of organized collective action. This action is the privileged location where we can encounter, get to know and share Jesus Christ. B) To awaken, develop and sustain at all levels of the Movement a veritable workers' political consciousness, to be reached by means of actions which develop in the various facets of workers' lives. C) We know that the militant action of workers proceeds in the context of an economic, social, cultural and political system which dominates and crushes the working class. This situation calls for redoubled efforts to ensure that this learning process takes on a truly international dimension, so that the solidarity and true liberation which are part and parcel of the fundamental aspirations of humankind may become reality.[84]

Most national sections of the MMTC were now centrally involved in all major and minor working-class battles which appeared to be possible harbingers of the much-invoked 'new society', whether in factories or mines or in working-class neighbourhoods over issues such as housing or education. A statement by one of the Flemish organizations belonging to the MMTC, the KWB, prominently noted: 'Some of our local sections have been involved in concrete actions against the strategy of multinational enterprises, such as Ford-Genk, Akso, Enka-Breda, and above all in Ghent where activists from our movement have participated in the occupation of the ACEC-Westinghouse plant, following the example set by LIP (France).'[85] Similar accounts were penned by MMTC members from across Europe.

Perhaps the most telling proof of the fundamental change of course undertaken by the MMTC since its founding in 1966 can be gauged from a letter by MMTC chaplain Agostinho Jardim to a fellow priest in October 1974 during preparations for the Rome Assembly of 6–10 December. For each day of the assembly, a priest was chosen to hold Mass and celebrate the eucharist as part of the proceedings. On 4 October 1974, Father Jardim approached a Quebeçois colleague, Father Lorenzo Lortie, to prepare the celebration on the opening day of the congress. 'As far as you are concerned, we have "designated" you to be responsible for 6 December, for a celebration to be held in French, which should address the following topics: to celebrate a number of

[84] 'Plan de travail de quatre ans du MMTC', in 'Documents de Travail. Assemblée Générale MMTC 1974', pp. 2–3—MMTC 1.3/11.
[85] 'KWB Belgique. Réponse au Questionnaire: Conversations internationales. 1974', p. 2—MMTC, 4.3. For the remarkable wave of working-class radicalism in Belgium in the early-to-mid-1970s, see Rik Hemmerijckx, 'Mai '68 und die Welt der Arbeiter in Belgien', in Bernd Gehrke and Gerd-Rainer Horn, *1968 und die Arbeiter. Studien zum 'proletarischen Mai' in Europa* (Hamburg: VSA, 2007), pp. 231–51.

events which have occurred during the past four years which have found an international echo and which have engendered intensified working-class solidarity: the struggle at LIP, Chile, the Paris Peace Accords on Vietnam, the decolonization of territories under Portuguese domination, the events in Quebec . . .'[86]

Small wonder that relations between the MMTC and the various Catholic national bishops' assemblies and the Vatican hierarchy rapidly went from bad to worse. It did not help matters that, in full flight towards new and unexplored horizons, the MMTC chose as their new General Secretary a Belgian activist from Ghent, Luc Vos, president of the KWB, whose organization had, back in 1968, publicly criticized the highly controversial papal encyclical, *Humanae Vitae.* For a period of time diplomatic relations between the MMTC and the Vatican came to a complete halt and financial support by the Holy See was cut off. When, by the mid-1970s, the MMTC made efforts to reopen channels of negotiation, concrete links improved, but the root causes of the mutual alienation did not disappear overnight. A protocol of a 1977 discussion between a visiting MMTC delegation and a leading representative of the Vatican Secretary of State's office provides elegant testimony to the tense atmosphere which continued to cast a shadow over such conversations.

The MMTC spokespersons had laid out their overall strategic approach, which had not changed significantly since their radical turn at the onset of the decade. Giovanni Benelli, who had made his visitors wait for two hours in his antechamber despite an agreed-upon appointment, listened carefully, thanked his interlocutors, but then launched his counterattack. 'As to the identification with the workers' world, that is all well and good. But this identification must not be complete, it cannot be total, or there will be nothing Christian left. This is not possible. We must be the yeast in the dough, but not adapt completely to the workers' world. The working class is socialist, socialist in the Marxist sense of that term. We cannot accept this. Socialism is opposed to Christianity. First of all because socialism means division; Christians strive for unity. [. . .] If the Christian workers' movement adulterates itself, then it is not worthy of its existence. Your specificity as Christians is to contribute something Christian, to promote the Word of God [. . .] The need for justice—there is nothing wrong with it; but it must be fought for also with love, patience, pardon and all the other virtues [. . .] As to your insistence on autonomy: the Church is like a mother, and your Movement is the child. The mother cannot abandon her responsibility [. . .]'

---

[86] Letter by Agostinho Jardim to Lorenzo Lortie, 4 October 1974—MMTC, 1.3/8. The mention of 'events in Quebec' refers to a series of social movements which gripped the francophone province in Eastern Canada in the early 1970s, which made Quebec into a hotbed of radical activism in North America, comparable to countries in Mediterranean Europe.

At this point the MMTC's Luc Vos interjected the following comment: 'And if the child becomes a mother one fine day?' Giovanni Benelli immediately retorted: 'This is impossible. There will always remain a difference in levels of authority. It is the Good Lord himself who has arranged things in this manner. Even the Pope cannot do anything about this.' Luc Vos now almost lost his cool: 'I do not think that it was Jesus Christ who drew up the regulations which are supposed to govern the internal affairs of our organization!' Giovanni Benelli shot back in this conversation which had been conducted in French: 'Stop these wisecracks, Monsieur . . .'[87]

---

[87] 'Visite du Bureau a Mgr. Benelli, Secrétaire d'État, le 13 mai 1977'—MMTC, 2.3/11.

Conclusion

A VIRTUOUS CIRCLE

The dramatic change of direction set in motion by Vatican II created an unexpected window of opportunity for progressive sentiments within the Catholic church. At first cautiously, just like the bishops in the run-up to the council, then determinedly, a new spirit arose within Catholic communities. Taking at face value the injunction of conciliar documents to tackle the burning issues facing the world of their day, the ageing activists of the first wave of Left Catholicism, coming to the fore in the mid-to-late-1940s, suddenly were joined by a rapidly swelling new cohort of young grassroots believers determined to seize the day—all of them encouraged by what they began to regard as the spirit of Vatican II.

Soon a classic mechanism which frequently operates within social movements began to click in: a radicalization process, a virtuous circle of ever-larger expectations and ever-more-daring demands. Progressive priests often began their mobilization cycle over the issue of celibacy. Yet, in the process of addressing this topic, they rapidly began to draw ever-larger circles and more far-reaching conclusions, soon agitating for democratization of the church, eventually advocating the declericalization of the priesthood. Students initially often focused on local, campus-related conflicts, and only subsequently did they begin to tackle society-wide and global relationships of inequality and injustice. Base communities usually initiated their attempts to fashion a Christian community by targeting ecclesiastical issues. Yet, before long, the remit of their concerns widened considerably, and they became committed agitators for a better world. Catholic workers, likewise, did not set out to create a paradise on earth from the outset of their multiple efforts to give concrete shape to the message emanating from Vatican II.

In fact, the 'spirit of Vatican II', operating on multiple levels and in appropriately mysterious ways, soon began to be subject to multiple interpretations. As the cycle of activism propelled by Christian inspirations got under way, Vatican II soon was used as a metaphor for any number of possible blueprints for radical actions. It was not the precise wording of council declarations which counted, but the intentions that may have been hidden behind those words. Indeed, even prior to May '68, the concrete manifest-ations of the spirit of Vatican II often far outpaced the specific suggestions that could be legitimately culled from the pages of the relevant documents. Just as post-conciliar theology often far outdistanced the textual meaning of most conciliar declarations, Catholic activists creatively took matters into their own hands. This astounding ferment within communities of Catholic believers accounts for the fact that, in many countries throughout Western Europe, a large number of social movements—of which student movements were often only the most visible component—in the mid-to-late-1960s were animated to a significant extent by Catholics.

And then one of those unforeseen and unpredictable 'signs of the times' occurred: the spark of rebellion and contestation suddenly began to affect *secular* society-at-large as well. A parallel process of gradual radicalization, under way since—at least—1956 and slowly giving rise to a powerful and imaginative New Left, dramatically made itself felt in often spectacular actions in country after country, the respective causes often differing from case to case. In the United States, the Vietnam War was the key catalyst, but the earlier Civil Rights Movement—where religious leadership was key—had crucially already taught white Americans the politics of protest and associated tech-niques. In Spain, the conditions of dictatorship in the midst of the Free World were responsible for the precocious vitality and volatility of protest cultures—notably animated by progressive Catholics—from 1956 onwards. In Belgium, the peculiar conditions of francophone cultural and economic domination of an increasingly vocal and restless Flemish community, with the Catholic curia consecrating this unequal relationship, led to the outburst of youthful enthu-siasm as early as May 1966. The French May 1968 was by no means the first general societal conflagration to mark European (and world) politics in the long sixties—though it became the shot that was heard around the world. Religious and secular radical currents now engaged in a joint race to the top, mutually reinforcing each other, creating a seemingly unstoppable dynamic.

THE ITALIAN CAULDRON

Much attention has been devoted in the five chapters of this book to the case of Italy. A few comments are thus in order to attempt to provide an explanation for the particular vibrancy and colourful presence of the Italian variant of second wave Left Catholicism south of the Alps. At the risk of doing injustice to the inner force and outlook of *il dissenso cattolico*, I believe that a compre-hensive answer to this question has to take into account the peculiarities of Italian politics and society in general. The key to the astounding (if, ultimately, temporary) ascendancy of Italian Left Catholicism in the turbulent central years of its existence—the 'red decade' of 1965/6 to 1975/6—is due above all to features of Italian culture as a whole.

The polarization of Italian society and politics as such, with the western world's most powerful Communist Party—in a position of ideological hegemony in many walks of life—confronting a staunchly conservative Christian Democracy in a quasi-permanent stand-off from the 1950s to the 1970s accounts for much of the local colour of conflicts throughout the Italian boot. In addition, the dislocations of European society resulting from massive waves of migration from south to north probably affected no other country as centrally as Italy. Countless southern Italians in search of employment fled to Northern European states, but for a huge number of such migrants their journey north ended within the confines of the Italian state. Northern Italian cities thus lived the conflicts and contradictions associated with this massive influx of migrants just as much, if not more, than Europeans further north. In Northern Italy, however, such southern migrants spoke the same language and were more readily integrated into protest cultures emerging autonomously in Italy's North than their brothers and sisters who travelled to the far side of the Alps.

No Western European country had given rise to a similarly powerful and militant antifascist resistance movement in the closing years of World War II as had Italy. To the west of the subsequent Iron Curtain—with the exception of Greece at the southeastern tip of the post-1945 'free world'—no other country saw a more deep-going and literally all-encompassing development of radical antifascist activities than was the case in Italy. And this truly popular Italian resistance was by no means solely a result of the particular vibrancy of the Communist tradition. Socialist, dissident socialist, radical Catholic, and secular radical democratic currents (e.g. the Partito d'Azione) all contributed their fair share—and shared in the attendant sacrifices and bloodletting—to the liberation of Italy and the creation of a forceful and upright tradition favouring self-reliance and autonomous action. The legacy of this unique constellation of forces centrally affected social movement discourse and practices all the way up to—at the very least—the 1970s. The particular poignancy of Italian Left Catholicism in the Italian *sessantotto* arose out of this highly unusual and, indeed, unique conjuncture and concatenation of circumstances.

Italy, however, may stand for only *one* example of the creative confluence of secular and Catholic cycles of radicalization in the course of the late 1960s, which created a unique opportunity for innovative experiences. The remarkable story of the rapid growth and efforts at national coordination of Italian *gruppi spontanei* may stand merely as *one* exemplary showcase incident of secular and Catholic radical sentiments working in tandem to find solutions to the vexed questions of the day. For a brief moment, it appeared as if progressive Catholics would be able to link arms with the spirit emanating from the nonconformist secular Left in the search for a New Jerusalem in a great variety of Western European states.

In fact, when looked at more closely and placed in a comparative perspective, a whole series of such efforts to coordinate secular and religious forces can be discerned in the period under review. In underground Spain, it should be highlighted once more, the traditional deep-seated hostility between Catholicism and the secular Left was finally beginning to be overcome. And the conditions of illegality ensured that such new alliances did not just link Catholics to the New Left, but crucially to the Communist Old Left as well. In Leuven, for more than half a dozen years after 1968, it may be recalled, Left Catholic student groups became mainstays of the vibrant local protest culture, demonstrating in the city streets alongside Trotskyist and Maoist agitators from the Far Left.

THE BACKLASH

What all these natural and unnatural alliances also brought about was a climate of growing division within the Catholic Left. For by no means every Catholic parishioner was willing to go along all the way in this process of free-flowing reinterpretations of the spirit of Vatican II. The clearest indication of such new divisions internal to the Catholic Left could be found within the community of theologians who had initially closed ranks to defend and publicize the change of course announced at Vatican II. By the late 1960s, the erstwhile bloc of reform-minded theologians began to unravel. As the process of radicalization began to become seemingly irreversible, several leading theologians within the progressive camp—Jean Daniélou, Henri de Lubac, Hans Urs von Balthasar, Joseph Ratzinger come to mind—began to form their own more moderate network, separate from the ardent defenders of a more radical course. And a similar reshuffling of allegiances took place in the world of Catholic parishes and communities as well—and not all of them had been affected by the proverbial spirit of Vatican II in the first place.

I have elsewhere described in greater detail how such second thoughts, in the face of the seemingly boundless radicalization of some Catholic believers in the wake of 1968, led to a moderation of course by the Catholic church under Pope Paul VI, who had earlier on—notably in the decades prior to Vatican II—been a steadfast defender, if not a direct supporter himself, of the first wave of the Catholic Left.[1] And this new division within the camp of

---

[1] Gerd-Rainer Horn, 'Les Chrétientés catholiques à l'épreuve des *sixties* et des *seventies*', in Yvon Tranvouez (ed.), *La Décomposition des chrétientés occidentales 1950–2010* (Brest: Centre de Recherche Bretonne et Celtique, 2013), pp. 23–35.

advocates of the spirit of Vatican II naturally put wind in the sails of conservative groups in the curia. The Italian and Spanish hierarchy had, for instance, never been seriously affected by the spirit of Vatican II in any of the latter's multiple and conflicting manifestations. Now, in the wake of a partial retreat by Paul VI and others in the aftermath of 1968, the conservative networks began to regain the upper hand. Long before the advent of the period of open reaction characterizing the pontificates of John Paul II and Benedict XVI, the spirit of Vatican II had become an evanescent dream.

The crushing of the Spanish Catholic Left after 1966 was thus merely a precursor of what happened elsewhere in Europe in subsequent years. A promising period of open-ended experiments was artificially cut short. The link-up between progressive Catholics and the nonconformist secular Left thus never occurred, understandably leading ever-greater numbers of formerly Catholic grassroots activists to concentrate exclusively on family, career, and the private sphere, abandoning social movement engagements, and, frequently enough, discarding their faith along the way. If they did continue to be active in socio-political affairs, they now quite often carried out such work in secular organizations of the political Left.

In the short run, then, the spirit of Vatican II led to a renewal of Catholic engagements with progressive social issues on a scale unprecedented in recent history. In the medium term, the rising curve of activism was followed by disillusionment and resignation, and a powerful reinforcement of the trend towards secularization, which had begun to affect European societies for quite some time prior to Vatican II. But, inasmuch as many erstwhile Catholic activists now shifted their attention and their energies towards the secular Left, a new set of consequences can be discerned.

SOME HIDDEN CONSEQUENCES OF SECOND WAVE LEFT CATHOLICISM

Dutch civil society, for instance, prior to the sixties, was one of the most socially and culturally conservative national communities in Europe. In the late 1960s and beyond, the Netherlands became one of the most permissive societies in all of Europe. It would be too far-fetched to ascribe this massive switch entirely, or even primarily, to the small-scale revolution carried out within the Dutch Catholic church. But the remarkable change of direction carried out by an unusually progressive Dutch hierarchy in conjunction with a grassroots flock largely supportive of such changes surely must have contributed its own fair share to this drastic reorientation of the cultural climate in the Low Countries in subsequent decades.

The radicalization of significant sections of grassroots Catholic communities in post-1965 Italy was probably on a scale unprecedented in postwar Europe, leaving aside the case of Spain under Franco. To be sure, here too, the New Jerusalem remained out of reach. Yet, by the mid-1970s, the impact of such sentiments could be felt in unforeseen, if refracted, ways. Leaving aside the highly polarized electoral contest of 1948 where the Italian Communist Party (PCI) obtained 31.0 per cent of the popular vote, the highpoints of postwar election results for the flagship party of the Italian secular Left, the PCI, were the elections of 1976 and 1979, in which the PCI obtained 34.4 per cent (1976) and 30.4 per cent (1979). The mid-to-late-1970s were precisely the years when many Catholic activists, previously concentrating their efforts on the battalions of the Italian New and then Far Left, began to switch their allegiance (and, often enough, their membership) to the only remaining game in town, the PCI. Thus, the successes of the flagship Eurocommunist party in the second half of the 1970s probably in no small part occurred as a result of the redirected energies of the forces emerging out of the disintegration of the Catholic Left.

In France, one of the regions which underwent a most profound political mutation in the postwar period is Brittany. A traditional stronghold of Catholic conservatism 'since time immemorial', Brittany had for a long time been a safe reservoir for electoral successes by conservative parties. Since the 1970s, this constellation of forces has been spectacularly reversed, and Brittany has become a bastion of the political Centre Left.[2] Again, it would be wrong to ascribe this role reversal of Brittany's politics to the impact of radical Catholics in the post-Vatican II era alone. But the bitter contestations of Left Catholic forces in Brittany in the long sixties must surely be counted as *one* of several important factors.

And how can one explain the fact that Belgium, a country which had a rock-solid conservative Catholic pillar, certainly in its northern half well into the 1960s, has in recent decades become one of the socio-culturally most liberal countries in Europe? In the 1950s, Catholic conservatives twice almost brought Belgium to the brink of civil war, first during the controversy surrounding the return of Leopold III to the Belgian throne, then on the question of state support for Catholic education. Today, issues such as gay marriage, which give rise to huge controversies elsewhere in Europe, barely raise an eyebrow and certainly lead to no visceral and divisive national debates. Once again the explanation cannot be exclusively sought in the legacy of radical Catholic movements erupting in Belgium in the wake of Vatican II. But

---

[2] On the vicissitudes of Catholicism in Brittany, see Brigitte Waché (ed.), *Militants catholiques de l'Ouest. De l'action réligieuse aux nouveaux militantismes* (Rennes: Presses Universitaires de Rennes, 2004), and Yvon Tranvouez, *Catholiques en Bretagne au XXè siècle* (Rennes: Presses Universitaires de Rennes, 2006).

perhaps enough has been said to suggest that the medium-to-long-term impact of such sudden paradigm shifts within (in this case, Belgian) Catholicism should become an object of historical and social scientific study.

THE SILENCES OF HISTORIOGRAPHY

This monograph has addressed an entirely different set of questions, attempting to draw attention to a much-neglected blank space in history when a Catholic Left became an important player in church affairs but also in national politics in a whole host of countries for about a dozen turbulent years. The ultimate defeat of such efforts has ensured that serious studies of this phenomenon are few and far between. There certainly is an astounding absence of any studies that look at this complex issue from a comparative and transnational perspective. Nothing works as efficiently to excise a subject matter from historical memory as a historical defeat. And, although it would be absolutely incorrect to suggest that progressive Catholicism has vanished completely since the late 1970s, it is true that there has yet to emerge a viable 'Third Wave' of Left Catholicism in the most recent decades. In that sense, the Second Wave was, to date, the last major occurrence of progressive Catholicism in Western Europe on any larger scale.

Another factor helping to explain the lack of attention to the very real—and, after all, relatively recent—incidents of Left Catholicism on Western European soil is related to the socio-political background and training of 'radical' or open-minded historians in recent years. Today's historians of the Left mostly hail from the secular Left and thus have neither the ideological arsenal of tools nor the relevant political background and interest to discover a religious undercurrent of radical change which appeared to go against the tide. Church historians likewise have little incentive to discover such a nonconformist past, given that most will have been socialized within a Catholic church which, since the 1970s, has been firmly in the hands of conservative and traditionalist forces. Nor are there any institutional benefits to be expected by researching and writing about a period which most members of the Catholic hierarchy would rather forget about and consign to the dustbins of history or, to quote Karl Marx, the gnawing criticism of mice.

Still, it is in no way my intention—far from it—to deny or to belittle the survival—and, on occasion, even expansion and growth—all the way until the present day of progressive Catholic thought and, more importantly, circles of activists. In virtually all countries covered in this monograph, by no means insignificant numbers of individuals, loose associations, and organized groups continue to profess—and to live in accordance with—Left Catholic convictions. To be sure, their outlook and agenda have changed in important ways since the heyday of second wave Left Catholicism forty years ago or more, in accordance with the ongoing evolution of society, the church, and the corresponding 'signs of the times' in the late twentieth and early twenty-first centuries. It is certainly fair to say that today's progressive Catholic networks have less reason to be regarded as endangered species than their co-thinkers and antecedents were in the dark days of the final decade of the pontificate of Pius XII. In fact, there are grounds for optimism. The recent surprise election of Pope Francis has created a new dynamic which is, if anything, on balance rather favourable to many of the designs of today's Catholic Left. Predictions of the definitive demise of progressive Catholicism are therefore ill-advised and by all means subject to the verification of actual developments in upcoming years.

THE ROLE OF UTOPIA

What, then, may ultimately explain the conjunctural importance of progressive Catholicism in the long sixties? To be sure, the happy circumstance of Vatican II occurring just a few years before the explosions of '1968', discussed in the opening sections of this Conclusion, is the obvious and easy answer to this question. But there is another possible explanation. There exists an intellectual attraction and a distinct fascination with the thoughts and deeds of Catholic activism and associated Catholic intellectuals of that time, which goes beyond their involvement in the multiform social movements of their age.

When assessing the original contributions of conciliar declarations and post-conciliar developments in theology, traced in Chapter 1, it is astonishing to note the regularity with which the messianic, eschatological, utopian dimension comes to the fore. If there is a red thread which links Yves Congar to José María González Ruiz via Karl Rahner and Johann Baptist Metz, it is their emphasis on the importance of the link between salvation and liberation, the need for equal attention to the tasks of human liberation in the present and the utopian Kingdom to Come. Moreover, time and time again it becomes clear with regard to all the theologians whom I earlier discussed that the real driving force in this creative admixture of earthly and millenarian pursuits is their firm belief in ultimate redemption. The utopian goal is what energized Catholics to devote their actions to the improvement of their present circumstances and their concrete socio-cultural and political environments in the here and now.

And this is where the utopian, messianic dimension of Catholicism overlapped with secular ideals prominently at work behind the scenes in the long sixties. Utopian goals were all the rage in the social movements and political battles of that period. Marxist and/or anarchist dreams of classless societies were then common currency in many countries across Europe and the wider world, precisely at the same time that his apocalyptic eschatology propelled Johann Baptist Metz to front-line status in the galaxy of European radical Catholicism. Both messianic Catholicism and utopian Marxism captured the imagination of an entire generation and mutually influenced each other. There is no better proof of purchase of this creative confluence than the conjunctural radiance of a figure such as Ernst Bloch, the philosopher of the West German New Left who, in turn, crucially shaped the outlook of the Protestant Jürgen Moltmann and the Catholic Johann Baptist Metz.

In that sense, the long sixties can be compared to another period in modern European history, the period known in German-speaking areas as the *Vormärz*, the period between the 1815 Vienna Congress and the Revolutions of 1848. In particular the 1830s and 1840s were decades of great expectations and hopes in the coming springtime of peoples and a radically different organization of life. Not only Marx and Engels—as well as Heinrich Heine and Georg Büchner—then came of age, but so did Bakunin and Proudhon. Some of the earliest shoots of organized feminism (Flora Tristan) can be traced back to this period as well. Even the comparatively quieter first half of the Vormärz had seen its share of visionary projects. The entire panoply of utopian socialists in France and England (Saint-Simon, Fourier, Owen) then developed and put into practice their respective schemes. In short, the Vormärz, in particular the years between 1830 and 1848, saw a similar proliferation of utopian dreams and concrete plans as did the dozen years preceding and immediately following 1968.

As long as those hopes and aspirations appeared to incorporate real possibilities, the associated ideologies continued to hold sway over ever-larger segments of the relevant generations. Once those dreams were dashed, the formerly influential belief systems were rapidly discarded. It would be interesting to see what role the failures of the revolutions of 1848 and the revolts of 1968 played in this process. For, in neither case were these moments of crisis and opportunity successful in obtaining the much-invoked dreams, which had energized countless activists and thinkers in the preceding years. Once the realization settled in that the springtime of peoples and the revolts of 1968 had not ushered in the New Society, the plug was pulled and the energies, tirelessly amassed in prior decades, dissipated into thin air.[3]

Second wave Left Catholicism was, thus, part and parcel of a period of rising expectations fuelled by utopian goals. Developing in synchrony with concrete social movements assembling secular and religious actors, both cohorts benefited from this synergy. (It may be useful in this context to draw attention once again to the internationally significant inspiration and pioneering role

---

[3] Daniel Francisco Álvarez Espinosa has put forth some stimulating remarks to this effect in his 'Cristianismo y marxismo. ¿Un diálogo de otro tiempo?', *Historia Actual Online* 18 (Winter 2009), pp. 161–77, where he casts light on the Spanish dimension of this problematic.

The Spirit of Vatican II
262   *The Spirit of Vatican II*

performed by the United States Civil Rights Movement in the long sixties, a social movement in which religious leaders and messianic visions played primordial roles.) Once the bubble burst—or, as the case may be, once defeat was snatched from the jaws of victory—utopian visions rapidly lost their purchase. When, by the early-to-mid-1970s, the painful realization set in that redemption might be further away than imagined, Left Catholic utopian ideals became increasingly unattractive—much as nonconformist New and Far Left ideologies lost their audience at the very same time.

Symptomatically, the definitive closing moment of Spanish Left Catholicism as an influential social movement, slowly revitalized after the curia-induced backlash and paralysis of the period 1966–70, was—figuratively speaking—the morning after Franco died. When it became clear that the new society following the much-anticipated death of the dictator was not exactly the New Jerusalem eagerly fought for by generations of anti-Franco activists, the apocalyptic visions quickly perished along with the associated cherished ideals. A similar process affected secular utopian ideals. It should provide food for thought that the long period during which notions of self-management (*autogestion*) had fuelled secular and Left Catholic activists in post-1968 France came to a sudden halt precisely in the wake of the 1981 victory of the Union of the Left. Confronted with the mismatch between long-cherished ideals and the humdrum results of the Mitterand years, the hopes died along with their utopian ideals.

Second wave Left Catholicism was a sign of the times. As a serious mass movement, it vanished along with the hopes and ideals of the long sixties. Who is to say where the next empowering set of utopian goals will come from, which 'signs of the times' will inspire future generations? What would be utterly surprising, however, would be a scenario where such a revitalization of system-transcending ideologies—be they secular and/or religious—would simply no longer occur. For, as Marie-Dominique Chenu, following Hegel and Marx, astutely observed: 'History consists of collective, yes indeed, massive leaps forward by human beings, leading to qualitatively new levels of consciousness, a reorientation by means of which humanity suddenly steps into mental spaces of whose existence it had, for very long periods, not the faintest idea.'

Index

Printed and bound by CPI Group (UK) Ltd, Croydon, CR0 4YY